To Pat,

Best wishes

Bob

Many happy
returns!
Theresa

The Fund Industry

How Your Money Is Managed

ROBERT POZEN AND
THERESA HAMACHER

Foreword by
Don Phillips

WILEY

John Wiley & Sons, Inc.

Published by John Wiley & Sons, Inc., Hoboken, New Jersey.
Published simultaneously in Canada.

The Fund Industry is an expansion of Robert C. Pozen's *The Mutual Fund Business*, Second Edition, published by Houghton Mifflin Company. Copyright 2002.

For general information on our other products and services or for technical support, please contact our Customer Care Department within the United States at (800) 762-2974, outside the United States at (317) 572-3993 or fax (317) 572-4002.

Wiley also publishes its books in a variety of electronic formats. Some content that appears in print may not be available in electronic books. For more information about Wiley products, visit our web site at www.wiley.com.

Library of Congress Cataloging-in-Publication Data:

Pozen, Robert C.
  The fund industry : how your money is managed / Robert Pozen and Theresa Hamacher ; foreword by Don Phillips.
      p. cm. – (Wiley finance series)
  Rev. ed. of: The mutual fund business / Robert C. Pozen ; editorial assistance by Sandra D. Crane. 2nd ed. 2002.
  Includes bibliographical references and index.
  ISBN 978-0-470-63425-7 (cloth)
  1. Mutual funds–United States.   2. Mutual funds.   I. Hamacher, Theresa.   II. Pozen, Robert C. Mutual fund business.   III. Title.
  HG4930.P63 2011
  332.63'27–dc22

                                                                    2010032743

Printed in the United States of America

10 9 8 7 6 5 4 3 2

Contents

S cores of books tell investors how to choose a mutual fund. Dozens more feature famous fund managers recounting their investment glories. A handful of texts even offer thoughts on how to reform and improve the fund industry. But there's no other book that gives readers such a thorough overview of how the fund industry operates, its evolution, its regulation, and what makes it tick. If you want to truly understand today's mutual fund industry, there's no finer text than the one in your hands.

Mutual funds have become the investment vehicle of choice for investors around the world, and with good reason. No other investment offers the same level of convenience and diversification at such an affordable price. Funds revolutionized and democratized the investment landscape. Yet the industry itself goes largely unexamined. Small investment partnerships and family businesses have morphed into global financial powerhouses seemingly overnight, dramatically altering the investment landscape, yet few fully understand the fund industry's structure, its distribution methods, and its back-office workings.

If you are one of the millions of fund investors and you want to know how your money is processed and managed, not just which funds had the highest return, this book is for you. Similarly, if you work for a fund company, are involved in fund distribution, or work perhaps as an independent director for a fund, this text has much to offer. If you are an auditor, lawyer, or custodian or work for one of the many data services companies involved with the fund industry, this text will be invaluable. Moreover, journalists, policymakers, and professors following the industry and its transformational role in capital markets will find this text an indispensable reference.

Of course, all that I've said here applies to the earlier editions of this text as well. What makes this third edition special? For one, it features much more coverage of funds outside the United States and much more material on other types of pooled investments, such as hedge funds, exchange-traded funds, and separate accounts. But I'd argue that the most significant upgrade is the involvement of Theresa Hamacher, one of the sharpest and classiest people I know in the industry. Terry perfectly complements Bob Pozen's considerable expertise to form a dream duo to guide readers through the world of funds.

I first met Terry when she ran a top-performing convertible-bond fund back in the 1980s. Convertibles are an odd niche of the financial world that demands expertise in both equity and fixed-income management. Terry brought not only formidable intelligence but great creativity to the task, and her fund delivered fine results to shareholders. Her hands-on expertise in portfolio management shines through in the investment-management sections of the text. Terry went on to even greater successes, first in managing other investment professionals, and more recently in heading NICSA, the National Investment Company Service Association, which is the organization of service providers to the fund industry, where she's fought for ever-higher professional standards. No one knows portfolio management and back-office operations like Terry. As importantly, Terry brings an educator's touch that translates arcane information into easily understood and readily assimilated insights. She's an ace.

Bob Pozen is similarly impressive. My defining memory of Bob came from the late 1990s when Bob headed up Fidelity's asset management arm. The scene was an industry conference devoted to how the Internet would change everything. The conference was abuzz with New Economy fever, and rival fund executives boasted of money pouring into their recently launched Internet-themed investment funds. Against this background, Bob was asked when Fidelity would launch its Internet fund; after all, Fidelity was a leader in sector funds and already had funds investing in such specialties as air transportation and property and casualty insurance. Bob's answer shocked the audience. He said Fidelity wouldn't be launching an Internet fund at that time because he didn't want to take the calls in five years from investors who had bought the fund in the midst of the current euphoria. To me, Bob's sentiment embodied the notion of stewardship over salesmanship. While many of his peers were eager to push what was then easy to sell, Bob recognized that the most valuable asset of any fund manager is its reputation and that short-term gains that come at the cost of long-term reputational damage aren't worth taking.

Coupled with his deep-seated commitment to stewardship, Bob's expertise in the legal aspects of fund management and his passion for public policy fully round out this book's impressive parentage. Like Terry, Bob has continued to flourish in the industry, moving on from Fidelity to guide the venerable MFS organization back to its historic position of industry leadership. He stands today as one of the industry's most revered statesmen. His insights help shape financial regulation, and he's a thought leader in the debate surrounding retirement-planning issues. With this text, he generously gives back to the industry in which he's enjoyed such success, sharing a lifetime of accumulated wisdom with future industry leaders. Just as veteran stock fund managers prize their tattered copies of Ben Graham and David Dodd's *Security Analysis*, coming generations of fund industry leaders will cling to this essential text. It's that good and that important a book.

Don Phillips
Managing Director,
Morningstar, Inc.

Preface

Mutual funds play an integral role in daily life. In 2009, more than 87 million Americans invested their money through mutual funds, using them as vehicles to save for such important life goals as the purchase of a home, a child's college education or a comfortable retirement.[1] Many businesses rely on money market mutual funds for help in managing their cash balances. And mutual funds are an increasingly popular savings vehicle in Europe, Asia, and other regions of the world.

In the United States alone, more than 157,000 individuals worked directly for fund management companies—among them call center representatives and credit analysts, wholesalers, and portfolio managers. Firms providing critical support to funds—including audit, custody, legal, and technology services—employed hundreds of thousands more. Yet these jobs in the United States represent only a fraction of worldwide employment in the fund industry.

It's a highly complex industry, offering more than 7,600 funds with different investment objectives and approaches to consumers through multiple distribution channels—through intermediaries, direct sales, and retirement plans. It's governed by detailed laws and regulations that are continually evolving.

The Fund Industry explains how this industry works in practice. We examine how mutual funds are structured and discuss the key laws and regulations governing their operations. We go behind the scenes at fund management companies to explain how they select investments for fund portfolios, sell fund shares around the globe, and provide service to fund shareholders.

We wrote this book for anyone who's unfamiliar with the mutual fund industry but would like to know more. All we ask is that readers understand key economic and tax terms such as interest rates and capital gains; knowledge of basic investment concepts—such as the difference between stocks and bonds—is helpful, but not required. We explain the jargon and try to assemble the various components of the fund industry into a coherent whole. Callout boxes highlight key definitions and recent controversy or give you a feel for what it's like to work for a fund management company.

This book doesn't just update the second edition of Bob Pozen's *The Mutual Fund Business*—it adds much new material to address the tremendous changes in the industry in the eight years since that book was published. Among the enhancements are:

- A revised first section explaining how investors can research and evaluate funds to find the ones that fit with their preferred asset allocation
- A separate chapter on money market funds, a category that has received much more attention as a result of the credit crisis of 2008
- A completely revised chapter on securities trading, reviewing the tremendous growth in virtual exchanges and automated trading
- A chapter on exchange-traded funds and hedge funds, investment vehicles that have soared in popularity recently
- Two additional chapters on the global fund industry, summarizing trends in asset gathering outside the United States

Despite these additions, this book has fewer pages than its predecessor because we've established a companion web site for the book at www.wiley.com/go/fundindustry. Rather than including supplementary materials in an appendix to each chapter, we've posted them online; you'll see references to these materials throughout the text. There's a special section of this web site for teachers; it contains review and discussion questions and suggestions for readings and case studies.

One area that we wished we could have covered in greater detail was derivatives, but space was simply too short to do justice to this complex topic. Instead, we've just made brief mention of their impact on mutual funds, especially during the credit crisis of 2008. The web site provides a list of reference materials if you'd like some background reading. Another omission: a glossary—in this case without regrets—since it's now so easy to look up definitions online. One of our favorite sources for basic financial information is Investopedia.

This book is divided into five sections:

1. *Section I: An Investor's Guide to Mutual Funds* looks at funds from an investor's perspective. We review the advantages and disadvantages of mutual funds, explain how they operate, and discuss how investors can gather information about potential fund investments. We also explore the different categories of mutual funds and review how investors might choose funds within each.
2. *Section II: Mutual Fund Portfolio Management* examines how funds manage their investments. We discuss portfolio management in stock, bond, and money market funds and then examine how funds implement

investment decisions through trading. We conclude with an overview of how mutual funds exercise their responsibilities as substantial stock investors.

3. *Section III: Selling Investment Funds* reviews how mutual funds are distributed to investors in the United States. We discuss sales through intermediaries, directly by funds and through retirement plans, examining issues within each channel as well as those affecting all channels. The final chapter in this section reviews the inner workings of two other investment vehicles that have become increasingly important: exchange-traded funds and hedge funds.

4. *Section IV: Operations and Finance* explains how the fund industry provides customer service and keeps portfolio records. We also review the financial dynamics of mutual fund management companies, examining factors that drive their profitability, and trends in mergers and acquisitions.

5. *Section V: The Internationalization of Mutual Funds* looks at cross-border investing and asset gathering. We take a look at the investment and operational issues faced by U.S. mutual funds investing outside the United States. We examine the special challenges involved in distributing funds across the world and discuss how the European Union has increased cross-border distribution. We end with a survey of the asset management industry in Asia and in the Americas outside of the United States, with a focus on China and Chile.

Supplementary materials mentioned throughout the text—plus a guide for teachers—are available online at www.wiley.com/go/fundindustry.

Acknowledgments

We would not—and could not—have undertaken a project of this scope without the help of experts in the disciplines that this text covers. We want to thank the many volunteers who made this book possible.

We'd especially like to thank the contributors who put in the long hours to draft or revise chapters. They are:

Chapter 5 on stock funds: Deborah H. Miller

Chapters 6 and 7 on bond and money market funds: Dwight Churchill and Claire M. Churchill

Chapter 8 on trading: Eric Roiter

Chapter 9 on proxy voting: Matthew R. Filosa

Chapter 10 on mutual fund sales: Alexander C. Gavis

Chapter 11 on retirement plans: John Kimpel

Chapter 12 on competition: Karl-Otto Hartmann on ETFs and Michael Pereira on hedge funds

Chapter 14 on portfolio recordkeeping and valuation: Virginia M. Meany

Chapter 15 on fees and expenses: Maria Dwyer

Chapters 17 and 18 on the internationalization of mutual funds: Christopher Bohane and Robert F. Hynes, Jr.

We want to thank our dedicated group of reviewers who commented on the draft manuscript. Their suggestions were invaluable: Carl Baldassare, Susan Christoffersen, Larry Cranch, Dwight Churchill, Lena Goldberg, Kathleen Miskiewicz, Betsy Pohl, Brian Reid, Craig Tyle, and Elizabeth Watson.

Many people provided input on particular chapters: Kino Clark, Catherine Coyne and her colleagues at NQR, Rhonda Dixon-Gunner, Mark Fischer, Joseph C. Flaherty, Jr., Stuart E. Fross, Annelise Goldberg, Laurie Gruppuso, Martin Guest, Giulia Hamacher, Van Harlow, Judy Hogan, Brett MacLeod, Charles Muller, Betsy Palmer, Gary Palmer, Mary Podesta,

Fred Quatrocky, Richard A. Schlanger, Peggy C. Schooley, Edgar Wallach, Michael Woodall and his associates at Putnam, Eric Woodbury, the trading team at MFS (Donald M. Mykrantz, Jeff Estella, and Greg Heller), and the trading team at Pioneer (Robert F. Gauvain and Mark Phillips).

A special thanks to the Investment Company Institute for their help in updating data, particularly Shaun Lutz.

Bob thanks MFS Investment Management for giving him the flexibility of time to work on the third edition of this book.

Theresa would like to thank the NICSA staff and the NICSA board for their support. She also thanks her mom.

But our biggest thanks go to our spouses. Without their love and patience, this book would have been completely impossible.

ROBERT POZEN
THERESA HAMACHER
November 2010

One

An Investor's Guide to Mutual Funds

Mutual funds are designed to make life easier for investors. Funds give savers of even modest means access to top-quality investment management combined with a high level of convenience and service, all at a reasonable price.

Since the mission of funds is to serve investors, we start this book by taking a look at mutual funds from an investor's perspective. We give an overview of mutual funds by focusing on four critical questions:

1. Why invest through mutual funds?
2. How do mutual funds work?
3. How do investors research a potential mutual fund purchase?
4. How do investors choose a mutual fund that's right for them?

This section has four chapters:

Chapter 1 provides an introduction to investing through mutual funds. It reviews their advantages and disadvantages, summarizes their history, and discusses how they are used by investors today. It concludes by providing an overview of the entities that work to ensure that funds meet their obligations to investors: the government regulators and the industry associations.

Chapter 2 describes the basic structure and operations of a mutual fund. It begins with a discussion of two key fund features: daily liquidity at net asset value and pass-through tax status. It explains how funds operate through contracts with service providers supervised by a board of directors, and it discusses the ethical standards that apply to fund managers. Finally, it compares mutual funds to alternative methods of investing, either directly in securities or through other commingled investment vehicles.

Chapter 3 explains how investors can learn about potential mutual fund investments through information provided by the funds themselves. It begins with a review of the principle of disclosure. It then focuses on the summary prospectus of a mutual fund and then continues with an overview of the other parts of the prospectus and of the shareholder reports. It ends with a discussion of how investors can use this information to select mutual funds.

Chapter 4 discusses how investors might go about choosing a mutual fund. It places funds in the context of a personal financial plan, and then explains the various approaches to evaluating fund performance results. It next reviews each type of mutual fund and ends with a discussion of the factors investors should consider when choosing a funds in that category.

CHAPTER 1

Investing through Mutual Funds

The odds are high that you already own a mutual fund. You're in good company: at the end of 2009, some 87 million people in the United States had invested at least a portion of their money through a fund.[1] Notice that we say that you invest *through* a mutual fund rather than *in* a fund. That's because a mutual fund isn't really an investment itself; it's just an intermediary—a financial intermediary.

Mutual funds have made it easy for individuals (you, me, anyone with some money to invest) and institutions (corporations, foundations, pension funds) to pool their money to buy stocks, bonds, and other investments. A fund is *mutual* because all of its returns—from interest, dividends, and capital gains—and all of its expenses are shared by the fund's investors.

Funds offer investors advantages over buying and selling securities directly, including:

- Reduction of risk by investment diversification
- Ability to sell your investment daily at no cost
- Access to the expertise of a professional money manager
- Ability to participate in investment strategies that might not otherwise be available to smaller investors
- Administrative convenience and shareholder services
- A high level of investor safeguards
- Full reporting that allows easy comparisons among funds

These benefits have proven to be very popular with investors around the world; they held a total of $23 *trillion* in fund assets at the end of 2009. American households now put more of their money in mutual funds than they do in banks, making mutual funds an integral part of financial planning for many people.[2] We describe a few typical fund buyers in "Mutual Fund Investors."

MUTUAL FUND INVESTORS

Are you—or is someone you know—in a similar position to one of these typical mutual fund investors?

- A middle-aged couple looking to retire sometime in the next 10 to 15 years. He works for a technology company, while she runs her own consulting business. They're building a retirement nest egg by investing in stock mutual funds through his company's 401(k) plan and her individual retirement account.
- A grandmother who wants to help finance the college tuition of her two baby granddaughters. She opens college savings plan accounts for both, with the intent to make annual contributions to them. She puts the assets in each account into a balanced mutual fund that holds a mix of stocks and bonds.
- A young professional tired of paying rent for his small apartment in the city. He has a goal of moving into his own condo in a few years and has started setting money aside for the down payment, through automatic deductions from his paycheck. His savings go into a bond mutual fund recommended by a financial adviser.
- The executive director of a small nonprofit looking to earn a return on her organization's modest surplus. An institutional money market fund managed by a national bank provides both a competitive yield and easy access to the funds if they're needed to meet any unanticipated expenses.

This chapter provides an introduction to investing through mutual funds. It reviews:

- The advantages and disadvantages of investing through mutual funds
- Their history and their use by investors today
- The regulators and industry associations that play a key role in the fund industry

ADVANTAGES AND DISADVANTAGES OF MUTUAL FUNDS

Mutual funds have gained such acceptance in household finances because they offer many advantages that include:

- *Greater diversification.* Through a mutual fund, investors may be able to own more securities than they could if they were acting just for themselves. Plus, investors can diversify even further by buying more than one fund. In the United States alone, there were more than 7,600 funds to choose from in 2009 with many different investment profiles—from bond funds to emerging market funds. (See "The ABCs of Risk" to understand how diversification helps investors.)

THE ABCs OF RISK

Reducing your investment risk is simple—all you have to do is buy more than one investment. This strategy of not putting all your eggs in one basket is technically known as *diversification*.

To understand why it works, it's useful to think of securities as having two kinds of risk: beta risk and alpha risk. Beta (often referred to by the Greek letter b or β) is the risk of the market overall. Alpha (Greek a or α), or idiosyncratic risk, is the ups and downs related to a specific investment. Looking at how they work together in a single stock, the price of that stock will tend to rise and fall with the stock market (beta). At the same time, the fortunes of the particular company issuing the stock will also have a big impact (alpha). As a general rule, a company's stock will do better than the market when the company news is good and worse when it is not.

Diversification reduces overall risk by reducing alpha risk. That's because when you hold a diversified portfolio, the good news on one security might offset bad news on another. Diversified investors don't have to worry as much about being wiped out when one investment goes sour—when, for example, the buggy whip manufacturer they've sunk their money into goes bankrupt after years of declining sales.

On the other hand, diversification doesn't help at all with beta risk. A diversified portfolio of U.S. stocks, for example, will still be likely to go down in price when the U.S. stock market is doing poorly.

Truly diversified investors spread their savings not just among individual investments but also among markets. Not sure whether the economy is getting stronger or weaker? You could decide to buy both stocks and bonds, since stocks tend to do well in a strong economy, while bonds tend to do well in a weak one. Believe there's a chance that the United States is losing its competitive edge? You might apportion your account into stocks around the world to increase the chance that you have at least some money invested in the country that's gaining market share.

While the principle of diversification is simple, implementation can be more complex. For example, it's not entirely clear how many securities are needed to eliminate alpha risk. In the U.S. stock market, for example, many professional investors will tell you that holding 20 to 30 securities is sufficient. The scholarly research, on the other hand, suggests that the number of stocks you need to completely eliminate idiosyncratic risk is both much higher than the practitioners' rule of thumb and rising over time. Although one study from the early 1990s calculates that 50 stocks will do the trick, the subtitle of a 2007 article asserts that "100 Stocks Are Not Enough"—while another study published that same year concludes that for certain types of stocks, such as smaller companies, maybe even 170 holdings won't provide complete diversification.[3]

- *Daily liquidity.* Investors in mutual funds have the right to sell their position back to the fund at the end of every business day at a price equal to the value of their share of the fund's holdings. No need to find another buyer or negotiate a sale price.
- *Professional management.* Funds hire professional investors with a high level of expertise to buy and sell securities on their behalf. Because these managers are working on behalf of a large number of investors, they can afford the top-notch analysts and sophisticated technology that can help them identify investments with higher returns.
- *Access to investment opportunities.* Individuals who want to invest overseas often find this easier to do through a mutual fund. Also, some securities are available only to investors with significant assets. For example, some stocks and bonds can purchased only by qualified institutional buyers responsible for at least $100 million in assets. While most mutual funds meet this test, very few individuals do. But by investing through mutual funds, which usually have minimum investments in the

range of only $5,000 to $10,000, individuals are able to participate in these opportunities.

- *Administrative convenience and shareholder services.* Funds offer their shareholders an easy way to invest, either over the phone or through the Internet, often 24 hours a day. Fund owners can also take advantage of a host of other services, such as tax reporting, check writing, automatic purchase programs, or access to retirement planning and other educational materials.
- *Investor protections.* A system of government regulation ensures that mutual fund assets are legitimately invested. In the United States, this includes oversight by an independent board of directors. As a result, investors in funds have less to fear from Ponzi schemes and other forms of theft.
- *Transparency and comparability.* Mutual funds are required to report to their investors regularly on their holdings and investment strategy, so that investors have a very good idea of what they're getting into when they invest their money through a mutual fund. Just as importantly, funds provide all of this information in a standardized format, which makes it easy to compare offerings.

Mutual funds have disadvantages as well. These include:

- *Fees.* Investors pay for all these benefits. In 2009, stock fund investors on average paid a little under 1 percent—0.86 percent to be precise—of the value of their fund assets for a year's worth of basic management services, including investment management and administration, together with annual marketing charges known as 12b-1 fees. Excluded from the 0.86 percent figure are the trading commissions that funds paid as they bought and sold stocks. Also excluded: sales loads—paid by some investors when they purchase shares of a fund—and program fees for using mutual funds as part of certain investment plans, such as wrap programs provided by brokerage firms or variable annuities offered by insurance companies.

   How much a shareholder will pay to own a fund varies widely, depending on the type of fund and the way the fund's shares are distributed to investors. Annual expenses on a money market fund in a 401(k) plan at work may be only 0.28 percent or 28 basis points. (See "Basis Points" for a definition of that term.) The fees may be 63 basis points per year on a bond fund bought directly from a fund company. But a small investment in a fund that buys high-growth start-up companies purchased through a financial adviser could cost 1.65 percent in annual fees plus a one-time sales load of 5.3 percent. (For a full explanation of mutual fund fees, see Chapter 15.)

BASIS POINTS

Mutual fund expenses are often expressed as a percentage of fund assets. Two decimal places are typically required for sufficient precision—for example, 1.07 percent.

Another way to express expenses is in *basis points*, often referred to casually as *bips* or *beeps*. A basis point is one-hundredth of a percent, so that "107 basis points" is the same as "1.07 percent."

Offsetting some of this cost, annual fees are subtracted from a fund's taxable income, making them effectively tax-deductible. In contrast, an investor who owns individual securities can't deduct investment-related expenses unless they add up to more than 2 percent of the investor's adjusted gross income for that year, a floor that few investors exceed.

- *No control on timing of gains.* Mutual funds don't allow investors to control the timing of capital gains. Investors who own individual stocks or bonds can choose when to sell a security to recognize a tax gain or loss. If they're not quite ready to pay taxes on the gain from a stock that has gone up, they can simply decide to wait—maybe until they can sell another stock at a loss to offset the gain. Shareholders in U.S. mutual funds, in contrast, don't have that option. The manager of the mutual fund decides when to sell the securities the fund holds, and the investors in the fund are required to pay taxes on the net capital gain that same year, even if they haven't reduced their investment in the fund. We talk more about fund taxation in the next chapter.

- *Less predictable income.* Dividend and interest income are less predictable in mutual funds, which means that investors who place a priority on steady income might be better off owning individual securities. They can buy bonds and hold them until maturity, knowing that they will receive the same interest payment regularly until the bonds are redeemed. In contrast, because a mutual fund buys and sells bonds often, the income it generates will vary, depending on the specific combination of securities owned on any given date.

- *No customization.* One final drawback to mutual funds: They don't allow for any customization. Instead, everyone in a fund gets exactly the same deal. An investor who objects to owning a particular stock can't insist that it be sold out of just his account. A large investor can't get a break on annual fees, which isn't available to other large investors. In fact, whenever one fund investor has been given special treatment, it often leads to scandal in the industry.

HISTORY AND GROWTH

The growing recognition of the advantages of mutual funds has led to a significant change in the way that Americans invest. U.S. households have been steadily increasing their positions in mutual funds while reducing their direct holdings of individual stocks. Let's take a look at how mutual funds evolved to become such a key element in individuals' financial plans.

Early History

The mutual fund is a fairly recent invention, dating back only to the beginning of the twentieth century.[4] That's when Boston law firms began to form trust divisions to manage the assets of wealthy local families. When their wealth became dispersed as it was passed down through the generations, the mutual fund came into existence as a way to jointly manage multiple family accounts. The year 1924 saw the introduction of a new type of fund, the *open-end* fund that was to become the standard for the industry, innovative at the time because it stood ready to accept new money and honor redemption requests from investors on a daily basis. "Funds from the 1920s" provides background on the two oldest funds.

Though the growth of the mutual fund industry was soon stymied by the stock market crash of 1929 and the Great Depression, legislation enacted in the 1930s and 1940s, as part of Franklin Roosevelt's New Deal, created a more regulated, less freewheeling financial industry—an environment that played to funds' strengths. In particular, the Investment Company Act of 1940 established strict operating standards for mutual funds and other types of investment companies, combining limits on fund promotion and portfolio investing with minimum requirements for reporting and pricing. The Act didn't mean much change for open-end funds, which had already adopted most of its provisions, but it did level the playing field by eliminating competition from less scrupulous investment managers.

Nevertheless, the growth rate of mutual funds was modest from the 1940s through the 1970s. Funds invested largely in stocks over this period,

FUNDS FROM THE 1920s

The recent explosive growth of the industry means that the vast majority of mutual funds today are veritable infants. Of the 7,600-plus funds registered at the end of 2009, fewer than one in five are more than 25 years old. Yet a few funds have very long histories. The two oldest U.S. funds are:

Massachusetts Investors Trust. This is the fund that started it all, the first open-end mutual fund, established in 1924. From its very beginning, Massachusetts Investors Trust adopted the shareholder protections that would only later become standard in the industry, including a willingness to redeem investments every day and to disclose its holdings regularly. MIT opened its own offices and hired its first full-time employee during the Great Depression, and by 1959, when *Time* magazine featured it in a cover story on mutual funds, it was the biggest fund in the industry, with assets of $1.5 billion. Today, MIT is part of the MFS family of funds. It invests in high quality companies with superior growth characteristics, whose stocks are selling at reasonable prices.

The Pioneer Fund. In 1928 Philip Carret, then a journalist working for *Barron's*, started a small, family-funded investment trust, originally called the Fidelity Investment Trust. Carret managed the portfolio himself for 23 years with a goal to "buy values—not fancy names."[5] Today's Pioneer Fund pursues reasonable income and capital growth by investing in stocks as part of the Pioneer fund family.

meaning that their fortunes were tied to the ups and downs of the market. As a result, the industry experienced a small growth spurt during the late 1950s and 1960s, when the economy was strong and stock prices were rising. But the mini-boom turned to prolonged bust when stocks plummeted in 1973. In the ensuing recession, it became very difficult, if not impossible, to sell stock mutual funds.

By the end of the decade, with the stock market still moribund, the action was in interest rates. From 1979 through 1982, interest rates soared into double digits, seldom dropping below 10 percent, and at one point rising to almost 20 percent. But most individual investors couldn't earn these high returns at the bank, because banking regulations—specifically Regulation Q under the Federal Reserve Act—capped the rates that a bank could pay on savings and checking accounts to less than 5 percent. Fat rates of interest were available only on $10,000 Treasury bills and $100,000 certificates of deposits, investments beyond the reach of the average American.

Enter the money market fund. By pooling together money from many investors, money market funds could afford to buy these high-yielding securities, making the attractive returns available to those of moderate means. The introduction of check-writing privileges made these funds even more competitive with bank deposits. The public was happy to move money out of their low-yield bank savings accounts into the new alternative: between 1977 and 1982, total assets held in money market funds grew from less than $4 billion to more than $200 billion. By the end of that period, three-quarters of the mutual fund industry's assets were in money market funds.

The dominance of money funds was short-lived, lasting only until the early 1980s. That's when Regulation Q was phased out, allowing banks to start paying competitive rates of interest again, and when the nascent bull market in stocks and bonds brought other types of mutual funds into the public eye. But money market funds remained a key financial tool for both businesses and individuals. And they played a critical role in positioning fund managers for the future. They did this by enabling funds to expand their reach among individual investors, who could exchange easily from money market funds into other types of funds when market conditions were right.

The Surge in Growth in the 1980s and 1990s

Once investors had been introduced to the advantages of money market funds, they were quick to turn to mutual funds for other investment needs. From 1984 to 2009, U.S. mutual fund assets increased 30-fold, from $370.7 billion to $11.1 *trillion,* a compound annual growth rate of 15.0 percent. Adjusted for inflation, that's an annual growth rate of 11.3 percent, significantly higher than the 2.8 percent per year gain in real gross domestic product over that same period.[6] Perhaps even more remarkably, total fund assets declined in only two of those 25 years, as a result of post-bubble declines in the stock market in 2002 and 2008. (The growth trajectory is shown in Figure 1.1.)

The steady expansion in fund assets was primarily the result of three factors: the bull market in stocks and bonds, new product introductions, and expanded distribution. We take a look here at each.

Growth factor 1: The bull market for both stocks and bonds. Rising prices for stocks and bonds from 1984 to 1999 increased the value of the savings already invested in mutual funds. At the same time, the very

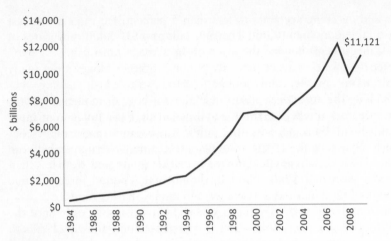

FIGURE 1.1   Growth in U.S. Mutual Fund Assets
Source: Investment Company Institute.

favorable market environment in the 1990s encouraged more individuals to take their money out of savings accounts and begin investing in bonds and stocks. The boom times ended with two market crashes, the collapse of the Internet bubble and the credit crisis. (See "The Crashes" for an introduction to both.)

THE CRASHES

There have been two times in the past 15 years when stock prices rose dramatically—and eventually fell even more dramatically. The first was the Internet bubble, which developed in the late 1990s in lockstep with the public's growing awareness of the potential of the World Wide Web. This bubble popped in March 2000 when it became clear that going virtual was not a guarantee of real profits.

Much of the hot air released from Internet stocks was to find its way into real estate. House prices around much of the world ballooned through most of the first decade of the new century, inflated by the easy-to-obtain mortgages that banks offered to even the most unsuitable buyers. When overextended property owners defaulted on their loans in startlingly high numbers, real estate prices fell with a thud—seriously wounding many financial institutions in the process. The shakeout in 2008 has come to be known as the *credit crisis*.

Growth factor 2: New product introductions. Encouraged by the success of the money market fund, management companies created new types of funds to meet investor needs and win market share from other financial institutions.

- *Tax-exempt funds.* Tax-exempt funds were developed in the late 1970s, after legislation was enacted that eliminated a tax penalty on municipal bonds owned through a mutual fund.[7] Tax-exempt funds were to become popular in the 1980s, after Congress curtailed many of the other strategies that individuals had used to reduce their tax bills.
- *Sector funds.* The 1980s also saw the introduction of sector funds focused on particular industries, appealing to investors who might otherwise purchase individual stocks.
- *International funds.* The launches of new types of international funds in the following decade brought consumers to a field of investing formerly available only to large institutions.
- *Target-date funds.* More recently, the development of target date funds, a type of hybrid fund investing in varying amounts of both stocks and bonds, has created a new alternative for individuals saving for retirement.

This broad range of offerings has ensured that the fund industry can provide options for all economic environments. Figure 1.2 shows how, from

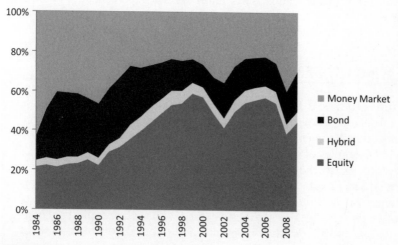

FIGURE 1.2   Share of Assets by Fund Type
Source: Investment Company Institute.

1984 through 2009, assets have shifted among the four main types of mutual funds: stock funds, bond funds, money market funds, and hybrid funds. While money market funds were still predominant in 1984, the interest rates paid on these funds were already beginning to decline, and assets subsequently shifted toward bond funds. Stock and hybrid funds moved to center stage at the start of the 1990s, so that by the end of the decade, they were almost two-thirds of the fund industry. Since then, their popularity has tracked the rise and fall of the stock market. Money market and bond funds have generally provided a haven for investors in those periods when stock funds are out of favor. At the end of 2009, equity and hybrid funds together accounted for 50 percent of the mutual fund industry, and money market funds 30 percent, with bond funds making up the balance.

Growth factor 3: Expanded distribution. Over the past 30 years, fund management companies have reached out to new groups of investors through new distribution channels. Until the 1970s, almost all mutual funds were sold to the public through intermediaries; in other words, they were managed by one company, but sold to the public by another, usually a *broker-dealer.* ("Dealing with Brokers" provides key definitions.) Brokers at these firms would make personalized investment recommendations to their clients, who were generally quite wealthy. At that time, brokers were normally compensated for giving this advice through commissions, which were fees charged to the investor on a purchase or sale transaction. In the case of mutual funds, the commission is called a *front-end sales load* or *front-end sales charge* and is deducted from the investment before it goes into the fund; in the 1960s, sales loads were 8.5 percent of the amount invested.

DEALING WITH BROKERS

A *broker-dealer* is firm that buys or sells securities, either for clients or for its own account. Broker-dealers are sometimes called *brokerage firms.* Merrill Lynch, Morgan Stanley Smith Barney, and Edward Jones are all examples of broker-dealers.

In the past, the salespeople employed by broker-dealers were referred to as *brokers.* Today, however, they are usually called *financial advisers* or *account executives.* In legal parlance, they are *registered representatives,* because they are licensed with the appropriate regulatory agencies. That's why one publication targeted at brokers is titled *Registered Rep.*

This traditional method of distribution through intermediaries began to change with the advent of money market funds. These funds were sold without a front-end load directly to the public, who became aware of them through advertisements and mailings. Eventually, some mutual fund management companies began to sell all of their funds, including stock and bond funds, directly to the public, avoiding intermediaries altogether. Because they did not involve a sales load, direct sales became very popular with cost-conscious investors who were comfortable making their own investment decisions without the help of a broker.

The introduction of 401(k) plans in the 1980s—combined with the tremendous growth in individual retirement accounts, or IRAs—created another, and perhaps the most significant, way to distribute funds: through retirement accounts. Mutual funds became the preferred investment option in these accounts, while fund management companies became leading providers of the detailed recordkeeping and customer service capabilities retirement plans require. The services provided have been so popular that retirement accounts now make up more than one-third of industry assets. At the same time, mutual funds have become a critical component of the nation's retirement system, accounting for 25 percent of retirement plan assets at the end of 2009.

Distribution through intermediaries has evolved. Today, both banks and insurance companies sell funds to the public, the latter often through variable annuity contracts or life insurance policies. Registered investment advisers, unaffiliated with a broker dealer, have also become a major factor in fund distribution. Their entry into mutual fund distribution sparked a new trend: charging clients an annual fee based on assets rather than a front-end load triggered by a purchase. Broker-dealers have responded with similar programs that incorporate mutual funds, purchased without a sales load, into a complete financial solution which charges an additional and separate fee for participation.

Mutual fund distribution has gone global, too. Fund management companies have set up shop around the world, opening funds for local investors. And with the growing acceptance by many governments of the European Union's harmonized fund format, funds can now be distributed across borders, as we see in Chapter 17. At the end of 2009, investor ownership of mutual funds outside the United States exceeded a total of $11 trillion in more than 40 countries.

Mutual Fund Ownership in the United States Today

The combination of attractive features and broad distribution has made mutual funds a compelling alternative to direct investing in securities. In

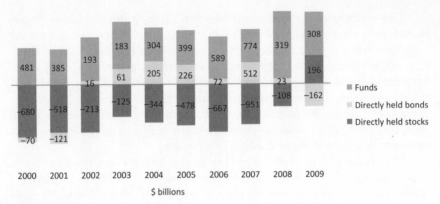

FIGURE 1.3 Household Net Investments in Funds, Bonds, and Stocks[8]
Source: Investment Company Institute.

9 of the past 10 years, U.S. households have increased their positions in mutual funds while reducing their direct holdings of individual stocks. Figure 1.3 shows the recent data on household investment in funds, bonds, and stocks.

This shift toward mutual funds has occurred in the context of increasing household interest in investing savings, as opposed to leaving them in the bank. In 1989, only 39 percent of U.S. households owned bonds and stocks. That figure soared to 57 percent in 2001, before tailing off to 49 percent. Many of the investors buying stocks and bonds for the first time made their purchases through mutual funds.

By the end of 2009, some 43 percent of all U.S. households—50.4 million in total—had invested at least some of their assets through funds. As Figure 1.4 illustrates, the proportion of households owning mutual funds zipped upward in the 1980s and 1990s and has remained steady at 40 percent to 45 percent in the past decade.

So who are these individuals? In 2009, they were likely to be employed college graduates of middle age; most had a spouse or a partner sharing responsibility for financial decision making. Their median household income was $80,000, with median financial assets (excluding their home) of $150,000. Mutual fund owners did not generally fall into the ranks of the very wealthy: only 22 percent had financial assets exceeding $500,000 and just 16 percent earned more than $150,000 annually.

A few more facts: The average fund-owning household had invested $80,000 in four different funds.[9] Funds represented the majority of financial assets for 66 percent of these households. Their most important reason by

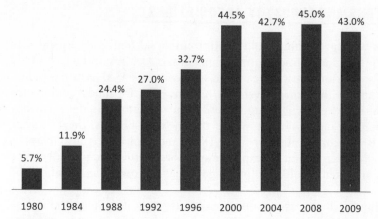

FIGURE 1.4 Percentage of U.S. Households Owning Mutual Funds
Source: Investment Company Institute.

far for investing in funds was to prepare for retirement, although they were also concerned about reducing taxable income, meeting emergency needs, financing education, providing income, and saving for a house or other large purchase. More than 80 percent participated in a retirement plan sponsored by their employer, with more than a quarter owning funds only as a part of that plan. Table 1.1 provides the data.

TABLE 1.1 Profile of Mutual Fund Investors (2009)

Demographic Characteristics	
Median age	50
Married or living with a partner	76%
Employed, whether full-time or part-time	73%
College graduates	47%
Partners share financial decision making	61%
Financial Characteristics	
Median household income	$80,000
Less than $50,000	23%
Between $50,000 and $150,000	61%
More than $150,000	16%
Median household financial assets (excludes primary residence, but includes employer-sponsored retirement plan)	$150,000
Less than $500,000	78%
Participate in employer-sponsored retirement plan	82%

Source: Investment Company Institute.

REGULATORS AND INDUSTRY ASSOCIATIONS

With such widespread household interest in mutual funds, it's critical that they fulfill their commitments to their investors. As a result, mutual funds have become the most strictly regulated segment of the U.S. securities industry. The entity with primary oversight responsibility for funds' compliance with all of the relevant laws and subsequent regulations is the Securities and Exchange Commission; it works closely with FINRA, the Financial Industry Regulatory Authority. The Department of Labor also plays a role through its regulation of employer-sponsored retirement plans. Finally, the states are often involved in investigating and prosecuting violations of the rules.

The fund industry associations play a key role in helping the industry handle the high level of regulatory oversight. The Investment Company Institute is the principal advocate for the industry with legislators and regulators, while NICSA, the National Investment Company Service Association, provides educational programs on the implementation of new regulations.

Securities and Exchange Commission

The Securities and Exchange Commission, or SEC, was created by Congress in 1934 as the agency primarily responsible for administering federal securities laws. Its mission is "to protect investors, maintain fair, orderly, and efficient markets, and facilitate capital formation."[10] Five commissioners are responsible for overseeing its operations. They are appointed by the president of the United States to five-year terms; these terms are staggered so that one commissioner is appointed each year. To ensure bipartisanship, no more than three serving commissioners may be of the same political party.

The SEC has five divisions:

1. The *Investment Management Division* has the greatest impact on the mutual fund industry. It oversees investment companies and the investment advisers that manage them.
2. The *Division of Trading and Markets* monitors the buying and selling of securities through regulation of broker-dealers and exchanges. Of particular relevance to mutual funds, this division oversees the shareholder service division of fund managers, known as the *transfer agent*.
3. The *Division of Enforcement* investigates potential violations of the law, recommends action when it believes there has been a violation, and negotiates settlements with offenders. It often acts on the basis of

referrals from the Office of Compliance Inspections and Examinations, as described in "SEC Inspections."

SEC INSPECTIONS

To make sure that firms are complying with regulations, the SEC's Office of Compliance Inspections and Examinations conducts reviews of securities firms. Problems detected by OCIE (often spoken of as "*Oh*-see") may be referred to the Division of Enforcement for follow-up action. OCIE examiners may appear in offices at any time, sometimes as the result of a tip, if there is cause to believe that a firm is violating a significant rule. OCIE can also ask for information from many firms at one time as part of a *risk-focused*, or *sweep*, exam, looking at a new issue in the industry.

4. The *Division of Corporation Finance* ensures that publicly traded corporations provide investors with the information needed to make informed decisions. As significant holders of corporate securities, mutual funds are beneficiaries of this division's work.
5. The *Division of Risk, Strategy, and Financial Innovation* was created in 2009. It studies longer-term trends in the financial markets and makes recommendations on how the SEC might adapt its regulatory approach in light of them.

By law, the SEC must follow a lengthy procedure whenever it considers new regulations. This process works as follows:

- First, the SEC staff issues a proposed rule, which explains the need for the regulation and its specific terms.
- In most cases, the SEC will then request comments on the proposed regulation, during a specified comment period. Although anyone can comment on an SEC proposal, it's typically firms in the industry that provide input, both on the advisability of a new regulation and on the feasibility of its technical provisions. Occasionally—usually when a new regulation represents a significant break with the past—the SEC will actively solicit comments before issuing a proposed regulation. In such cases, it issues a "concept release," giving a broad overview of the potential change and requesting input.

■ The SEC staff reviews the comments received and makes any appropriate changes to the proposed rule. The rule becomes a final rule after it has been voted on by the SEC commissioners and approved by at least a majority.

This lengthy rule-making process is designed not just to ensure that all technical issues have been addressed—which facilitates implementation—but also to build consensus around the new regulation. As a result, while new regulations can be approved by a simple majority of the SEC commissioners, they almost always receive their unanimous support. The few instances when a decision has been made over the dissent of one or two commissioners have been newsworthy. A split decision did occur in 2010 when the commissioners divided over whether to pursue an enforcement action against Goldman Sachs. (They voted three to two to proceed.) But the last time it happened before that was in 2004.[11]

After a final rule is issued, management companies and other industry firms can seek informal interpretive advice from the SEC in the form of *no-action* letters. The requesting organization writes a letter to the SEC, essentially asking, "Will the SEC take any enforcement action if we do such-and-such?" and describing some activity they would like to undertake but aren't sure is permitted. The SEC staff studies the proposed action, and, if they feel that it does not violate a statute or rule, the Office of the Chief Counsel of the appropriate division issues a no-action letter. The letter generally says that the staff "will not recommend to the Commission that it take enforcement action" related to the proposed activity. These letters—while not technically binding on the Commission—serve to alleviate concerns on the part of requesting organizations that their proposed action might lead to enforcement action.

For example, in a recent no-action letter it issued, the SEC staff said that it would not recommend enforcement action if Bear Stearns Asset Management, after its emergency acquisition by J.P. Morgan during the credit crisis, continued to act as the investment adviser to the mutual funds it managed before the acquisition. The no-action letter was needed because Bear Stearns's contract to manage the fund was legally terminated upon the change in ownership, and the takeover happened so swiftly that there wasn't time to prepare a new contract and seek approval from fund investors in advance.

Most no-action letters address subtle or arcane issues in the interpretation of the regulations—or unique situations (as in the Bear Stearns case)—that defy easy categorization. They provide the industry and the SEC with a valuable tool for resolving the inevitable ambiguity associated with complex securities laws.

More information on the SEC is available on its web site: www.sec.gov. All of the SEC's recent proposed rules, final rules, concept releases, and no-action letters are posted there.

FINRA

The mission of FINRA (*Fin*-rah), the Financial Industry Regulatory Authority, is "to protect America's investors by making sure the securities industry operates fairly and honestly."[12] FINRA took on its current name when its predecessor, the NASD (National Association of Securities Dealers, once part of the NASDAQ stock market) merged with the enforcement division of the New York Stock Exchange in July 2007. It oversees the activities of broker-dealers and their registered representatives, specifically with regard to their sale of securities to the public. Its web site is www.finra.org.

Of most importance to mutual funds, FINRA regulates much of their distribution activity.

- It licenses those individuals who participate in the selling of mutual funds and securities. FINRA requires the licensing of individuals who sell only mutual funds (through the Series 6 exam and registration), those who sell mutual funds and other securities (Series 7), and the supervisors of the selling brokers (Series 24). It has also proposed that many operations professionals, especially those dealing with customer accounts, be licensed as well.
- It reviews almost all sales and advertising materials produced by the funds and may bring disciplinary proceedings against firms or individuals for violations of fund advertising or sales rules.
- It limits the sales loads on securities that broker-dealers sell, which effectively enables it to set maximum limits on the sales loads the funds charge. This maximum is currently 8.5 percent of the amount invested.

Unlike the SEC, FINRA is not a governmental agency but a self-regulatory organization. SROs typically come about when industry members join together to police themselves, in an attempt to throw out bad apples in advance, rather than have the government come along and root through the entire barrel. An SRO can acquire and exercise quasi-governmental authority, subject to SEC oversight, and this is what has happened with FINRA. The SEC, through the Division of Trading and Markets, has delegated a portion of its responsibilities to FINRA, those having to do with the regulation of broker-dealers doing business with the public. Another SRO in the investment industry is the Municipal Securities Rulemaking Board, which monitors the market for municipal bonds.

Department of Labor

Why would the Department of Labor be involved with the regulation of mutual funds? Because the DOL is responsible for overseeing employer-provided retirement plans. As we've seen, retirement plans have come to represent a significant proportion of mutual fund assets. Acting through its division of Employee Benefits Security Administration or EBSA, the DOL sets rules regarding plan terms and reporting to participants, which include both current and retired employees. Mutual funds offering retirement plans must be cognizant of DOL regulations. For more on the DOL's role in retirement plans, go to www.dol.gov/ebsa.

State Regulators

State regulation of mutual funds has changed significantly over the past 15 years. Until 1996, most states maintained their own regulatory agencies with their own rules—often inconsistent with those established by the SEC. To bring some order to the chaos, Congress enacted the National Securities Markets Improvement Act. NSMIA preempted state authority in most areas, giving the SEC the sole regulatory authority on most substantive issues. In doing so, it relieved funds of a considerable burden in responding to fragmented and conflicting state regulatory requirements.

Yet NSMIA explicitly preserved local authority to investigate and prosecute fraud involving mutual funds, and the states have recently been flexing their muscles in this regard. For example, in 2003, the New York State Attorney General's office was instrumental in uncovering and pursuing abuses regarding trading in mutual fund shares, as is discussed in Chapter 14. Also, under NSMIA, funds interested in selling shares in a state must usually register with and pay a fee to that state's regulators.

Investment Company Institute

The Investment Company Institute is the industry's primary trade association. Founded shortly after the passage of the Investment Company Act of 1940, the ICI's membership today includes almost all of the fund complexes in the United States. At the end of 2009, ICI member firms managed funds with assets representing over 93 percent of the industry total. Its web site is www.ici.org.

This broad base of support has allowed the fund industry to speak with one voice before Congress, the SEC, and other regulators, making the ICI an effective advocate for industry interests. The ICI devotes considerable resources to advocacy. According to the Center for Responsive Politics, in

2009 it spent $5.5 million on lobbying and employed nine in-house staff in lobbying activities. Its political action committee made $695,000 in contributions to federal candidates in the 2008 election cycle.[13]

The ICI has a critical educational mission as well. Its research department is a primary source of information on investment industry trends, covering topics as diverse as the retirement plan market, investor demographics, and fund fees. In 2009, it produced close to 150 reports with statistics on the mutual fund business (many of them cited in this chapter). The ICI also holds well-attended conferences for industry participants and generates materials for investor education.

NICSA

NICSA (*Nick*-sa), the National Investment Company Service Association, helps fund management companies and service providers respond to new regulations. Established in 1962 as an informal forum for operations and shareholder service professionals, NICSA's mission is solely educational. Like the ICI, it is a membership organization; unlike the ICI, it does not engage in any lobbying. Instead, it organizes both live conferences and webinars that brief managers on the latest business developments. It also sponsors discussion groups that develop and codify best practices for complying with regulations.

NICSA's web site at www.nicsa.org has information on its programs.

CHAPTER SUMMARY

Mutual funds enable investors to pool their funds together to buy stocks, bonds, and other investments. All of the fund's returns and all of its expenses are shared by the fund's investors.

Mutual funds have gained considerable acceptance in household finances because they enable investors to diversify more—both in numbers and types of securities—than they would if they were investing on their own. Funds are also a convenient way to invest: they allow investors to sell their holdings daily, provide professional investment management and a range of other investor services. Mutual funds are subject to extensive government regulations that provide a high level of protection for investors. On the negative side, mutual funds charge fees for these services, and there is little opportunity for investors to customize a fund to fit their situation.

While the first mutual funds were established in Boston in the 1920s, most of their growth has occurred within the past three decades. The bull market for both stocks and bonds in the 1980s and 1990s boosted the value of fund assets and encouraged more individuals to invest, often through mutual funds. Fund management companies expanded the market for mutual funds by introducing new types of funds and opening up other channels for distribution—through direct sales and through retirement plans as well as through financial intermediaries. Today, mutual funds are held by 43 percent of U.S. households.

Mutual funds are subject to strict government oversight. The Securities and Exchange Commission, or SEC, is the primary regulator of the fund industry, though FINRA, the Department of Labor, and the states also play a role. The industry associations help the industry handle this high level of regulation. The Investment Company Institute is the principal advocate for the industry with legislators and regulators, while NICSA, the National Investment Company Service Association, provides educational programs on the implementation of new regulations.

CHAPTER 2

How Mutual Funds Work

Now that we've discussed how mutual funds can help investors, let's take a quick look inside mutual funds to understand exactly how they are organized and operate. At first glance, there doesn't seem to be anything out of the ordinary about a mutual fund. Each mutual fund is a separate corporation, often referred to as an *investment company* or *registered investment company,* or RIC.[1] Like other corporations, mutual funds issue shares to the public. These shares represent proportional ownership of the fund: own 10 percent of a fund's shares, and you effectively own 10 percent of both its assets and its liabilities. Investors who decide to place their money in a particular fund do so through buying its shares, becoming shareholders in the process. This is why the terms *investors* and *shareholders* are used interchangeably throughout the fund industry.

On closer examination, however, mutual funds are quite unusual public companies. Their shares do not trade on a stock exchange. As a general rule, they neither pay taxes nor have any employees. In addition, they are protected by particularly strict ethical standards. Let's take a closer look at each of these features and see how they compare to other options for investing.

This chapter reviews:

- How investors buy and sell fund shares at net asset value
- The pass-through tax status of mutual funds
- How funds organize their daily operations under the supervision of a board of directors
- The ethical standards that govern fund operations
- The alternatives to mutual funds available to individual investors

Note that, from this point on, we focus on U.S. mutual funds. We return to non-U.S. funds in Chapter 17. For those interested in learning more about the laws and regulations we discuss, see the list of legal citations that is posted on this book's web site.

BUYING AND SELLING FUND SHARES

Mutual funds are unique because their investors don't go to a stock exchange to buy and sell their shares: they go directly to the fund itself. As a result, a fund's share price isn't established by traders in the marketplace. Rather, it's equal to the fund's *net asset value,* or NAV, which is calculated daily using the formula described in "Navigating NAV." When making a purchase of a share, investors pay the NAV plus the sales load, if any, which together are known as the *offering price.* When selling, they receive the NAV, reduced by any redemption fees.

NAVIGATING NAV

A fund's net asset value or NAV (pronounced as one syllable rhyming with *have*) equals fund assets minus fund liabilities divided by the number of shares outstanding.

$$NAV = (Assets - Liabilities)/Number \ of \ shares \ outstanding$$

A fund with $100 million in assets, $10 million in liabilities, and 10 million shares outstanding has net assets of $90 million and a NAV of $9.00.

Of course a fund has assets, but what are its liabilities? Certain complex investment strategies, such as short selling or option writing, generate liabilities. If a fund borrows money for any reason—to meet redemptions or to create leverage—the borrowings will also appear as liabilities. Finally, a fund will accrue liabilities for the fees that it will pay to providers of services such as investment management.

Most funds make shares available for purchase every business day. They are not required to do so, however, so that on occasion funds will refuse additional money from investors. This is most likely to occur when a fund has grown to be very large and is concerned that it will not be able to find opportunities for investing new cash.

By law, though, a mutual fund must be willing to buy back, or redeem, its shares from its investors every day the New York Stock Exchange is open. If a fund wants to suspend redemptions—because of dire emergency or severe disruptions in the markets—it must first receive permission to do so from the SEC. (There is an exception for money market funds that allows them to stop redemptions without SEC approval. We discuss this exception—and the events that gave rise to it—in Chapter 7.)

Obviously, the ability to sell a mutual fund position almost instantaneously is a tremendous benefit for investors: investors can notify the fund's shareholder service provider any time during the day that they'd like to sell their shares, and the fund will send cash equal to the value of those shares based on the NAV calculated that evening.[2]

While a boon for consumers, daily redemptions make life considerably more difficult for a fund, in two ways. First, a fund must be able to compute its NAV daily. While the formula is simple, the process is anything but. Entering securities transactions, reconciling holdings, recording liabilities, and then valuing all positions accurately—on an extremely tight schedule—is a major undertaking for any fund, but especially for those holding a large number of positions or more complex investments. We review the challenges of NAV calculation in depth in Chapter 14.

But it's not just operational infrastructure that must be prepped to accommodate daily redemptions: funds must also structure their investment portfolios in a way that enables them to raise cash quickly and easily meet any level of withdrawal requests. Rules regarding portfolio structure were included in the Investment Company Act of 1940, one of the laws that supported the creation of the fund industry. (See "The Cornerstones" for more information on this early legislation.)

THE CORNERSTONES

Two pieces of legislation created the mutual fund industry as we know it today. The Revenue Act of 1936 established the guidelines that allow funds to pass through taxation to shareholders. The Investment Company Act of 1940, usually referred to as the 1940 Act, determined their structure. The principles of both laws continue to govern fund operations today.

While the Revenue Act may have been "the most important event in mutual fund history," as industry historian Matt Fink asserts, it's the 1940 Act that gets the press.[3] Funds are often called '40 Act Funds to distinguish them from other types of commingled funds. And lawyers that specialize in mutual funds? They're '40 Act attorneys, of course.

The 1940 Act limits portfolio holdings in two ways:

1. *It limits borrowings.* A fund is limited in how much money it can borrow. By law, the value of its borrowings may not exceed one-third of the value of its assets. Fund borrowings are collateralized, or *secured,* by fund assets, which means that those assets can't be sold until the loans are paid off. As a result, limited borrowing equals limited impediments to fast security sales. Today, most funds borrow only to meet short-term cash needs—to be able to send checks to redeeming shareholders, for example, while they wait for proceeds from the sale of fund holdings to come in.

2. *It sets standards for diversification.* Most funds elect to qualify as *diversified.* Under the 1940 Act, one of the key pieces of legislation governing mutual funds, diversification is defined as a negative. Specifically, with respect to 75 percent of their assets, diversified funds do *not* put more than 5 percent of total fund assets in a single investment and they do *not* own more than 10 percent of the voting securities of a single company.

   They have complete freedom with regard to the other 25 percent, however, so in theory they could invest 25 percent of assets in one issuer and then 5 percent in each of 15 other issuers. In practice, however, most diversified mutual funds hold more than 50 positions and rarely invest more than 10 percent of their assets in any one issuer. Since smaller positions are easier to sell than larger ones, the thinking goes, diversified funds are better positioned to meet redemption requests.

   Nondiversified funds, which concentrate their investments in a smaller number of issuers, could have a tougher time raising cash when needed. Funds that focus on a single industry sector or in very small high-growth companies often elect to be nondiversified.

The SEC has established additional limits to ensure that funds are able to meet redemption requests. For example, funds may not invest more than 15 percent of their assets in illiquid securities, which are those that cannot be sold within seven days. The limit is even lower—5 percent—for money market funds. In other words, the great majority of fund holdings must be available for sale at short notice if needed to meet redemptions.

In short, the ability to redeem at any time carries a cost. The limitations on fund concentration, borrowing and illiquid securities mean that mutual funds cannot use the most aggressive investment strategies, strategies that can result in higher returns. That's okay with mainstream investors, but it does mean that those interested in high risk–high reward approaches often prefer alternatives such as hedge funds.

THE PASS-THROUGH TAX STATUS OF MUTUAL FUNDS

Another way that mutual funds are unique: they are corporations, but don't pay corporate taxes. Funds pass all tax liabilities on to their shareholders. This may not sound like much of a benefit, but contrast the tax situation of a mutual fund to that of a typical corporation. The earnings of an operating company are taxed twice. First, the company pays corporate income taxes, and then shareholders pay personal income tax on any dividends that the company has paid out of its after-tax income. At least mutual fund owners pay taxes only once!

The Internal Revenue Service obviously collects more money if it imposes taxes twice, so it has established tests to prevent operating companies from transforming themselves into mutual funds. These tests are included in Subchapter M of the Internal Revenue Code. (Not surprising, then, that tax attorneys refer to mutual funds as "Subchapter M corporations.") Two of these tests should be familiar from our discussion of the 1940 Act diversification standards:

- *Diversification.* With respect to 50 percent of their assets, mutual funds may not invest more than 5 percent of total fund assets in a single investment; with respect to the other 50 percent, they may not invest more than 25 percent in any one issuer. (Similar to the 1940 Act. See "Test Taking" for details on how the two requirements differ.)

TEST TAKING

Which diversification test is easier to pass: the 1940 Act test or the IRS test? It depends. The tax test requires the fund to own fewer issuers, it's true, but the IRS requires funds to satisfy its test at the end of every calendar quarter. The test in the 1940 Act, on the other hand, applies only at the time of purchase.

An example: On March 1, assume that the Avon Hill Fund invests 24 percent of its assets in Windy Corner stocks. (All other holdings are well below 5 percent of assets.) Windy Corner's stock takes off, and by March 31, the fund's investment in this company has risen to 40 percent of the fund. That's not a problem under the 1940 Act, because the position was under the 25 percent limit at the time it was bought. But the fund will need to sell part of its position to comply with the tax test, which looks only at the portfolio's holdings at the end of the quarter.

- *Limited ownership of voting securities.* With respect to 50 percent of their assets, Subchapter M corporations may not own more than 10 percent of the voting securities of any one issuer.

The other tests are specific to the Internal Revenue Code:

- *Distributions.* To qualify for pass-through tax treatment, funds must distribute at least 90 percent of the interest, dividends, and net realized capital gains they earn every year. Taxpayers then include these distributions in their individual tax returns. To help them prepare those returns, funds report the income to shareholders on Form 1099-DIV, which is also sent to the IRS. Distributions retain their character when they pass into the shareholder's hands; if they were long-term capital gains to the fund, they are long-term gains to the investors.

  In practice, funds pay out *all* of their income every year. That's because they must pay an excise tax if they distribute less than 98 percent of their income. To discourage funds from distributing just 98 percent of income every year, any undistributed income is carried over into the next year's calculation.

- *Qualifying Income.* One final requirement under Subchapter M: at least 90 percent of income before expenses must come from the business of investing in securities and currencies (and in commodities, if proposed legislation passes). A fund may not invest most of its assets in apartment buildings or factory equipment or gold mines and still receive favorable tax treatment.

Sounds fair, right? Investors in a mutual fund pay the same taxes that they would pay if they owned the securities directly. Except that fund investors don't control the timing of their tax payments. If they held a stock in their brokerage account, *they* would decide when to sell to recognize a capital gain or loss. When they hold that same stock through a mutual fund, it's the investment manager who makes the timing decision—and fund shareholders have no choice but to pay the resulting tax bill when it comes due.

Making matters worse, funds are not allowed to distribute the benefits of any net realized capital losses; these can only be used to offset fund gains in future years. If a shareholder would like to take advantage of a loss in a mutual fund holding to offset a gain in another portfolio position, she must sell fund shares to make that happen. In other words, funds are not perfect pass-through vehicles.

To help alleviate the tax burden, many funds use investment strategies that minimize the recognition of capital gains—and the tax bill that comes with them. Index funds, in particular, have become very popular in part because they do very little trading of the securities in their portfolios: no trading, no capital gains, no taxes.

So maybe fund taxation is less fair than it seems at first glance. In fact, most other developed countries have adopted a different approach, as "A Taxing Comparison" explains.

A TAXING COMPARISON

It's all a matter of perspective. While U.S. corporations may yearn for the tax rules that apply to mutual funds, investors in the rest of the world see the U.S. mutual fund tax regime as draconian. Most foreign investment funds are not required to distribute capital gains to shareholders. Instead, all gains accumulate within the fund, and investors pay taxes on them only when they redeem their shares, giving shareholders more control over the timing of their tax bill.

So at least from a tax perspective, U.S. mutual funds are not very attractive to non-U.S. savers who have better alternatives at home. And while *offshore* mutual funds, meaning those set up in another country, may look good to U.S. investors, the SEC won't permit their sale to individuals here.

As a result, the global mutual fund industry has effectively split into two parts: U.S. versus non-U.S. We review the business implications of this divide in Chapter 17.

One final caveat: annual taxation on distributions isn't an issue for over half of the assets in mutual funds.[4] That's because 44 percent of fund assets are held within tax-deferred vehicles, like retirement accounts or variable annuities. Income received in these accounts is not taxed until it is withdrawn. And another 8 percent of assets is invested in tax-exempt municipal bond funds. The interest income on these bonds is generally not subject to federal income tax.

A VIRTUAL CORPORATION

Mutual funds differ from operating companies in another important respect: they generally don't have any employees. Rather, they are virtual corporations that retain other companies to do all the work. The fund's board of directors is responsible for negotiating contracts with these service providers and monitoring their performance under them.

So mutual funds are exactly like other corporations in at least one respect: they all have a board of directors.[5] In 2008, the average fund board had eight members.[6] Like corporate boards, mutual fund boards represent the interests of shareholders, and fund directors have the same general duties as corporate directors—the duty to manage with care and the duty of loyalty to the fund.

Both corporate boards and mutual fund boards must refer certain issues to shareholders for a final decision. To do this, they send out a *proxy statement* that explains the questions that investors are being asked to weigh in on. Shareholders then say yea or nay on each question, casting one vote for each share that they own at a meeting called for this purpose. The entire process is often called *proxy voting*, because shareholders can submit their vote by absentee ballot, or *proxy*. They don't have to be present in person to make their views known.

While a corporate board must hold a shareholder vote annually—whether there's something important to decide or not—mutual fund boards only consult their investors when there are particularly meaty questions on the table. Fund shareholders are not required to vote on routine matters, such as the reappointment of the same audit firm or the reelection of already serving directors. Instead, fund shareholders vote on relatively few substantive issues. These include changing fundamental investment policies, increasing the management company's fees or hiring a new management company or auditor. Fund directors can even serve for a time without being elected, because the current board can appoint its own replacements as long as at least two-thirds of the directors have been approved by shareholders. When the percentage of investor-approved directors falls below that figure, a vote must be taken. (See "The Price of Democracy" to learn why funds are not required to hold annual shareholder votes.) Links to sample fund proxies are available on this book's web site.

THE PRICE OF DEMOCRACY

Funds don't hold annual shareholder votes for one main reason: it's a matter of cost. Because most funds have lots of individual shareholders and few large institutional investors, they often have a tough time collecting the minimum number of votes required by law to make a quorum. To ensure that votes are cast for enough shares, funds usually pay proxy solicitation firms to make phone calls. The SEC has concluded that this is not worth the expense when only routine matters are being considered.

On issues that don't require shareholder approval, both corporate and fund boards have broad authority to supervise and manage the business, though they handle this responsibility in very different ways. For corporate boards, a primary role is the hiring, firing, and compensation of the company's chief executive officer. Corporate directors normally act through the CEO to influence strategy and policy. As mentioned, fund directors manage relationships with service providers.

The single most significant contract the board signs is with the fund management company, also referred to as the *fund sponsor*. The management company is critical for three reasons:

1. *Fund creation.* The management company is usually responsible for the creation of the fund, providing seed capital at the time of its incorporation.
2. *Brand name.* The fund sponsor normally lends its brand name to the fund. In most cases, the sponsor has contracts with more than one fund; together, these funds form a *fund family* or *fund complex.* For example, the Avon Hill Value Fund and the Avon Hill Global Bond Fund would both be part of the same family of funds, with Avon Hill Investments as the management company. The same board of directors will normally oversee a subset of the funds—if not all of the funds—within a fund family.
3. *Investment management.* Most importantly, the management company is responsible for investing fund assets in a portfolio of securities. It's often referred to as the *investment adviser,* or *investment manager,* when it's acting in this capacity, and its agreement with the fund is the *advisory contract.* While most management companies handle this function internally, some may hire an independent firm or *subadviser* to make investment decisions. These arrangements are called *subadvisory relationships* and must be approved by the board of directors.

The contract with the management company comes up for renewal every year, and the annual review is a significant undertaking for the board. Directors scrutinize detailed reports analyzing the fund's expenses and performance and question management about business plans and profitability. (See "The Gartenberg Standard" to learn about the factors that they consider in their review.) Once the board decides to negotiate a contract with the management company, the board must document the reasoning behind its decision, writing down the factors it considered and the conclusions it drew. This record of the board's deliberations is published in the fund's annual report to shareholders.

THE GARTENBERG STANDARD

When evaluating a proposed management contract, virtually every fund board refers to what's known as the *Gartenberg* standard. It's named after a lawsuit filed by Irving L. Gartenberg, alleging that a Merrill Lynch money market fund had charged excessive fees. His case was struck down by the Second Circuit Court of Appeals.

In its 1982 decision, the court established standards for determining whether a fee being charged is "so disproportionately large that it bears no reasonable relationship to the services rendered and could not have been the product of arm's-length bargaining."[7] It listed six factors that courts should take into consideration when hearing cases on fund fees. They are:

1. The nature and quality of the services provided
2. The profitability of the fund to the adviser
3. Any fallout benefits to the adviser, which are indirect profits that are somehow due to the existence of the fund
4. The extent of economies of scale as the fund grows
5. Fees charged on comparable funds
6. The independence and conscientiousness of the directors

Gartenberg established a road map for the board's annual review of the management contract. Its approach was reaffirmed in 2010 by the U.S. Supreme Court in the *Jones v. Harris Associates* case, which elaborated on the application of these factors.

But the management company is only one of the many service providers that the fund board must supervise. These fall into three broad categories:

1. *Links with investors.* The *distributor* sells fund shares to investors, either directly or through intermediaries. The *transfer agent* keeps track of shareholder positions and answers questions from investors.
2. *Portfolio administration.* The *custodian* holds the securities in the fund's portfolio. The *fund accountant* maintains the fund's books and records and computes the NAV nightly.
3. *Professional services.* Legal counsel provides guidance on complying with relevant regulations. The auditor helps the board evaluate the accuracy of the financial statements and the adequacy of its operational procedures.

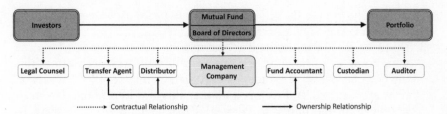

FIGURE 2.1 Typical Mutual Fund Service Provider Relationships

Some of these services must be provided by firms other than the management company. For example, the auditor must be independent, and virtually every fund has independent legal counsel. But other services can be—and often are—provided by the management company. A large fund complex may handle distribution of its own shares and fund accounting—together with some of the transfer agent's work—in addition to portfolio management. A smaller fund sponsor, on the other hand, may outsource everything but the selection of investments for the fund's portfolio. Figure 2.1 provides an overview of how these service providers might interact on a fund in a larger complex.

Regardless of how the work is packaged together, before signing any contract, the fund board must conclude that shareholders will get reasonable value for their money. Then, after the contract is in place, directors must make sure that those services are delivered as promised.

The board must also make sure that the fund management company does not favor the interests of its business affiliates at the expense of the fund. To limit the risk of this happening, the 1940 Act generally prohibits transactions between a fund and an affiliate of the management company unless specifically exempted by the SEC. *Affiliated transactions*, as they are called, normally qualify for an exemption only if they are subject to monitoring by the fund's directors.

Here are three examples of typical affiliated transactions that directors monitor:

1. A fund management company is owned by a bank. The investment adviser may not buy shares of the bank for the fund's portfolio.
2. Now assume that the bank also owns a brokerage firm, and the management company would like to use that firm to execute buy and sell transactions for the fund's portfolio. Directors must first determine whether trading with the affiliate is in the fund's best interest. If they conclude that it is, they must review the trades to make sure that the commissions

paid by the fund to the affiliate are fair compared to those paid to third parties on other similar transactions.

3. Directors must also decide if it's permissible for two funds within the same complex to buy and sell securities directly with each other; this can be a cheaper way to trade since no commissions or other transaction costs are incurred. If directors authorize this type of trading, they must scrutinize all the purchases and sales that actually do take place to determine that they have been in the best interests of both funds.

To sum it all up, directors must be responsible purchasing agents for fund shareholders. They must negotiate a fair price for services, make sure those services have been delivered, and then confirm that there are no hidden charges.

To ensure that boards keep shareholder interests front and center as they do this job, the SEC effectively requires that more than half of their members be *independent*.[8] The balance of the board members may be employees of the management company. While the official definition of independence is quite detailed, broadly speaking, *disinterested* or *noninterested* directors (alternate terms for independent directors) have no close connection to the management company or other service providers to the fund. It's a tough standard—tougher than comparable rules for industrial companies.

Independent directors have special responsibilities to fund investors. Only they may approve the advisory contract. A majority of the independent directors (as well as a majority of all board members) must authorize certain agreements and transactions, including any of the affiliated transactions that we just reviewed. Not everyone believes that the independent directors discharge these responsibilities well, as "Lapdogs or Watchdogs?" explains.

LAPDOGS OR WATCHDOGS?

Fund boards are intended to be the vigorous protectors of shareholders, yet some vocal critics allege that fund directors are like cocker spaniels in a situation that calls for Doberman pinschers—the implication being that boards are populated with individuals willing to comply with the wishes of the management company, rather than advance the interests of investors. It's a critique that's hard to ignore, coming as it does from fund visionary John Bogle, founder of the Vanguard fund family, among others.

The Critics' Case

The critics have three specific concerns:

Problem 1 is the large fees that directors earn. While the fee for overseeing a single fund is modest, the same board usually serves for many, if not all, of the funds within a complex, earning a separate fee for each one. As a result, a director's total remuneration can exceed $115,000 annually at a good-sized fund group.[9] Critics claims that directors are more interested in protecting that income than in tussling with management.

Problem 2 is directors' lack of personal investment in the funds they oversee. "Without skin in the game, how can directors relate to shareholders' interests?" the critics query. While more and more boards are requiring directors to buy shares in the funds they oversee, board members are still unlikely to have a large ownership stake in most of their funds.

But it's Problem 3 that's the real sticking point. If directors were acting in shareholders' best interests, the critics posit, they would be aggressively driving down the fees paid to the management company. Yet funds' boards almost never solicit competitive bids for the advisory contract or replace one management company with another.

The Economists' Rebuttal

Many economists argue that cutting fees shouldn't be a primary function of fund boards. They believe that the market for mutual funds is highly competitive; for supporting evidence, they point to the 7,600 fund offerings available. And they note that it's easy for consumers to make an informed choice of fund manager, given the wealth of information available about fund investment approaches and fees—a choice that boards shouldn't presume to override. Some of these economists even suggest that funds don't need directors at all.

The Practical Middle Ground

In practice, most fund boards tread a middle ground between the activist approach advocated by the critics and the laissez-faire attitude of certain economists. Boards generally acknowledge that shareholders have chosen to invest with a particular management company and seldom force a change in that company.

At the same time, directors annually negotiate with the fund sponsor to advance shareholder interests. They confirm that the fees being charged are reasonable, by comparing them to fees on comparable funds, and they often press management companies to share economies of scale with shareholders by reducing fees as funds grow. For funds with poor investment performance, boards may advocate a change in portfolio manager or investment approach. Management companies seldom disregard pointed advice from the fund board, knowing that the directors do ultimately have the authority to replace them.

Fund directors also note that they do more than just examine fees: boards have an exemplary record in protecting shareholder assets against theft. U.S. mutual funds were not among the victims of the Ponzi schemes exposed during the credit crisis.

With independent directors playing such an important role, shareholder advocates assert that an even higher level of board independence is needed to protect investor interests. They continually suggest a higher percentage of disinterested directors on the board and independent committee chairs, among other measures.

In 2004, the SEC staff responded to their arguments by presenting a proposed rule that included, among other things, a requirement that the chair of the board must be an independent director. Fund management companies objected to this provision and fought back. They argued that there was absolutely no empirical evidence that shareholders did any better when a fund board had an independent chair. One firm even commissioned a study to show that investors paid lower fees and experienced better investment performance when a management company representative sat at the head of the board table. After a pitched battle, waged in the media as well as SEC comment letters, the proposed rule was ratified by the commissioners in an unusual split decision—though the SEC later abandoned its most contentious components after losing a court case that raised questions about the SEC's rulemaking process.

Only some procedural elements of the proposed rule survived the fallout. Today, fund boards must meet at least once a quarter. The independent directors on a board must meet separately, without the presence of the interested directors, at least as frequently. Boards must also be able to hire staff directly if they conclude that they need direct access to information or support. Finally, fund boards must conduct an assessment of their own performance every year.

But while the controversy did not lead to a change in regulation, it did result in a quiet change in board practice: many fund boards have voluntarily increased their level of independence. According to a 2009 study published by the Investment Company Institute and its affiliate, the Independent Directors Council, most fund complexes—88 percent to be exact—had boards in which at least 75 percent of the seats were held by independent directors, well above the minimum requirement. And almost two-thirds of board chairs were disinterested.[10]

Stay tuned. . . . The debate continues.

ETHICAL STANDARDS

An independent board of directors is not the only safeguard protecting shareholders from malfeasance. Mutual fund operations are also governed by very strict ethical standards.

Specifically, the managers of mutual funds are *fiduciaries* with a special set of duties to their investors. It's a considerable responsibility. Fiduciaries are expected to use their expertise to advance their clients' interests and may not gain personally at their clients' expense. They must be completely candid with their clients, presenting all material facts and explaining any conflicts that they might have. In short, fiduciaries must always put their client's interests ahead of their own. An exacting standard—in fact, it's the highest legal duty that one party can have to another. While it's a tough standard, it's also a vague one, providing no concrete guidance for management company employees confronting ethical dilemmas.

ANOTHER 1940 ACT

The Investment Company Act was not the only major piece of financial market legislation to be enacted in 1940. The Investment *Advisers* Act was also passed in that year.

Under the provisions of the Advisers Act, firms that get paid for counseling others on investing in securities must register with the SEC. They do this by filing Form ADV, which describes the types of services provided and the fees charged.

There are exemptions from the registration requirement, but not for mutual fund managers. As a result, 1940 Act funds are always managed by *registered investment advisers*.

To help them make the right choices, the SEC requires registered investment advisers—which include all fund management companies—to adopt and enforce a written code of ethics that applies to all of its associates. (See "Another 1940 Act" for an introduction to registered investment advisers.) This code must be distributed to all employees, who are required to acknowledge—in writing—that they have received a copy. Many firms repeat the process annually. A few firms post their codes online, usually in the "About Us" or "Corporate Governance" section of their web site.

The SEC has established guidelines about what should be included in a code of ethics, though advisers still have discretion over many aspects of it. An adviser's code of ethics generally contains the following five core components:

Component 1: Standard of business conduct. A code of ethics opens with a general statement about the expected standard of business conduct. At the very least, staff members must be required to comply with all relevant laws and regulations. But many adviser codes go far beyond this bare minimum, asking associates to protect the firm's reputation by avoiding even the appearance of impropriety as they go about their duties.

Component 2: Protection of material nonpublic information. Advisers must take steps to protect the confidentiality of information about client portfolios and transactions—information that can be quite valuable. Traders who knew that a large mutual fund was about to purchase a substantial position in a particular stock might line their own pockets by buying shares for their own account first, hoping that the fund's activity would drive up the price and allow them to sell at a profit in short order. As a result, advisers limit access to this type of information to those with a real need to know and then prohibit them from trading in their personal accounts based on this knowledge.

While the emphasis here is on use of client-related information, this section also applies to material nonpublic information regarding potential investments—*material*, because it is likely to be important to investors; *nonpublic*, because it has not been made available to all investors. Acting on this information is taboo: Those who do so can be accused of insider trading, which carries stiff civil and criminal penalties.

Mutual fund management companies that are part of larger financial firms must be particularly careful about insider trading issues. They may be affiliated with an investment bank that routinely learns material nonpublic information as it works with clients issuing securities. These firms must adopt procedures that create an information barrier—sometimes called a *firewall*—between the fund managers and the bankers. [11]

Component 3: Limits on personal securities trading. Advisers must take steps to ensure that those employees with access to material nonpublic information are not using it for personal gain. Note that these provisions do not apply to all employees—just to *access persons,* as they are dubbed in the regulation. This group normally includes the portfolio management team, the traders, the administrative staff who have daily access to transaction information, and the senior executives who supervise the investment process. (Note that many of the rules that apply to access persons also apply to members of their household.)

At most advisory firms, access persons must receive prior written approval of any trades they'd like to make in their personal accounts. *Preclearance,* as it's called, is far from a mere rubber stamp process. Approval to buy or sell a particular security will be denied if the individual has access to any material nonpublic information. It will also be denied if any fund in the complex is currently trading or has recently traded that security—or maybe even one similar to it.

Advisers may exempt certain types of securities, such as U.S. government bonds, from pre-clearance requirements. On the other hand, purchases of initial public offerings and private placements must always be pre-cleared. These latter investments can be quite lucrative—while the opportunities to own them can be very limited—so the SEC wants to make sure that they are not being handed to access persons as a thank-you for business done by the fund. Initial public offerings in particular can be so problematic that many investment advisers never allow their purchase in personal accounts under any circumstances.

Other types of transactions may be prohibited as well. Access persons are generally not allowed to engage in short-swing trading, meaning buying and selling within a short time period, typically defined as 60 days. Also, portfolio managers may not personally buy or sell stocks that were just traded in the accounts they manage.

Access persons give up a great deal of privacy when it comes to their finances. To confirm that they are complying with the policies in the code of ethics, they must regularly report on their securities transactions and holdings.

By now, it should be clear that it isn't easy for access persons to trade in their personal accounts. Some fund managers avoid the hurdles altogether by putting all their own money in their firm's mutual funds. Management companies generally encourage this practice as both easier administratively and better for shareholders.

Component 4: Limits on gifts and entertainment. Most firms impose limits on business gifts and entertainment in their codes of ethics.[12] Staff

DOUBLE DUTY

The SEC requires that every investment adviser and every mutual fund have a chief compliance officer. It's an important position. CCOs make sure that the adviser and the fund adhere to—or, in industry parlance, are "in compliance with"—all relevant laws and regulations. The CCO has "full responsibility and authority to develop and enforce policies and procedures" to make this happen.[13]

The CCO for a mutual fund reports to its board of directors and is paid by the fund for his services. But while part of his compensation comes from the fund, he is generally an employee of the management company and often serves as its CCO as well. Their work for the fund is usually only part-time.

ADDITIONAL REQUIREMENTS FOR CFAs

Analysts and portfolio managers who are Chartered Financial Analysts must comply with the *Code of Ethics and Standards of Professional Conduct* of the CFA Institute, the organization that grants the CFA charter. It establishes guidelines in seven areas:

1. Professionalism
2. Integrity of capital markets
3. Duties to clients
4. Duties to employers
5. Investment analysis, recommendations, and actions
6. Conflicts of interest
7. Responsibilities as a CFA Institute member or CFA candidate

These standards are quite demanding. Not only must CFA charter holders place client interests above their own, they must also strive to continually improve their professional competence.

CFAs must file an annual Professional Conduct Statement disclosing any litigation, customer complaints, or disciplinary proceedings related to their work. The CFA Institute investigates each of these cases. If it determines that misconduct has occurred, it may impose penalties ranging from a cautionary letter to summary suspension of membership.

Interested in becoming a CFA? You'll need to have four years of experience working in an investment area and to pass a series of three challenging exams. For more information, visit the CFA Institute web site at www.cfainstitute.org.

members are normally not permitted to give or accept any gifts of cash or other gifts worth more than $100 from anyone they do business with. Entertainment must be consistent with customary practice and not be excessive. Some advisers require their associates to file a report on all gifts and entertainment given and received.

Component 5: Violations of the code. The code must require prompt reporting of any violations to the adviser's chief compliance officer. The chief compliance officer or CCO has responsibility for enforcement, usually consulting with a committee of the firm's senior executives. This group may determine the consequences of violations of the code, imposing penalties that can range from a written censure to monetary fines to termination of employment. (See "Double Duty" for more on the CCO.)

One final note: management company associates may be subject to other codes of ethics, in addition to the one adopted by their employer. This is often the case for individuals with professional accreditations, such as accountants with CPAs. See "Additional Requirements for CFAs" for a summary of another code of ethics that applies to many investment managers.

ALTERNATIVES TO MUTUAL FUNDS

As we've seen, mutual funds provide investors with a high level of convenience and protection. But how do funds compare to other means of investing available to investors? We conclude this chapter by looking at the two principal alternatives available to individuals: investing directly in securities or participating in another type of commingled investment vehicle.

Direct Investing through Individual Accounts

Individuals always have the option of owning securities directly, without going through an intermediary such as a mutual fund. Individuals have traditionally had two alternatives if they wanted to buy and sell securities themselves: a brokerage account or a trust account.

Option 1: A brokerage account. Many investors buy stocks in an account that they have opened at a brokerage firm, such as Merrill Lynch or Charles Schwab, giving specific instructions to buy or sell securities at the time they believe is advantageous. This option makes sense for the investor who wants a great deal of control, but not for the investor who is most concerned about diversification or professional management.

Brokerage account costs vary widely. Investors using a low-priced discount firm and making decisions on their own can pay less in fees than they would in a mutual fund. That may not be the case if they opt for a full-service brokerage firm that provides personalized advice from a financial adviser along with the execution of buy and sell orders.

Option 2: A trust account. Consumers who are interested in platinum service often opt for an account professionally managed by the trust department of a bank or by an investment adviser who caters to high net worth individuals. *High net worth* points to the main drawback here: these accounts are for the very well-heeled only. Minimum account size can be $2 million or more, and the fees charged reflect the large number of services provided, which for some investors can include handling their bills, paying their kids their allowances, and helping them find a mortgage.

Within the past 20 years, a third choice has developed:

Option 3: A separately managed account. The separately managed account was designed for individuals who like the concept of a trust account but lack the bank balance to justify one. SMAs are sometimes called, by among other names, *individually managed accounts, managed accounts,* or *wrap accounts.* (Note that they are different from mutual fund wrap programs, which are discussed in Chapter 10.)

As with trust accounts, investors in an SMA actually own the specific securities in their account, rather than a share of a communally owned portfolio. Like trust accounts, SMAs are professionally managed, and investors have the opportunity to customize the security choices. They can, for example, give instructions to avoid selling securities that have gone up in price and would generate a capital gain, or they can prohibit the purchase of alcohol, tobacco, or gambling stocks if they object to supporting these industries. In an essential departure from trust accounts, however, the size minimums for SMAs are significantly lower, in the range of $100,000 to $250,000—though that's still much higher than mutual fund minimums.

SMA programs are generally sponsored by brokerage firms. As sponsors, the firms are responsible for keeping portfolio records, preparing performance reports, and buying and selling securities in the accounts. They also select the investment managers for the program. "Surfing for SMAs" describes an online alternative to brokerage firm–sponsored programs that has recently become available.

Not surprisingly, making professionally managed, individualized portfolios affordable for smaller accounts entails compromises. Most notably, the customization of the security selection is in actuality quite limited. In the preponderance of SMA programs, each investor is assigned to a model portfolio determined by the investment manager or managers. A computer program then buys and sells substantially the same securities for the thousands of accounts based on that model, making minor adjustments for the tax and other preferences of the owner. (SMAs weren't really possible until computers had become powerful enough to manage this algorithm easily.)

SURFING FOR SMAs

If you're intrigued by separately managed accounts, but don't have a relationship with a financial adviser, Internet entrepreneurs hope that you'll surf the net for portfolio advice. They've launched a number of web sites that provide model portfolios much like the ones that are used as a basis for SMAs. These web sites are usually linked to an individual brokerage account, so that any changes in the model are automatically mirrored in your own personal portfolio. That's the easy part.

Choosing a model portfolio is a much tougher task, given the large number of options available. You can track stocks chosen by:

- A best-selling financial author
- Well-known hedge fund and mutual fund managers
- Quantitative selection techniques (see Chapter 5 for more on these techniques)
- Small money managers
- Other investors like you.[14]

But shop carefully! Fees vary wildly—from just $29 a month to 3 percent of assets per year.

Another compromise: SMA investors do not receive all the personal services that a bank trust department client might demand. Even after implementing these economies, SMAs can be expensive. According to Cerulli Associates, average annual fees in 2009 were 1.7 percent of assets.

Assets in SMAs have held relatively steady over the past decade. The Money Management Institute estimates that they were approximately $525 billion at the end of 2009. Figure 2.2 shows the trend.

Other Commingled Investment Vehicles

Individuals can also invest in one of the other types of *commingled investment vehicles*. Like mutual funds, all of these vehicles allow savers to *commingle,* or *pool,* their money to make joint investments. Closed-end mutual funds, exchange-traded funds, unit investment trusts, and hedge funds are all commingled vehicles available to consumers.[15]

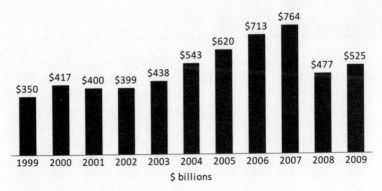

FIGURE 2.2   Assets in Separately Managed Accounts
Sources: Money Management Institute, Dover Financial Research.

One clarification: so far in this chapter we've been talking about *open-end mutual funds* or *open-end investment companies*. Only open-end funds allow investors to redeem their shares every business day, and, as we've discussed, most sell their shares to the public every day as well. There are two other types of 1940 Act investment companies, *closed-end funds* and *exchange-traded funds*. They differ from open-end funds in the way they handle share sales and redemptions. For a quick comparison of open-end funds with the other vehicles we discuss, take a look at Table 2.1.

Closed-end funds. Closed-end funds normally collect money from investors and issue new shares only once, at their creation. Their shares are then listed for trading on a stock exchange, such as the New York Stock Exchange. Shareholders who wish to convert their investment to cash can't just turn them in to the fund; they usually must find a buyer on the open market. The price they receive for their shares is determined by supply and demand and is often lower than NAV.

In the early years of the industry, closed-end funds were more common than open-end funds, but their popularity has declined sharply. At the end of 2009, there were fewer than 650 in existence.[16] Investment managers like the closed-end format, because it gives them a pool of assets to manage that doesn't change dramatically in size because of purchases or sales by shareholders. But investors favor the open-end format, because when they invest through open-end funds they don't need to worry about selling shares at a discount to NAV.

Exchange-traded funds. Exchange-traded funds, or ETFs, are the newest type of mutual fund, having been introduced successfully in the United States only in 1992. They combine features of both open-end and closed-end funds.

TABLE 2.1 Comparison of Commingled Investment Vehicles

Feature	Mutual Fund (open-end)	Closed-End Fund	Exchange-Traded Fund	Unit Investment Trust	Hedge Fund
Daily redemptions at NAV	X	Open market sale	Open market sale	X	No
Pass-through tax status	X	X	X	X	X
Ongoing professional management	X	X	X	No	X
Supervision by independent directors	X	X	X	No	No

Like closed-end funds, ETF shares are traded on a stock exchange, and investors make purchases and sales throughout the day on the open market. But ETFs resemble open-end funds in that they're able to adjust the number of shares outstanding. The happy result is that trades on the exchange normally occur at close to—but not necessarily exactly at—a fund's NAV.

ETFs have a reputation for being very tax-efficient. Most use a passive investment management approach, based on an index, which generates little by way of capital gains and therefore creates few unexpected income tax bills. It's important to note, though, that the tax regime applied to ETFs is the same as that for open-end funds.

Investors have come to appreciate the virtues of ETFs—so much so that they are now the fastest-growing type of commingled fund. At the end of 2009, there were more than 750 ETFs trading with more than $750 billion in assets. Compare that to slightly over 150 just five years earlier, and only one in 1992! We take an in-depth look at this growing alternative in Chapter 12.

Unit investment trusts. The 1940 Act authorizes one other type of commingled investment vehicle: the unit investment trust. UITs are significantly different from other mutual funds because they don't hire an investment manager. Instead, when it creates the UIT, the sponsor selects a portfolio of securities that then doesn't change significantly throughout its life. (UITs normally have a limited life span, determined at the time the trust is started up.)

Investors who want to get their money out of a UIT can simply cash in their shares at NAV, as with an open-end mutual fund. But they have other options as well. They may be able to sell their positions on the open market. Or they can wait until the trust liquidates its entire portfolio on its termination date.

Their appeal: Owners of a UIT know exactly which securities they will own. Because there is no trading in the portfolio, UIT investors never receive an unexpected distribution of capital gain income. And UITs can be very cost effective—with no trading, there's no need for an investment adviser or a board of directors—which means that ongoing expenses are very low. On the flip side, investors usually pay a sales load when they buy a UIT, which can offset much of the annual cost savings.

Despite their virtues, UITs have been eclipsed by their more glamorous mutual fund cousins. At the end of 2009, all UITs combined had only $38 billion in assets. While that may sound substantial, it's less than half of their asset base just a decade previously. Many more UITs are being liquidated than are being launched.

Hedge funds. One more investment vehicle is worth taking a look at: hedge funds, the only commingled vehicle that we discuss that is not regulated under the 1940 Act. As long as they pass certain tests, hedge funds are not even required to register with the SEC. Until recently, managers of hedge funds weren't required to become registered investment advisers, though that changed in 2010 with passage of the Dodd-Frank Wall Street Reform and Consumer Protection Act, which we refer to throughout this book as the *Dodd-Frank financial reform legislation.*

Hedge funds differ from mutual funds in significant ways:

- Investors in hedge funds may not cash in their holdings at will. Instead, they're usually only permitted to redeem on certain dates once or twice per year and then only after they've been invested in the fund for some minimum period.
- Hedge funds are not subject to investment limitations of the kind imposed by the 1940 Act or Subchapter M. On the contrary, they are known for using aggressive investing techniques such as leverage, often investing borrowed money substantially in excess of shareholder contributions. As a result, they appeal to investors looking for high returns and willing to accept high risks.
- Most U.S. hedge funds do not have an independent board of directors supervising operations and protecting shareholder interests.

Hedge funds and mutual funds do have something in common: they are both pass-through entities, though they achieve the same result in different ways. As we've seen, mutual funds are corporations; hedge funds, on the other hand, are structured as partnerships, governed by Subchapter K of the Internal Revenue Code. Note that partnerships are not required to distribute their income to mutual funds annually, as are mutual funds. Yet investors are liable for the tax on their share of the partnership's income, reported annually to them on Schedule K-1, so hedge funds usually distribute enough cash to cover most of the tax liabilities they generate for their limited partners.

Over the past decade, hedge funds have moved from a little-known option for the truly wealthy to a much-discussed alternative for the just well-off. According to HedgeFund.net, even in a weak market environment, industry assets have more than doubled, from $0.8 trillion at the end of 2003 to $2.2 trillion at the end of 2009. That's still small relative to the mutual fund industry, but hedge funds continue to benefit from a perception that they are more likely to deliver extraordinary returns to investors in all market environments. We spend more time discussing hedge funds in Chapter 12.

CHAPTER SUMMARY

Each mutual fund is a separate corporation. Investors who decide to place their money in a particular fund do so through buying its shares directly from the fund itself. They pay a price per share that equals the value of the fund's investments minus its liabilities divided by the number of shares outstanding. This price, known as the net asset value or NAV, is computed at the end of every business day. Investors have the opportunity to sell their shares back to the fund at the NAV every business day. To ensure that a fund always has enough cash available to pay redeeming shareholders, the Investment Company Act of 1940 places restrictions on the fund's investments.

Mutual funds do not pay corporate taxes themselves. Instead, they pass all tax liabilities on to their shareholders. To qualify for this pass-through tax treatment, funds must adhere to certain restrictions on their investments and must pay out virtually all income to their shareholders at least annually.

Rather than hire employees, mutual funds generally retain other companies to do all the work. The fund's board of directors is responsible for negotiating contracts with these service providers. The most important contract is with the management company which is the firm that normally lends its brand name to the fund and that manages the fund's investments. The fund board's role in negotiating this management contract is a subject of controversy.

Mutual fund operations are governed by very strict ethical standards. The managers of mutual funds are fiduciaries that are expected to use their professional expertise to advance their clients' interests. The SEC requires that each fund manager have a written code of ethics that describes its standards of business conduct for its employees.

Individuals who are not interested in investing through an open-end mutual fund have the choice of owning securities directly, through a brokerage account, trust account, or a separately managed account program. They may also prefer another type of commingled investment vehicle, like a closed-end fund, an exchange-traded fund, a unit investment trust, or a hedge fund. These alternatives to mutual funds differ along several dimensions: costs to investors, account size minimums, degree of professional management, ability to redeem, opportunity to customize features, and level of regulation.

Researching Funds: The User Guides

Now that we've studied the advantages and disadvantages of mutual funds and taken a look at how they work, you're ready to begin researching a potential fund investment. Much of the information you'll need will come directly from the fund itself. In fact, funds are required by law to disclose essential information to investors in the fund—providing what are, in effect, user guides for potential buyers. This chapter examines the documents that funds prepare to do just that. Looking ahead, in the next chapter, we'll take a look at independent sources of information that you can consult to learn even more about possible fund choices.

This chapter reviews:

- The principle of disclosure and how it applies to mutual funds
- The content of the summary prospectus, the key document that funds provide to prospective buyers
- The other documents that must be prepared by funds: the statutory prospectus, the statement of additional information, and the shareholder reports
- How investors can use the information in these documents to help select funds for their portfolios

MUTUAL FUNDS AND DISCLOSURE

The underlying principle of U.S. securities regulation is *disclosure,* the concept that the seller of a security has an obligation to tell potential buyers essential facts about the investment. Under U.S. law, anyone who wants to sell a security to the public must:

- Register the offering of the security with the SEC
- Provide buyers with a document called a *prospectus*, which discloses material information about the investment, meaning information that's likely to be important to the investor
- Report periodically to buyers about their investment after the security has been issued

See "Landmark Legislation" for information on the source of these rules.

LANDMARK LEGISLATION

The first two pieces of securities legislation passed as part of President Franklin Roosevelt's New Deal remain the cornerstones of U.S. securities regulation today:

1. *Securities Act of 1933.* Because this 1933 law mandated disclosure of material information through a prospectus, it is sometimes referred to as the *truth in securities* act. The Securities Act also established the requirement for registration of securities.
2. *Securities Exchange Act of 1934.* The Exchange Act set down annual and quarterly reporting requirements for issuers of securities. It is also the legislation that created the SEC.

Disclosure creates transparency, an environment in which potential investments are not black boxes but glass houses, whose inner operations are easily seen and analyzed. Buyers benefit from transparency because they have ready access to the data they need to make an informed decision about a potential investment. And because all sellers must disclose similar information, investors are able to compare offerings fairly easily.

Note that the responsibility for making disclosure falls fully on the shoulders of the seller. Even though the seller must file a draft, or preliminary, prospectus with the SEC, the agency never actually approves any prospectus—though it may, on some occasions, prevent the issuance of a prospectus if it fails to meet the relevant requirements. But the SEC is not opining on the accuracy or completeness of the content. In fact, every final prospectus includes the disclaimer that:

> *Neither the Securities and Exchange Commission nor any state securities agency has approved or disapproved of these securities or determined whether this prospectus is truthful or complete. Any representation to the contrary is a crime.*

The burden of disclosure does carry an offsetting benefit: sellers who make full disclosure enjoy considerable protection against lawsuits. Buyers can't sue the issuer of a security simply because the security has gone down in price. Instead, they must prove that a seller omitted or misrepresented an important fact from the relevant disclosures—called a *material misstatement*—either intentionally or because they failed to exercise sufficient care in preparing their documents. Buyers must also demonstrate that they relied on misinformation in the offering documents when making their purchase decision and that they suffered a financial loss as a result.

As a result of this protection, sellers are willing to offer a wide range of securities. If they were afraid of litigation every time the price of a security went down, they'd limit offerings to only the safest of bonds, investments that would be unlikely to provide much by way of potential return. Instead, under a disclosure regime, sellers are more willing to offer securities with even very high levels of risk.

And that, in turn, is good for buyers, who have access to a greater number and variety of investment opportunities—and who are given the information they need to judge for themselves whether the potential reward justifies the risk involved. For society as a whole, disclosure leads to more active securities markets.

Because they are considered issuers of securities, mutual funds are subject to all of the requirements of the disclosure rules. They must register their shares with the SEC, prepare a prospectus for potential buyers, and provide periodic reports to investors.

Disclosure poses particular challenges for mutual funds, in two ways. First, because most funds sell shares to the public every business day, they must have an accurate prospectus available at all times. Contrast that with the typical operating corporation, which needs to raise money from the public only every few years. That company will prepare a prospectus just before issuing stocks or bonds. After the offering is completed, they needn't worry about the prospectus until they are ready to raise capital again.

Prospectuses for mutual funds, on the other hand, are continually in use. Funds review them regularly, doing a complete update roughly once a year, but also amending them during the year if there have been any significant changes. These intra-year amendments are informally called *stickers,* because state law used to require that they be literally stuck to the paper version of the prospectus. In an electronic version, you'll usually see them first as you scroll through the document. (See "Prospecting for Fund Documents" for a guide to online access.)

PROSPECTING FOR FUND DOCUMENTS

Finding fund documents is easy online. There are two places to look them up on the Web:

Option 1: Visit the management company's web site. Since a sponsor generally offers many funds—sometimes many, many funds—you'll need to find the page for the particular fund you're interested in. In some cases you may need to look for a navigation element labeled *documents,* or *literature.* When you do find what you're looking for, usually only the current document set will be available.

Option 2: Ask EDGAR. That's the Electronic Data Gathering and Retrieval system maintained by the SEC. It's available online at www.sec.gov/edgar.shtml. Here you can access absolutely *all* the filings the fund has made with the SEC over roughly the past 15 years—not just the key disclosure documents we look at in this chapter.

The second disclosure challenge for mutual funds is the diversity of the investors they serve, in terms of the type of information they or their representatives would like to receive. Some shareholders—those buying through their 401(k) plan, for example—may be comfortable with just a broad overview of the fund. These individuals may want to know only about the fund's general investment approach, its risks, and its costs. Others—possibly corporate gatekeepers who decide whether to include the fund as an investment option in that same 401(k) plan—may be interested in all the details, such as the specific investment techniques that may be used or the qualifications of the members of the board of directors.

As a result, over the years, the SEC has developed a tiered approach to fund disclosure. Funds prepare a series of documents describing the fund and its policies with varying levels of detail; investors then choose the document that best suits their needs. The prospectus now comes in three different forms. From shortest to longest, they are the:

1. *Summary prospectus.* As the name implies, this is a brief document, typically only three or four pages long, designed for the investor who

wants just the highlights. It must be written in plain English. (See the "Plain-Speaking Prospectuses" for the SEC's definition.)

PLAIN-SPEAKING PROSPECTUSES

The SEC encourages companies to use plain English in their disclosure documents and even requires its use in the summary prospectus. It offers some specific guidelines on how to make disclosure documents readable. The SEC suggests that writers:

- Use active (not passive) voice
- Write in short sentences
- Use definite, concrete, everyday words
- Use tables and graphics, rather than text, to explain complex material whenever possible
- Avoid legal jargon and highly technical business terms
- Avoid multiple negatives

More generally, the SEC asks prospectus writers to know their audience, to highlight the information that is most important and to design the layout of the prospectus in a way that's easy and inviting to read. The SEC provides a 77-page manual titled *The Plain English Handbook: How to Create Clear SEC Disclosure Documents*, with guidance on writing in plain English. It's available at www.sec.gov/pdf/handbook.pdf.

2. *Prospectus.* The full, or *statutory,* prospectus contains all the material information that the SEC believes is needed for an investor to make an informed purchase decision. The content of the summary prospectus forms the first section of the full prospectus.
3. *Statement of additional information.* Again, the name says it all. The SAI provides potential buyers who are interested in detail with quite a lot of it. It is technically Part II of the prospectus.

We focus on the summary prospectus, and then take a quick look at the other two forms of the prospectus and the shareholder reports that funds prepare at least twice a year.

THE SUMMARY PROSPECTUS

The summary prospectus is the key user guide for the mutual fund investor. It provides an overview of the fund's investment objective, strategies, and risks, summarizes its past performance, and provides administrative information that is particularly relevant to shareholders.

The summary prospectus is fairly new; funds were first permitted to use it only in March 2009. Industry observers expect that it will eventually become the document most funds send to investors making a purchase of shares. (There is an alternate way of providing the necessary information, which we explain when we discuss the full prospectus.)

To ensure that the summary prospectus is a disclosure document and not a marketing document, its specific content is mandated by the SEC. To help investors make comparisons among funds, every summary prospectus must contain the following items in this exact order:

- Heading or cover
- Investment objectives and goals
- Fee table
- Investments, risks, and performance
- Management
- Purchase and sale of fund shares
- Tax information
- Financial intermediary compensation

We review the most important components of each section in turn. We've posted a sample summary prospectus on this book's web site.

Section 1: Heading or cover. The summary prospectus opens by laying out the fund's vital statistics. The first things the reader sees, either on the first page or a separate cover page, are:

- The fund's name.
- The date of the summary prospectus.
- The classes of shares.
- The exchange ticker for each class (see "Keeping Your Funds Straight" for a definition).
- Information on how to get a copy of the full prospectus. Funds must offer to send the prospectus to you by either e-mail or snail mail, and they also must provide a web address for an online version.

We just mention share classes here. We cover them in depth in Chapter 10.

KEEPING YOUR FUNDS STRAIGHT

With more than 7,600 mutual funds available, it would be easy to mix up one with another. To prevent confusion, each mutual fund offered to the public (and each class of shares for that fund) has a unique identifier called an *exchange ticker*—similar to a Social Security number for individuals or an ISBN number for books. This ticker consists of five letters, often ending with X. For example, the exchange ticker for the BlackRock Equity Dividend Fund, Class A, is MDDVX.

You can use a fund's ticker to look up information quickly on stock information services. Enter MDDVX in the "get quotes" box at the top of the Yahoo! Finance page, and you'll be given basic statistics about the fund, including NAV.

Disclosure about key features of a fund actually begins with its name. The SEC has strict standards when it comes to names applied to mutual funds: in short, fund names cannot be deceptive or misleading. As is its custom, the SEC has laid down a number of specific rules and guidelines in this regard, which are outlined in Table 3.1. These rules cover only fund names that indicate the type of investments the fund plans to hold. Names that describe an investment strategy (such as *growth* or *value*) or generic names (like Voyager and Destiny) have not been defined by the SEC, though names may not under any circumstances paint a false picture for investors. For instance, Rock Solid or Super Safe would never pass muster as fund names.

Section 2: Investment objective. The body of the summary prospectus begins with a simple declaration of the fund's investment objective, which is the type of return it is seeking to generate. Table 3.2 provides some examples. And if the name hasn't already done the job, a fund may clarify which category it falls into (money market, tax-exempt, equity, and so on). We review the types of mutual funds in more detail in Chapter 4.

Section 3: Fee tables. The SEC wants investors to be well aware of the costs of owning a fund, so information on fees comes next, even before a discussion of risk and return. This section includes tables enumerating the annual operating expenses—in both percentage and dollar terms—and the sales loads, if the fund imposes them. (Remember that front-end sales loads or sales charges are fees paid when shareholders purchase shares.) Funds must also explain:

- If investors can reduce sales charges by increasing the size of their investment in the fund, a price reduction called a *breakpoint discount.*

TABLE 3.1 Limitations on Mutual Fund Names

If the fund's name...	Then the fund must...
implies that it will focus in a particular industry or type of securities...	keep at least 80 percent of its assets invested in that industry or type of investment. A biotechnology fund, for example, must put at least 80 percent of its assets in the biotech industry.
says it focuses in a particular country...	invest at least 80 percent of its assets in securities economically tied to that country.
contains the word *foreign*...	hold at least 80 percent of its investments in securities economically tied to countries outside the United States.
contains the words *tax-exempt, tax-free,* or *municipal*...	have at least 80 percent of its holdings in tax-exempt securities. Alternatively, at least 80 percent of the fund's income must be exempt from taxes.[1]
describes the fund's maturity (as short-term, long-term, and so forth)...	maintain a portfolio of fixed income securities with an average portfolio maturity consistent with that name. For example, short-term funds should have an average weighted maturity of less than three years.
represents it as *balanced*...	hold a mix of equities and fixed income assets. Specifically, it must have at least 25 percent of its assets in bonds and at least 25 percent in stocks.

- How portfolio *turnover*—meaning buying and selling securities within the fund—will affect costs. Turnover can increase costs in two ways. First, executing some trades involves the payment of transaction costs—an expense to the fund. Second, selling securities might generate capital gains, which could increase the shareholder's tax bill for the year.

TABLE 3.2 Sample Investment Objectives

Type of Fund	Typical Investment Objective
Money market	Maintain $1 value of its share while providing income
Investment grade bond	Current income
Tax-exempt or municipal bond	Current income exempt from federal income taxes
Equity income fund	Long-term capital appreciation and income
Aggressive growth equity fund	Long-term capital appreciation

Taking our lead from the summary prospectus, we're providing only the briefest of overviews here of fund expenses. We discuss the subject in detail throughout the book and provide a compilation of all fund expenses in Chapter 15.

Section 4: Investments, risks, and performance. This is the heart of the summary prospectus: It describes the fund's investment approach, the risk of that approach, and the fund's past success with that approach.

This section opens with a description of the types of securities the fund will buy and its method of choosing them. One fund may invest in U.S. equities that its managers believe to be undervalued, while another may

THE DIFFICULTY OF DEFINING RISK

How best express the risk associated with a mutual fund?

Good question. Academics have long defined investment risk mathematically, by measuring the variability in an investment's past returns. A U.S. Treasury bill has a narrow range of potential returns, while a biotech stock has wide range of potential returns.

Investors themselves define risk much less crisply, however. A 1996 survey by the Investment Company Institute explored investors' thoughts about the risks of mutual fund investing.[2] Asked to define risk, respondents said that it was the chance of:

Losing some of the original investment (57 percent)

Investment not keeping up with inflation (47 percent)

Value of the investment fluctuating up and down (46 percent)

Not having enough money at the end of the investing period to meet one's goals (40 percent)

Income distribution from the investment is declining (38 percent)

Investment not performing as well as a bank CD (30 percent)

Investments not performing as well as an index (27 percent)

Losing money within the first year (23 percent)

Only 16 percent of respondents chose only one definition, while 55 percent chose three or more.

The multiple descriptions of risk in a prospectus—in both text and graphics—are designed to help investors determine whether the fund's profile matches their own conception of risk.

buy stocks of companies based or doing business in the developing world that appear to have the potential for high growth. If a fund concentrates its investments in a particular industry or group of industries, it will be noted here.

The summary prospectus then goes on to describe circumstances that are reasonably likely to have a negative impact on the fund's yield or return. The specific concerns vary widely depending on the type of fund. The prospectus for a blue chip stock fund might describe only two main risks: that the stock market overall may decline and that the stocks chosen for the portfolio may not do well. An emerging market equity fund may be concerned about foreign currency fluctuations or political risk in the countries it invests in, while a high yield bond fund might list many risk factors including a downturn in stocks, a rise in interest rates, defaults by issuers, and potential difficulties in selling the bonds the fund holds. The narrative also provides information on the fund's best and worst quarterly returns. ("The Difficulty of Defining Risk" explains why the prospectus includes several different depictions of a fund's risk.)

Funds must also include a bar chart showing the fund's return in each of the past 10 years. (The period can be shorter if the fund hasn't been in operation that long.) The ups and downs of the graph provide investors with a snapshot of how much fund shares can fluctuate in value which, in turn, gives investors some sense for the variability of that fund's returns. Figure 3.1 gives a hypothetical example.

To make it absolutely and positively clear that there is risk involved in mutual fund investing, the SEC also requires that all funds, except money

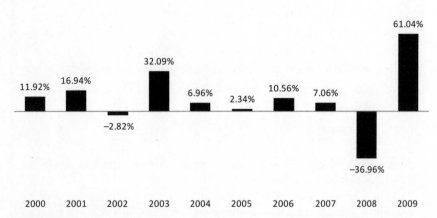

FIGURE 3.1   A Sample Risk/Return Bar Chart

market funds, state simply and explicitly that the value of fund shares may decline. Many fund documents say flatly:

You can lose money by investing in the fund.

After describing risk, this section of the summary prospectus concludes with a review of the fund's past returns. To prevent funds from displaying only the most favorable numbers, the SEC strictly defines the return data to be included. As a general rule, the summary prospectus must show annualized return for the past 1, 5, and 10 years (or since the startup of the fund if it has been around for less than 10 years). The calculation must be done in three different ways:

1. Showing the effect of sales loads only, if there are any
2. After sales loads and taxes on distributions
3. After sales loads, taxes on distributions, and taxes on sale of fund shares[3]

The return figure used is always *total return,* which is defined in "Adding Up Return." A detailed description of the calculations is available on the web site that accompanies this book.

ADDING UP RETURN

Even though mutual funds come in a variety of flavors, their results are all evaluated using the same measurement: total return, which incorporates *all* the elements of return—both income and price appreciation—in one computation. For mutual funds, total return includes:

- Interest and dividend income, minus the annual operating expenses. As we learned in Chapter 2, this income must be distributed to shareholders annually.
- *Realized* gains or losses on securities that have been sold already, which must also distributed annually.
- *Unrealized* gains or losses on securities still held in the portfolio. These gains and losses are reflected in the fund's NAV.

To help buyers put these return numbers in context, the fund must also provide the return of an appropriate market index for the same periods. We talk in depth about the value of this type of comparative analysis in the next chapter.

Section 5: Management. Here, the summary prospectus names names. It's at this point that we're given the name of the company managing the investments—which isn't always the company on the front cover of the prospectus. We also learn the names of the portfolio managers—who are the specific individuals at that firm who are responsible for buy and sell decisions—and we find out how long they've been managing the fund. (This information is not required for money market funds). Mutual fund cognoscenti keep a close watch for amendments to this section, since a change in portfolio manager can sometimes mean a significant change in investment approach.

Section 6: Purchase and sale of fund shares. For investors who are still interested in the fund, this section gives an overview of how to buy or sell fund shares. Some funds may offer only one option, but many present a whole menu of ways to invest, which could include:

- Through a broker or other financial representative
- Through a systematic investment program, making regular deductions from a checking or savings account or a paycheck
- Through the Internet
- By phone
- By mail
- By wire transfer

Minimum investment amounts are discussed here, along with basic information on redeeming your shares, such as how the proceeds of a sale will be paid to you.

Section 7: Tax information. For those unfamiliar with how a mutual fund works, the summary prospectus explains that the fund will distribute its income every year and that shareholders may have to pay taxes on those distributions.

Section 8: Financial intermediary compensation. The summary prospectus ends with another discussion of costs. (It should be obvious by now that the SEC wants disclosure in this area to be crystal clear.) If a fund—or its adviser and or an affiliate—pays intermediaries, such as brokerage firms, to sell its shares or to provide services to investors, it must declare that:

These payments may create a conflict of interest by influencing the broker-dealer or other intermediary and your salesperson to recommend the fund over another investment.

And that's it. All other information must go into either the statutory prospectus or the statement of additional information; it can't be added here.

BEYOND THE SUMMARY PROSPECTUS

Some potential buyers want more detail than the summary prospectus provides. Funds prepare the full prospectus and statement of additional information for them. Investors who already own shares need regular updates on how the fund is faring, which they can find in the semiannual shareholder reports. Let's take a closer look at these documents. Samples are posted on this book's web site.

Prospectus

Until March 2009, the full, or statutory, prospectus was the document that all mutual funds sent to buyers. It had been carefully designed to include all material information that investors needed to know before diving into a mutual fund.

Unfortunately, there wasn't a lot of evidence that investors actually read the full prospectus. In fact, a 2006 survey conducted by the Investment Company Institute found that only one-third of fund investors had consulted the fund prospectus before investing.[4] Recommendations from financial advisers were much more likely to influence decisions.

PAPERBACK WRITING

The fund prospectuses that arrive in a fund owner's mailbox can rival a paperback novel in weight and page count. The statutory prospectus for even a single fund can run to 40-plus pages if formatted in a reader-friendly way. And adding to the weight of the documents—literally—fund families often present several related funds together in the same prospectus. This saves on printing, mailing, and legal fees, but does little to prevent shareholders from being overwhelmed by excess information.

To cut back on the deluge of information, the SEC has decreed that the summary prospectus must stand on its own: it may contain information about only one fund.

The sheer quantity of information included in the prospectus seemed to be part of the problem. The same ICI survey found that about two-thirds of shareholders thought the prospectus contained too much information and was difficult to get through. And despite the SEC's best efforts to make the language in it understandable, one professor of English termed it *unreadable*.[5] Given all the criticisms, many industry observers began to endorse the idea of a shorter document that made key information more accessible. (See "Paperback Writing" for more on the sheer weight of prospectuses.)

Concluding that there must be a better way, the SEC created the summary prospectus and offered funds a choice. Beginning in March 2009, they could send either the full prospectus or the summary prospectus to buyers. If they opted for the latter, they would have to post on their web site all the documents we discuss in this chapter: the summary prospectus, the statutory prospectus, the statement of additional information and the fund's most recent annual and semiannual reports. And they would have to make sure that investors could easily navigate both within and among these online documents, using tools like a table of contents or links.

Since most funds already posted key documents online, moving to the summary prospectus offered substantial savings on printing and mailing costs. In fact, by April 2010, a little over a year after its endorsement by the SEC, more than 4,300 standalone summary prospectuses had been filed, according to NewRiver, Inc. which has tracked the filing data.[6]

Still, the statutory prospectus has its adherents. It necessarily includes more information than the summary prospectus for the simple reason that it includes the summary prospectus in full—as its leading section. The balance of the statutory prospectus contains:

- More detail on investment strategies and risks.
- Information on the time the fund calculates its NAV, which is usually right after the New York Stock Exchange closes. Investors need to have their buy or sell order in before that time if they'd like them to be processed on the same day.
- Specifics about limits on transactions by fund shareholders, especially short-term trading. Funds discourage investors from buying and selling fund shares frequently, since it imposes costs on all the owners of the fund but benefits only a few.
- All the nitty-gritty detail on sales charges.
- A financial highlights table, with data on NAV, returns, and expenses in each of the past five years.

If a fund wants to put an attractive outside cover, or *wrapper*, around the prospectus, it must prevent any confusion by including the disclaimer that "This page is not part of the prospectus." For the guidelines on the content of these wrappers and other fund promotional material, see "Truth in Advertising."

TRUTH IN ADVERTISING

While the SEC wants investors to use the prospectus as their sole source of fund information, many potential buyers are first exposed to a fund through an advertisement. Fund management companies advertise heavily to attract assets to their funds.

Like every other aspect of the mutual fund business, investment company advertising is strictly regulated. And it's not just conventional TV, radio, or print ads that are subject to controls. Restrictions apply to anything a fund distributor sends out to promote itself or its fund offerings, whether a sales brochure or even the reprint of an article appearing in the *Wall Street Journal*. This includes a firm's entire Internet presence, from its web site to blog posts to messages left on social networking sites.

Fund distributors must file every last bit of this material with FINRA within 10 business days of its first use.[7] (For an overview of this self-regulatory organization, refer back to Chapter 1.) FINRA reviews all submissions to determine if they are fair and balanced and provide a sound basis for evaluating the fund. In addition, materials may not include any "false, exaggerated, unwarranted or misleading statement or claim" or any predictions about future performance.[8] Ads promoting a particular fund must also refer the reader to the prospectus. If the FINRA reviewer finds shortcomings with the material, she may suggest changes, require revisions, or, in the case of serious deficiencies, issue a "Do Not Use" letter that calls for a written response from the fund distributor.

While a few ads are designed to build brand and do not include any numbers, most focus on fund performance and are, therefore, subject to particularly stringent standards set by the SEC. As in the prospectus, management companies have no choice about which numbers to present. If they want to include performance information at all, they must show data for 1, 5, and 10 years (or since inception if the fund has been in existence for less than 10 years) as of the most current quarter end. And these ads must always remind investors that:

Past performance does not guarantee future results.

So, fund ads are accurate, but are they useful in making a decision about a future investment? Remember that fund management companies are not required to publish ads; it's something they do only when they believe they'll increase fund sales. And that's usually when the fund has been doing particularly well, either because of astute choices by the fund's portfolio manager or strong gains in the types of securities the fund holds or both. But that's not necessarily the best time for making an investment in that fund. At the same time, ads don't include the full discussion of risk and expenses that investors can find in the required disclosure documents.

Best to follow the advice that at the bottom of almost all fund ads, and:

Read and consider the prospectus carefully before investing.

Statement of Additional Information

Some investors scoff at the idea that the prospectus is too detailed—they argue that it's not detailed enough: the statement of additional information is the fund document geared for this group. It's a small audience, though—so small that one large mailing house, serving many fund families, reported that investors had requested a total of six SAIs over the course of one calendar year. Because of the limited demand, funds are not required to provide SAIs unless someone specifically asks for them. These days, most fund families make them available on their web sites—and remember that they *must* make SAIs available online if they send out the summary prospectus as a standalone document.

While the SEC has, as usual, established detailed guidelines for the SAI, in practice, funds include everything in it that they believe some investors might want to know. For example, many funds provide additional detail on how portfolio securities are valued, even though this is not specifically required by the SEC.

Much of the SAI tends to be legal boilerplate, included to make sure that the fund has disclosed absolutely everything to the investor. For example, the list of investment strategies will normally describe every transaction that the fund might possibly engage in during the year, whether they'll use those strategies regularly or not. Then there's the list of things the fund may not do, called *investment restrictions*. These are usually mandated by law and apply to all funds.

There is not much in any of these sections to distinguish one fund from another. There are, however, important pieces of information in the SAI. Among them are:

- *Board of directors.* The SAI provides the detail that helps investors assess how well the board members' interests are aligned with their own. We learn specifics about the directors' occupations, the other boards they sit on currently or have served on in the past five years, the compensation they receive from this fund specifically and from all the funds in the fund family combined, their ownership of shares in this fund and other funds in the family, and their financial transactions with the fund management company. More generally, the board must explain why each of the directors is qualified to serve on the board at this time. (Refer back to Chapter 2 for a review of the ongoing debate about fund directors.)

  This section also provides insights into the board's inner workings. There's a description of the leadership structure: whether the chair of the board is an interested or disinterested director or whether there's a designated lead independent director. The fund must also explain the board's role overseeing risk management—a critical issue for investors.

  These disclosures about boards are not unique to mutual funds; the SEC requires them of all publicly held corporations. Missed them in the SAI? They are also included in the proxy statement prepared whenever there is a shareholder vote.

- *Portfolio managers.* Here investors can learn more about the individuals making investment decisions for the fund. The SAI gives details on how many other accounts they manage—both mutual fund and non-mutual fund— which is relevant because those accounts may compete for the manager's time, attention, and best investment ideas. It provides a description of the methodology used to determine the manager's compensation (though not the actual dollar amount) and the amount of the portfolio manager's ownership of the fund's shares, if any. As with the section on members of the board, investors are being given information that helps them assess whether the portfolio managers' interests align with their own.

- *Contracts.* The fund must describe the contracts for services it has signed. This discussion is useful for understanding the fund's expense structure and for identifying any potential conflicts of interest.

■ *History.* If the fund has changed its name, it must mention that here—important for anyone tracking down an old fund position. The SAI also discloses any tax-loss carryforwards; these are net losses on securities sold in prior years. (They may appear in the fund's annual report as well.) Loss carryforwards will reduce the taxes on any gains taken this year, so information on them is valuable to investors.

Shareholder Reports

The disclosure of important information doesn't end once an individual has bought fund shares. Funds keep their shareholders up to date by providing them with at least two reports every year, the semiannual and annual shareholder reports.[9] These reports give investors the information they need to evaluate both whether the fund has met their expectations and whether it should continue to be part of their financial plan in the future.

At the most basic level, the shareholder reports update the key information provided in the prospectus to reflect the most current data. They include expense and performance numbers, although they're presented a bit differently here than in the other disclosure documents. For example, past performance is displayed in a line graph as well as presented in a table. All very helpful, but not particularly new information.

It's the narrative discussion of the raw data that makes these periodic reports especially useful to shareholders.

Portfolio commentary. The most important part of a shareholder report is the commentary from the fund's portfolio manager, usually in the form of a letter or an interview. Here the manager discusses how well—or poorly—the fund did over the period being covered compared to both a relevant market index and to similar mutual funds. The review highlights the investment decisions that had the biggest impact on that performance, both positive and negative, and any major changes that were made in the portfolio over the period. The portfolio commentary normally ends with a discussion of the future—a very rare item indeed in a fund's disclosure documents. The manager will review, in broad terms, his outlook for the relevant markets and explain how the fund is positioned to profit from the expected environment.

President's letter. The shareholder report often includes a letter from the chief executive of the management company, covering nonportfolio issues that might affect shareholders. This letter might review changes in the executive suite at the management company or in the fund's boardroom. If the fund management company has been involved in any mergers or acquisitions, this letter may describe the expected impact on investors. Or the president may explain how the fund might fit into a personal financial plan in the year ahead.

The quality of these letters varies widely. The weaker ones seem to be more interested in marketing than informing. But even then they're an important source of the latest news.

Board discussion of contract renewal. Finally, in the annual report only, investors hear directly from the fund's board of directors, which is required to explain why it signed a contract with the management company. Essentially, the independent directors are justifying the fee that they've agreed to. Most boards follow a template for this section, changing only the numbers from year to year and fund to fund. Despite its limitations, this material does give investors a sense of the factors that have come into play in the board's conversations with management. (Turn back to Chapter 2 for a review of the *Gartenberg* standard that applies to those discussions.)

Two other elements of the shareholder reports are worth highlighting:

Holdings list. All funds (except money market funds) are required to include at least their top 50 holdings in their shareholder reports, although most include the full roster.[10] Holdings are grouped by economic sector, geographic region, or other classification scheme appropriate to the fund.

Since the holdings list can be overwhelming—especially for a large fund—funds must include at least one graphic element summarizing the fund's positioning. This could be, among other examples, a pie chart showing the percentages invested in stocks versus bonds or a bar graph showing the distribution of stocks by sector.

Financial statements. The income statement, balance sheet, and statement of cash flows are included, though for mutual funds they're called the *statement of operations, statement of assets and liabilities,* and *statement of changes in net assets.* They are audited once a year. The annual report will include a letter from the fund's audit firm, describing their review and expressing their opinion on the accuracy of the financial statements.

USING THE USER GUIDES

So the fund's disclosure documents contain a lot of information. What's most important? When you're beginning to research a fund, here are a few of the things to focus on:

- *Investment objective.* First turn to the prospectus or summary prospectus and the discussion of investment objective and strategy. Make sure that the investment approach matches your goals and fits well into your long-term plan for your portfolio.

- *Risk.* Staying with the prospectus, read through all the risk descriptions and assess the overall risk level of the fund. There are two ways to gauge this quickly: Number 1—if the fund has a fairly long history, look at the bar graph of annual returns to see the fund's volatility. Less reliable, but still useful, especially within fund families, is Number 2— notice how much ink is devoted to describing the risks. The lawyers drafting prospectuses generally include more disclosure on funds they consider riskier within a fund family. These two factors combined allow you to begin to judge whether you're comfortable with the expected level of risk.

- *Sales load.* If you think you're still interested, study the table on expenses. Will you need to pay a front-end sales charge to invest in the fund? That might not make sense if you're making all your own investment decisions, though it can be appropriate if you're working with a financial adviser who is providing valuable advice. There are usually lots of rules in this section, but be sure to check them all out; you may be eligible for a reduced sales charge.

- *Performance snapshot.* Finally, take a quick look at the performance data. Overall, has performance been very good or very bad—or just mediocre? You'll want to make sure you understand why . . . which leads to our next step.

- *Performance analysis.* Now you're ready to take out the annual or semiannual report. Read through the portfolio commentary. Does the explanation of past performance make sense? Is it consistent with the performance numbers that have been presented and the list of holdings, as best you can determine? Pull up the management discussion and analysis in a shareholder report from a year or two previously—preferably from a time when performance wasn't that great. You'll want to make sure that the investment approach has been consistent over time. It's particularly important to look back if the portfolio managers are new to the fund. (Remember that the prospectus will tell you about their tenure.)

- *Portfolio manager investment.* Next, turn to the statement of additional information and read about the qualifications of the portfolio team. Check whether the managers have invested their own money in the fund—it's a good sign if they have.

Next, you'll want to evaluate both performance and expenses compared to other funds. For this, you'll need to turn to outside information sources. They're the subject of our next chapter.

CHAPTER SUMMARY

Mutual funds must comply with U.S. disclosure rules. They must register offerings of their shares with the SEC, provide buyers with a prospectus describing the investment, and then report periodically to owners about their investment. Funds usually provide three types of prospectuses: the summary prospectus, the statutory prospectus, and the statement of additional information. Each has a different level of detail. Investors can choose the prospectus type that best matches their informational needs.

The key disclosure document is the summary prospectus. It provides an overview of the funds' investment objective and risks as well as the costs of owning the fund. It also gives potential investors information about the management of the fund, how to buy and sell fund shares, taxes associated with fund share ownership and compensation paid to intermediaries who sell the fund.

The statutory prospectus contains the summary prospectus in full. It also includes more information about the investment strategy and risks, the calculation of the fund NAV, sales charges and limits on purchases and sales of fund shares. Any other information that funds believe investors should know is placed in the statement of additional information. Details about the fund's board of directors and portfolio managers can be found there.

Funds keep investors up to date by sending them at least two shareholder reports every year. These reports contain the latest statistics on the fund's performance and expenses, together with a list of the fund's holdings. Most importantly, these reports include the portfolio manager's explanation of past returns and review his outlook for the future.

Investors considering a mutual fund investment can learn much of what they need to know about their potential purchase by reading these three types of disclosure documents. Fund advertisements are less complete. Most are designed to tout past performance, without an explanation of how that performance was achieved or whether it's likely to continue.

CHAPTER 4

Comparing Mutual Funds

To sort through the 7,600-plus funds available in the United States today, you'll want to go beyond the disclosure documents supplied by any single mutual fund. If you'd like to follow the lead of experienced investors, you'll follow a two-step process. First, you'll specify your investment objectives so that you can divide your investment dollars among four broad categories of funds, in a process called *asset allocation.* Second, you'll choose specific funds within each of the four categories, by using third-party sources of information to compare the merits of these funds.

In making your first decision about asset allocation, you'll use categories based on the main types of securities the funds hold. While we provide a detailed review of the many types of funds in each group later in this chapter, the four main categories are in brief:

1. *Money market funds.* Money market funds are the investment vehicle most like bank savings accounts, though these funds are not insured by the federal government. They pay relatively low rates of interest, or, put another way, their yield is low. As an offset to their modest return, these funds afford a high degree of safety. In fact, they ordinarily have a stable NAV of $1 per share. When you invest in a money market fund, you can reasonably expect that its value will only grow and not diminish over time.

2. *Bond funds.* Bond funds normally pay a higher rate of interest than money market funds but without the same level of security: the value of your investment in a bond fund can vary from day to day. The bonds these funds hold are, in essence, loans to a government or a corporation that promises to repay the money—with interest—by a fixed date known as the *maturity date.* The value of that promise will vary with the economy, the current level of interest rates, and the financial health of the issuer of the bond.

3. *Stock funds.* Stock funds, unlike money market and bond funds, generally don't provide much income. Instead, most investors own stock funds in the belief that their NAV will appreciate in value as the prices on the stocks they invest in go up. Own a share of stock, and you own a small piece of a corporation; the value of this ownership stake will swing up and down with the company's prospects. Those swings can be quite significant, so that, at least in the short term, stock fund investing is normally much riskier than bond fund investing. But the rewards of holding an ownership stake can be quite significant over time. In consequence, investors should plan to hold stocks for an extended period, so that they can ride out the ups and downs to better reap the long-term benefits of stock ownership.

4. *Hybrid funds.* Hybrid funds invest in a combination of bonds and stocks. As we'll see, they allow investors to delegate many aspects of their asset allocation decisions to the fund manager.

After making the big picture asset allocation decision, you'll delve into the four categories of funds to choose the specific funds that make sense for you. Each category contains multiple subgroups, all with a different investment focus. You'll want to emphasize those subgroups—and their constituent funds—that both fit well with your financial plan and offer good prospects for future performance.

This chapter reviews:

- Factors to weigh as you develop your asset allocation plan.
- Methods of evaluating fund performance and risk.
- The four categories of mutual funds together with the key characteristics differentiating funds within each.

DELINEATING YOUR OWN INVESTMENT OBJECTIVES

To develop an asset allocation plan, you'll start by tackling the challenge of evaluating your own financial needs and investment preferences. Are you in your twenties and saving for the down payment on a car or a condo? In your thirties and worried about funding the kids' college education? In your fifties and building a retirement nest egg? In your seventies and looking for income to supplement your Social Security check? Of course, you may have more than one investment objective at the same time. Each one of these objectives may be best served by a different type of fund.

A comprehensive examination of investment objectives is beyond the scope of this book. Nevertheless, we encourage you to be more precise about your investment objectives by focusing on the following factors:

Liquidity needs. Begin the asset allocation process by specifying your liquidity needs—that's the cash you need on a regular basis to buy food and gas, write a check for the mortgage, and pay tuition bills. You'll want to put the dollars you need for those immediate expenses into money market funds, with their stable NAV and checking privileges. But if you have a substantial amount in savings above your current liquidity needs, you should be able to invest at least some of that cushion and let it grow undisturbed for a number of years. If that's the case, you'll want to consider buying stock funds or bond funds, with the specific choice depending on your time horizon. That's the next thing to contemplate. . . .

Time horizon. Looking beyond the dollars you need for short-term liquidity, estimate how long you'll be able to leave your money in the investments you select. The longer your time horizon, the larger the portion of your portfolio that you can allocate to stocks and other investments that have higher risk, but also a higher return potential. If you're setting aside money to buy a house or a car in a few years, you could think about investing in high-quality bond funds that provide more income than money market funds, though with some risk that you may lose money. If you're planning for retirement, your time horizon could easily be five or six decades long: the 30 or 40 years you'll still be working and earning an income plus the 20 or so years you'll be drawing on your savings after you've stopped. If leaving a significant estate to your heirs is an important goal, you'll need to think even beyond retirement.

Return expectations. Your outlook for the future returns of cash, bonds, and stocks will influence your asset allocation as well. To estimate those returns, you might start by looking at how well the various categories of funds have done in the past. This information is readily available, but as fund advertisements will remind you, past returns don't necessarily predict future returns, especially over relatively short periods. The future performance of most funds is determined largely by trends in the economy, such as the direction of interest rates and corporate earnings. For example, a rise in interest rates will lower the returns on bond funds, while a fall in rates will increase them. For stock funds, it's rising corporate earnings that boost returns and declining earnings that dampen them.

Risk tolerance. If you, like many people, are uncertain about where the economy is going, you might want a diversified portfolio of mutual funds to include a U.S. stock fund, an international stock fund, a corporate bond fund, and a money market fund. The weightings within this diversified portfolio should be heavily influenced by your own appetite for risk. If you're willing to take a chance of losing some money in exchange for the possibility of making a great deal more, your asset allocation should tilt toward stocks. On the other hand, if one of the things you dread most is watching the value of your savings decline, you should emphasize money market and bond funds in your investing.

In sum, the less your need for liquidity, the longer your time horizon, the more optimistic you are about the future and the greater your risk appetite, the larger will be your allocation to stock funds. If income from your investments is critical, you'll want to emphasize bond funds. And with a very short-term focus, money market funds are probably your best bet. Of course, it's very possible that you'll be saving for three very different goals at one time. You might have a money market fund with funds set aside for the next mortgage payment, bonds to pay for your daughter's tuition when she heads off to college five years from now and stocks in your retirement plan at work.

Even this short synopsis illustrates that arriving at the asset allocation that matches your needs is a complex process—involving many variables and much soul-searching. Furthermore, you'll need to carefully consider how your proposed asset allocation can be achieved on the most tax-efficient basis. For many people, making the maximum contributions to their retirement plan is the most tax-efficient method of investing in funds. These contributions are usually excluded from income taxation until they are distributed to you in retirement. There are also tax-efficient vehicles for achieving specific investment objectives. For example, you can withdraw money from a Section 529 plan without taxation if it's used to pay college tuition.

Most fund managers provide tools that help you determine an appropriate asset allocation and choose individual funds. These tools include online computer models that allow you to examine your projected financial position under multiple scenarios. Fund managers will also supply you with summaries of the relevant tax laws that are likely to affect your investment strategies—though they will not customize a tax analysis to your specific situation. To give you a sense of the materials available to help fund investors, we've compiled an illustrative list on this book's web site.

With these tools—and with the time and inclination—you can make the asset allocation decision and select funds within each category for yourself. However, some investors do not have time to do all this homework, while others may feel that they'd benefit from access to specialized expertise, especially when it comes to complicated issues like taxes. Investors who'd like advice about asset allocation, fund selection, and tax-efficient vehicles can consider hiring a financial planner to guide them through the process. Of course, as we review in Chapter 10, professional advice is more expensive than the do-it-yourself approach.

At this point, we assume that you have an asset allocation plan in place and are ready to start choosing specific funds with the asset categories.

EVALUATING PERFORMANCE

To be better able to choose specific funds, we need to understand how to evaluate mutual funds—how to judge their returns and risk. When making investments, most people want to maximize their returns and minimize risk. While this is a simple goal, it isn't easy to achieve because high returns almost always mean high risk and vice versa. The price of the stock of a new biotech company could zoom up (high return)—though it might just as easily fall to near zero (high risk). Conversely, money in a checking account won't earn high rates of interest (low return), but it's not likely to disappear (low risk)—without someone having written a check, of course. Understanding the trade-off between the two is critical.

When we talk about risk and return in the context of mutual funds, we'll always use the following definitions:

- *Return.* Return will always be *total return,* which combines all the sources of returns from an investments, namely:

  Total Return = Interest Income + Dividend Income +/− Realized
  Capital Gains (or Losses) +/− Unrealized Capital Gains (or Losses)

  The calculation of total return for mutual funds also normally reflects a deduction for annual operating expenses, such as management fees and 12b-1 charges, but there are some exceptions to this norm, as we see a little later in this section.

- *Risk.* As we discussed in the last chapter, risk means something slightly different to each investor. But for the purpose of evaluating performance, we define risk precisely as the variability in fund returns. Mathematically, this is the standard deviation of return, a measure of how much those returns differ from the average return. For example, two funds may both achieve a 6 percent annual return over 10 years, a return that is in line with the average fund in the group. But Fund A never deviated significantly from the average return, while Fund B did wildly better than average in 5 of the 10 years and much worse in the other half of the decade. In this hypothetical scenario, Fund A has a lower standard deviation of return than Fund B. Therefore, under our definition, Fund A is less risky than Fund B.

With these definitions of return and risk in hand, we can explore the three key methods used by experienced investors to assess fund performance.

These are: peer group comparison, index comparison, and risk-adjusted performance calculation. We discuss each method in turn, and then review the special roles that yield and expenses play in fund evaluation for some investors.

Peer group comparison. The first evaluation method is to compare fund performance to the returns of its subcategory of funds, called its *peer group,* or *competitive universe.* A peer group is a set of mutual funds, all with similar investment objectives and approaches that can reasonably be vying with each other for investor attention and dollars. A peer group can be quite broad—funds investing in U.S. stocks, for example—or quite narrow, such as funds focusing on Minnesota state tax-exempt bonds.

A fund's performance can be stacked up against the peer group in two ways. First, its return is compared to the average return for all funds in the group, generally for several different time periods. Second, all the funds are ranked in order of return: the higher the fund is in this ranking, the better. For this purpose, the competitive universe is often divided into quartiles, with the better performing funds (top 25 percent) composing the top quartile and the poorer performers (bottom 25 percent) making up the fourth, or bottom, quartile.

Two firms, Morningstar and Lipper, dominate in the business of maintaining peer groups and publishing data about their returns. Of the two, Morningstar has the higher general name recognition and makes much of its content available at a fee that is affordable for most investors. Lipper is more often used by management companies because Lipper provides a broader menu of peer groups and more options for customized reports. More information is available on their web sites: www.morningstar.com and www.lipperweb.com.

Index comparison. The second way to look at a fund's performance is to compare it to that of a market index or *benchmark.* (Remember from Chapter 3 that the SEC even requires that funds provide this comparison in shareholder reports.) An index is a hypothetical portfolio of securities chosen to represent an entire market or some segment of it. Like peer groups, they can be very broad—the Barclays Capital Global Aggregate Index covering bond markets around the world, for example—or quite specific, such as the Morgan Stanley Retail Index, which, as its name suggests, measures the return of retail company stocks.

Again, like peer groups, indexes are maintained by independent firms that periodically publish return data and information about the securities that are included in them. These firms also select the stocks that are put into the indexes, based on criteria that they usually publish on their web sites. Some of the best-known index providers are Barclays Capital (formerly Lehman), Dow Jones, J.P. Morgan, MSCI, Russell Investments, and Standard & Poor's.

To get a fair assessment of performance, each fund is compared against an index that reflects its investment objective. A general U.S. stock fund might be stacked up against the S&P 500 index, while a high yield bond fund might be measured against the J.P. Morgan Developed High Yield Index. The comparison itself is very simple: if the fund's return is higher than the return of the relevant index, the fund is said to *outperform;* conversely, it *underperforms* whenever its return falls short of the index return. Note, however, that the index return does not include any expenses—not even the brokerage commissions required to buy any stocks in the index. As a result, a fund with an investment return equal to the index will necessarily have a lower total return than the index once expenses have been deducted.

Not all investors believe that this analysis versus an index make sense. Rather, they expect that funds generate a positive, absolute return, after adjusting for inflation, in all market environments. Some investment managers have developed funds that use certain investment techniques to help them achieve that goal. These techniques have most often been used in hedge funds, though some management companies have recently introduced mutual funds that use a similar approach.

Indexes can serve as a point of comparison for more than just performance evaluation. Fund managers often use indexes as a reference point when making decisions about which securities to hold and in what proportions. For some funds, the index even becomes their entire investment strategy. These *index funds* or *passively managed funds,* as they're known, simply try to track the performance of the index, by holding all the stocks included in the index with exactly the same weightings or by buying a representative sample of the index stocks. (Contrast this with *actively managed funds,* which try to outperform the index by selecting securities with superior prospects.) While index funds are available to both bond and stock investors, they have been much more controversial in the stock arena. We review the debate in detail when we discuss choices of stock funds later in this chapter.

Risk-adjusted performance calculation. There's a third way of evaluating fund returns—by comparing a fund's return with the risk that it has assumed, using a risk-adjusted performance calculation. To some degree, both peer group and benchmark index comparisons take risk into account because they compare funds and indexes that all invest in similar securities and therefore have similar risk in a rough sense. As a result, performance against a peer group or benchmark alone is a rough measure of risk-adjusted return. But many investors want to capture the effect of a fund's deviation from the average more precisely.

In its simplest form, a risk-adjusted performance calculation divides a fund's return in any given period by the standard deviation of that return over the same period.[1] The result is tracked over time and compared to other funds. In practice, fund managers often use a more complex approach that compares both return and risk to these measures for a benchmark index before doing the long division. This result is called an *information ratio;* it's often used by fund managers and the consultants advising large investors to assess portfolio positioning and performance.

The general public may be most familiar with risk-adjusted performance through the Morningstar star ratings: a scale of from one to five stars—five being best—designed to give investors a quick way of evaluating funds. To arrive at its well-known ratings, Morningstar divides fund performance by a proprietary measure of variation of returns, calculated by putting a heavier weight on underperformance versus the index as compared to outperformance. (Morningstar is making the reasonable assumption that investors are more concerned about price

SHINING STARS

Star ratings have an intuitive appeal. Whether it's hotels, restaurants, or movies, a five-star rating is a symbol of high quality and therefore likely to draw consumers' attention—and their dollars.

And so it has proved with mutual funds: earning a Morningstar five-star rating may be the surest way to draw investor assets into a fund. One influential study found that an initial five-star rating led to fund sales that were 53 percent above average.[2] With stars generating such a high payoff, fund managers have been eager to publicize any top rankings they have received. Fund advertisements, as a result, frequently feature Morningstar rankings.

As an investment tool, the stars have not been quite as reliable. Like many similar systems, Morningstar uses past performance to predict future results, which is a tricky endeavor since the economic environment can change dramatically over time – meaning that an investment strategy that works today might not be as successful tomorrow. As a result, the star ratings—again, like similar systems—have worked better for some types of investments than others and better in some markets than others. According to Morningstar's own analysis, the star ratings have proved the most predictable indicators for U.S. stock funds in relatively stable market environments. Their record with other types of funds has been more mixed.[3]

movements that can cause losses.) The star rating incorporates a peer group comparison as well: all the funds in a category are ranked on risk-adjusted return, then the top 10 percent are assigned five stars, the next 22.5 percent are given four stars, the next 35 percent three stars, and so on. The Morningstar system has been extremely influential. (See "Shining Stars" for more.)

Throughout this section we've been talking about total return, which, as we've discussed, equals investment income received by the fund plus its realized and unrealized capital gains minus its operating expenses. But some investors focus on only one part of this definition of total return—either on the yield from investment income or the expenses incurred by investors.

Yield. Investors who are concerned about income often zero in on a fund's yield, the portion of its return that comes from interest and dividend payments. Looking at yield to the exclusion of other sources can be highly misleading for all but money market funds, with their stable NAV, since swings in fund values can be a significant factor determining total return. For example, a bond fund may have yielded 5 percent in a year, but its NAV could drop by 3 percent over that same period, resulting in a total return closer to 2 percent.

Nevertheless, many investors base their decisions about funds on yield, so fund management companies include yield information in their advertising, especially in ads for bond funds. To help consumers make informed comparisons across funds, the SEC provides detailed instructions for the calculation of fund yield, which require that annual expenses be deducted from interest and dividend income to arrive at the quoted figure.

Expenses. The costs of owning a fund play a critical role in the selection decision for many investors. "Investment performance is unpredictable," they assert, "but expenses are not. Therefore, the easiest way to improve returns is to lower costs." Expense-conscious investors won't buy funds charging a sales load, and they screen no-load funds for low annual expenses before considering any investment. Many of these frugal investors end up owning index funds because of their low costs.

Expenses are a particularly important component of money market and bond fund performance, for two reasons. First, the dispersion of returns of fixed income securities—a term that includes both money market instruments and bonds—is not particularly wide. In other words, the gap in performance between the best-performing bond and the worst-performing bond in many categories will often not be very large. With so little difference in the returns of the securities, the returns of fixed income funds investing in them will cluster tightly together before expenses are deducted. As a result, expenses will often be a major determinant of bond or money market fund rankings. They're less important in rankings of actively managed stock funds—where returns vary more widely—though they're perhaps the single biggest factor separating passive and active stock fund returns, as we'll see later in this chapter.

At the same time, bond and money market returns are normally a lot lower than stock returns, so that expenses in fixed income funds generally reduce net returns by a larger percentage than they do in stock funds. Expenses have had an especially large impact in the recent low interest rate environment. Management companies are sensitive to the ratio of a bond or money market fund's expenses to the yield on the securities it holds, and they will often waive a portion of their fee and maybe even pay some of a fund's other expenses so that it can maintain a competitive yield. (Chapter 15 discusses waivers and subsidies in greater depth.)

A final word about expenses: It's extremely important to understand which expenses are—or are not—included in any performance calculation presented. The calculations may include:

- *Annual expenses only.* Some performance calculations include only the annual expenses that are deducted from income, specifically annual operating expenses and 12b-1 distribution charges. (We explain more about 12b-1 charges in Chapter 10.) This is the way that Lipper incorporates expenses when making its peer group rankings.
- *Annual expenses plus sales loads.* In contrast, Morningstar includes sales charges paid by the shareholder in its calculations, arguing that this approach better represents the returns that the consumer actually earns when investing in a fund. If, for example, the fund charges a front-end sales load and Morningstar is calculating three-year performance, it will deduct the full sales load at the beginning of the three-year period. Fund managers argue that this methodology unduly penalizes returns for shorter periods, especially one-year results. They note that shareholders often do not pay the full load because of load waivers, breakpoints, and other factors. (Again, these are discussed in detail in Chapter 10.)
- *No expenses at all.* A mutual fund's board of directors may review performance calculations that have been adjusted to exclude all expenses. Fund managers believe that these *gross* performance numbers—as opposed to figures *net* of fees—give a better indication of their success in choosing securities. This is particularly true when making comparisons with benchmark indexes, which do not include any sort of expense charges.

THE TAXONOMY OF MUTUAL FUNDS

With our performance measurement tools firmly in hand, we're ready to delve into the details of the subcategories of mutual funds. Like a biologist, we'll divide the four general classes of funds into orders, families, genuses, and species that are relevant for asset allocation decisions.

Money Market Funds

With only a small number of subgroups, the money market fund, or *money fund,* category is the simplest of all the fund categories. (Management of money market funds is another story. It's quite complicated, as Chapter 7 reveals.) Figure 4.1 shows the classification system.

Investors have a choice between two major types of money market funds: tax-exempt funds and taxable funds.

- *Tax-exempt funds.* Tax-exempt funds invest in securities backed by municipal and state governments. They are tax-exempt because the interest income from these securities is not subject to federal income tax. Within this subcategory, investors can choose either a national fund that invests around the country or a fund that focuses on securities issued within a single state. Distributions from the latter will also be exempt from state income taxes.

  Tax-exempt funds are also known as *municipal,* or *muni,* funds, and fund managers use the terms interchangeably in everyday conversation. There is, however, a technical distinction between the two: municipal funds may invest in securities that are subject to the alternative minimum tax or AMT, while tax-exempt funds may not. We discuss the AMT in Chapter 6.

- *Taxable funds.* Investors interested in taxable funds are also faced with two options. They can go for a fund holding only U.S. government

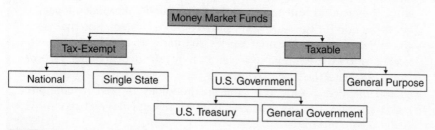

FIGURE 4.1   Money Market Funds

securities. (Chapter 7 explains the subtle difference between the two types of government money funds in the chart.) Or they can elect a general purpose money market fund that owns corporate securities as well as governments, providing a higher yield but with a little bit less safety.

Which is a better fit for a particular investor is simply a question of after-tax yield, computed as described in "A Taxing Calculation." As a general rule, tax-exempt funds make sense only for investors whose income places them in a high tax bracket or who live in a state with very high tax rates. For other investors, taxable funds will provide better after-tax returns in most environments.

A TAXING CALCULATION

To determine which fund type is right for you—taxable, national tax-exempt, or single state tax-exempt—you'll need to do some math. You'll calculate your after-tax return for a fund in each category and compare the results. Ready to do the numbers? For this calculation, you'll need the returns for funds in each group and your federal and state tax brackets: that's the percentage tax rate you pay on your last dollar of income, or your *marginal* tax rate.

Let's look at two theoretical taxpayers. Jack earns $80,000, placing him in the 25 percent tax bracket for federal tax purposes (for 2010). Jill earns considerably more, so she pays federal income taxes at the top rate of 35 percent (for 2010). They both live in California and pay 9.55 percent of their income to the state.

The returns on the three funds they're considering are in Table 4.1. To compute her after-tax return on the taxable fund, Jill will subtract 41.21 percent from the 4.00 percent return. That equals her 35 percent federal tax bracket plus the 9.55 percent state tax rate minus 35 percent of the 9.55 percent state tax rate—Jill will probably get a federal income tax deduction for the state taxes she pays, so the calculation makes an adjustment for that potential benefit. Similarly, to compute her after-tax return on the national tax-exempt fund, she deducts 6.21 percent from the return (the 9.55 percent state tax rate adjusted for the possible federal tax deduction). The same methodology is used to compute Jack's after-tax returns. The results of all the calculations are in the last two columns in the table.

TABLE 4.1 After-Tax Returns

Fund	Taxes Deducted	Return	Jill's After-Tax Return	Jack's After-Tax Return
General taxable	Federal and state	4.00%	2.35%	2.71%
National tax-exempt	State only	2.80%	2.63%	2.60%
Single state tax-exempt	None	2.65%	2.65%	2.65%

For Jill, both the national and the single state tax-exempt funds provide significantly better after-tax returns than the taxable fund. Jack, on the other hand, gets a slight return advantage from the taxable fund. But all three returns are so closely bunched together for him that Jack might want to make his investment decision based on nontax considerations. For example, the taxable fund might provide greater diversification than the tax-exempt funds.

Money market fund choices are quite straightforward in another way: investors generally are not offered a choice of money funds managed by different fund managers. The firm maintaining the investor's account normally puts him in one of its own money market funds, so that an investor with an Arch Street brokerage account, for example, will often have access only to Arch Street's money funds. This is typically not the case in the other fund categories.

On the flip side, making things more complicated, many fund sponsors actually offer two sets of money market funds: a *retail* series for individual investors and an *institutional* series for larger investors. The institutional funds have higher minimum investments and lower expenses and often provide special services that help businesses and governments manage fluctuating cash positions. On the other hand, most do not offer check-writing privileges, which are a common feature in retail money market funds.

Two other unique aspects of money funds: Morningstar does not publish any information on them. Instead, peer group comparisons are provided by Lipper and iMoneyNet.[4] Also, fund managers are not required by the SEC to publish benchmark index comparisons for their money market funds.

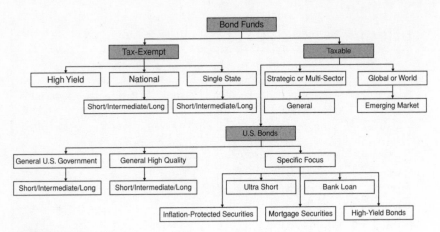

FIGURE 4.2   Bond Funds

Bond Funds

In marked contrast to the austere money market fund segment, the bond fund category confronts investors with a plethora of alternatives. (See Figure 4.2 for an overview.) Yet at the highest level, the classification of money and bond funds is quite similar. Like money market funds, bond funds are divided into tax-exempt, or municipal, funds and taxable funds, depending on the securities that the particular fund holds.

Within the tax-exempt segment, investors have a choice of either a national fund—exempt from federal income tax—or a single state fund—exempt from both federal and state income taxes—though there's also often a high yield option for tax-exempt bonds. High-yield muni funds focus on the bonds that finance specific state- and city-sanctioned projects, as opposed to the general obligations of the state or local government. Again, as in the money fund category, tax-exempt bond funds often will make sense only for investors paying taxes at one of the highest rates.

Turning to the taxable segment, bond fund investors confront a choice not available within money funds: they must decide whether to keep their money within the United States or whether to roam the globe in search of higher returns, by buying a world bond fund. Investors who are particularly excited about the prospects for the developing world can maximize their exposure to those countries through an emerging markets bond fund.

Within the U.S.-focused funds, investors again face a choice between a U.S. government fund or a general fund that invests in both high quality corporate bonds and governments. That's similar to the options in the money fund category, though here again, the bond category is much more diverse, providing numerous subcategories concentrating in particular types of securities. These specialized portfolios range in risk level from quite aggressive—such as high yield funds that invest in companies with high levels of debt—to very conservative, such as the inflation-protected securities that provide protection against increases in consumer prices usually associated with a rise in interest rates.

A distinguishing feature of bond fund taxonomy is that each of the more general subcategories is further broken down into *short, intermediate,* and *long* based on a fund's average maturity, which is the number of years until the maturity date for the average bond in its portfolio. Morningstar defines *short* as less than four years and *long* as more than 10 years, with *intermediate* filling the gap in between. Funds with long maturities are more sensitive to fluctuations in interest rates and are, therefore, riskier than funds with shorter maturities.

Within most of the bond fund subcategories, there are index fund alternatives, though they may not look all that different from actively managed funds. The distinction between passive and active management is less of a bright line in the bond category than it is in stocks. That's because bond indexes contain a very large number of securities, many of them hard to buy in any sizable quantities. As a result, index fund managers must often substitute similar bonds for the ones that are specifically identified in the index, adding an element of active management to these funds. At the same time, many actively managed bond funds hew very closely to the indexes that they use as a benchmark.

The number of choices can be overwhelming. To simplify life, many investors just buy the fund with the highest yield available, assuming this strategy will lead to the highest return. In some environments, that assumption will be correct, but in others it can prove to be a disastrous mistake, because it can mean taking on a relatively high level of risk at the wrong time.

Why? Bonds with higher yield also have higher risk. Maybe they've been issued by a company in a less-than-stable financial position. In that case, interest payments on these bonds are often at risk in a weak economic environment. Or they may have a long maturity, meaning that their value can fall significantly if interest rates rise. The key to successful bond investing is to choose the right type of risk at the right time in the economic cycle.

Other investors delegate the decision making by buying a strategic or multisector bond fund. The managers of these funds look for opportunities throughout the bond universe and allocate fund assets to the most compelling ones.

TABLE 4.2 Sample Peer Groups and Benchmark Indexes for Bond Funds

Fund Type	Peer Group	Benchmark Index
National municipal	Municipal national long funds	Barclays Capital Municipal Bond Index
General high quality	Intermediate-term bond funds	Barclays Capital U.S. Aggregate Index
Strategic	Multisector bond funds	Barclays Capital U.S. Universal Index
Emerging market bond	Emerging market bond funds	J.P. Morgan EMBI Global Index

Table 4.2 provides sample peer groups and benchmark indexes for different types of bond funds. We review bond fund investing in depth in Chapter 6.

Stock Funds

At first glance, the taxonomy of stock funds seems much simpler than that of bond funds. There's no separation between taxable and tax-exempt in this category. As we've discussed, stocks are inherently tax-efficient because they have little current income in the form of dividends. Instead, most of their return comes in the form of price appreciation—which is not taxable until the stock is sold and then usually at the lower tax rates that apply to capital gains. The taxonomy of stock funds is illustrated in Figure 4.3.

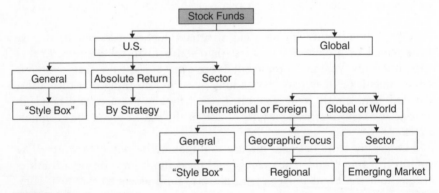

FIGURE 4.3 Stock Funds

Like taxable bond funds, stock funds are divided between those that stay at home and those that venture abroad, though here there are three categories:

1. U.S. funds.
2. International or foreign funds, investing in non-U.S. stocks only. International funds may focus on a particular region, such as Europe or Asia, or on the emerging markets.
3. Global or world funds, combining U.S. and non-U.S. stocks.

The decision on U.S. versus non-U.S. investing can be an important one, since many market observers believe that growth prospects—and, therefore, stock returns—are higher in other countries than here in the United States. We talk more about investing overseas in Chapter 16.

For investors who are excited about the prospects of a particular industry, sector funds are available. A *sector* is a group of related industries; for example, pharmaceutical and biotech and health care equipment and services are the industries in the health care sector. The term *sector fund* applies to a fund that focuses on a sector (such as health care), an industry (pharmaceutical and biotech), or a subindustry (just biotech stocks). Sector funds can be found in both U.S. and international varieties.

Now things really start to get complicated: general U.S. and international funds are further broken down into what has become known as a *style box*. This classification system, though long in use previously, was popularized by Morningstar in the 1980s. Today, virtually all rating services evaluating stock portfolio performance, including Lipper, have some version of one. A quick look at the schematic for the Morningstar system, shown in Figure 4.4, will explain the name.

The style box classifies funds in a grid along two dimensions. The first dimension is size, as measured by market capitalization. See "A Matter of Value" for a definition.

The second dimension is *style,* a classification that summarizes the types of stocks the fund invests in. Style is usually sorted into three categories: value; growth and core or blend. As their name implies, growth funds invest in stocks of fast-growing companies. Value funds, on the other hand, prefer to buy stocks that look cheaply priced, as may be the case when a company has experienced some problems. Core funds—often called blend funds—favor neither growth nor value: their portfolios tend to gravitate around the benchmark index for that size segment. We talk more about style in the next chapter, which reviews stock fund investing.

A MATTER OF VALUE

When stock market investors talk about a company's size, they're not referring to the number of employees or the level of revenues; they're usually talking about the total value of the company's stock, termed its *market capitalization,* or *market cap,* for short. Market cap equals the stock price times the number of the shares outstanding.

Stocks are often sorted by market cap into three categories: large cap, mid cap, and small cap. (Some systems also have a micro cap category.) While the dividing line varies with market conditions, small cap stocks generally have market caps below $2 billion, large cap stocks have market caps above $10 billion, and mid cap stocks comprise everything in between.

Style box classifications are based on a fund's actual holdings. This is a fundamentally different approach to classification than the other systems we've reviewed so far; all the other approaches are based on the objectives and constraints which are set forth in the prospectus, without looking at the actual portfolio. In fact, in these other systems, even if the holdings should

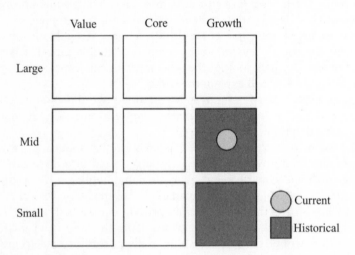

FIGURE 4.4   Morningstar Style Box
Source: Morningstar.

diverge from the objective—which can happen for a variety of reasons—the fund will still remain in its original category as determined by the prospectus.

In the style box approach, however, funds may move between style boxes as portfolio characteristics change. That may be the result of the portfolio manager actively changing holdings by buying or selling stock, or it may happen because stock prices have moved. For example, a small cap fund that has been extremely successful and bought stocks that have outperformed by a wide margin, could find that it has become a mid cap fund solely because of the price appreciation of its stocks. (Figure 4.1 illustrates how a fund might move between style boxes.)

The proponents of the style box make two arguments for it:

1. *Apples to apples comparisons.* First, accurately assessing investment acumen requires comparing one manager against another operating in the same portion of the grid. Let's say that a small cap value manager outperforms a large cap growth manager. An analytically minded investor would want to know whether the superior results came about because small cap stocks in general did well, because the value style did well, or because the manager did a great job picking stocks. By comparing small cap value managers against one another, neither market cap nor style come into play, leaving only investment skill as the cause of the performance differential.
2. *Diversification.* Sorting funds into these classifications helps investors diversify their portfolio into different segments of the equity market. With a style box system, it's harder to inadvertently buy two large cap value funds. Rather, it's easy to identify funds with varying approaches and investment universes.

Critics of the style box express concern at the pressure that it creates for fund managers to remain firmly within one segment of the grid. Funds that move between boxes may be shunned for being subject to *style drift,* the mutual fund equivalent of leprosy; a shift can be interpreted as inconsistency on the part of the fund manager. Yet, funds may move between boxes for two quite legitimate reasons.

1. *Fluid style categories.* First, investment style is more of a concept—a way of thinking about stock selection—rather than a hard and fixed rule. Stocks and industries can move between growth and value—or even be both at the same time—based on the economic environment. There are even periods when the entire market can look like value, as was the case after the bursting of the Internet bubble. Style boxes came into vogue in the 1980s and 1990s when the division between growth and

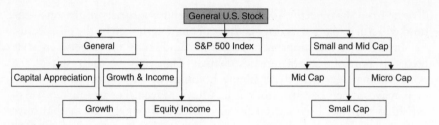

FIGURE 4.5 Lipper Alternative Scheme for Classification of U.S. Stock Funds
Source: Lipper.

value was very clear cut; in other periods, definitions have been much more fluid. In other words, rigid adherence to style box classifications doesn't reflect market reality.

2. *Opportunity cost.* Even more importantly, the critics contend, investors who insist that funds remain in a single box may be losing out on money-making opportunities. The best stock picks may often be found just over the border in an adjacent box. Fund managers' top ideas may be going to waste if they are overly restricted.

Some investors find the style box system so constraining that they reject it altogether. They prefer instead to evaluate funds using broader classifications based on their investment objectives. One of these alternative classification systems, the one used by Lipper for U.S. funds, is shown in Figure 4.5.[5] In this scheme, funds that specialize in small and mid cap stocks are classified according to their size predilection. S&P 500 index funds are also classified separately.

Other U.S. stock funds are sorted by general category of objective. These are:

- *Capital appreciation.* Uses an aggressive investment approach to generate capital gains.
- *Growth.* Invests for capital gains, but less aggressively than capital appreciation funds.
- *Growth and income.* Looks for capital gains, but with some level of dividend income.
- *Equity income.* Emphasizes a high level of dividend income.

Note that none of these category definitions are based on either style or market cap. (The term "growth" here refers to the fund's objective of seeking capital gains rather than to its investment approach.) See Table 4.3 for

TABLE 4.3 Sample Peer Groups and Benchmark Indexes for Equity Funds

Fund Type	Peer Group	Benchmark Index
Large cap value (style box)	Large cap value funds	Russell 1000 Value Index
Large cap value (alternative)	Growth & income funds	S&P 500 Index
Mid cap growth (style box)	Mid cap and growth funds	Russell MidCap Growth Index
Mid cap growth (alternative)	Mid cap funds	S&P MidCap 400 Index
Emerging market stock	Emerging market funds	MSCI Emerging Markets Investable Market Index

sample peer groups and benchmarks for funds classified using both the style box and alternative approaches.

Another group of investors avoids the style box debate altogether by putting their money into index funds. Index investing has passionate and vocal adherents. Foremost among them is Jack Bogle, the founder of Vanguard, the fund management company that has popularized index fund investing. Some index fund groupies even style themselves "Bogleheads" in his honor.

Index fund advocates contend that most investors would be better off over the longer term simply by aiming to match index returns, rather than trying to outperform the market by making active stock selections. They make their case with four arguments:

1. *Market efficiency.* Proponents of index funds argue that the U.S. stock market is so efficient that it's impossible to outperform an index for any length of time. "Acting Efficiently" provides a brief explanation of the theory behind their thinking.
2. *Expense advantage.* In fact, stock index funds haven't just matched the performance of their actively managed funds cousins—they've done better. Much of that differential is the result of the higher fees charged by active managers, fees that reflect their higher costs. Active management often involves large teams of analysts and portfolio managers trained to find attractive investments and manage risk. Managing a stock index fund is a much simpler task: a very small staff can recreate a benchmark. (Note that the cost dynamics are starkly different for bond index funds, as we discussed earlier.) Also, actively managed funds buy and sell stocks much more frequently than index funds, meaning that they incur much higher trading costs.

ACTING EFFICIENTLY

Planning to spend Saturday night looking for a good stock pick? One group of economists—the advocates of the Efficient Market Hypothesis—suggests that you may as well go to the movies instead, since the search for undervalued stocks is just so much wasted effort. They argue that so many people are spending so much time researching possible investments that the market for any widely traded security is incredibly efficient. By that they mean that the price of a security already reflects everything that's publicly known about its earnings prospects.

They explain that their research shows that stock prices move in a random walk, in which tomorrow's change in price—up or down—has no predictable connection to today's price. For example, if Windy Corner stock is selling for $40 per share today, tomorrow it's just as likely to sell for $41 as it is to sell for $39. That's because today's price of $40 incorporates all the public information about Windy Corner as a company and as a stock. As a result, any change in Windy Corner's stock price can only result from the release of new information, and investors can't tell in advance whether this new information will be positive or negative. In other words, to the disappointment of those trying to find a better deal in the market, the efficient market advocates suggest that there's no such thing as an undervalued security.

The savings from owning index funds instead of actively-managed funds can be significant. In June 2010, looking only at funds without a sales load, over a third of U.S. index funds for large cap stocks had expenses of less than 25 basis points per year; only 4 percent of the actively-managed funds investing in the same type of stocks had expenses that were that low.[6]

3. *Tax efficiency.* Another advantage of passive management is that it is extremely tax-efficient. Because index funds rarely buy and sell stocks, they rarely realize capital gains. No realized capital gains, no capital gains distributions, no unexpected tax bills. Instead, index fund investors can choose exactly when to realize capital gains through the sale of their fund shares.

4. *Lack of performance persistence.* Still, even if the average active fund lagged the benchmark, active management might still make sense if there were a significant number of actively managed funds that regularly

outperformed. In other words, if superior performance were persistent, shareholders could do well by identifying managers who consistently beat the averages. But here again, index fund fans like to throw cold water on active management enthusiasts, by pointing to a raft of academic studies that provide little support for sustained outperformance.[7] According to these studies, performance persistence, if it exists at all, is a short-term phenomenon and is largely confined to the worst-performing funds, not the ones that anyone would want to include in their portfolios.[8]

The proponents of active management have their own five arguments in rebuttal:

1. *Performance persistence.* Active management advocates argue that good performance does in fact persist, but that the academic studies fail to detect it because of all the noise from the ups and downs of mediocre managers. These fans point to research showing that there is, in fact, a group of highly skilled, experienced managers who do outperform over time.[9]
2. *Cycles in performance.* Perhaps more importantly, index funds don't outperform in every environment. Instead, there are cycles in the relative returns of active and passive management as shown in Figure 4.6. Active

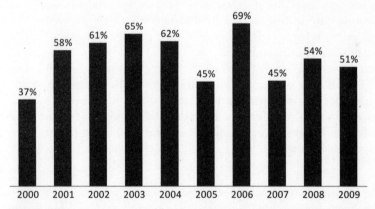

FIGURE 4.6 U.S. Large Cap Stock Funds Outperforming the S&P 500
Source: Standard & Poor's Indices Versus Active Funds (SPIVA) Scorecard, Year-End 2009 (March 2010). © 2010 Standard & Poor's Financial Services LLC is a wholly-owned subsidiary of The McGraw-Hill Companies, Inc. All rights reserved. STANDARD & POOR'S, S&P, and SPIVA are registered trademarks of Standard & Poor's Financial Services LLC.

managers tend to do well when the performance of the stock market is driven by stocks of every capitalization, as opposed to a narrow band of the largest cap stocks. On the other hand, when the market is led by the largest 40 or 50 stocks in the S&P 500—the ones that dominate that index—index funds tend to do better than the average active manager. Active managers appear to add value by finding opportunities among the smaller stocks in the index and by investing in stocks that are technically outside the benchmark universe. They may, for example, buy some mid cap stocks in a large cap fund. (Sound similar to the argument against style boxes?)

3. *Tax time bomb.* Supporters of active management point to a potential time bomb that might make index investing unattractive over the long term. They note that, while index funds are very tax efficient right now, that's partly because the total assets in these funds are growing, so that there are no net redemptions by shareholders that force the funds to sell securities to generate cash. If index funds should ever start shrinking, they could be forced to start generating enormous capital gains for investors.

4. *Free riders.* Active managers like to point out that it's their work that makes index fund investing possible. Markets are efficient only because so many analysts are digging for information that will give them an edge. With so many eyes trained on every security, it's hard for mispricings to last for very long. But if index funds became the predominant form of investing, the securities they held would frequently be under- or overvalued. In other words, index fund investors are free riders on the backs of the more industrious.

5. *Irrational markets.* Finally, fans of the active approach contend that markets are not as efficient as index fund proponents suggest. Instead, they're predictably irrational, leaving lots of room for active managers to find good values. This view is supported by the work of researchers in the field of behavioral economics. See "Financial Myth Busters" for more on their findings.

Who is winning the argument—the index fund advocates or the supporters of active management? It's hard to say. Actively managed funds still predominate, accounting for 86 percent of equity mutual fund dollars at the end of 2009. But index funds' share of assets has risen to 14 percent, from less than 4 percent just 15 years earlier.[10] As you can see in Figure 4.7, the gain has not been steady, but has tended to follow the trends in relative performance.

FINANCIAL MYTH BUSTERS

Researchers studying behavioral finance are the myth busters of the economics world. Their work is based on the premise that people don't always act rationally. While that may seem obvious, the assumption is a radical departure from previous work in the field. Classical economic theories—including the Efficient Market Hypothesis—are based on the idea that individuals always advance their financial best interest.

Behavioral finance research rejects that notion and demonstrates how people act in predictably self-defeating ways. Their studies have shown, for example, that investors are more reluctant to sell losing investments than winning ones, even if selling losing investments would help them reduce their income tax bill. They offer explanations for why stocks tend to go up on sunny days, down after the home team has lost in soccer's World Cup tournament and, more importantly, why out-of-favor stocks with low price-to-earnings ratios consistently do better than average. In an efficient market, stock prices would be affected only by new information and would not follow predictable patterns like these.

So, there is hope for active managers. By identifying these patterns of irrationality, they have a chance of finding undervalued investments.

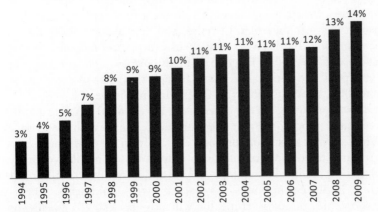

FIGURE 4.7   Index Fund Share of Stock Mutual Fund Assets
Source: Investment Company Institute.

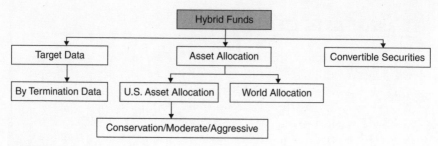

FIGURE 4.8 Hybrid Funds

Hybrid Funds

The taxonomy of hybrid funds—shown in Figure 4.8—is uncluttered, as befits a category that aims to make life simple for investors. With the exception of convertible funds, which specialize in a particular type of security, all the subgroups in this segment have portfolios that combine bonds, stocks and, to a limited extent, cash.[11] They may do this by investing directly in those securities, or they may buy shares of other mutual funds that specialize in those categories, a structure known as a *fund of funds*. In a very literal sense, then, hybrid funds take care of the fund asset allocation decision for investors. Individuals who find investment decision making a chore or who just don't have the time to focus on asset allocation often gravitate toward hybrid funds.

This category contains one of the fastest-growing types of funds: *target date*, or *life cycle*, funds. These funds gradually decrease their exposure to stocks and increase their exposure to bonds as they approach a specified, or target, year—hence their name. Investors choose a fund with a target date that's close to the year they plan to retire, and they automatically get an asset allocation fund that becomes more conservative and income-oriented as they get closer to that time. Target date funds have become quite popular in employer-sponsored retirement plans, though they disappointed many investors in 2008. We return to target date funds in Chapter 11.

Asset allocation funds, on the other hand, have a fixed baseline allocation between stocks and bonds that does not change simply with the passage of time. While an asset allocation fund may deviate from the guideline to capitalize on an investment opportunity or to prevent losses, it will eventually move back to the baseline. For example, a fund that normally has 70 percent in stocks and 30 percent in bonds, may increase stock holdings to 80 percent if the economic outlook is strong, but will move back to 70 percent—or even lower—when growth starts to slow. Funds with baseline allocations of roughly a 60/40 split of stocks and bonds are often called *balanced* funds.

TABLE 4.4 Sample Peer Groups and Benchmark Indexes for Hybrid Funds

Fund Type	Peer Group	Benchmark Index
Target date 2030	Target date 2026–2030 funds	70% Russell 3000, 15% Barclays Capital U.S. Aggregate Index, 15% MSCI All Country World ex-U.S. Index
Balanced	Balanced funds	60% S&P 500 Index, 40% Barclays Capital U.S. Aggregate Index

Within these funds, the international orientation (or lack thereof) of a fund is a key differentiator. World allocation funds, which have significant non-U.S. investments, are a separate subgroup here. U.S.-oriented funds are further broken down into conservative, moderate, and aggressive funds, based on their baseline weighting in stocks. Conservative funds have the lowest commitment to the stock market, while aggressive funds have the most. Aggressive funds may also make larger and more frequent changes in their stock allocation when they see the chance to improve returns.

No single index is right for these very varied funds. Therefore, hybrid funds combine indexes from the separate asset categories to generate a benchmark that matches the baseline allocation. For example, a 60/40 stock and bond balanced fund may publish a benchmark that gives a 60 percent weight to a stock index and 40 percent weight to a bond index. Table 4.4 shows sample peer groups and benchmark indexes for hybrid funds.

CHAPTER SUMMARY

Experienced investors use a two-step process when choosing mutual fund investments. First, they specify their investment objectives and divide their assets among the four main categories of funds. As part of this first step, they evaluate their investment objectives and constraints, considering factors such as their liquidity needs, time horizon, return expectations, and risk tolerance. Once they have established an asset allocation, they then select specific funds within each category.

Most investors evaluate a mutual fund's returns using three different techniques. They may compare its performance to the returns of a peer group, which is a set of funds with similar investment objectives and approaches. They may measure its results against the returns of a market index representative of the fund's investment universe. Or they may calculate the fund's risk-adjusted performance, comparing the fund's return to its risk level. The Morningstar star rating is an example of a risk-adjusted measure of performance. A few investors may focus almost exclusively on yield or expenses when evaluating funds.

Money market funds are the funds that are most like bank savings accounts, except that money market funds are not government-insured. There are two principal types of money market funds: taxable and tax-exempt. Investors must calculate a tax-adjusted yield to determine which makes most sense for them.

Bond funds provide a higher rate of interest than money market funds, but without the same level of security. There is a wide variety of bond funds. They are categorized by tax status (taxable versus tax-exempt), geographic focus (U.S. versus non-U.S.), credit quality (investment grade versus high yield), and maturity of their bond holdings (short, intermediate, and long).

Investors buy stock funds in the belief that their NAV will appreciate in value; these funds don't provide much income. Funds that focus on a specific sector or industry are evaluated separately. General stock funds are then categorized by geographic focus and then assigned to a style box by evaluating their portfolios along two dimensions—investment style and market capitalization. The style box classification approach is controversial; some investors reject it altogether in favor of a system based on prospectus objective.

Passively managed stock index funds attempt to mirror the return of an index, while actively managed funds try to do better than the index. Supporters of index funds argue that they provide better returns at a lower cost. Proponents of active management contend that experienced fund managers can outperform the index, especially in certain market environments.

Hybrid funds invest in both stocks and bonds, taking care of the asset allocation decision for investors. Target date funds gradually decrease their exposure to stocks over time, while asset allocation funds have a fixed baseline allocation between stocks and bonds.

Two

Mutual Fund Portfolio Management

Shareholders own mutual funds for one main reason: to earn an attractive investment return. That return may come from interest income or dividend income or capital gains or all three combined. Whatever the precise source, investors believe that by putting their money in a fund, they will be able to see their assets grow in value.

This section focuses on how mutual funds generate those investment returns. First some terminology: The investments that a fund purchases are together referred to as its *portfolio*. The process of choosing those investments is called *portfolio management* and is overseen by *portfolio managers*. *Analysts* research the details of particular investments, while *traders* implement portfolio managers' decisions by arranging the purchase and sale of individual investments.

Chapter 5 reviews the management of stock funds. The first half of this chapter discusses different approaches to researching investments, techniques that apply not just to stocks, but to other types of investments as well. The second half focuses on portfolio management. It contrasts the management of index funds with active management, explaining how benchmark indexes play a critical role in both. It also reviews the importance of risk management in portfolio construction and the role of attribution analysis in understanding performance results.

Chapter 6 turns to bond funds. It opens with a review of the types of securities that bond funds invest in. It then discusses strategies used in the portfolio management of actively managed bond funds and how they are implemented by bond fund managers.

The appendix to Chapter 6 looks at the basics of bond investing for those readers who need a refresher on the terms used in Chapter 6. It reviews the defining characteristics of bonds, the key measures used when analyzing them and their principal risks.

Chapter 7 examines money market funds and their unique features. It discusses the rationale for the stable $1 NAV and how it works in practice. It surveys the securities held by money market funds and then reviews the research, trading, and portfolio management of money market funds. It concludes with a discussion of the role that money funds play in the U.S. financial system and the questions raised about that role as a result of the 2008 credit crisis.

Chapter 8 reviews trading—the actual buying and selling of securities— and its importance to mutual funds. Focusing on trading in stock funds, it reviews the dramatic restructuring of the stock markets that has taken place in the past decade and its impact on mutual funds. It then discusses the role of the trader in executing buy and sell transactions while ensuring that the fund complies with a complex set of regulations. The final section briefly reviews the trading of bonds.

Chapter 9 discusses the role that mutual funds have as substantial owners of stock and the responsibilities accompanying that role. It reviews how funds vote as shareholders in corporate elections, comparing the approach of mutual funds to that of other shareholders. Next it summarizes the current issues in shareholder voting, such as advisory votes on executive pay and advocacy for social change. The chapter concludes with an overview of shareholder rights outside the United States.

CHAPTER 5

Portfolio Management of Stock Funds

For many, the capstone of the investment process is the management of stock funds. The performance of these funds often garners headlines—soaring when the business news is good and dropping in times of financial crisis. While their average returns are usually strong—at least when looked at over the long term—stock funds can show significant losses in any single period.

If stock fund returns are volatile, that's because the stocks they own participate directly in the ups and downs of the economy. Buy a stock, and you're buying a proportional *share,* or an *equity stake,* in a company. (The terms *stock, share,* and *equity* are used interchangeably.[1]) Own 100 shares in a company that has 10,000 shares in total outstanding, and you own rights to 1 percent of that firm's assets and 1 percent of its profits. If the company does well, whether because of a booming economy or astute management decisions or a favorable regulatory environment, you as an investor do well, too.

Ownership of stock carries voting rights. Shareholders are empowered to elect a board of directors; in turn, the board hires the firm's top executives and oversees its business. Shareholders also vote on other significant matters, such as the implementation of a stock option plan or a merger proposal. (Chapter 9 has a detailed discussion of shareholder voting.)

Most firms sell their stocks to the public—after having registered the securities offering and filed a prospectus with the SEC, of course—usually with the help of an investment bank.[2] After the offering is completed, investors may then buy and sell the shares with each other, in what is known as the *secondary market.*[3] The first time a company issues stock is called an *initial public offering,* or IPO. (Chapter 8 covers secondary market trading in detail.)

Stockholders can make money from an investment in stocks in two ways. First, the company may pay out a portion of its earnings to shareholders in the form of *dividends*. These payments are made at the discretion of the company's board of directors and may be eliminated if business conditions deteriorate. Even in good times, many companies prefer to retain their earnings and reinvest them in the business rather than pay dividends. For U.S. stocks, dividend income has historically been a less important component of return.

As a result, stockholders normally own shares for their capital appreciation potential, which is the chance that the price of the shares will increase in value. That's likely to happen if the firm's business improves and if investors are optimistic about its prospects. Over time, stock price performance tends to reflect the company's underlying business performance. Business fundamentals and stock price trends, however, can diverge, often significantly and sometimes for extended periods.

The key to managing a stock fund is to recognize when these divergences occur for particular stocks—while monitoring the overall risk of a portfolio composed of many individual investments. Simple in theory, though extremely difficult in practice.

This chapter reviews:

- The different approaches to researching stocks as potential investments
- The techniques used in managing a stock fund

STOCK RESEARCH

The equity investment process begins with research: analyzing the relationship between a company's business and its stock price. There are many different research techniques, but most fall into one of three categories: fundamental analysis, quantitative analysis, and technical analysis. Professional investors usually focus on one methodology, although they may incorporate some elements of all three in their research. (Note that these general approaches apply to all types of investments, not just stocks.)

- *Fundamental analysis.* Fundamental analysts rate stocks based on their evaluation of a company's business prospects. They examine its operations and finances, gathering information that will help them estimate its future earnings. Their sources include the firm's financial statements and other filings with the SEC, interviews with company management and industry sources, including trade journals and reports from competitors. Direct observation plays a role, too. Fundamental analysts will visit the company they are studying and even use its products and services if at all possible. The process involves one industry or even one stock at a time.

- *Quantitative analysis.* In contrast, quantitative analysts examine large groups of stocks. They work with probabilities, wanting to know whether particular business characteristics or trends are more or less likely to result in superior returns. To confirm their hypotheses, quantitative analysts use computers loaded with vast amounts of data on factors such as a company's earnings growth, its return on capital and the price momentum of its stock.
- *Technical analysis.* Technical analysts believe that stock price movements follow certain patterns, reflecting the predictable irrationality of investor behavior. They study charts of stock prices and trading volumes to develop investment recommendations, looking for changes in trends that signal that the price has reached an inflection point. They watch for stocks that have breached an important *resistance level* on the upside—or *support level* on the downside—and have begun to trade in a new range.

For example, a technical analyst looking at the chart in Figure 5.1 would see a stock that traded in an uptrend in period A, rising to about six times

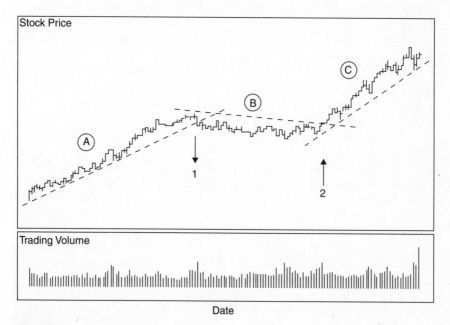

FIGURE 5.1 Technical Analysis in Action

its original value, then meandered around in period B, not doing much of anything. It then broke out on the upside, for a four-fold increase in period C. A technical analyst would explain that the shifts in trend were visible at the time, because they were accompanied by substantial increases in trading volumes at points 1 and 2.[4]

Despite its intuitive appeal, technical analysis has many detractors, especially among equity investors.[5] Academic researchers have raised serious questions about the value of technical research in selecting stocks. As a result, many fund managers today do not have dedicated technical analysts on their staffs, though individual analysts and portfolio managers may use technical analysis to determine the right time to buy or sell a stock.

Therefore, we will focus only on fundamental and quantitative research, the most important types of securities analysis for the majority of mutual fund managers. See the "Career Track" box for more on the job of the equity research analyst.

CAREER TRACK: STOCK ANALYST

Interested in becoming a stock analyst? You might work directly for a fund management company. Most larger fund managers have in-house analysts who produce proprietary research for the exclusive use of their own funds. This is referred to as *buy-side* research, since the managers buy stocks for their clients' funds.

Or you could work for an independent research firm that provides your ideas to the buy side for a fee. Or you might be employed by a broker-dealer on what's casually referred to as the *sell-side,* or *the Street*—short for Wall Street, naturally. You'll supply your research reports to clients who hire your firm to execute trades or provide other services.

Longevity counts in equity research. Analysts often follow, or cover, the same industry for years, building in-depth expertise. But for those interested in becoming a portfolio manager, researching several different industries over time is a great place to start. In fact, most equity portfolio managers began their investment career as analysts.

Equity research is a multifaceted job. You'll be judged not just on the success of your recommendations but also on your ability to persuade others to buy them, especially if you work on the sell side. Writing research reports and talking with fund managers about your ideas will be a large part of your job.

Fundamental Research

Fundamental equity research evaluates a company's prospects, looking at its competitive position within its industry, as well as the outlook for the industry as a whole. Analysts aren't just looking for facts; they're looking for something that will help them stand out from the crowd, either a little-known relationship or an unusual interpretation of very public information. Remember from the last chapter that markets are very efficient, so that common knowledge is already reflected in the stock price. To find stocks that stand out, analysts must take positions that defy conventional wisdom.

Analysts gather the information they need to make those assessments from three primary sources: the company itself, industry experts, and other analysts. Let's look at how analysts use each to develop an opinion on a stock.

Information from the company itself. As with a mutual fund, a wealth of information about an operating company comes from the documents that it's required to file with the SEC. Analysts often start the research process by reviewing these filings.

- *10-K.* The annual report—usually called a *10-K* after the SEC form it must be filed on—provides an overview of the company's business and describes the risks it faces. Like a mutual fund annual report, the 10-K includes a letter from management discussing results over the past year, together with the company's audited financial statements. The analysts will examine the numbers closely, looking for trends in profitability to see if business conditions are getting better or worse. And they'll read the footnotes carefully to gauge whether a company's reported earnings give a good sense of underlying business reality. That's not a given, because some companies take advantage of flexibility in accounting rules to boost their short-term results. Analysts try to avoid companies with a poor *quality of earnings,* as it's called, since academic research has demonstrated that they tend to have relatively weak performance in the future.[6]
- *10-Qs.* The quarterly reports, or *10-Qs,* give analysts updates on results during the year. The components of the 10-Qs are similar to those of the 10-K, although they are less detailed. The financial information they contain is not audited. Both the 10-Ks and 10-Qs are available on-line, through the company's web site or the SEC's EDGAR database.
- *Proxy statement.* Companies must prepare a proxy statement before the annual shareholder vote. In addition to describing the issues being presented to shareholders, the proxy statement contains detailed

information about a company's management and board of directors, including their compensation. Analysts use this information to evaluate the qualifications of the management team and to determine whether its interests are aligned with shareholders'.

- *Prospectus.* The prospectus is prepared whenever a company sells its shares to the public. It's especially important for IPOs, since it's the first complete description of the company available to the public.

But analysts are not content with hearing from company management through documents; they want to talk with them directly. They'll

FAIR DISCLOSURE

The owner of a single share of stock is entitled to the same information from company management as the owner of one million shares. So says the SEC, a principle it has solidified in Regulation Fair Disclosure, known as *Reg FD*, issued in October 2000.

Q: *What does Reg FD say?*

A: When a company discloses to any person information that would likely be material to most investors, it must make that same information available to the public.

Q: *Why did the SEC issue this rule?*

A: During the booming stock market of the late 1990s, the press reported several instances of companies releasing the inside scoop to large investors first; these large investors were then able to profit on the information at the expense of individual stockholders—who were kept in the dark until the stock price had already moved. The SEC became concerned that this practice could undermine investor confidence in the markets and be used by company managements to reward analysts for making favorable recommendations. The SEC wanted to make it clear that a selective release of information was just as serious a violation as insider trading.

Q: *How have companies responded to the rule?*

A: Almost all companies now make significant announcements, such as reports on quarterly earnings, in a public forum. This is usually done by holding a conference call or webinar that is open to all shareholders and maybe even the public at large. The company will also simultaneously issue a press release with the news.

attend presentations given by the company—in person, on the phone, or by webcast—and, if at all possible, they'll arrange to meet with the CEO one on one. And they won't just listen—they'll ask questions about recent performance and future strategy. Throughout, they'll be judging the reasonableness of the company's approach and the capabilities of its management team.

Information from the company is a necessary—but not sufficient—component of the research process. That's because analysts can't get much of a competitive advantage from communications with management. As "Fair Disclosure" explains, companies must provide the same material information to all investors—who now have easy access to it over the Internet. That's a significant change from even a decade ago, when company documents were much harder to obtain, and investors who wanted to hear a company management had to travel to do so. In that environment, professional investors—who had the resources to track down information—had a bigger edge.

Insights from industry sources. To get information that is not available to the public at large, analysts must turn to other sources within the industry. They'll read the trade publications, and they'll consult with industry experts. In fact, some analysts have once worked in the industry they now cover, so that they have an insider's view of its trends and prospects.

Whenever possible, analysts will go directly to the users of the company's products and services to assess the outlook for future sales. They might do this systematically through a survey—asking doctors whether they plan to prescribe a new drug, for example—or anecdotally by talking with a small user group. And, if possible, they'll be a consumer themselves, tasting a food company's new line of soups or taking their family to shop at a remodeled retail store.

Research from other analysts. But are the insights gleaned really unique? To answer that question, analysts must be familiar with the general opinion of the company and its stock. They'll read the coverage of the company in the press. They'll talk with analysts at both independent shops and sell-side firms and read their research reports.

Fundamental analysts must then turn this carefully gathered information into numbers. First, they estimate earnings and cash flow per share using a *model*, which is a quantitative representation of a company's operations, typically created in a computer spreadsheet. The analyst populates the model with estimates of the company's revenue, expenses, margins, growth rates, and other key variables, separated into key product lines or geographic areas.

A model serves two important purposes: it allows an analyst to forecast a company's earnings, the primary driver of stock price performance, and it provides a framework to evaluate new information about the company. Suppose an analyst reads that the European Union is considering the adoption of stringent standards regarding the disposal of electronic equipment. Two proposals have been floated—one imposing a sales tax to cover the costs of municipal recycling, another requiring manufacturers to arrange for recycling of all of their own equipment. The former would raise prices and, therefore, potentially push down demand, while the latter could significantly increase manufacturers' costs. An analyst following a global manufacturer of PCs could estimate the impact of the different regulations by adjusting

---

FUNDAMENTAL RESEARCH IN ACTION

Behind every fund success story is a good research idea. For proof, look no further than the following quotations from the annual shareholder reports for three top-performing funds in 2009. All three discuss the fund's best stock pick during the year:

> "ASML, the world's leading provider of lithography systems for the semiconductor industry, was among the Fund's top contributors during the year. Despite a difficult business environment, a recent sales rebound and improved cost trends have returned the company to profitability."[7]
>
> "Communications tower company Crown Castle International provided the Fund's largest gains. . . . We had added to holdings in Crown Castle during the credit crunch in the late 2008, correctly believing in the company's business model and its ability to service a fairly large debt load."[8]
>
> "Our holdings in Apple were especially beneficial, as the company continued to generate impressive revenue growth and better-than-expected earnings thanks to record sales for Mac computers and iPhones."[9]

Note the common theme: in each case the investment team had identified something about the company that other investors had failed to appreciate—sales did well despite the weak environment, the debt load proved manageable, earnings were "better than expected." This ability to see beyond the consensus is the key to successful stock selection.

the model to see what would happen to the firm's operating results in either scenario. A well-constructed model allows an analyst to quickly test a variety of assumptions and scenarios.

Analysts will compare the earnings estimate from their model to *consensus earnings,* which is the average or median of the earnings predicted by Wall Street analysts. It's available through Thomson Reuters First Call or Zacks Investment Research.

If the model-generated earnings estimate is significantly different from the consensus, there is potential for an earnings surprise—a positive earnings surprise if the estimate exceeds consensus, and a negative earnings surprise if it falls short. Earnings surprises can be powerful drivers of stock price performance. That's partly because it's rare to see just one earnings surprise at a company—one Wall Street analyst compared them to cockroaches for that reason. Instead, companies will tend to do better—or worse—than the consensus expects for several quarters in a row. As a result, analysts will usually place a buy or sell opinion on a stock whenever they believe there will be an earnings surprise. "Fundamental Research in Action" gives some real-life examples of analysis identifying earnings surprises.

Valuation

While in many instances a model will not predict an earnings surprise, an analyst may still recommend a stock based on its valuation. Let's review a few of the measures used in valuing stocks. Because all are ratios of stock price to another factor, valuation work using these measures is called *ratio analysis:*

- *Price/earnings or P/E ratio.* The P/E ratio, also known as the *P/E multiple,* is the price of a share of stock divided by its earnings per share—sometimes the earnings most recently reported, sometimes those estimated for the future. This ratio gives an indication of how much investors are willing to pay for a company's earning power. The higher the multiple, the more expensive the stock.

  Stocks are often classified by their P/E ratio. Those with a high P/E ratio—which can be 30 or 40 times earnings or more—are usually young or fast-growing companies, while those with a low P/E—generally under 10 times—are typically low-growth or in mature industries. The stocks of companies that have experienced problems recently often have a low P/E.

- *Price/cash flow ratio.* The price to cash flow ratio equals stock price divided by cash flow per share, which is usually defined as net income plus depreciation and other noncash expenses, all on a per-share basis. P/CF is often used to supplement P/E as a valuation measure, since cash flow is less subject to accounting distortions than are earnings. It's particularly important in industries that have recently spent considerable amounts on plant and equipment and have high depreciation charges as a result.

- *Price/book ratio.* Price to book also uses stock price in the numerator, but here the denominator is *book value,* meaning the company's assets minus its liabilities per share. If a company has a relatively high P/B, investors are signaling that they see more profit potential than the hard assets on the company's books would suggest. For example, a software company with a high P/B ratio may not own any physical assets—other than a few servers—but may still have fabulous prospects. Conversely, if a company has a relatively low P/B, its hard assets may not have good prospects of generating future earnings. A typical low P/B company is a manufacturer that has an enormous factory, but one churning out products that have lost their competitive edge.
- *Price/sales ratio.* In this ratio, price is divided by sales per share. P/S can be particularly useful in looking at stocks in cyclical industries that are extremely sensitive to the ups and downs of the economy. Because sales are relatively easy to count, P/S is less sensitive to accounting policies than the other measures we've discussed so far.
- *Dividend yield* is the annual dividend of a stock divided by its market price. Yield represents the cash return of a stock, as measured by dividends. For example, a stock selling for $50 per share that pays an annual dividend of $1 has a dividend yield of 2 percent ($1 divided by $50). In contrast with the ratios we've just discussed, stocks with higher dividend yields are considered cheaper than stocks with lower yields. As a general rule, low P/E stocks have higher dividend yields than high P/E stocks, which may pay no dividends at all.

Analysts look at all of these measures within the context of their assessment of a company's prospects. A stock may be undervalued even at 40 times earnings if its outlook is extremely promising. On the other hand, a stock with a P/E of 8 times might be too expensive if its business is rapidly deteriorating.

Much of the debate about individual stocks comes down to valuation. Take the case of Amazon.com, which has often sported a P/E ratio north of 50 times. Its proponents justify the lofty valuations by pointing to the company's strong and steady growth—growth that they believe is likely to continue because of Amazon's dominance in online retailing. Critics counter that a lower multiple is warranted, because the larger Amazon gets, the harder it will be to grow at the same rate. And a bigger Amazon will be more vulnerable to economic downturns, competitive threats, and increased regulation. Shoppers online may even have to start paying sales taxes one day, the naysayers note. Overall, the doubters argue, Amazon is "priced to perfection," meaning that its value will fall dramatically should business conditions prove anything less than ideal.

Analysts don't look at the valuation of a stock in isolation. Instead, they study a stock's valuation over time relative to other stocks in the same industry and then look at the industry's valuation relative to that of the market as a whole. This approach is called *relative valuation.*

Relative valuation makes sense because the valuation levels for the overall equity market have fluctuated significantly through time. Figure 5.2 shows how widely the valuation level of the S&P 500 has ranged around a rising trend line over just the past 20 years. Three factors in particularly influence the overall level of equity market valuation: economic strength, interest rates, and investor sentiment.

Analysts will even assess the valuation of the overall market, taking into consideration the strength of the overall economy, the direction of interest rates, and the mood of investors.

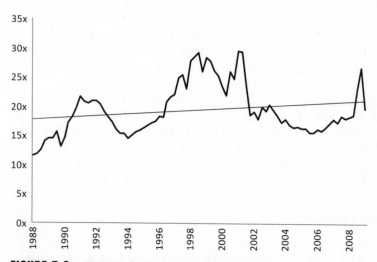

FIGURE 5.2   S&P P/E Ratio on Operating Earnings
Source: Standard & Poor's. Standard & Poor's Financial Services LLC is a wholly-owned subsidiary of The McGraw-Hill Companies, Inc. All rights reserved. STANDARD & POOR'S, S&P, and S&P 500 are registered trademarks of Standard & Poor's Financial Services LLC.

Economic strength. The value of the stock market as a whole equals the present value of all the constituent firms' earnings combined. If investors' expectations for earnings growth increase, so too will prices and valuations. As a result, in strong economic times, with estimates of growth rates rising for many companies, the P/E ratios for both individual stocks and market indexes tend to increase.

Interest rates. Rising interest rates tend to depress equity valuations. Because higher rates make it more expensive for companies to borrow money, they can slow down the economy enough to put future earnings growth in doubt. Also, rising rates can signal higher inflation ahead—another scenario that can often lead to lower earnings growth, because companies often find it hard to raise prices to their customers as quickly as prices of raw materials are rising. Adding insult to injury, higher rates mean higher yields on bank deposits and fixed income securities, making them more attractive as alternatives to equities. Conversely, declining interest rates tend to support higher equity valuations.

Investor sentiment. Psychology plays a role in setting equity valuations. If the economy and the political scene are stable, investors perceive risk to be low and are willing to pay more for stocks. When fear reigns, however, P/Es can come down quite quickly. Notice how in Figure 5.2 the market's P/E plunged when the Internet bubble popped, from over 29 times at the end of 2001 to less than 19 times just nine9 months later.

Because the irrationality of investor sentiment can have such a dramatic effect on market valuations, many analysts reject the relative valuation approach altogether. Instead, they prefer to use *dividend discount models* and other *discounted cash flow* approaches. Analysts use these techniques to project dividends and cash flows into the future, then compute the present value of those payments. If a stock's price is significantly below the value calculated, it's a buy. While these models have strong adherents, other analysts reject them as too dependent on future projections and, therefore, less reliable than relative valuation, which is largely observable currently.

Analysts update their opinions as stock prices move and as news is released. Figure 5.3 provides an actual example of a quarterly update.

Quantitative Research

While fundamental analysis zeroes in on individual companies, quantitative research looks for patterns affecting many stocks at once. Quantitative analysts—fondly known as *quants*—all use the same general process:

- *Hypothesis.* Quants always start with a hypothesis, a theory of what determines stock performance. A simple hypothesis might be that the

MFS RESEARCH NOTES

DU PONT E I DE NEMOURS & CO COM (DD)

Rating: 2-Hold (Reaffirmed); Quant Rank: 38   **Basic Materials, Chemicals**
Previous Close: $28.47 Mkt Cap: $25,590M Avg. Daily Vol: 8.9M

Div Yield	5.8%	Price to Book	3.5
% of Index (SPX)	0.306%	ROE	6.3%
MFS Price Target	--	EV | EV/Sales	34,006M | 1.2
MFS Downside Risk	--	LT EPS Growth Est.	4.1%

Estimates - FYE Dec 31	2008	2009	2010	2011
P/E	10.2	16.3	13.9	11.9*
EV/EBITDA	--	8.6*	7.8*	7.2*
* Consensus Estimates Used				
Earnings (MFS)	2.78	1.75	2.05	--
Revenue (MFS)	--	--	--	--
EBITDA (MFS)	--	--	--	--
Earnings (Consensus)	--	1.71	2.04	2.40
Revenue (Consensus)	--	26,498.18	28,167.02	30,099.50
EBITDA (Consensus)	--	3,973.26	4,343.72	4,714.02
Earnings Growth (MFS / Consensus)		7% / 19.83%		
Revenue Growth (MFS / Consensus)		-- / 6.30%		
EBITDA Growth (MFS / Consensus)		-- / 9.32%		

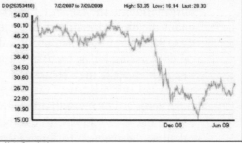

Business Description

E. I. du Pont de Nemours and Company (DuPont) operates as a science and technology company in various disciplines, including agriculture, industrial biotechnology, chemistry, biology, materials science, and manufacturing. It operates in five segments: Agriculture & Nutrition, Coatings & Color Technologies, Electronic & Communication Technologies, Performance Materials, and Safety & Protection. The Agriculture & Nutrition segment offers benzene and carbamic acid related intermediates, copper, insect control products, natural gas, soybeans, soy flake, soy lecithin, sulfonamides, corn, and soybean seeds. The Coatings & Color Technologies segment provides automotive finishes, industrial coatings, and titanium dioxide white pigments. The Electronic & Communication Technologies segment offers a

Note Conclusion

DuPont reported a slightly better quarter and maintained annual EPS and cash flow guidance. They saw a seasonal sequential uptick in volumes of Q1 lows, though no improvement in y/y volumes vs. Q1'09 and Q4'08. They did declare an end to de-stocking in their short cycle businesses, and expect up volumes in Q4'09 vs. easy comps. Declining raw materials and aggressive cost-cuts led to a 97% q/q incremental margins in their core chemical businesses.

Note Conclusion

DuPont reported a slightly better quarter and maintained annual EPS ($1.70-2.10) and cash flow ($2.5b) guidance. They saw a seasonal sequential uptick in volumes off Q1 lows, though no improvement in y/y volumes vs. Q1'09 and Q4'08 (-19-20% in each). They did declare an end to de-stocking in their short cycle businesses, and expect up volumes in Q4'09 vs. easy comps. Declining raw materials and aggressive cost-cuts led to a 97% q/q incremental margins in their core chemicals businesses.

Relative to my model, DuPont's revenues were light but margins better. I am leaving '09 expectations unchanged. The opportunity for relative EPS upside versus peers primarily comes from a second half auto production recovery, and the biggest downside risk is pricing in performance materials and the longer-cycle nature of safety/protection.

The implication from DuPont's report for other specialty chemicals companies is favorable. DuPont's peers will benefit from lower raws & aggressive cost-cutting, but should have 'less-bad' volumes due to less auto, longer-cycle, and commodity exposure than DuPont. Therefore, I anticipate the trend in '09 estimates for specialty chemicals companies to be more "up" vs. DuPont's "flat".

As of 7/21/2009

The dated MFS Equity Research example above should not be considered a recommendation to buy or sell any security.

FIGURE 5.3   An Actual Research Update

stock of companies whose CEOs have doctoral degrees do better than average.

- *Data for modeling.* The analyst then identifies sources for data to rigorously test this hypothesis for a large number of companies. Sometimes this is easy. In this hypothetical example, data on U.S. stock returns are readily available. But other data are not so easy to come by—such as information on the doctoral degrees of company CEOs. The theoretical quant might need to approximate the information sought, by screening CEO names for the title *Dr.*, broadening the test to include both medical doctors and PhDs. Or at larger investment advisers, the fundamental research analysts may be asked to provide the data for the companies they cover.

- *Back testing.* The test will divide the universe of stocks into two halves: companies with CEOs with doctoral degrees and those without. It will calculate the average stock price gain in the past for each group; because the test uses historical return data, it is called a *back test*. To help with the analysis in the next step, quants will test different time periods and break down the results by industry.

- *Analyze results.* The results of the back test allow the analyst to judge if the hypothesis worked: Did the stocks of companies with CEOs with doctoral degrees do better than the average stock? Whatever the answer, quants will look for patterns in the results. For example, if a large percentage of the CEOs of biotech companies have PhDs and biotech stocks have done extremely well recently, results could suggest—incorrectly—that buying stocks with a "Dr. CEO" is an easy way to make money.

    If that's the case, the quant will look to see whether the hypothesis works within industries, as well as for the market as a whole. Another avenue to explore is whether the hypothesis works better in some market conditions than in others. For example, do companies with PhDs at the helm surge ahead when the market is rising, and investors may be willing to pay more for products with a high technology content? Or do they do better when the market is falling, and investors take refuge in firms that are more likely to hold lots of patents?

- *Implementation.* Once quantitative analysts have drawn a conclusion about the validity of a particular hypothesis, they will continue to monitor its performance in the future, since a theory that worked in a back test may not continue to work prospectively.

Where quants have an advantage is in their dispassionate approach to investing—the application of tested models in a disciplined fashion. They may thus avoid some of the predictable pitfalls that have been analyzed by behavioral finance.

PUTTING IT ALL TOGETHER: MANAGING A STOCK FUND

Once the analysis has been completed, the individual stock ideas are combined into a fund. This is the job of the portfolio manager (discussed in more detail in the "Career Track" box). There are two main approaches to portfolio management: passive management and active management. The contrasts between the two are starkest in stock investing, where the differences in returns, risks, and costs can be quite dramatic. While we reviewed the debate about which approach is better in Chapter 4, we discuss here the process of managing both types of portfolios. We take a quick look at passively managed, or *index* funds, and then turn our attention to actively managed portfolios.

CAREER TRACK: STOCK PORTFOLIO MANAGER

If you're an equity portfolio manager, you have a job that carries a high level of responsibility. You're helping to ensure the financial well-being of hundreds—if not thousands—of investors.

It's a stressful job. The results of your work are measured constantly—even posted online every day if you're in charge of a mutual fund. Your returns will be stacked up against your competitors' monthly, quarterly, and yearly.

You may carry the responsibility on your own as the sole manager. Or you may work as part of a portfolio team and be in charge of a portion of a fund—often referred to as a *sleeve*—possibly in an area in which you have particular expertise. For example, you might make decisions about a fund's cyclically sensitive sleeve, while another team member handles the consumer sectors and yet a third manages the financial exposure. Whether working on your own or as part of group, you'll be in constant contact with the analysts to discuss trends at companies and industries.

Passive Portfolio Management

In passive portfolio management, the objective is simply to match the return of a stock market index. As we've learned, an index is a hypothetical portfolio of stocks designed to represent the market as a whole or a segment of it. These hypothetical portfolios are maintained by independent research firms that calculate their value daily. In the U.S. equity world, prominent providers of indexes include Standard & Poor's, Russell Investments, and Wilshire Associates.

Passive managers try to minimize *tracking error,* meaning the deviation of the fund's return from the return of the index. For many equity indexes, including the S&P 500—which, as its names suggests, contains 500 stocks—this is normally done by purchasing all of the component securities of the index in those same proportions in the fund, a practice known as *replication.*

But some indexes contain such a large number of stocks that replication is impracticable. An example is the Wilshire 5000, which includes more than 4,000 stocks. In those cases, passive managers may purchase only a representative subset of stocks in the index, in a practice known as *sampling.* Through quantitative modeling, they can assemble a basket of securities whose risk profile approximates that of the index. That means that its return should also approximate that of the index most of the time, though there's no guarantee of that. Performance of a passively managed fund using sampling can differ significantly from that of the index, especially when there's a high degree of volatility in the market or in key stocks.

Although an index fund manager does not make active investment decisions on individual stocks, most index funds must still trade each day in response to shareholder activity. The manager must buy securities in the index when shareholders purchase shares of the fund and must sell securities in the index as shareholders redeem—while keeping the fund closely aligned with its index. One key to minimizing the impact of shareholder cash flows on tracking error is to have good advance information about the magnitude and direction of the transactions. Most fund complexes have sophisticated cash management systems that monitor pending shareholder activity during the day.

Once funds have accurate information on the cash coming in or out, they use various techniques to minimize the cost of investing inflows or of selling stocks to meet outflows. They may buy or sell stock index futures contracts rather than trading in the stocks themselves. Or they might engage in a *basket trade,* which we describe in Chapter 8. Or they might establish a relationship with an investor who agrees to trade stocks for cash or cash for stocks in what is called an *in-kind exchange.* Exchange-traded funds use a similar technique for managing cash flows, as we see in Chapter 12.

Another big headache for an index fund manager is a change in the composition of the index itself. Whether because of a merger, bankruptcy, or a desire by the index provider to include a more representative security, index changes are common. The Russell indexes, for example, are ordinarily rebalanced annually at the end of June. When that happens, hundreds of stocks can move in and out of the Russell 2000, one of the most popular indexes measuring the performance of small-capitalization stocks. Even the

TABLE 5.1 Changes to the S&P 500 Index Constituents in 2009

Additions		Deletions	
Airgas	MetroPCS Communications	American Capital	Ingersoll-Rand
CareFusion	Monsanto	Centex	Jones Apparel
Cliffs Natural Resources	Priceline.com	Ciena	KB Homes
Denbury Resources	Quanta Services	CIT Group	Manitowoc
DeVry	Red Hat	Convergys	MBIA
Diamond Offshore	Roper Industries	Cooper Industries	Rohm & Haas
First Solar	Ross Stores	Covidian	Schering-Plough
FMC	SAIC	Developers Divers Realty	Sovereign Bancorp
FMC Technologies	Time Warner Cable	Dynegy	Tyco Electronics
Health Care REIT	Ventas	Embarq	Tyco International
Hormel Food	Visa	ENSCO International	Weatherford International
Mead Johnson Nutrition	Western Digital	General Motors	Wyeth

Source: Standard & Poor's.

most widely used index, the S&P 500, has a surprising number of changes in a year, as shown in Table 5.1.

Index fund managers must decide whether to buy stocks in advance of their inclusion in the index or whether to wait for the changes to be finalized. Acting early can save the fund some money: stocks that are to be included in the S&P 500 index, in particular, tend to do well in the period leading up to their addition to the index.[10] But the strategy of buying in advance can be dangerous, since there might be some bad news that causes a stock's price to tumble down before it officially becomes part of the index.

Active Portfolio Management

Active management seeks to beat the return of an index through insightful security selection. Industry insiders often call this *generating positive alpha*. (See "Endlessly Seeking Alpha" for an explanation of this terminology.) It's the portfolio manager of an actively managed fund who oversees the selection process: evaluating which ideas generated by the research team should be included in a portfolio, assigning them a weighting, and then making the call on when precisely to buy or sell.

ENDLESSLY SEEKING ALPHA

Another way of saying that active managers are looking to beat the return of the market is to say that they're looking to generate positive alpha. Remember from Chapter 1 that returns from investments can be broken down into two components: beta and alpha. A quick refresher: *beta* is the return of the market as a whole. An index fund, which seeks to match the return of the market, provides only beta. *Alpha* is the difference between the market return and the return on the portfolio investments.[11] The return of a fund will have alpha whenever its portfolio varies from the index—in other words, whenever the manager makes active investment decisions.

Of course, managers always prefer that a fund's return be higher—rather than lower—than the index return. In other words, they want positive—and not negative—alpha. *Outperform* is another term for the same happy result; managers want to avoid underperforming.

Some managers take the concept even further. They aim to give their clients only alpha return—the return that comes from their investment decision making—and eliminate all the beta return. (This is one of the *absolute return* strategies that we reviewed in Chapter 4.) To accomplish both objectives, they create a *long-short* portfolio. In brief, the manager buys a *long* portfolio of stocks and at the same time sells *short* another portfolio of stocks of equal value. The positive beta on the long portfolio and the negative beta on the short portfolio should cancel each other out, theoretically leaving only alpha exposure. The popularity of long-short portfolios has been increasing.

For regulatory reasons, the long-short approach is easier to implement in hedge funds than in mutual funds. We go into detail when we review hedge funds in Chapter 12.

Investors who want to own a general equity fund—as opposed to a fund that focuses in a specific industry or sector—often look for portfolios that concentrate in a particular type of stock usually evaluated along two dimensions: market capitalization, or *market cap* and *style*. As we saw in Chapter 4, market cap equals the value of a company's outstanding stock. Let's take a closer look at style now.

A style is a framework for choosing investments, essentially a set of rules that help an investor determine whether a stock fits in a portfolio. Because a style is a disciplined approach to investment decision making, most professional investors use one. The most common styles are growth, value, and growth at a reasonable price.

- *Growth* managers look for companies that are expected to have higher-than-average earnings growth in the future, usually because revenue—or *top line*—growth is strong. They are the luxury goods shoppers of the investment world; they are willing to pay high prices for companies with premium products or brand names. Because growth stocks often come with high multiples, they can be very sensitive to downturns in the market. As a result, this style tends to do best later in the economic cycle when growth is particularly strong.
- *Value* managers, on the other hand, are shoppers who hunt for bargains, looking for companies with low multiples and high dividend yields. They understand that the merchandise might be slightly damaged, but they believe that, even if it's irregular, the company will still generate enough in earnings to more than justify the price paid. Value managers seek out companies on the rebound, whether from a tough economic environment or bad management decisions or both, so it's no surprise that this style often outperforms when the economy itself is recovering from a recession. Through their research, value managers try to dodge the dreaded *value trap*: companies that have cheap stocks but also have businesses that are going from bad to worse.
- *Growth at a reasonable price* managers—also known as *GARP,* or *relative value* managers—want the best of both worlds. They're looking for stocks with decent growth prospects that aren't extremely expensive.

Portfolio managers often categorize their style along a third dimension as well: top-down versus bottom-up.

- *Top-down* managers form a big picture, or *macro*, view of the economy and financial markets and use that as a basis for identifying attractive sectors, industries, and securities. (Remember from Chapter 4 that a *sector* is a group of related industries.) For example, a top-down manager who expects that economic growth is slowing may sell holdings in *cyclical* industries like autos that are very sensitive to the ups and downs, or *cycles,* in the economy. She may buy companies in the consumer and health care sectors instead. Because the manager looks at individual stocks only after the big picture decisions are made, this approach is often associated with *sector rotation*. Many growth managers incorporate top-down elements into their styles.
- *Bottom-up* managers, in contrast, begin with the selection of individual securities. They choose securities with the most attractive investment

prospects, with little regard for macroeconomic forecasts. Value managers generally use a bottom-up approach.

Any of these styles can be implemented using fundamental and quantitative analysis or both. Many portfolio managers today combine the two techniques, using quantitative *screens* to narrow down the list of ideas for further fundamental research or monitoring overall portfolio risk with quantitative estimates of tracking error. (We review risk control in a moment.)

Portfolio Construction

Okay, you've just been appointed the portfolio manager of an actively managed equity mutual fund. There's a lot you'll need to know before you make your first buy or sell decision.

Investment objectives, style, and restrictions. First, you'll want to read the fund's prospectus. As we reviewed in Chapter 3, this document sets forth the fund's investment objectives, gives a brief description of its style, and lists some important constraints that you must adhere to.

Benchmark index. Pay particular attention to the market index that is mentioned there. (You'll see it in the table providing performance information.) This index is your *benchmark,* and your returns will be evaluated in relation to the returns of this index. The specific index chosen will match the objective and style of the portfolio. For example, if your portfolio primarily invests in small capitalization U.S. growth stocks, the index will represent that area of the market.

Next, you'll study the composition of the index. Portfolio managers carefully weigh decisions to *overweight* or *underweight* a security compared to the index.[12] In an overweight, the fund holds a larger position in the security—measured as a percentage of the portfolio—than that same stock's representation in the index. Avoiding a stock entirely or holding a relatively small position is an underweight and can be just as risky as holding a large overweight in another stock—because if the absent stock turns out to be one of the stronger performers, it can cause the fund to lag the index. Yet another type of decision is to hold a security not included in the index. This is called an *out-of-benchmark* position.

Let's assume that Windy Corner stock is the largest position in the S&P 500 with a 3 percent weight. Let's also assume that your outlook for the company is quite positive—that you expect earnings to grow significantly. If your analysis is correct, you'll need to have more than 3 percent of the fund invested in Windy Corner for you to gain ground on the index. Concerned about Windy Corner's future? You'll want to put less than 3 percent of assets into the stock. If you're very negative, you won't own the stock at all.

TABLE 5.2 Sector Weights for the Avon Hill U.S. Equity Fund

Sector	Fund Weight	S&P 500 Weight	Over(under)weight
Energy	13.7%	10.9%	+2.8%
Materials	6.2%	3.5%	+2.7%
Industrials	14.3%	10.4%	+3.9%
Consumer Discretionary	12.2%	10.0%	+2.2%
Consumer Staples	7.5%	11.3%	−3.8%
Health Care	13.1%	12.3%	+0.8%
Financials	9.5%	16.3%	−6.8%
Information Technology	16.9%	18.8%	−1.9%
Telecommunications Service	4.9%	2.9%	+2.0%
Utilities	1.7%	3.6%	−1.9%
	100.0%	100.0%	0%

But if you just believe that the stock will tread water, you might decide to limit your risk versus the index by buying a 2 percent position. So, it may be that a stock that you have a poor opinion of may still appear as a significant holding in your fund.

The key point is that all weightings are evaluated in relation to the index weightings. Check the math yourself: a 1 percent position in an out-of-benchmark stock will have the same impact on performance relative to the index as a 4 percent position in Windy Corner.

Just as fund managers can over- or underweight individual stocks, they can also decide to over- or underweight a sector in an index. Table 5.2 shows the weights for the hypothetical Avon Hill U.S. Equity Fund compared to the sector weights for the S&P 500 index. As you can see, this fund is overweighted in sectors that traditionally do well when the economy is strong, including industrials, energy, and materials. It has relatively little exposure to financials and consumer staples, both sectors that usually lag when the economy rebounds. (Financial company earnings are often hurt by the interest rate increases that accompany economic recovery.) This portfolio should outperform if economic growth is robust.

Benchmark peer group. Finally, you'll want to know which peer group of competing mutual funds you'll be measured against. (See Chapter 4 for more about peer rankings.) Since you won't have up-to-date information on the portfolios of your competitors, you can't use their holdings as a basis for making your day-to-day weighting decisions. But you'll want to know something about their approach to investing, so that you can understand how yours may differ and how your decisions might affect your ranking in the peer group. If you manage a growth-style fund, for example, your competitors are likely to have heavy weightings in technology stocks. Should you turn negative on technology and reduce your positions to an underweight, your performance will probably be very different from the average performance of competing funds. You'll have a chance to shine if technology stumbles, but you could well end up falling in the rankings if technology rallies. Your peer group ranking will also play an important role in determining what you will be paid, as explained in "Relative Compensation."

RELATIVE COMPENSATION

The benchmark index and benchmark peer group will determine more than just your portfolio's weightings: they'll also be the basis of your compensation as a portfolio manager. At most fund advisers, you'll receive an attractive base salary, but you'll stand to earn a much larger amount as an annual bonus if your fund does better than both of its benchmarks. Good performance tends to lead to strong sales of fund shares, which, in turn, leads to higher revenues, so portfolio managers try hard to produce superior fund returns.

You usually won't get top dollar if your fund's gains are a one-year phenomenon. Bonus calculations normally put the most weight on three-year performance and may even consider results over longer periods as well. They may also take into account your department's performance or possibly the results of all the funds run by the firm—that's to encourage you to share your ideas with your colleagues.

And while your bonus will be largely determined by the numbers, more subjective factors may play a role at the margin. Your compensation may be boosted somewhat if you've helped market the funds, recruit trainees, or mentor new analysts.

Even if you've earned a top bonus, don't plan to spend it all right away. To encourage you to stay at the firm, many fund advisers defer payment of a portion of cash bonuses for one or more years. And there are other reasons why you may not consider the offer of a job from your competitor. You may have been given an ownership stake in the management company that won't vest for some time, or you may have signed a noncompete agreement that makes it difficult for you to take clients away from your current employer.

If you want to learn more about how portfolio managers are paid, all you need do is turn to the statement of additional information for any mutual fund. The SEC requires that firms describe their compensation methodology there.

Risk Management

Up until now, your security selection decisions may have focused on maximizing potential return; but before you put in your buy or sell orders, you'll want to make sure that the portfolio's level of risk is appropriate for its investment objective. The risk of the overall portfolio is not simply the average of the risk of each of its component securities.

That's because the stocks won't always be moving in the same direction; some will be going up while others are going down. As an example, consider the relationship between oil producers and airlines. While falling oil prices will hurt the stock of the oil companies, they help airline stocks, which are big users of energy. In technical parlance, oil producers and airlines are *negatively correlated*. A portfolio holding stocks in just those two industries should be at least somewhat insulated from changes in the price of oil. That's not the case if you invest in just oil producers and energy service companies, which are the firms that help producers drill for oil. These groups are *positively correlated,* and should track the price of oil fairly closely.

The number of stocks you hold will affect overall risk. As a general rule, the fewer stocks you hold, the riskier the fund. Most portfolio managers try to limit the number of fund holdings. That's because managers tend to have strong convictions about a relatively small group of stocks. Also, while a large number of positions may reduce risk by increasing diversification, they can tax the ability of even the most diligent manager to keep on top of them all. As Figure 5.4 shows, in June 2010, more than a quarter of actively managed stock funds had concentrated portfolios with fewer than

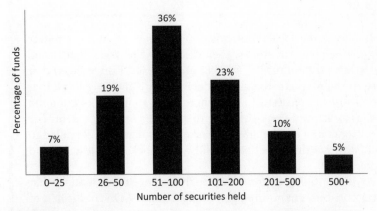

FIGURE 5.4 Number of Securities in U.S. Stock Funds (June 2010)[13]
Source: Morningstar.

50 holdings. Over half of the funds owned between 50 and 200 securities. Only a small percentage of funds held more than 200 positions.

The decision on the number of stocks in the portfolio is not just a matter of portfolio manager preference; practical considerations will play a role, too. Funds focusing on hard-to-trade securities such as small cap stocks will tend to hold more names, as will funds with a large asset base. Another consideration: fund complexes limit the percentage of the outstanding shares of a company that they will hold in all funds combined, forcing you to seek out new ideas once the maximum position has been reached. (This can easily be the case with small cap stocks.) For example, many funds groups do not want to own, in total across all funds, more than 15 percent of any company's stock.[14] Cash flows are another factor that comes into play. Steady inflows of money to a fund may compel you to look for ways to invest that cash quickly, possibly by buying more names.

To help you assess risk objectively, you'll most likely use a computer system to calculate your expected, or *ex ante*, tracking error. ("Beyond Beta" provides more information on a commonly used risk assessment tool.) This system will predict the standard deviation of the differences between the portfolio return and the index return. If your portfolio is broadly diversified and includes many of the stocks in the index at close to their index weightings, its tracking error will be low. But if your portfolio is quite concentrated, holding only a few stocks from the index together with a few out-of-benchmark positions, your predicted tracking error will probably be quite high.

BEYOND BETA

As researchers in the 1970s took advantage of faster computer power to study the behavior of stocks, they discovered patterns that defied the theory behind the Efficient Market Hypothesis. They noticed that exposure to the market—the classic beta—wasn't the only thing that made stocks move together. In fact, there were a number of common factors that influenced stock behavior to a greater or lesser extent. For example, stocks of a similar size or market capitalization all tended to go up and down at the same time, as did value stocks with low P/E and price/book ratios.

From this insight, quantitative analysts developed models that measure a portfolio's exposure to all of these factors. One of the first of these models—and still the most widely used—is the Barra risk model.

While the specific Barra risk factors vary by market, they normally include:

- *Momentum,* which is a stock's recent performance.
- *Volatility,* how sensitive a stock is to the ups and downs of the market, a measure that includes a stock's beta.
- *Value,* based on many ratios such as P/E, price/book, and price/cash flow.
- *Size,* equal to market capitalization. Because the size effect becomes more pronounced as market cap grows bigger or smaller, a *size nonlinearity* factor is included as well.
- *Growth,* looking at historic and estimated earnings growth.
- *Liquidity,* a stock's trading volume.
- *Financial leverage,* the amount of debt on a company's balance sheet.

Exposure to common factors can often explain much of a fund's tracking error against an index. For example, if a fund has a heavy weighting in stocks with lots of financial leverage—compared to the index, of course—it will do well when market conditions favor this type of company.

Portfolio managers want to ensure that their factor exposure is consistent with their portfolio's objective and approach, especially since style drift can be a major source of concern for many managers. For example, a value-style manager would expect to have greater-than-average exposure to value and low exposure to high growth and positive momentum.

You'll then assess whether the estimated tracking error is appropriate for your fund. An index fund should have a tracking error of close to zero. An aggressive fund might be expected to have a performance variation from its index of 5 to 6 percent. In between these two extremes are broadly diversified funds that make active decisions always keeping the benchmark in mind.

Performance Analysis

Now the investment decisions are made and begin to generate performance results. Your results will be dissected by pundits in the media rating, rating firms such as Lipper and Morningstar, and fund shareholders—but nowhere more extensively than within your fund management company itself. Portfolio managers always analyze past performance with the goal of learning from both their successes and mistakes. And as a portfolio manager, you'll make plenty of mistakes. Even outstanding fund managers will find that only two-thirds of their stocks are winners, while the rest are losers—relative to the benchmark, that is.

Performance attribution. Performance analysis begins with *performance attribution,* the process of calculating the contribution of each decision to the fund's returns. Again, all of this work is done relative to the benchmark. For example, you may have chosen to overweight financial stocks in the fund compared to their weight in the benchmark index. If financial stocks outperformed the overall index during the subsequent period, the decision was a good one. Performance attribution captures that benefit, measuring the effect of both the size of the overweight and the degree of outperformance. The combination of the two factors is the decision's relative contribution to the fund's performance, which is measured in basis points.

Specialized computer programs generate reports that will enable you to see how even single securities contributed to return. If, for example, the fund holds a 1 percent position in a stock that is not included in the benchmark and that stock outperforms the index by 20 percent, that holding contributed 20 basis points to outperformance (1 percent times 20 percent equals 20 bp). But if the fund holds a 1 percent position in a stock with a 1 percent weight in the index, the holding makes no contribution to relative performance, since its returns are already incorporated in the index's returns. Similarly, having no exposure to an index stock that does well will detract from relative performance. Table 5.3 shows a sample attribution report for the hypothetical Avon Hill U.S. Equity Fund at the sector level. Information on how the contributions are calculated is available on this book's web site.

While portfolio attribution tries to isolate each factor contributing to a fund's performance, the interaction of these factors is quite complex. A portfolio manager can make an incorrect call on sector allocation but recover through good security selection decisions. For example, as you can see in Table 5.3, the manager of the Avon Hill Fund was underweighted in information technology, a sector that did relatively well, which caused the fund to lag the index by 9 bp (the sector weight contribution). However, the specific stocks the fund held in that sector outperformed modestly for a positive contribution of 12 bp. The positive security selections compensated for the incorrect sector decision, resulting in a combined total relative contribution of 3 bp from the fund's technology positions.

TABLE 5.3 Sample Performance Attribution for the Avon Hill U.S. Equity Fund

	Fund Weight	Index Weight	Relative Weight	Fund Return	Index Return	Relative Return	Contribution in Basis Points		
							Stock Selection	Sector Weight	Total
Energy	13.7	10.9	2.8	18.7	17.9	0.8	10	36	47
Natural Resources	6.2	3.5	2.7	1.9	9.0	−7.1	−44	11	−33
Industrials	14.3	10.4	3.9	21.4	13.2	8.2	117	32	149
Consumer Discretionary	12.2	10.0	2.2	18.7	11.2	7.5	92	14	105
Consumer Staples	7.5	11.3	−3.8	−6.0	−3.6	−2.4	−18	33	15
Healthcare	13.1	12.3	0.8	−1.3	−1.9	0.6	8	−5	2
Financials	9.5	16.3	−6.8	−2.1	−6.1	4.0	38	75	113
Info Technology	16.9	18.8	−1.9	10.2	9.5	0.7	12	−9	3
Telecomm Services	4.9	2.9	2.0	1.3	2.7	−1.4	−7	−5	−11
Utilities	1.7	3.6	−1.9	2.1	−0.2	2.3	4	10	14
Total	100.0	100.0	0.0	9.0	5.0	4.0	212	192	404

You'll look at the contribution of both individual stock and sector decisions and then try to identify patterns in the returns. Maybe you'll conclude that you've had great stock picks, but didn't put enough of the fund's assets in them. To adjust, you'll increase the weightings of your top picks—though you'll have to be careful not to increase your tracking error too much.

Risk-adjusted performance. As a final step, you'll look at your risk-adjusted performance. To do this, you'll divide your alpha by your actual tracking error. The result is the *information ratio.* The higher it is, the greater the return for the risk taken. Top-ranked equity funds may have an information ratio of about 0.5, meaning that they deliver about half of their tracking error in outperformance.

CHAPTER SUMMARY

The managers of stock mutual funds mainly rely on two types of investment research: fundamental research and quantitative research. Fundamental research analysts look closely at individual companies or industries to find little-known relationships or to identify situations in which the consensus opinion appears to be wrong. Information provided by the companies themselves, insights gathered from industry sources, and research reports from other analysts help them develop a model to project future earnings. Fundamental analysts will generally recommend purchase if a company is expected to have a positive earnings surprise or if its stock is attractively valued. Conclusions about valuation are commonly based on ratio analysis using P/E and other metrics.

Quantitative analysts sift through data on large numbers of stocks to identify patterns in performance. They develop a hypothesis about factors that determine stock price performance, and then back test that hypothesis using historical data.

Index funds use one of two different portfolio management techniques. They may replicate the index by owning all the stocks in the index in the same proportions as their weightings in the index. Or they may use *sampling,* meaning that they buy a representative sample of index stocks that is expected to provide similar performance to the index as a whole. Index fund managers must have good information about daily cash flows and handle them efficiently.

The portfolio managers of actively managed funds generally focus on a particular style of investing when selecting stocks for a fund. The most popular styles are growth, value, and growth at a reasonable price. Growth managers look for companies with higher-than-average earnings growth, while value managers seek out companies with low multiples and high dividend yields. Growth-at-a-reasonable-price managers look for stocks with decent growth prospects that aren't exceptionally expensive.

Active managers evaluate their positions in relation to the benchmark index. They may overweight or underweight the stocks in the index or hold out-of-benchmark positions. Risk control tools help managers predict the overall volatility of a portfolio, considering the correlations among its holdings. Many managers use a model that analyzes exposure to common factors that influence stock price behavior. Performance attribution analysis enables managers to precisely measure the impact of specific decisions on portfolio performance.

CHAPTER 6

Portfolio Management of Bond Funds

I n this chapter, we review the portfolio management of bond funds. These funds are also called *fixed income funds,* a name that refers to the relative predictability of the returns of the bonds held in the funds. Because the issuers of bonds are contractually obligated to make specified payments to investors on fixed dates, bond returns are generally more stable than stock returns.

This chapter reviews:

- The principal types of securities held in bond fund portfolios
- The main approaches to the portfolio management of bond funds

> **Note:** Before you read on, please note that we assume throughout this discussion that you are familiar with how bonds work and are comfortable with fixed income terminology. If that's not the case, you might want to turn first to the appendix to this chapter, which reviews bond basics.

BOND FUND HOLDINGS

Bond funds are divided into two major segments: taxable and tax-exempt. Taxable funds invest in a variety of bonds that pay interest subject to federal income tax, while tax-exempt funds invest in bonds issued by states and municipalities that are exempt from federal income taxes and sometimes state income taxes. This section reviews the types of securities that are often found in the portfolios of each category of bond fund.

Holdings in Taxable Bond Funds

As we saw in Chapter 4, taxable bond funds have a wide variety of investment objectives. Some funds have a very broad mandate to invest in many kinds of bonds, while others specialize in a particular type of bond or in a specific range of maturities: short, intermediate, or long term. All invest in one or more of the following different categories of bonds:

U.S. Treasuries. Treasuries are bonds issued and guaranteed by the U.S. government through the Department of the Treasury. They have maturities of up to 30 years and generally do not have call provisions (which are explained in the appendix). Because the United States is a wealthy country and the U.S. government has the power to tax its citizens to raise money to make interest and principal payments on these bonds, most investors consider Treasuries to be credit risk-free. They are, however, still subject to market risk and will fluctuate in value as interest rates change, with the degree of variability depending on their duration.

Treasuries accounted for about one-quarter of the U.S. bond market at the end of 2009, as shown in Figure 6.1.

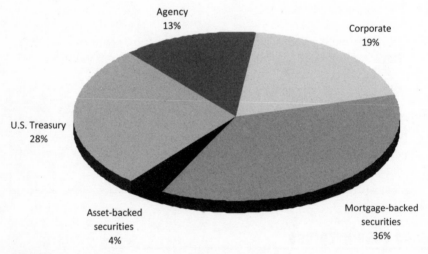

FIGURE 6.1 Overview of the Taxable Bond Market
Barclays Capital U.S. Aggregate Index
December 31, 2009
Maturity = 6.8 years[1]
YTM = 3.7 percent
Duration = 4.6
Source: Barclays Capital.

Agencies. Agency securities are the obligations of either federal government agencies or of *government-sponsored enterprises,* often referred to as GSEs. Major issuers of agency bonds are the Federal National Mortgage Association and the Federal Home Loan Mortgage Association, better known as Fannie Mae and Freddie Mac, respectively. Agencies accounted for about 13 percent of the U.S. bond market in 2009.

Debt issued by GSEs, which are private corporations, is not guaranteed by the U.S. government. Even so, most investors still consider it to have minimal credit risk because they believe that the federal government will provide support for these issues should problems arise. That turned out to be true during the credit crisis in 2008, when the government assumed control of Fannie Mae and Freddie Mac, which were both major mortgage lenders and experienced large losses when housing prices collapsed. While the government takeover validated the assumption of Treasury support, it also changed the agency landscape dramatically. Issuance of agency securities has fallen off sharply, as Congress debates the future of the home loan agencies.

Historically, agency debt has offered a slight yield premium over Treasuries. This yield advantage is not large, but does reflect the additional credit and liquidity risk of agency securities.

Mortgage-backed securities. Mortgage-backed securities, or MBS, are a collection of a large number of residential mortgages assembled together in a pool. Mortgages included in these pools must meet certain criteria with regard to size and quality. Similar to shareholders in mutual funds, investors in MBS own a proportional share of all the mortgages in the pool, which passes through the mortgage payments made by the homeowner to the bondholders. These payments are often guaranteed by a government agency or by a GSE—either Fannie Mae or Freddie Mac or possibly the Government National Mortgage Agency, known as Ginnie Mae.[2] MBS are very popular: close to half of all mortgages in the United States are pooled in this fashion, creating a highly liquid market of high quality securities. MBS represented more than one-third of the U.S. bond market in 2009, making them an extremely important investment option for bond funds.

A distinguishing feature of MBS is that they have considerable call or prepayment risk. That's because most homeowners can—and often do—pay off all or part of their mortgage at any time. If their mortgages are part of an MBS pool, those payments are passed on to the bondholders. Unfortunately, since homeowners are more likely to prepay their mortgage when interest rates are falling—and it makes sense to lower their costs by refinancing—that means that MBS holders will have to invest the cash received in lower-yielding securities. As a consequence, investors in MBS may find that their return falls short of what they originally expected. MBS holders try to manage this risk by using sophisticated models to quantify prepayment risk and estimate returns under various interest rate scenarios.

Asset-backed securities. Like MBS, asset-backed securities are also based on pools of debt, though usually without the guarantee of a government agency. The different types of ABS go by different names, depending on the nature of the underlying IOUs. Some of the varieties of ABS are:

- Traditional ABS, based on home equity loans, car loans, or credit card balances.
- Collateralized mortgage obligations, or CMOs, based on home mortgages. While many CMOs use loans that qualify for MBS, others package together mortgages that don't qualify for inclusion in a mortgage pass-through, either because they are large (*jumbo* mortgages) or because they are of lower quality (*subprime* mortgages). A mortgage may be considered subprime if it was made to a borrower with a poor credit history, if it is large relative to the value of the home because the down payment was small (*high loan-to-value*), or if the borrower was not required to document his income (*no doc, low doc,* or *Alt-A* mortgages).
- Commercial mortgage-backed securities, or CMBS, based on mortgages made to businesses for commercial properties.
- Collateralized loan obligations, or CLOs, based on bank loans to businesses.
- Collateralized debt obligations, or CDOs, based on a variety of bonds including—believe it or not—other ABS. CDOs using subprime mortgage-backed securities played a significant role in the credit crisis.[3]

While these are some of the better-known types, ABS can be based on almost any type of debt. For example, the first ABS, issued in 1985, was backed by the credit that a computer manufacturer extended to its customers to enable them to purchase its equipment.[4]

ABS are an important part of the U.S. financial system, allowing banks and nonbank lenders to better manage their risk. Let's take the example of a bank that has made a large number of car loans in a particular city and has decided that it has too much exposure to an economic downturn affecting the industries in that area. The bank would like to continue making loans there—rather than give their competitors a foothold in the market—but it would like to reduce its risk. The easiest way to do this is to sell the loans already on the books. Unfortunately, few investors have interest in buying the loans outright, since that would mean taking responsibility for collecting payment on and accounting for thousands of car loans. To get around this issue, the bank can *securitize* the loans by creating an ABS.

Unlike their mortgage-backed cousins, ABS are not pass-throughs, with a share-and-share-alike approach. Instead, ABS are *structured securities* which means that different investors in the pool can face different risk-and-return profiles, depending on the specific *tranche* (pronounced *trawnch*) they have purchased. Tranche is French for *slice,* or *section,* and each tranche in an ABS is entitled to a different slice of the risk and return. This tranching approach became a major factor contributing to the credit crisis, so let's take a closer look at it.

An ABS starts with a *special purpose entity,* or SPE—usually a trust or limited partnership—that holds a pool of loans or fixed income securities. The SPE generally issues several tranches of securities that are ranked from top to bottom. (There are single-tranche ABS, though these are less common.)

We'll discuss an ABS with four tranches: Tranche A is at the top, while Tranche D is at the bottom. (See Figure 6.2 for a schematic of our hypothetical ABS, which explains why the structure of an ABS is often called a *waterfall.*) Tranche A is the senior tranche, while Tranche D is the junior tranche.

Each tranche gets a different share of the income and losses. Tranche D is the riskiest. If there are losses on the underlying loans, Tranche D will take them first.[5] Only after Tranche D has been extinguished—essentially wiped out—after absorbing all of the losses related to loans in the pool will Tranche C experience losses, and only after Tranche C has been extinguished by the next set of losses will Tranche B get hit, and so on. Because Tranche

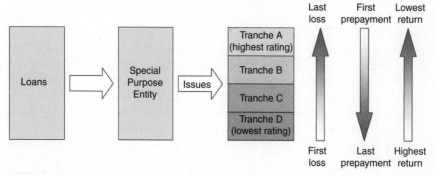

FIGURE 6.2 Structure of an ABS

D is so risky, it is usually held by the financial institution that has created the ABS, or possibly by a hedge fund prepared to take that risk for a high potential return.[6]

Prepayments flow down in exactly the opposite direction. When borrowers on the underlying loans pay off their debt, the money goes first to Tranche A, then to Tranche B, then to Tranche C, and so on. This makes Tranche A the safest: because prepayments are allocated to them first, holders of this tranche have the best chance of seeing a return of their principal. (On the other hand, Tranche A will have considerable prepayment risk, but, as we've seen, investors will anticipate this risk and factor it into the return they demand from the tranche.)

Because Tranche A is the safest, it gets the highest credit rating and a lower share of the income produced by the underlying debt. Conversely, Tranche D will have the lowest credit rating—or maybe even no rating at all—and a higher share of the income.

However, if the pool of underlying loans is of poor quality and defaults in large numbers, it's not just Tranche D that will suffer losses. This is what happened in the credit crisis, when even the most senior tranches of ABS, based on subprime mortgages, crumbled when housing prices collapsed.

These subprime mortgage ABS and CDOs had been the fastest-growing category of ABS in the years leading up to the credit crisis, a reflection of the surge in subprime mortgage issuance. In 2006, for example, over 39 percent of all new U.S. mortgage loans could be considered subprime, compared to about 9 percent only five years before.[7] Analysts with little experience with these loans seriously underestimated the potential for defaults. Nowhere was this more true than at the credit rating agencies, which gave high ratings to the senior tranches of subprime ABS. ("Reforming the Credit Rating Agencies" reviews the proposals that have been made to prevent a repeat of the problem.)

In 2009, ABS accounted for less than 5 percent of the U.S. bond market—a decline in share resulting from the poor performance of recent issues and increased skepticism about the reliability of the credit ratings on new issues. Provisions in the Dodd-Frank financial reform legislation may help reinvigorate the market and increase investor confidence in ABS by establishing new requirements for securitization. For example, the creators of a new ABS are now required, with some exceptions, to retain at least 5 percent of the risk of loss from the entire issue—an incentive to keep credit quality high.

Corporate bonds. Large corporations often issue bonds to finance ongoing operations or new acquisitions. Public utilities, transportation

REFORMING THE CREDIT RATING AGENCIES

The credit agencies' broad misjudgments on securities based on subprime mortgages have generated some serious accusations—that the rating agencies were co-conspirators in the credit crisis—and other even more serious calls for change. The critics of the rating agencies have focused on their oligopoly status and their compensation model of *issuer pays*. Specifically:

Oligopoly status. The SEC and other financial industry regulators require the use of credit ratings for certain purposes. For example, as we see in the next chapter, money market funds must invest most of their assets in securities of the highest credit quality, as determined by a rating agency. Only a small group of rating agencies—technically known as *nationally recognized statistical rating organizations,* or NRSROs—have been recognized by the regulators. That has created an oligopoly with very limited competition, dominated by three firms: Fitch, Moody's, and Standard & Poor's. While some critics want to eliminate credit ratings altogether, individual investors, state pension plans, and some insurance companies rely on them quite heavily.

"Issuer pays" compensation model. The major rating agencies are chosen and paid by bond issuers—not by the bond investors who rely on the ratings as an indication of quality. Since issuers want a high rating to make their bonds attractive to the public, this model encourages the agencies to go easy on companies in the hope of attracting their business. Critics even contend that issuers go "ratings shopping," pitting the agencies against one other and choosing the one that is most likely to supply the highest rating. The agencies themselves counter that this is not the case and that they have strong internal processes that protect the integrity of the ratings process. In any event, the perception persists that agencies serve issuers more than they do investors.

Congress has addressed both of these concerns in the Dodd-Frank financial reform legislation of 2010. The legislation directs regulators to remove many references to ratings in the federal statutes, thus reducing the rating agencies' special status. It also directs the SEC, after conducting a study, to establish a mechanism to prevent bond ratings shopping.

companies, industrials, telecommunication companies, banks, and finance companies are typical issuers. They issue bonds as an alternative to borrowing from banks, usually lowering their interest costs by going directly to investors. Corporate bonds make up almost one-fifth of the U.S. market.

All corporate bonds have a risk of default, so careful credit research is essential in this segment. This is particularly true for lower-rated, or *junk*, bonds, which are often considered a separate sector of the bond market. There are many funds that focus on junk bonds exclusively, and they appeal to many investors because of their fat yields. (See "Sorting through the Junk" for more detail on *high-yield* bonds, as they are often called.) With all corporate bonds—investment grade or junk—in addition to assessing default risk, analysts look for mispricings, meaning yield spreads that are too high or too low considering the expectations for the financial condition of the issuer

SORTING THROUGH THE JUNK

The high-yield bond market has changed significantly over the course of the past 30 years. In the 1970s, most junk bonds were *fallen angels*, formerly investment-grade issues that had fallen from grace. The companies that had issued these bonds had tumbled from the credit-rating heights when their businesses suffered serious setbacks.

In the 1980s, investors began to notice that past returns for diversified portfolios of lower-rated bonds were quite attractive, more than compensating for higher losses from defaults. They began to buy junk bonds in quantity, and it wasn't long before demand for high-yield issues exceeded the supply of fallen angels. That left an opening for companies with below-investment-grade ratings to issue bonds, something they had generally not been able to do in the past. New issues poured into the market, visibly championed by the Drexel Burnham Lambert investment banker Michael Milken. Unfortunately, "junk" turned out to be an accurate characterization of many of the bonds issued during this boom period, and the high-yield market crashed at the end of the 1980s when many of these bonds defaulted.[8]

But the high-yield market survived the fallout and soon began to thrive again. Returns over the past 20 years have been attractive, although very volatile, and more often correlated with the returns of stocks than those of investment-grade bonds. Figure 6.3 shows the ups and downs of annual issuance of high-yield debt since 1985.

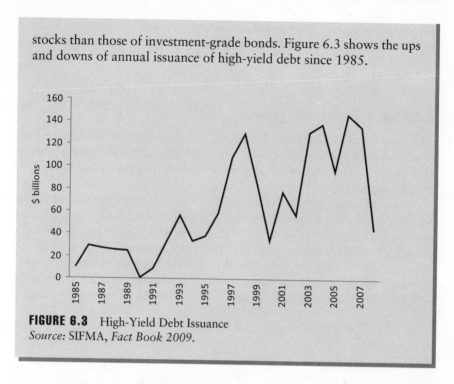

FIGURE 6.3 High-Yield Debt Issuance
Source: SIFMA, *Fact Book 2009*.

Non-U.S. bonds. As we've seen, many bond funds can invest outside the United States. If they do, they have a wide choice of bonds issued by foreign governments, international agencies, and companies incorporated in other countries. In some cases, these bonds are priced, or *denominated,* in U.S. dollars. Analysis of these *Eurodollar,* or *Yankee bonds,* as they are often called, is quite similar to that of U.S. bonds.[9]

However, most bonds issued outside the United States are not denominated in U.S. dollars. For these bonds, *currency risk*—the risk that the value of the foreign currency declines against the U.S. dollar—can be significant. Therefore, holding foreign currency bonds can add significantly to a portfolio's volatility. We discuss the risks of cross-border investing in more detail in Chapter 16.

Derivatives. Derivatives are contracts that derive their value from an underlying security or group of securities. Many bond fund portfolio managers use them as a low-cost way to adjust a portfolio's exposure to interest rate or credit risk. The most widely used fixed income derivatives are bond futures contracts, interest rate swaps, and credit default swaps. We discuss credit default swaps in more detail later in this chapter, but a comprehensive review of derivatives is beyond the scope of this book. For those who would like to do some reading on the topic, we have placed a brief bibliography on our web site.

Holdings in Tax-Exempt Funds

The tax-exempt, or municipal, bond market is less diversified than the taxable market. It is made up of only two basic types of bonds: general obligation bonds and revenue bonds. Figure 6.4 shows the breakdown of the U.S. municipal market.

General obligation bonds. General obligation bonds, often referred to as GOs, are issued by states and local governments (the latter are called municipalities) that pledge their taxing power to repay investors. This is a valuable promise, making GOs the least risky segment of the tax-exempt sector. Unlike Treasuries, however, they are not considered credit risk-free, and local issuers have defaulted on their obligations on occasion. As a result, investors make distinctions among tax-exempt issuers, requiring higher

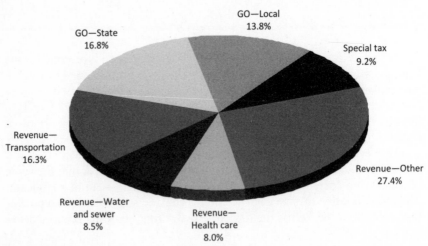

FIGURE 6.4   Overview of the Tax-Exempt Bond Market
Barclays Capital U.S. Municipal Bond Index
December 31, 2009
Maturity = 13.5 years
Yield = 3.6 percent[10]
Duration = 8.3
Source: Barclays Capital.

yields from those who are weaker financially. In 2009, GOs made up about one-third of the municipal bond market.

A separate category of debt issued by states and municipalities are *special tax* bonds, which are backed by revenue from a specific tax such as a gasoline tax. Since these bonds are not supported by the issuer's general taxing power, they are not GOs, but their credit quality is still considered to be very high. They were about 9 percent of the tax-exempt bond market in 2009.

Revenue bonds. Revenue bonds, in contrast, do not have a claim on the government's taxing power. They are issued to fund a specific project, and only the revenues associated with that project are available to repay investors. Revenue bonds may be used to finance the construction of water or sewer facilities, toll roads, hospitals, and municipal power plants, among other projects. They accounted for over half of the market in 2009.

Within revenue bonds, there are two subcategories:

1. *Alternative minimum tax bonds.* The interest from some revenue bonds is subject to the alternative minimum tax; these bonds are known as AMT bonds. The AMT was introduced in the late 1960s; it was designed to prevent wealthy taxpayers from lowering their tax bill to zero by taking advantage of the exemptions, credits, and deductions in the tax code—including the tax exemption on municipal bond interest. Not all revenue bonds are subject to the AMT—only those that are deemed *private activity* bonds because they are used to finance airports, stadiums, or other private-use facilities that do not have a clear public purpose. AMT bonds generally have higher yields than other revenue bonds, both because they are subject to the tax and because they are backed by projects that are more sensitive to the ups and downs of the economy.
2. *High-yield municipal bonds.* As in the taxable market, high-yield municipal bonds are those with lower credit ratings. Most are fallen angel revenue bonds, whose project revenues have fallen short of expectations.

Insured bonds. Even though most municipal bonds are considered quite secure, many state and local governments choose to increase the appeal of their bonds to investors by purchasing bond insurance. These policies, which are issued by specialized companies, guarantee repayment of interest and principal as it comes due. "The Faded Appeal of Municipal Bond Insurance" explains why this coverage was once very popular and why it's no longer as common.

THE FADED APPEAL OF MUNICIPAL BOND INSURANCE

To understand the appeal of municipal bond insurance, let's consider a bond with an underlying credit rating of single A. If the issuer purchases insurance, this bond's rating jumps to AAA, which equals the rating of the insurer providing the protection. The rating upgrade appeals to buyers interested in reducing their risk. But the upgrade can make sense for the issuer, too—financial sense, that is. Higher-rated bonds can be issued with lower yields—meaning lower interest costs to the issuer. These cost savings are often more than the price of the insurance policy. Municipal bond insurance made so much sense to both buyers and issuers that, at its peak, in 2006, about half of all municipal issues were insured.

Insurance also made sense to the companies issuing the policies. In fact, because the default rate of municipal bonds is low, writing municipal bond insurance was a very profitable business. It was so stable and profitable that the insurers companies felt comfortable expanding into other areas. Unfortunately, many of their initiatives—which included forays into the subprime mortgage market—were badly hurt during the credit crisis. As these newer lines of business began accumulating huge losses, the municipal bond insurance market was thrown into turmoil. All of the insurers, including market leaders Ambac, FSA, and MBIA, suffered multiple credit rating downgrades, some to junk levels. As a result, the bonds they insured no longer automatically carried the all-important AAA rating. These downgrades, in turn, made insurance far less attractive to investors and issuers, and volumes fell off dramatically in consequence.

Pre-refunded bonds. One last category of municipal bonds: pre-refunded bonds, often referred to as *pre-res,* which are backed by a portfolio of U.S. Treasuries. Issuers generally can't retire a municipal bond before its call date. Instead, to benefit from lower interest rates, the issuer buys enough Treasury bonds to cover all the remaining payments on the current bonds and then places the Treasuries into a separate escrow account, drawing on this account as needed to make those payments. The cash to buy the Treasuries comes from the issuance of another bond, often at a coupon rate lower than that of the bond that is being pre-refunded. The result is that the old bonds are *defeased* and taken off the books of the issuer—which is reasonable because the Treasuries are there to fund the payments on the bonds—while the new, lower-cost bonds remain outstanding. After-tax yields on pre-res are slightly higher than after-tax Treasury yields.

PUTTING IT ALL TOGETHER: MANAGING A BOND FUND

So far, we've been talking about the many factors that any investor should consider when purchasing an individual bond. In this section, we review the challenges of selecting a portfolio of bonds that will achieve a fund's objective. This task falls to the bond portfolio manager.

NOT ENTIRELY PASSIVE

While stock index funds have captured much of the limelight, bond index funds play an equally important, if less-heralded role for investors. As we reviewed in Chapter 4, passively managed funds look to match the return of a benchmark index. To do this, portfolio manager sometimes simply replicate the index by buying investments in the same proportions as their representation in the relevant benchmark.

That's easy in theory, but next to impossible in practice—at least for bond indexes, which contain an extremely high number of securities. A taxable bond index can include thousands of issues, and the number rises into the millions for some tax-exempt benchmarks!

As a result, bond index managers generally use sampling techniques that seek to match the return of an index while holding only a portion of its securities. They may start by eliminating the very smallest issues from consideration. Then they'll use computer models to determine which bonds are likely to have very similar or homogeneous returns, then choose only a few representative bonds from that group. In this latter step, they may incorporate some of the techniques used by active managers. For example, they may try to eliminate bonds with the highest call risk. Finally, they'll look at the overall positioning of the portfolio they've selected to make sure that it aligns with index in regard to duration, yield curve exposure, overall credit quality, and other key characteristics.

Investment Strategy

The portfolio managers of bond funds use different strategies to produce a competitive total return. Some emphasize a big-picture, or top-down, approach, such as duration management, yield curve positioning or sector selection, while others work from the bottom up, focusing on credit analysis or on predicting calls or prepayments. We focus here on how these strategies are used by active managers, those who seek a total return that is higher than that of the benchmark index and ranks high in its peer group. By contrast, managers of bond index funds use only a few elements of these approaches when they attempt to replicate an index, as "Not Entirely Passive" explains.

Strategies for actively managing bond portfolios include:

- *Duration management.* Portfolio managers can dramatically influence the return of a bond portfolio by adjusting its sensitivity to anticipated interest rate movements, a practice commonly referred to as duration management or *interest rate anticipation.* This strategy involves altering the average duration of the fund based on the outlook for interest rates based on an assessment of the macroeconomic situation. If interest rates are expected to fall, portfolio managers buy longer duration bonds, which would benefit more from a decline in rates, while selling shorter duration bonds. Conversely, if portfolio managers expect yields to rise, they lower, or shorten up, their funds' average duration.

  The most obvious way to adjust the duration of a portfolio is to replace short duration bonds with longer ones or vice versa. This can be a very inefficient approach, however, especially when the bonds are difficult and costly to buy and sell. As a result, portfolio managers often modify a fund's interest rate exposure by using a derivatives transaction, either a bond futures contract or an interest rate swap.

  Duration management is a powerful performance tool. If a manager predicts the level of interest rates accurately and makes appropriate portfolio adjustments, her fund will likely beat the market handily. Unfortunately, predicting the direction of interest rates consistently is very difficult to do in practice.

- *Yield curve positioning.* Portfolio managers may also try to predict shifts in the shape of the yield curve. The yield curve is constantly moving up and down, reflecting the change in the level of different interest rates. Sometimes all interest rates across the maturity spectrum will go up or down by the same amount; this is called a *parallel shift in the yield curve.* At other times, interest rates for different maturities change

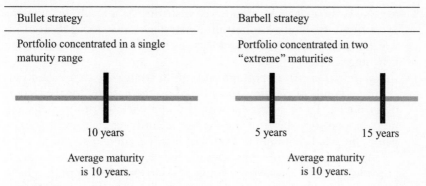

Bullet strategy	Barbell strategy
Portfolio concentrated in a single maturity range	Portfolio concentrated in two "extreme" maturities
10 years	5 years · · · 15 years
Average maturity is 10 years.	Average maturity is 10 years.

FIGURE 6.5 Two Common Yield Curve Strategies

by different amounts. For example, if 30-year Treasury bonds are in particular demand, their yield may be less affected by a general rise in interest rates than the yield on 10-year Treasury notes. In other words, the yield on a 30-year bond will rise less than the yield on the 10-year note. In that circumstance, the yield curve is said to *flatten*. It *steepens* when short rates fall faster or rise more slowly than longer-term rates.

Portfolio managers can adjust the positioning of a portfolio to match their outlook for the yield curve shifts. If they anticipate that either short- or long-term rates will move without affecting the balance of the yield curve, they may opt for a *bullet* strategy, concentrating holdings in a narrow maturity range. If they think that the yield curve will steepen, they may use a *barbell* strategy, splitting the fund's holding between longer or shorter durations. Figure 6.5 illustrates bullet and barbell portfolios.

- *Sector selection*. With a sector selection strategy, the portfolio manager tries to take advantage of performance differences among the various bond market sectors. For example, the portfolio manager of a taxable bond fund who expects that the economy will get stronger may emphasize corporate bonds over U.S. Treasuries, while a tax-exempt manager might choose lower-rated bonds or revenue bonds in weaker states or cities. (Why? A stronger economy will likely lead to improved financial health of most companies and municipalities—which will reduce credit risk and, in turn, lead to lower yields and higher bond prices.)

All of the top-down strategies—duration management, yield curve positioning, and sector allocation—can have a significant impact on the relative performance of a bond fund. But success with all of these strategies—which often depends on accurately predicting economic trends—is difficult to accomplish consistently. As a result, many managers prefer to emphasize bottom-up strategies that focus on security selection, keeping duration and sector allocation close to that of the benchmark.

- *Credit selection.* An important bottom-up strategy is credit selection, choosing bonds of certain issuers based on the outlook for their creditworthiness. To be successful with this approach, portfolio managers must be one step ahead of the market, identifying changes in a company's financial condition not yet seen by other investors.

Again, the most obvious way to change credit exposure within a portfolio is to sell less-favored bonds and buy ones that appear to have brighter prospects. However, some portfolio managers use a derivative transaction—in this case called a *credit default swap* (described in "Popular, but Controversial")—to accomplish the same thing.

POPULAR, BUT CONTROVERSIAL

A credit default swap is like an insurance policy: the buyer of the CDS pays a premium to a *counterparty*—usually a bank or a broker-dealer—to protect against credit risk on a bond. The policy pays off if the bond goes into default. They are a recent financial innovation, tracing their origins back only to the 1990s, and were initially used by banks with large corporate loan portfolios, which wanted to limit their exposure to borrowers facing potential financial difficulties. CDS allowed the bank to continue its relationship with a troubled corporation, while reducing or eliminating the cost of a potential default. The market for CDS has since expanded well beyond banks, as many investors have found them to be an effective tool to adjust credit risk exposure.

They have become so popular that, at their peak in 2008, the CDS market was many times the size of the actual corporate bond market! That had some advantages for investors. Given the breadth and depth of the market, CDS became a very good barometer of investor opinion regarding the outlook for a particular company. And they often provided an easier and cheaper way for portfolios to adjust credit exposures.

But the ballooning market raised more than a few eyebrows, as well. Market observers became concerned that CDS encouraged excessive speculation. That's because it's possible to buy a policy on a company even without owning the underlying bond. (This is the big difference between a CDS and a true insurance policy.) With the prospect of a big profit if the firm should go bankrupt, owners of a CDS had an incentive to bring about that very event by undermining public confidence in a company. Critics also pointed out that CDS involve substantial counterparty risk—the risk that the bank or broker-dealer providing the insurance would be unable to meet its obligations to policyholders. Unfortunately, their worst fears were realized when American International Group, also referred to as AIG, a substantial CDS counterparty, ran into financial trouble and could not pay its obligations to the parties on the other side of the CDS it had written. AIG was ultimately bailed out by the federal government to prevent its collapse from spreading to other firms.

In response, the Dodd-Frank financial reform legislation mandates that most standardized derivatives be traded on an exchange or swap execution facility and settled through a clearing corporation. Writers of CDS will need to make margin deposits, marked to market daily, to ensure that they are able to fulfill their commitments to the buyers of the CDS.

■ *Predicting calls or prepayments.* Managing the level of call or prepayment risk is another bottom-up approach. It's especially important for MBS, which have a high prepayment risk. To assess this risk, portfolio managers use mathematical models to estimate the expected prepayments and to calculate the value of the imbedded call option based on that estimate. The manager then compares the value of the bond calculated by the model to its market price to determine whether the bond is a buy or a sell.

Portfolio Construction

In this section, we give you a chance to grapple with some of the challenges of managing a large bond fund. All of the investment strategies we've described can be used separately or in combination. Their implementation is within your province as portfolio manager, working on your own or as part of the portfolio management team. Your responsibility to the fund's shareholders means that you have to manage the risks carefully, while doing everything you can to provide a competitive return. For more on the job of the bond portfolio manager, see the "Career Track" box.

CAREER TRACK: BOND PORTFOLIO MANAGER

Wonder what it's like to be a bond portfolio manager? Here's a scenario you might face on a typical day:

Your portfolio holds a large position in an exceptionally good corporate bond. It's not a well-known company or bond, so it doesn't trade often, and it has taken you the better part of a year to build the position with small purchases. A highly experienced credit analyst walks over and talks with you about their most recent report covering the issuer of this bond. The analyst says there's a concern about a pending lawsuit that could have a devastating impact on the company.

You start weighing your options:

Option 1: Sell your position. To try to sell the entire amount of your holdings might move the market substantially, causing the price to drop considerably, because it's a large position relative to normal trading activity. In further discussions with the analyst, you find that while an unfavorable outcome in the case could really hurt the company's financials, maybe permanently, it's not a likely scenario. If the lawsuit does not succeed, the company is expected to continue to do well.

Option 2: Do nothing. You could do nothing and just hope for the best. At this point, prices are stable, and the market doesn't seem concerned yet with the lawsuit.

Option 3: Reduce risk. Or, you could think about using a credit default swap to hedge against a big decline in the bond. (See the explanation of these derivatives in the preceding callout box.) If the legal problems of the bond's issuer are not yet widely known, the price of this insurance could be low.

To decide which option makes most sense, you'll need to quantitatively estimate the results of each outcome, considering the likelihood of the success of the lawsuit, the potential impact on the bond price, and the cost of implementation of each outcome. And you'll have to do it quickly, before other investors zero in on the same issue.

Assume that you've been put in charge of a multibillion-dollar taxable fund with a broad mandate to own investment-grade bonds of all types. Let's think through some of the factors you'll have to consider before buying a bond for the fund:

Prospectus objectives and restrictions. First and foremost, before buying any security, you'll need to make sure that its selection complies with the guidelines set down in the prospectus. For example, if your prospectus states that the fund must invest at least 80 percent of its assets in high quality debt securities rated BBB or better, it's your responsibility to ensure that actual purchases comply with that restriction. (See Chapter 3 for a more detailed discussion of the prospectus and the types of limitations it normally contains.)

Index. Next, you'll need to know which benchmark index is being used for your fund. In this case, it's the Barclays Capital U.S. Aggregate Bond Index, which, like your fund, ranges across all sectors of the taxable bond market. You'll study the details of the index, including its sector weightings, its constituent bonds, and its average yield and duration.

That's because all of your positions will be evaluated relative to the index, which becomes your neutral position. If you're positive on the outlook of a sector or a particular security, you'll overweight it versus the index, meaning that its percentage weight in the portfolio will be higher than its weight in the index. Similarly, you'll underweight sectors and securities when your opinion is less positive. But you probably won't have a value-added idea every waking moment of every day. Therefore, when the ideas are in short supply, you'll need to know how to keep the fund neutral to the index.

We'll assume that you have studied the index and now know enough about how to neutralize the fund's risks. Well done; it takes most portfolio managers months or years!

Peer group. You'll also take a look at the peer group of competing funds that your fund is being compared against to see if you can learn anything from their strategies. (See Chapter 4 for a discussion of peer groups.) Peer groups and benchmark indexes are important for another reason: they'll be the basis for your calculation of your bonus.

Duration management. Now it's time to figure out which of the strategies fit with the strengths of your firm and your experience. The biggest question you'll face is how much emphasis to place on top-down strategies. Most managers of large bond funds have decided that using an interest rate anticipation, or *market timing,* strategy exclusively is not a winning approach over the long run. All bond managers can talk about a few times when they made a large shift in duration that served the portfolio and shareholders well, but they usually have an equal number of stories—not as well publicized—about times when a shift in duration hurt returns. But if you deemphasize the most powerful tool available to a bond portfolio manager, how will you focus your efforts?

Yield curve positioning. You can turn to a team of analysts armed with computer models to help you sort through the decisions regarding yield curve shape. You'll need to figure out where to own securities along the time line of the yield curve. Do you want the portfolio to be more of a bullet or a more of a barbell? And once you settle on your ideal positioning, implementing your decision is quite complicated in practice, very much interconnected with sector and credit choices. Certain securities lend themselves to certain positions on the curve. For example, mortgages tend to have intermediate durations because of a high probability of prepayment, whereas utility bonds tend to be longer term since they use the proceeds from bond sales to finance plant construction. Therefore, your choice of how to invest along the yield curve will influence the types of securities that may be available to the portfolio and vice versa.

Sector. Recognizing the impact of the yield curve decisions, you'll need to think more about the sectors that make the most sense for the portfolio. Do mortgages make sense? Do market prices reflect the levels of prepayments predicted in your modeling? Should you over- or underweight corporate bonds? Is the economy improving or deteriorating, and how will that affect corporate bond prices? And which industries within the corporate market will perform the best? There are lots of questions to sort through to invest in the right sectors and industries. For example, it wouldn't make much sense to find the best bond issued by an insurance company if the whole industry is under pressure. If one insurer's bonds are priced cheaply enough, they might still be a buy, but you have to own them recognizing that there is downside risk for the industry as a whole.

Credit. At the same time, you'll be working with the credit analysts to identify which securities represent the best values at the points on the yield curve and in the sectors that you are trying to emphasize. The credit analysts will let you know which bonds are most attractive, maybe because the issuers are stable or even improving financially—or maybe because they're priced right even if the issuer's prospects are deteriorating slightly. Once you start to narrow down the list, you'll need to decide which specific bond is best. In most cases, large corporate issuers will have many bonds outstanding. Choosing between a four-year or five-year bond of the same issuer if only one has a call option attached is when the process gets most interesting. All of the skills of the investment team will be needed to evaluate trade-offs in order to arrive at a final decision.

Liquidity and trading. Once your security selections are made, you'll need to consider your ability to actually buy them in your portfolio. Unfortunately, many corporate bonds trade in small amounts and can be costly to buy and sell. You'll work closely with your trading desk to actually implement your decisions. They'll give you an overview of a market, look for the right securities at the right prices, and try to identify attractive bids for the bonds in the portfolio that may no longer make sense to hold.

The dialogue among the traders, the analysts, and you needs to be constant. It's a dynamic process, particularly given that you are managing a multibillion-dollar fund with hundreds of positions together with daily inflows and outflows as shareholders purchase or redeem fund shares. We discuss bond trading in more detail in Chapter 8.

CHAPTER SUMMARY

Taxable bond funds invest in securities issued by the U.S. Treasury, by government agencies and government-sponsored enterprises, by U.S. corporations, and by non-U.S. governments and corporations. The credit quality of these issues can vary widely. U.S. Treasuries are considered credit risk-free, while high-yield, or junk, bonds have considerable default risk.

Taxable bond funds may also invest in mortgage-backed or asset-backed securities—which are backed by a pool of loans or other fixed-income securities. Mortgage-backed securities act much like a mutual fund, passing through payments of interest and principal to the bondholder. In contrast, asset-backed, or structured, securities are divided into a series of tranches. Each tranche receives a different share of the income and the losses from the underlying pool of securities.

The tax-exempt bond market is composed of two types of bonds: general obligation bonds and revenue bonds. General obligation bonds, or GOs, are issued by state and local governments that pledge their taxing power to repay investors. GOs are considered to have very high credit quality. Revenue bonds are riskier because they can be repaid only from the income generated by a particular public project, such as a water or sewer facility constructed using the money raised from the bond offering. Certain revenue bonds may also be subject to the alternative minimum tax. Both GOs and revenue bonds may be insured or pre-refunded.

Bond fund portfolio managers use various strategies to choose securities for their funds. Bond index fund management involves some active elements; that's because most bond indexes contain a large number of securities, which means that passive managers almost always use sampling techniques to try to match index performance. Active managers use a wider range of bond selection strategies. They may use a top-down approach and try to anticipate changes in interest rates or the relative returns of different types of bonds. While these big-picture strategies can have a significant impact on fund returns, they are very difficult to get right consistently. As a result, many bond fund managers use bottom-up strategies that focus on selecting specific securities by using credit analysis or predicting calls or prepayments.

Portfolio managers work closely with bond traders to implement buy and sell decisions. They often use derivatives transactions, such as credit default swaps, to reduce the transaction costs of implementing those decisions.

Appendix to Chapter 6:
Bond Basics

We start our review of bond basics with a definition. A *bond* is a formal IOU given by a borrower, such as a corporation or government, to the investors who have lent it money. This written IOU normally specifies that the borrower, or *issuer,* will:

- Repay the amount borrowed on a specific date, known as the *maturity date.*
- Make periodic interest payments until the maturity date.
- Promise to repay bondholders before paying stockholders. Put another way, bonds are senior to stocks when it comes to claims on a company's cash—most importantly, in bankruptcy.

The IOU is often tradable, meaning that it can be purchased and sold between one investor and another. While some investors may choose to hold bonds from issue date to maturity date, most buy and sell bonds during their term to meet their changing investment goals and to try to maximize total return.

The total return from a bond equals interest payments received plus—or minus—the change in price of the bond from time of purchase to time of sale. From the perspective of the IRS, the interest is considered ordinary income, while the change in price is capital gain or loss, which is generally taxed at a lower rate.

The bond market is immense, as measured by both dollar value and number of securities. At the end of 2008, the tradable bond market in the United States was estimated to include more than two million issues, worth some $30 trillion; in contrast, there are only 7,000 stocks listed on the exchanges in the United States, valued at only half that amount.[11] There are many more bonds than stocks because, while most firms have only one class of stock, governments and companies may issue more than one—and often many—different bonds, each with a unique set of attributes.

This appendix reviews:

- The characteristics of bonds
- The key measures used to evaluate and compare them
- Their principal risks

DEFINING CHARACTERISTICS OF BONDS

Every bond can be described by the combination of five key attributes, which are all described in the prospectus prepared when the bond is publicly issued. (The prospectus describes the provisions of the *indenture,* which is the legal document defining the terms of the bond.) The five defining attributes are: issuer, par value, coupon, maturity, and option features, if any.

Issuer. The issuer is the entity that has borrowed the money and is responsible for paying bondholders. An issuer is normally a corporation or a governmental organization. Bonds are said to be the *obligations,* or debt, of the issuer.

Par value. Par value is the amount that investors will be repaid when a bond reaches its maturity date; it is normally set at $1,000 per bond. Par value is also referred to as *face value, maturity value, principal amount,* or just *principal.*

Current market price, the price at which the bond can be sold to other investors, is expressed as a percentage of par value. Thus, a price of 97.5 for a $1,000 par value bond means that the investor pays $975 for each bond, equaling 97.5 percent of $1,000.

Coupon rate. The coupon rate specifies the amount of periodic interest the bond will pay. The term *coupon* originated in the days when investors were given a paper certificate as evidence of their ownership of a particular bond. To collect the interest owed, bondholders would *clip a coupon* from the edge of the certificate and turn it in to the company—or, more often, its bank—in exchange for cash. Today, most bonds are held in electronic form, a system called *book entry,* which enables bondholders to be paid automatically without requiring action on their part.

The coupon rate is usually expressed as an annual percentage of the par value. For example, an investor holding a $1,000 par value bond with a 6 percent coupon would receive $60 per year in interest payments—plus $1,000 in repayment of principal on the bond's maturity date, of course.

Most bonds pay interest semiannually, so that the owner of this bond would receive a payment of $30 every six months.

The bond in this example is a *fixed rate* bond; its coupon does not change during the life of the bond. In contrast, some bonds, known as *floating rate securities,* have coupon rates that are reset periodically using a formula. An example is a coupon rate adjusted every year to be 2 percent, or 200 basis points, higher than the yield on an interest rate index, such as LIBOR. (The London Interbank Offered Rate is the rate at which banks lend money to each other. It is pronounced "*Lie*-bore.") "The Case of the Missing Coupons" describes a unique type of bond with no coupon at all.

THE CASE OF THE MISSING COUPONS

As the name suggests, *zero coupon bonds* make no periodic coupon payments. Rather, they are issued at a discount, meaning at a price below par value, with their return coming solely from the change in price from the issue date until maturity. For example, a five-year zero coupon bond with a par value of $1,000 might be issued at a price of 80 or $800. While not providing any periodic interest payments, the bond should increase in value roughly $40 per year until maturity in five years, when it repays the par value of $1,000.

The tax treatment of zero coupon bonds deserves special mention. Because there are no coupon payments, an investor might suppose that the return from the change in price would be treated as a capital gain and taxed at potentially favorable capital gains rates. Unfortunately, it doesn't work that way. The IRS considers the expected annual increase in value—called the *accretion*—to be ordinary income each year. Therefore, the holder of a zero coupon bond, while receiving no annual cash interest payments, is still liable for taxes on the yearly accretion. For this reason, zero coupon bonds are best held in tax-deferred accounts, such as individual retirement accounts.

Maturity date. The maturity date is the day on which the bond comes due, when the issuer is required to repay investors the par value, or principal amount. Most bonds have a maturity date within 30 years of their issue date. There are rare exceptions to this general rule, including *century bonds* with

100-year maturity dates, as well as *perpetual bonds* with no set maturity date at all.

Bonds with one to five years remaining to the maturity are considered short-term, while long-term bonds have more than 12 years left to maturity. Those with maturities falling between 5 and 12 years are known as intermediate-term bonds. Bonds with maturities of from 1 to 10 years are often referred to as *notes.*

Option features. Many bonds contain features that give special rights to either the issuer or the investors that can alter their risk and return patterns significantly. Two types of options that are often imbedded in bonds are call and put features. The term *imbedded* simply means that the bond was issued with the option included.

Call provisions allow the issuer to redeem, or *call,* the bond and pay off bondholders before the final maturity date. This is by far the most common form of option included with bonds. Most homeowners are familiar with call provisions, since residential mortgages usually include them—in the form of a right to pay back all or part the loan at any time. Repayment is normally required when houses are sold, but homeowners also have to option to prepay when they can save some money by refinancing at a lower interest rate.

Like homeowners, companies and governments often want to take advantage of lower interest rates to lower their costs. To do this, they often include call provisions in the bonds they issue to enable them to retire higher-coupon bonds. They may fund the repurchase by issuing new bonds at a lower interest rate. Investors who buy bonds with call provisions understand that they are granting a valuable right to the issuer and want to be compensated for it. As a result, callable bonds generally have higher coupons than similar noncallable bonds.

Alternatively, *put provisions* place the power in the hands of the bondholders, giving them the right to sell their securities back to the issuer. Bond owners will often exercise their option if interest rates rise and other bonds then appear more attractive. The benefit here is to the investor, with the result that bonds with put options are usually issued with lower coupons than other bonds without those features. "Exercising Options" illustrates how option provisions work in practice.

There is a third type of option feature called a *conversion feature,* which allows investors to exchange bonds for shares of stock when prescribed conditions are met. Bonds with these features are called *convertible securities.* The conversion feature can be quite valuable, particularly if the stock price rises substantially, so convertible bonds often have much lower coupon rates than bonds without conversion features. Smaller or higher-risk companies are more likely to issue convertible bonds.

EXERCISING OPTIONS

When do bond options get used? (The technical term is *exercised*.) Let's take a look at a hypothetical bond, issued by Windy Corner Corporation, with a call feature. Here are the bond's vital statistics, as set forth in the prospectus at the time it was issued:

- Coupon = 7 percent
- Years to Maturity = 10
- Par Value = $1,000 = price of 100
- Callable no sooner than two years after issuance at a price of 107 (or 107 percent of par value)

Now we'll assume that it's three years after the bond was issued. Times have been very good indeed. The economy has done well, so Windy Corner is in great financial shape, and interest rates have fallen along with inflation. In this favorable environment, the bonds have increased in value, and are now trading at a price of 110. Management decides to exercise its option and call the bonds, paying the investors the stipulated price of 107. Maybe the company no longer needs the money, or it may plan to issue new bonds with a lower coupon rate. (We explain why the rate will be lower when we discuss the price and yield relationship in a bit.)

Now let's assume that instead of a call provision, the Windy Corner bonds have been issued with a put feature that allows investors to sell them back to the company at a price of 90 no sooner than two years after issuance. We'll also assume that—rather than being a boom time for Windy Corner—the last three years haven't been good at all. The economy has been in a recession, and the company just lost a major contract from a customer who can no longer afford its products. The price of the bonds plunges to 85, so bondholders *put* their bonds back to the company, requiring that Windy Corner redeem them at a price of 90 per bond.

A critical question: In this difficult environment, will the company have the money to buy the bonds back? It's not a sure thing. While put options are designed to reduce an investor's risk, they work only if the issuer has the financial strength to honor the put.

KEY ANALYTICAL MEASURES

Investors compare bonds using a number of measures. The most-used ones are: current yield, yield to maturity, option-adjusted yield, yield spread, and duration.

Current yield. Current yield, also called the *coupon rate,* equals the annual interest or coupon payments divided by the bond's market price. For example, a 5 percent coupon bond priced at 90 has a current yield of 5.6 percent, which equals 5 divided by 90. Simple to compute, perhaps, but simplicity comes at an analytical cost. Current yield captures only one source of a bond's return—its coupon payments—and ignores others, such as expected changes in price. For a more holistic view of a bond's value, a broader metric is needed.

Yield to maturity. Yield to maturity is the most often quoted yield measure. Generally, when the yield of a bond is cited, it is the YTM that is being referenced. YTM captures the value of current yield plus the expected change in price. Going back to our hypothetical bond, assuming that it has a par value of $1,000 and five years to maturity, its YTM is 7.5 percent. This figure captures the current yield of 5.6 percent plus the value of receiving $100 more than the price paid when the bond matures. (Remember that price is expressed as a percentage of par value. So this bond with a price of 90 will cost $900. It will be redeemed for $1,000 upon maturity.) Several easy-to-use YTM calculators are available online, but if you want to understand how they work, we've provided a detailed explanation of the YTM calculation on this book's web site. The "Price/Yield Relationship" describes how the price of a bond and its YTM are inversely correlated.

THE PRICE/YIELD RELATIONSHIP

The most basic principle of bond behavior is that the price of a bond and its YTM are inversely related. If the YTM on a bond increases, its price must fall, and if its YTM falls, its price must rise.

For example, let's look at a 5 percent fixed-rate coupon, 10-year bond selling at a price of 100. The YTM of this bond is 5 percent. Now let's assume that interest rates drop to 4 percent on similar bonds. Because our bond has a 5 percent yield—when rates on other bonds are only 4 percent—investors are naturally willing to pay more than par value for it. In fact, the price on the bond will increase until the

YTM on the bond falls to 4 percent. On the other hand, if interest rates rise to 6 percent, our bond's coupon will look paltry compared to alternatives; investors will respond by selling this bond to buy more attractive ones, and our bond's price will fall.

To repeat, the price of a bond and its yield always move in opposite directions. If a bond's yield rises, its price will fall; if the yield falls, its price rises. Figure 6A.1 shows this relationship graphically.

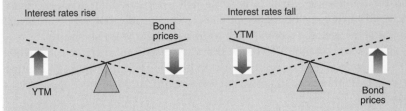

FIGURE 6A.1   The Price/Yield Relationship

How much will a bond's price rise or fall when interest rates change? The answer depends partly on the maturity of the bond. Bonds with longer maturities generally have larger price changes for the same change in the level of interest rates. In the case of the bond in our example, if interest rates fall to 4 percent, there would be a great deal of value in receiving a 5 percent coupon for 10 years, especially when everyone else is earning less. As a result, buyers will pay considerably more for this bond, so its price will move up significantly. But if our bond were to mature tomorrow rather than 10 years from now, buyers wouldn't be willing to pay much for a 5 percent coupon that will last for just one day, so there is a minimal price change. Although maturity gives us a rough idea of the volatility of the price/yield relationship, we'll need other tools, such as duration, to estimate it more precisely.

The calculation for YTM uses several key assumptions:

- The bond is valued at the current market price.
- The bond is held until maturity when it is redeemed at par value. We discuss situations when this doesn't happen later in the appendix.

- All coupon interest payments are made by the issuer. Again, this may not occur, as we'll discuss.
- Those coupon payments are reinvested by the bondholder in investments that earn a rate equal to the YTM.

This last assumption makes the calculation a bit circular, since it presumes that the coupon payments are reinvested at the YTM—the rate that is being calculated. However, it's a critical simplifying assumption, making it possible to compare bonds on an apples-to-apples basis. Note that the yield the bondholder earns in practice will probably differ from the theoretical YTM; it may be higher or lower, varying directly with the actual reinvestment rate. We'll come back to this reinvestment risk shortly.

On the other hand, YTM falls short as a useful measure of value when there are options (call or put options) imbedded with the bond. To capture the value of imbedded options, an even more sophisticated approach is required.

Option-adjusted yield. The option-adjusted yield is the YTM adjusted for the estimated value of the imbedded call or put option, if any. This value is calculated using a mathematical formula, or model, that takes into account the probability that it will be exercised. The best-known option-pricing model is the Black-Scholes model.

Yield spread. The yield spread of a bond is its YTM minus the YTM of a benchmark bond. Since the benchmark bonds used generally have little or no credit risk, the yield spread equals the compensation that investors require for taking on that risk. (We define *credit risk* shortly.). In the taxable market, the benchmark bond is most often a U.S. Treasury of similar maturity. In the tax-exempt market, the benchmark yield curve is usually the AAA-rated municipal scale, which is made up of the highest quality state-issued general obligation bonds.

Benchmark bonds of varying maturities are often displayed in a graph called a *yield curve,* with YTM on the y-axis and time to maturity (in years) on the x-axis. (There's an example in Figure 6A.2.) In most economic environments, longer maturity securities have higher yields; their higher projected returns compensate investors for lending money for longer periods of time. As a result, the yield curve is said to be normally *upward sloping.* A continuous curve fills in the gaps between specific issues, making it possible to compute a yield spread for almost any bond in the market.

As an example of how bonds are evaluated relative to the yield curve, let's look at a hypothetical Windy Corner bond. This 10-year corporate bond has a YTM of 6.0 percent, while the 10-year Treasury has a 5.0 percent YTM. That means that the Windy Corner bond has a yield spread of 100

FIGURE 6A.2   Hypothetical U.S. Treasury Yield Curve
Yields for U.S. Treasury Bonds of Different Maturities.

basis points, equal to its 6.0 percent yield minus the corresponding Treasury yield of 5.0 percent. If the yield of Windy Corner bonds increases while the corresponding U.S. Treasury yield remains the same, the yield spread is said to widen. Conversely, if the yield on Windy Corner bonds decreases in relation to the corresponding Treasury yield, the yield spread narrows, or tightens. A widening yield spread generally indicates that investors believe that risk has increased for that bond, while a narrowing yield spread points to lower risk. (More on the riskiness of bonds in a moment.)

Duration. Duration is an estimate of how much a bond's price will change if its yield increases or decreases by a small amount. (This measure is often referred to as *modified duration.*) For example, the Windy Corner bond has a duration of 7.66. Therefore, if interest rates fell by 1 percent, the bond's price should rise by about 7.66 percent, which equals 1 percent times 7.66. Similarly, if yields rose by 50 basis points, then the price would be expected to fall 3.83 percent, or 7.66 times .5 percent.

In essence, duration is the average amount of time it takes to receive all of the payments from the bond—the coupon payments plus the repayment of principal at maturity. These payments are weighted by their present value. Simply put, a payment made to an investor today is worth more than a payment made in the future. That's because the payment made today can be invested to earn a return. The present value calculation adjusts for this future earnings stream.

Since the repayment of principal is usually the largest payment, it gets the biggest weight in the duration calculation. Therefore, time to maturity generally has the biggest influence on duration. Not surprisingly then, the longer a bond's maturity, the higher or longer its duration.

Coupon rate also plays a role. The higher a bond's coupon rate, the lower or shorter its duration; conversely, a lower coupon rate leads to a longer duration. That's because the holders of bonds with high coupon rates receive more cash sooner from their investments than do owners of low-coupon bonds. A zero coupon bond, which provides no cash payments before maturity, has a duration equal to its time to maturity.

In sum, the higher a bond's duration, the longer it takes for investors in that bond to get paid in cash. That makes bonds with higher durations riskier than those with lower durations. (Getting cash sooner is always safer than waiting longer to receive it.) In particular, if interest rates rise, investors in high-duration bonds won't be able to take advantage of those increased rates because their cash is tied up. In comparison, owners of lower-duration bonds have more cash to put to work in higher-yielding investments. Therefore, when interest rates change, the prices of higher-duration bonds are much more affected than those of lower-duration bonds.

Figure 6A.3 provides a snapshot of how coupon and principal payments are factored into the duration, and we include a detailed explanation of the calculation on this book's web site. Duration calculators can also be found online.

As with YTM, duration needs to be recalibrated whenever options are present. If a bond includes a call feature, it may be called before its final maturity, shortening its expected life. Option-adjusted duration accounts for this reduction in the expected final maturity.

RISKS OF BOND INVESTMENTS

Like all investments, bonds carry their own special set of risks. These risks can be divided into six major categories: market, reinvestment rate, credit, call, liquidity, and event risk.

Market or interest rate risk. Market or interest rate risk is by far the largest single risk assumed by bond investors. Market risk is the risk that bond prices fall because interest rates are rising as a result of changing economic conditions. (Remember that inverse relationship between price and yield!)

Reinvestment rate risk. Bond investors also bear the risk that they will not be able to reinvest coupon payments at the YTM. Remember that the YTM contains some circular logic: it assumes that coupon payments received are invested to earn a return equal to YTM. Although this simplification makes it possible to compare bonds with different prices and coupons, it's not very realistic. Interest rates are more likely to vary considerably during the life of a bond, meaning that coupon payments will be reinvested

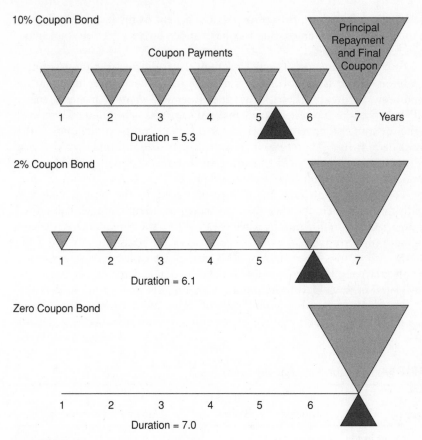

FIGURE 6A.3 Duration at a Glance[12]

at varying rates of return and not necessarily at the YTM. That can be a problem if interest rates fall, since in that circumstance the interest on interest earned from the reinvestment of coupon payments will be less than that projected by the original YTM calculation. As a result, the bond's actual return will end up being less than the expected return, meaning the YTM as originally calculated. A bond with a long time to maturity and a high coupon rate is most sensitive to reinvestment risk.

Reinvestment rate risk acts in the opposite direction to market risk. To illustrate how this works, we'll assume that interest rates are declining. As we've learned, falling rates will boost a bond's price, thereby increasing its total return. But at the same time, a fall in rates will also reduce the return on the reinvestment of the bond's coupons over the long term. That reduces the bond's total return, offsetting part the benefit of the higher bond price. In most cases, however, market risk has a much larger effect on total return than reinvestment risk.

Credit or default risk. Credit or default risk is the threat that the financial condition of the issuer of a bond deteriorates. The weaker the financial condition, the greater the risk that the issuer will *default,* meaning that it will fail to make interest or principal payments as scheduled. Bonds with higher default risk have higher yield spreads than comparable bonds with a lower default risk. Therefore, if credit risk increases, a bond's yield spread will increase; a higher yield spread, in turn, leads to a higher YTM for the bond, which will result in a lower bond price.

To assess default risk, many investors refer to the ratings issued by credit rating agencies, which are represented as a letter grade. Table 6A.1 summarizes the major ratings categories used by the three largest agencies. Ratings range from AAA—the strongest—to D, for bonds already in default. Bonds with ratings from AAA to BBB ratings are called *investment grade,* with a relatively low probability of default. Bonds rated BB or below are considered *high-yield,* or *junk* bonds, with a higher probability of default.

There are gradations within each of these major categories. Agencies may add a plus (+) or a minus (–) to a rating to indicate whether a credit is

TABLE 6A.1 Major Bond Ratings Categories

Fitch	Moody's	Standard & Poor's	Summary Description[13]
Investment grade			
AAA (Triple A)	Aaa	AAA	Highest quality
AA (Double A)	Aa	AA	Very low credit risk
A (Single A)	A	A	Low default risk
BBB (Triple B)	Baa	BBB	Low default risk but vulnerable to adverse conditions
Noninvestment grade, or *junk*, bonds			
BB (Double B)	Ba	BB	Faces higher level of uncertainty
B (Single B)	B	B	Able to meet obligations, but high default risk
CCC	Caa	CCC	Reasonable possibility of default
CC	Ca	CC	High possibility of default
D	C	D	In default

toward the top or the bottom of a category. Also, issuers may be placed on a *credit watch* for an upgrade or downgrade, giving investors some sense of future rating prospects for an issuer's bonds.

Call risk. If a bond has a call option feature, there is a risk that it will be redeemed, or called, prior to the stated maturity date. As we've seen, issuers are most likely to call bonds after interest rates have fallen. That creates problems for bondholders, because they'll need to reinvest cash just when other investments have become less attractive because of their lower yields.

Liquidity risk. Investors face liquidity risk if there's a chance that they will be unable to sell a bond when they want to raise cash. *Liquidity* describes how well a bond trades. A *liquid* bond can normally be bought and sold easily; an *illiquid* bond cannot. The liquidity of a particular bond is determined by its credit quality and the size of the issue—in terms of the number of bonds issued—among other factors. Larger issues, for example, often enjoy better liquidity than smaller issues.

Event risk. Events such as buyouts, corporate restructuring, natural disasters, or acts of war can have a significant adverse effect on bond values. By its nature, event risk is hard to predict with any accuracy, but it always lurks in the background.

CHAPTER 7

Portfolio Management of Money Market Funds

Money market mutual funds have become an essential cash management tool for both institutions and individuals. They were created in the 1970s for investors disappointed with the yields available on bank savings accounts, which at the time were limited by federal regulation.[1] Through money market funds, those investors could pool their funds together to buy higher-yielding short-term alternatives that were then generally available only in very large denominations. Money market funds quickly became a staple investment for both individuals and businesses. By the end of 2009, their assets topped $3 trillion, equal to roughly 30 percent of total fund industry assets.

While the benefits of owning a money fund have always been clear, the risks have been less so. Investors don't expect to take a loss on shares of a money market fund. They anticipate instead that every dollar put into the fund will be returned, plus interest. That's a reasonable expectation, because money market funds are designed to maintain a NAV of $1.00 per share. While the NAV of other types of mutual funds fluctuate daily, the NAV of money funds stays steady—usually, that is.

As investors learned to their shock in the 2008 credit crisis, the NAV of money market funds can indeed fall below $1.00—meaning that investors do bear a risk of loss, however small. This chapter explores the inner workings of money market mutual funds: how they maintain a steady NAV and the risks to that stability.

This chapter reviews:

- The stable $1.00 NAV and what can go—and has gone—wrong to make that NAV fluctuate
- The types of securities held by money market funds

- The investment process used to manage money market funds
- The role of money funds in the U.S. financial system, particularly during the credit crisis of 2008

Note: Before you read on, please note that we assume throughout this discussion that you are familiar with fixed income terminology. If that's not the case, you might want to turn first to the appendix to Chapter 6, which reviews bond basics. Both bonds and money market instruments are types of fixed income investments and, therefore, share the same fundamental characteristics.

HOW—EXACTLY—THE $1.00 NAV WORKS

At the end of each business day, money market funds, like all other mutual funds, must calculate and publish a NAV that equals the aggregate value of all of their holdings minus any liabilities. For all funds other than money funds, this NAV reflects the market value of the securities held in the fund.

But money market funds are different. If they meet certain tests, as set out in the SEC's Rule 2a-7, they can use the *amortized cost* accounting method to compute their reported NAV.[2] This method allows them to reflect the price paid for the security—rather than its current market value—in the NAV calculation.[3] No other mutual funds use this method.

Why is this treatment fair? Why don't money funds have to report a market value NAV? Because the securities in money market funds are of very high quality and have only a very short time to maturity. As a result, the odds are very high that investors will get their money back when the securities come due and that their values won't vary much between now and then. That means that the movements in the fund's NAV will be small—usually less than $0.005 or one-half cent per share. In fact, these fluctuations are immaterial enough that it's reasonable for the fund to keep the NAV at $1.00, a valuable convenience for investors. But that's true only if the fund sticks to high quality short-term investments.

Here's where Rule 2a-7 comes in. It keeps money market funds on the straight and narrow, by setting out detailed rules for money market portfolios—all designed to keep the NAV variation minimal. But it's important to note that it's not just Rule 2a-7 that keeps money fund management very conservative. Fund sponsors also want to make sure that they meet shareholders' expectations—and they definitely don't want to be called upon to provide financial support to their money funds, which could be the case if the NAV drops significantly. (We explain in a moment when that is likely to happen.)

Rule 2a-7 contains requirements for money funds in four areas: maturity, credit quality, diversification, and liquidity.

1. *Maturity.* The longest maturity of the securities held by money funds is limited to approximately one year. (Technically, the limit is 397 days, based on the market practice of issuing one-year securities with an initial maturity that is slightly longer than a year.) That may not seem like a long time, but one-year maturity instruments can experience a big swing in price with a large shift in the level of interest rates.

    If a money market fund put all of its assets into one-year securities, its NAV would be volatile—which is why 2a-7 also places a limit on the average maturity of the fund. Specifically, the weighted average maturity of all the securities held by a money fund may not exceed 60 days. If a fund holds longer maturity investments, they must be balanced with shorter maturities.

2. *Credit quality.* Credit quality is of paramount importance to a money market fund since the default of a security can be catastrophic, as we'll see. Rule 2a-7 states that money market investments must be of high quality, representing minimal credit risk. As of June 2010, it defines these as securities receiving ratings from the major credit rating agencies that place them in one of the top two short-term categories, or *tiers.* At least 97 percent of the fund's assets must be invested in securities in the top tier, the one that theoretically carries the least credit risk; the other 3 percent of assets may be invested in money market securities in the second tier. Table 7.1 shows the three highest ratings tiers for short-term taxable securities for the major credit rating agencies.

    The SEC is under pressure to establish quality standards for money market funds that do not refer to credit agency ratings. This should not

TABLE 7.1 Major Taxable Money Market Securities Ratings Categories

Fitch	Moody's	Standard & Poor's	Corresponding Long-Term Rating
F1	P-1	A-1	A or better
F2	P-2	A-2	BBB+ or A
F3	P-3	A-3	BBB

result in a significant change for most management companies, however, since Rule 2a-7 already requires that fund managers carry out independent credit analysis to verify that a proposed investment poses minimal credit risk. Under 2a-7, managers have never been able to rely solely on the opinion of third parties when judging credit quality.[4]

3. *Diversification.* Rule 2a-7 also places restrictions on a fund's exposure to the securities of nongovernment issuers. Specifically, money funds may not invest more than 5 percent of their assets in issuers in the top tier. If the issuer is rated in the second-highest category, the limit drops to 0.5 percent of assets per issuer. While Rule 2a-7 provides an upper bound, most management companies actually have tighter internal guidelines.

4. *Liquidity.* Money funds must be prepared to meet all shareholder redemptions without selling securities at a loss. (If a fund frequently locks in losses through sales, it violates the crucial operating assumption that it will usually get back what it paid for the securities it owns.) To make sure that money market funds will always have enough cash on hand, Rule 2a-7 requires that at least 10 percent of assets be *liquid* instruments with daily availability and that at least 30 percent of the fund be held in liquid instruments with weekly availability. (See "Trading Like Water" for definitions of these terms.)

TRADING LIKE WATER

Liquid instruments are securities that can be readily turned into cash in virtually any market environment. The SEC defines instruments with daily liquidity as:

- Cash, meaning investments with a maturity of one day
- U.S. Treasury securities of any maturity
- Certain other government securities with maturities under 60 days

For weekly liquidity, the SEC takes the preceding list and adds any security with a maturity within five days or that has a contractual provision that ensures that it can be sold in the same period.[5]

At the other end of the liquidity spectrum, Rule 2a-7 requires that no more than 5 percent of the fund be invested in *illiquid* securities, meaning securities that may take more than a week to sell at close to the current price. This 5 percent limit is much lower than the 15 percent limit applied to illiquid securities held in stock and bond funds.

Funds that pass all these tests may use amortized cost accounting to report a stable $1.00 NAV to the public.

Rule 2a-7 has another provision, however. Behind the scenes, funds must compute a daily NAV using market prices to value securities, rather than amortized cost. This market-value NAV is known as the *shadow price*. Funds must regularly compare the shadow price to the $1.00 NAV and report the difference to the fund's board of directors.

If the difference is under $0.005, the board will generally do nothing. That's because, even using market prices for securities, rounding keeps the NAV at $1.00. But if the difference is $0.005 or more, the board may need to take action.

- If the shadow NAV is higher than $1.04, no drastic action is required. The board will ask the fund manager to sell securities to generate realized capital gains and then distribute those gains to shareholders as part of the daily dividend. This is a very unlikely scenario, however, since money market securities rarely produce capital gains. Money funds also declare distributions daily, partly to prevent interest income from accumulating and drive the NAV above $1.00.
- But if the shadow NAV falls below $0.995, the board may decide to stop using amortized cost accounting and switch to a market value NAV calculation. At that point, the fund's reported NAV will fall below $1.00 per share, thereby *breaking the buck*.

    Why take this drastic action? Because fund directors want to en-sure that all shareholders are being treated fairly. If they don't lower the NAV, shareholders who are redeeming from the fund will reap a windfall—getting $1.00 for shares that are worth less—a bonanza that's paid for by the remaining shareholders. The pricing discrepancy could even encourage redemptions by savvy shareholders, creating a run on the fund. To prevent this, the board may suspend redemptions so that the fund can be liquidated in an orderly manner. This is the only time that a mutual fund can cut off redemptions without specific SEC approval.

Management companies can prevent funds from breaking the buck by stepping in to make good on the losses that caused the fund value to drop. The fund industry has been willing to provide this type of help when needed, because it wants consumers to continue to view money market funds as se-cure investments. Many fund sponsors provided that support in 1994, when

Orange County, California, surprised investors by declaring bankruptcy. Many California tax-exempt funds had large positions in its securities, and their shadow NAVs dropped below $0.995. Fund management companies stepped in and either bought the securities at amortized cost or guaranteed their value.

A crucial caveat: fund sponsors are not required to provide this support; they do so only voluntarily. They may not want—or even be able—to help

SECOND TIME UNLUCKY

The first time a money market fund broke the buck was in 1994, when the Denver-based Community Banker's U.S. Government Money Market Fund reported a NAV of $0.96. It had the misfortune of owning securities that fell sharply in value during the rapid rise in interest rates that year. Because this was a small fund held by a small number of institutional shareholders, the impact was limited.

It wasn't until the credit crisis of 2008 hit that a fund broke the buck in a dramatic way. This was the Reserve Primary Fund—the first money market fund in the United States. The Primary Fund was a $60 billion institutional money fund, open only to large investors.

Some of those shareholders kept a close watch on the Fund's holdings and noticed a large position in broker Lehman Brothers. These investors—sensing that the brokerage firm might be in trouble—decided to take their money out of the fund. To meet their redemption requests, the fund sold other securities—with the unfortunate result that the problematic Lehman securities became an ever-larger portion of the remaining assets.

As a consequence, when Lehman declared bankruptcy on September 15, 2008, the fund was hard hit, and the following day, the Primary Fund's board dropped the NAV to $0.97 per share. At the time, the fund needed permission from the SEC to suspend redemptions, which it received. It then eventually returned the balance of its assets to the remaining shareholders—amid a flood of lawsuits.

So ended the life of the first money market fund in the United States. The incident accelerated the credit crisis and prompted the federal government to provide support for all money funds. We discuss the consequences of the Reserve Fund collapse in more detail in the last section of this chapter.

out a fund if losses are large and permanent. In the Orange County case, as in the SIV example we discuss shortly, the problem securities had significant underlying value and eventually recovered. As a result, the ultimate cost to the management companies was modest.

This financial support from management companies—combined with conservative money fund portfolio management policies—has made breaking the buck an extremely rare event. In fact, it has only happened twice. "Second Time Unlucky" reviews those two occasions.

Fund boards of directors have unique duties when it comes to money market funds—duties that apply only to money funds and not to other types of mutual funds. In addition to checking the portfolio's shadow pricing and taking action if it drops significantly, the board must:

- Monitor credit quality and confirm that the fund manager's research practices are rigorous. Directors will usually be informed of credit downgrades in the portfolio.
- Review the policies and procedures that the fund manager uses to assure compliance with Rule 2a-7.
- Oversee *stress tests* that gauge the fund's ability to maintain a $1.00 NAV should interest rates rise, yield spreads widen, shareholder redemptions surge, or issuers default. These are all scenarios that could cause a fund to break the buck.

MONEY MARKET FUND HOLDINGS

Money market funds are divided into two major segments: taxable and tax-exempt. While both types of money funds invest in high quality, short-term instruments, there are significant differences in the types of securities they own.

Holdings in Taxable Funds

As we reviewed in Chapter 4, within taxable money market funds, there are three subcategories, each with a different set of permitted investments:

1. *U.S. Treasury funds* invest in U.S. Treasury securities only.
2. *U.S. government funds* invest in federal agency securities in addition to U.S. Treasuries.

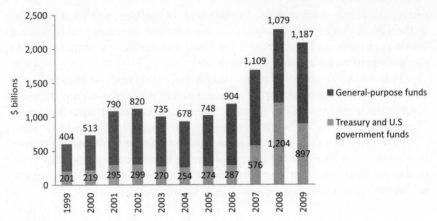

FIGURE 7.1 Institutional Money Market Fund Assets
Source: Investment Company Institute, *2010 Investment Company Fact Book.*

3. *General purpose funds* can hold a wide range of securities, and they often have exposure to all of the major taxable categories. Their predominant exposure is normally in commercial paper and certificates of deposits issued by banks or corporations.

Figure 7.1 shows the assets in Treasury and government funds as compared to general purpose funds since 1999 (looking at institutional money funds only). Because of their higher yield, general-purpose funds are normally more popular, though Treasury and government fund assets tend to spike up during times of turmoil, as during the credit crisis.

Taxable money market funds invest in the following types of securities:
Treasury securities. The U.S. Treasury has become the largest issuer of money market securities. It uses the proceeds from their sale to fund the U.S. budget deficit and to meet short-term imbalances between cash receipts and disbursements. While the U.S. Treasury securities have maturities out to 30 years, those attractive to money market funds are known as Treasury bills. T-bills are normally issued with maturities of 13, 26, and 52 weeks. They do not pay interest through coupon payments; instead T-bills are zero coupon securities that are sold at a discount to par value and reach par at maturity.

Because they are backed by the full faith and credit of the U.S. government, most investors consider T-bills to be credit risk-free. Their value will still fluctuate with interest rates, however. For example, a 52-week T-bill will rise and fall approximately 1 percent with a 1 percent change in interest rates. (Note that maturity and duration are roughly equal for short-term securities.)

Agency securities. Agency securities are the obligations of federal government agencies or government-sponsored enterprises. Generally, agency debt offers a slight yield premium over T-bills. Turn back to Chapter 6 for more on agency securities.

Commercial paper. Commercial paper, or CP, is issued by corporations (including banks) to finance short-term cash needs. While smaller corporations usually depend on bank loans for this type of funding, larger corporations with good credit ratings can access the CP market and often do so. By raising money from investors directly rather than from a bank, these companies can lower their borrowing costs.

CP is normally issued with maturities of 270 days or less, though most CP has maturities of 90 days or under. Yields vary with maturity and credit quality, but CP normally offers a higher yield than Treasuries or agencies. Because CP has such a short maturity, the companies that issue it are almost constantly raising money in the market, rolling over or replacing CP that has just matured, as part of a commercial paper program.

Since the CP market is generally open only to issuers with strong credit ratings, there have been few defaults over the years—but there have been some. As a result, credit analysis is important in this area, to identify problems early. "And the Little One Said, 'Roll Over' " describes a recent problem in the CP market.

AND THE LITTLE ONE SAID, "ROLL OVER"

Not all commercial paper is issued by large corporations. For a time, CP issued by a *specialty investment vehicle* was all the rage. A SIV is a type of issuer of an asset-backed security. (See Chapter 6 for an introduction to this class of investments.) The SIV owns longer-term bonds with higher yields, then issues CP with a lower yield backed by the value of the bond portfolio.

When they were first created in the 1990s, SIVs seemed to be a good deal for everyone. They were certainly a good deal for the sponsor of the SIV, which kept the bulk of the difference in yield as income. But they also seemed to be a good deal for the money market funds buying the CP, which thought they had found a way to enhance yield without taking significant risk. Rating agencies were convinced that the SIV model—which had worked well so far—would continue to work. In consequence, they published very high ratings for the CP issued by many SIVs.

Not everyone agreed with the rating agencies, however. Some money market analysts found that SIVs were too risky. Their big concern was the need to roll over or replace the CP every time it matured. (Remember that the CP had a much shorter maturity than the securities held in the SIV.) In other words, SIVs were dependent on the market for continued financing. If market participants didn't buy the next CP issue, the SIV would be in trouble.

While most analysts recognized the risks, many chose to focus instead on the value of the investment portfolio. They believed the SIV could easily sell those assets if CP funding became unavailable. This line of logic gave them a comfort level with SIVs that, in combination with attractive yields, caused explosive growth in the sector. By 2007, assets in SIVs had grown to approximately $400 billion.

This comfortable arrangement came to an end when the housing market collapse raised concerns about the quality of all asset-backed investments, including securities issued by SIVs. Money market funds soon stopped buying their CP. And then the doomsday scenario struck: when SIVs attempted sell a large part of their portfolio holdings to pay off the CP when it matured, they found that they couldn't.

Money market funds had to mark down the prices on any SIV-issued CP that they still owned, in the process threatening to break the buck. To keep that from happening, a number of fund sponsors provided support for the value of the SIV-issued CP.

Certificates of deposit. Money market funds also make deposits in banks through certificates of deposit. A CD, as the name implies, is a certificate that identifies a deposit with a specific banking institution, stating a maturity date and an interest rate. Certificates with banking institutions outside the United States—but still denominated in U.S. dollars—are known as Eurodollar CDs, or just Eurodollar deposits. CDs carry the federal deposit insurance provided by the FDIC, but because that insurance is capped at $250,000, it's of little value to a large money market fund.[6] As a result, good credit analysis of the bank issuing the CD is critical to avoid defaults.

Repurchase agreements. Repurchase agreements, or *repos,* enable broker-dealers to finance the huge blocks of securities that they hold as part of their business. These securities are used as collateral for a repo loan.

While almost any type of security can be used in a repo, funds prefer to have U.S. Treasury or other government obligations as the collateral for most of their transactions. For added security, the collateral must equal at least 102 percent of the loan amount.[7]

The transaction is called a *repurchase agreement* because the securities are actually sold to the lender or investor at the beginning of the period of the loan; the borrower agrees to repurchase the securities at the end of the loan term, usually at the same price. (That's different from a typical secured loan; for those loans, the collateral is simply set aside in a separate account and is transferred to the lender only if the borrower fails to fulfill its obligations under the agreement.) To be absolutely precise, the borrower (the seller of the securities) is actually doing the repo, and the buyer—a money market fund, for example—is engaging in a *reverse repo*. However, the term *repo* is often used for both sides of the transaction.

In a repo, the buyer is not interested in owning the securities for any length of time, so most repos have extremely short terms of only up to seven days, and many are just overnight. That makes them perfect for all types of mutual funds, especially money market funds, which have cash on hand to invest for a day or a week.

Holdings in Tax-Exempt Funds

The tax-exempt money market is more complex than the taxable money market. That's largely because of a supply-and-demand imbalance for very short-term municipal securities. There's a high level of demand for these issues—much of it coming from individuals who want to minimize their tax bill by placing their cash in a tax-exempt money market mutual fund. But supply is limited. States and municipalities generally prefer to issue longer-term securities, since the money raised is normally used to support long-lived projects such as roads or buildings or ongoing obligations, including the salaries of public employees. To provide a bridge between lenders and borrowers, a large derivatives market that synthetically creates short-term tax-exempt investments has evolved.

Tax-exempt money market funds invest primarily in the following securities:

Municipal notes. Municipal notes are issued by state and local governments with a maturity of one year or less. In some cases, these notes finance a specific project, while others are used to provide short-term cash flow, anticipating the receipt of revenues of some type. For example, a local government that needs money to pay for road construction now but also needs more time to prepare for a bond offering may issue a Bond Anticipation Note. When the bonds are eventually issued, the proceeds are used to pay off the BAN. Similarly, TANs, or Tax Anticipation Notes, provide short-term cash while a local government is waiting for tax revenues to come in. And RANs—the *R* is for *Revenue*—are issued when income from a specific project, such as a sewer facility, is expected in the future. In all of these cases, when the revenues clear, the notes are repaid.

Commercial paper. As in the taxable market, maturities of tax-exempt commercial paper are generally shorter than 270 days—most often 90 days or shorter. In the municipal market, however, CP programs are often backed by a letter of credit from a highly rated bank or insurance company, which guarantees repayment in the event of the default of the issuer. That makes CP more attractive to money market funds, all of which are seeking minimal credit risk.

Variable rate demand notes. Variable rate demand notes, or VRDNs—also known as *variable rate demand obligations,* or *tender option bonds*—represent the vast majority of securities used in tax-exempt money funds. A VRDN has two components:

1. A long-term tax-exempt bond, which may be guaranteed by credit insurance or a letter of credit from a bank.[8] While this is a long-term bond, it pays interest at the rate of a short-term security (which is almost always lower than the rate on a longer-term bond).
2. A short-term put option, or *demand feature,* that allows it to be sold back to the issuer at face value whenever needed. This put is backed by a bank or other financial institution.

This demand feature bridges the gap between borrowers and lenders. It allows governments to issue the long-term bonds they prefer, while making that debt eligible for purchase by money funds that must invest in short-term securities.

Sound like the SIVs we discussed earlier? VRDNs are like SIVs in many respects, but with some key differences. First, there is generally less concern about the credit quality of the bonds in a VRDN than the securities held in a SIV—governments are usually pretty good payers. Second—and most importantly—the credit guarantees and put options in a VRDN are provided by independent, high quality financial institutions, meaning that VRDN holders are not dependent on the issuer's ability to roll over its short-term funding. If the issuer can't find a new buyer, the VRDN may have to be liquidated—but money market investors will have already exercised their puts and been paid.

Despite these advantages, the VRDN market experienced significant volatility during the credit crisis, as investors worried about the health of the financial institutions that provided the crucial guarantees, although the disruption did not reach the level of the SIV crisis. To prevent a recurrence, the SEC has recently adopted news rules that require more disclosure from VRDN issuers.

PUTTING IT ALL TOGETHER: MANAGING A MONEY MARKET FUND

Now that we've reviewed the building blocks for money market funds, it's time to apply what you've learned. Imagine you've been given the task of managing a large multibillion-dollar money market fund. What would you do? Let's give it a try. We'll assume that the fund is a taxable general purpose money market mutual fund.

Your responsibility to investors means that you will to do everything you can to maintain the stable $1.00 NAV and to assure liquidity any time a shareholder wants to withdraw cash—while providing a competitive yield. You have to keep your eye on all of these objectives at the same time.

Research

You'll start by speaking with the analysts and reading their reports. (See the "Career Track" box for insights on the work of the money market credit analyst.) If the fund you're managing ranges beyond U.S. Treasuries, you'll need rigorous research to determine which securities provide minimal credit risk. You'll be investing in them for three to six months or longer and need to be confident that they'll repay the fund at the end of the period. If they fail to do so, the fund may be forced to break the buck and exit the business: an outcome you, your employer, and the shareholders are all keen to avoid.

At the same time, you'll work with the analysts to increase return. That means that you'll concentrate on the creditworthiness of the issuers of both commercial paper and CDs, which offer higher yields. You're probably going to try to buy as many of these issues as possible—assuming that the analysts can verify that the investments are high quality. Your fund has the flexibility to invest in a wide range of securities, and your competitors are doing just that, looking for higher returns.

To keep risk in check, you'll diversify broadly, with position sizes of 1 percent or less of the assets under management. In fact, many portfolio managers will seek to bring the positions to well under 1 percent for even more diversification. You may want to do the same, while recognizing that

CAREER TRACK: MONEY MARKET CREDIT ANALYST

Interested in becoming a money market credit analyst? Your job will be to identify issuers that carry minimal credit risk to the fund, meaning that they have a very high likelihood of repaying the fund when their securities mature. But within this group of very high quality companies, you'll be making distinctions, evaluating which securities should have a higher yield than others, and how much that yield premium should be.

To do this work, you'll review balance sheets, income statements, business plans, stock prices, and any other indicators of financial wherewithal, with a strong focus on short-term assets and liabilities. You'll look at the rating agency opinions as well as any other third party research. In short, a credit analyst in the money market area completes the same types of analysis as a bond analyst. In many firms, you'll research both bond and money market issuers, though at some larger firms, credit analysts specialize in the needs of the money market funds.

You'll work closely with both the portfolio managers and traders. More than in any other category of mutual fund, money fund portfolio management is a team effort.

you need to strike a balance between improving diversification and spreading the research analysts so thin that they can't be thorough enough in their analysis.

Keep in mind, though, that other market participants are doing this same work and may have come to the same conclusions. Therefore, you'll often find that the best credits in the market may well be the most expensive. The analysts will need to look out for unrecognized value, and you'll need to keep your eye on price trends. The credit opinions from the analysts generally do not change rapidly, but prices often do, which may create a buying opportunity one day.

Trading

Knowing the issuers you want to purchase is only half of the process—you then have to find the paper in the market. That's not always easy. Like bonds, money market securities trade over the counter, so you'll need to do some digging to find out what's available. Because securities in the fund mature almost every day, virtually all of the trading activity will be on the purchasing side. It's a rare day when a money fund sells a security, which usually only happens if a research opinion takes a dramatic turn to the negative—and it's not an easy thing to do in a market that normally does not buy securities back. You may monitor the market yourself, though at larger firms you'll be able to rely on the assistance of the money market trading desk.

The traders on the desk will contact broker-dealers to review their inventory of securities and keep them familiar with the needs of your funds. They'll also be in touch with corporations interested in issuing commercial paper directly to the buyers, without a broker-dealer as an intermediary.

The traders will also help out by monitoring the daily cash needs of the fund. They'll keep on top of which securities will be maturing that day, then add or subtract net shareholder inflows or outflows. (See Chapter 7 for more on trading.)

Portfolio Management

Now that you have a list of attractive securities from the credit analysts and a list of available securities from the traders, you'll need to combine them into a portfolio.

One of your first decisions will be about the maturities you'd like to buy. Remember that Rule 2a-7 limits money market funds to securities with maturities of 397 days or less. If you invest the entire fund at 397 days, you'd almost definitely have the best-yielding fund in the market, but you wouldn't be complying with Rule 2a-7. (Remember the 60-day limit on average maturity!) Moving all the holdings to a 60-day maturity would meet the SEC average maturity requirement, but would make it difficult to handle outflows.

Here's why: if the fund invested all its assets in 60-day paper, and tomorrow your shareholders wanted to withdraw some of their money, you would be forced to sell 59-day securities in what could be a weak market. To prevent this—and comply with Rule 2a-7—you'll need to hold at least a 10 percent cash position. To make sure that you're always in compliance, you'll stagger the maturities of the holdings in the fund, so that some securities are being paid off every day, providing a steady cash flow.

But there's even more to the maturity decision. Part of your role in managing the fund is to determine when it's appropriate to a hold a shorter portfolio—with an average maturity of, say, 30 days—and when extending the maturities is wise—up to maybe 45 or 50 days. That may not sound like a big shift, but there are hundreds of funds competing in this space, and your decision could significantly affect the ranking of the fund in its peer group.

The maturity decision will reflect your view of the direction of short-term interest rates over the coming weeks or months. You'll want a longer average maturity or duration when interest rates are falling and a shorter one when they're rising. A working knowledge of economics will help you sort through the market drivers that determine the direction of interest rates.

Once you've made the maturity decision, determining the optimal mix among U.S. Treasuries, agencies, commercial paper, CDs, and repos is still in front of you. If credit risk is too much of a concern, you can avoid it altogether by investing your general purpose fund entirely in U.S. Treasury bills. You'd have a very safe fund, but one that probably wouldn't be around for long, simply because its yield would be too low to be competitive. You'll talk constantly with research analysts and traders to choose higher-yielding securities that still have the financial health to meet their obligations. The combination will help the fund meet all of its objectives.

After you've figured out a good strategy and asset mix for that day, you'll have to start all over again, because your holdings are moving closer to maturity each day. In other words, your 45-day average maturity will fall to only 38 days in one very short week. The portfolio structure of a money market fund changes rapidly, faster than any other type of fund because of the short-term nature of its holdings. Managing a money market fund is a demanding job that requires the ability to continuously balance competing priorities in an ever-changing environment.

MONEY MARKET FUNDS AND THE FINANCIAL SYSTEM

Many investors use money market funds interchangeably with savings accounts. There are, however, clear distinctions between the two. Let's compare a retail money market fund and a bank deposit:

- *Immediate access to funds.* Provided by both.
- *Payment of competitive market interest rates.* Provided by both, but through different mechanisms. Money market funds provide a direct investment in securities yielding market rates of interest. The rates on bank deposits are set by the bank itself, which takes into consideration both market interest rates and the bank's need for funds.
- *FDIC insurance.* Carried by bank deposits, but only up to $250,000 per account. Balances over that limit are not insured and will likely incur substantial losses if the bank fails. Money market funds, in contrast, carry no guarantee, although they hold a diversified portfolio of high-quality securities to minimize the risk of significant losses.

- *Local convenience.* Banks have a local presence through bricks and mortar branches, while money funds don't. Instead, the convenience of mutual fund investing is derived from the Internet and telephone. But with more banking being done online, there is now less of a distinction between bank deposits and money market fund investments in this regard than there was in the past.
- *Banking services.* Banks have always provided a myriad of services, often bundled with their deposit and savings accounts. Money market funds provide bank-like services of their own, including check writing, bill pay, and other conveniences.[9] Making matters even fuzzier, many banks offer money market funds as an alternative to their traditional deposit accounts.

While the blurring of the lines between banks and mutual funds has generally benefited investors, it has created difficulties for regulators overseeing the financial system. The term *shadow banking* is now used for describing these banklike activities by nonbanks, including money market funds. And these activities are substantial. For example, money funds now manage 30 percent of the short-term assets of U.S. businesses, more than double their share 15 years ago. Figure 7.2 shows the trend.

While the growth of shadow banking has lowered the cost of borrowing, the enormous size of these activities in aggregate can create significant disruption when things go wrong, as happened during the credit crisis of 2008. The U.S. Treasury had actually considered getting involved

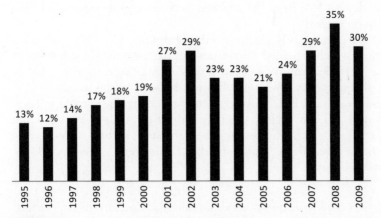

FIGURE 7.2 Money Market Fund Management of U.S. Businesses' Short-Term Assets
Source: Investment Company Institute, *2010 Investment Company Fact Book.*

with money funds during the SIV crisis in mid-2007 which we discussed earlier. While those problems were resolved without government intervention, both the Treasury and the Federal Reserve became acutely aware of the size of money market funds and their importance to the financial system.

It wasn't until after Reserve Primary Fund broke the buck that the government took direct action. In the weeks following that event, over $400 billion was withdrawn from general purpose money funds, principally by institutional investors. (Much of this money was moved to government money market funds.) The market for commercial paper was drying up, cutting off a critical source of funding for major U.S. corporations.

The federal government stepped in with a series of programs to reduce fund redemptions and stabilize the markets. While only the U.S. Treasury's Temporary Guarantee Program was directed specifically at money market funds, each of the programs in the following list played a significant role in alleviating the stress faced by money market funds.

- *September 19.* The U.S. Treasury established the Temporary Guarantee Program, which insured the value on that day of all the shareholder accounts of money market funds that chose to participate in the program. Virtually all funds signed up.
- *October 7.* The Federal Reserve created the Commercial Paper Funding Facility to provide support for issuers of highly rated commercial paper. The facility helped issuers who had been unable to roll over their commercial paper. As large holders of commercial paper, money market funds benefited from the renewed confidence in this segment of the short-term market.
- *November 21.* The FDIC instituted the Temporary Liquidity Guarantee Program, which provided a government guarantee for short-term debt issued by banks, improving their ability to raise money. The value of bank debt in money fund portfolios was boosted by this action.
- *November 25.* The Federal Reserve announced the creation of the Term Asset-Backed Loan Facility to provide relief to the asset-backed securities market, which was perhaps the hardest-hit sector. As owners of asset-backed securities, money market funds were helped by the increased liquidity.

The crisis raised basic questions about the basic structure and operations of money market funds, and in 2009 the SEC initiated a sweeping review of all of its regulation in the area. In the ensuing debate, three options for money market funds were presented:

- *Option 1: Bank-like regulation.* Money market funds could be regulated like banks. Their deposits would be insured with the FDIC, and funds or their management companies would guarantee fund values, holding capital to ensure their ability to support those guarantees.
- *Option 2: Floating NAV.* Money market funds could be treated like other mutual funds and have a floating NAV.
- *Option 3: Tighter restrictions.* Money market funds could continue to operate much as they had been, though maybe with some tighter rules.

As of late 2010, the SEC has so far gone with Option 3. The limit on holdings of illiquid investments was lowered from 10 percent to 5 percent, while 10 percent of a fund is now required to be invested in assets with daily liquidity. Furthermore, the average maturity of money market funds was reduced from 90 to 60 days. But the basic structure of the funds, including the reliance on amortized cost accounting, was left intact.

Yet more dramatic changes are still being considered. Money fund advocates argue that Rule 2a-7 has done a very good job in protecting investors for 30-plus years and that the SEC's recent tightening of restrictions is sufficient. Other industry observers and bank regulators counter that money market funds now pose a systemic risk to the financial system and that a completely different approach is required. The Investment Company Institute is developing the concept of a *liquidity bank*—to be established by the major fund sponsors—that would provide additional liquidity to money market funds in times of severe market disruption. The debate will continue for some time into the future.

CHAPTER SUMMARY

Money market funds may report a stable $1.00 per share NAV if they comply with the provisions of SEC Rule 2a-7. This rule limits their investments to only high quality, short-term fixed income instruments and places restrictions on the maturity, credit quality, diversification, and liquidity of money fund holdings. However, if the value of a money market fund's investments drops sharply, it may be forced to stop using the $1.00 NAV. This is called *breaking the buck,* and it has only happened twice in the history of money market funds. On other occasions when money funds have threatened to break the buck, fund sponsors have stepped in with financial support to enable funds to maintain the $1.00 NAV.

Taxable money market funds invest in Treasury bills, federal agency securities, and commercial paper and certificates of deposit issued by banks and other corporations. They also engage in repurchase, or *repo,* agreements with broker-dealers. The prospectus determines which securities are available to a particular fund.

The primary holdings in most tax-exempt money funds are variable rate demand notes, which are long-term tax-exempt bonds combined with put options that allow them to be sold back to the issuer whenever needed. Tax-exempt money funds also invest in municipal notes and commercial paper, although these are in limited supply.

Credit analysis plays a key role in money market portfolio management, especially for funds investing in commercial paper and certificates of deposit. Portfolio managers must also carefully manage the maturity structure of the fund's holdings to ensure both that cash is always available when shareholders wish to redeem and that the fund's yield is competitive.

Many businesses and individuals use money market funds interchangeably with bank deposits. As a result, money funds have become a critical part of the U.S. financial system, and problems at a few money funds aggravated the recent credit crisis. As a result of the 2008 problems, the SEC has tightened the Rule 2a-7 restrictions on money market fund investments. Regulators and fund sponsors are also considering alternative approaches to money fund operations and oversight.

CHAPTER 8

Implementing Portfolio Decisions: Buying and Selling Investments

F or mutual funds, *trading,* or buying and selling investments, is a critical final step in an integrated investment process that starts with research and carries through to portfolio construction. Here, we discuss how the decisions made in those first two steps are implemented through trading. Our focus is trading in stocks, although at the end of the chapter we outline how fixed income trading compares to equity trading.

Executing buy and sell orders is the province of the trader. Most larger investment managers have a trading division, or *desk,* that is separate from the portfolio management function. (At smaller advisers, portfolio managers may handle their own trading.) This division of labor allows the portfolio managers to concentrate on their primary task of selecting securities and structuring portfolios, normally with a time horizon measured in months or years. That, in turn, enables the traders to focus on the dynamics of the market, to gauge the appropriate day, hour, or even minute for completing a transaction. Separating the trading function from portfolio management has another benefit: it gets a second set of eyes involved in every transaction, which helps to ensure that a fund complies with all regulatory requirements.

The execution of trades is far from a mechanical process. It calls for close collaboration between portfolio managers and trading desks. Decisions on how, where, and when to send in trading orders require careful judgment, long experience, and intimate knowledge of the trading markets. Well-planned trading decisions can contribute significantly to a fund's investment returns.

This chapter reviews:

- The importance of the trading function to investment returns
- The evolution of stock trading in the United States
- The role of the stock trading desk
- Trading in bond funds

THE IMPORTANCE OF TRADING

Trading in either stocks or bonds can have a significant impact on fund performance. One influential academic study done in 1999 found that trading reduced returns in stock funds by almost 0.8 percent per year on average.[1] Fund managers today, with more choices open to them, work hard to push down transaction costs as much as possible, by using sophisticated trading techniques.

Yet, because funds often buy and sell securities in large amounts, they face considerable challenges when they trade, including:

- *Front running.* Other market players might learn about a fund's trading plans before they're fully carried out. If advance information about a fund's intentions becomes known to other traders, those traders can use that information to their advantage and a fund's disadvantage. For example, if traders learn that a fund is trying to acquire a large block of stock when the stock is trading at $10 per share, they might pay up a few cents to purchase the stock at $10.03, on the expectation that the fund will be willing to pay an even higher price to complete its purchase. This is called *front running.*
- *Market impact.* Even when other market participants are unaware of a fund's trading plans, the large size of a fund's purchases and sales alone can move the market in a stock—pushing up the price of a stock a mutual fund is trying to buy and driving down the price of a stock a fund is seeking to sell. This market impact is a particular issue for small cap stocks and other less-liquid securities in thin markets, which are markets with a low volume of trading.
- *Opportunity cost.* But there's another, countervailing risk: a fund that moves too slowly can incur an opportunity cost. It might miss out on a sharp increase in the price of a stock it's trying to buy or watch the price of a stock it's trying to sell tumble after bad news is announced.

A fund trading desk must weigh the relative importance of:

- Obtaining the most favorable price
- Protecting a fund's anonymity
- Obtaining a speedy execution
- Minimizing transaction costs

Trading decisions invariably call for the exercise of judgment in awarding greater weight to one factor over the others—and striking trade-offs when one trading goal must be sacrificed so that a more important one can be achieved. For example, a fund manager might be trying to acquire a substantial position in a thinly traded small cap stock or a less well-known bond. Recognizing the potential for market impact under these circumstances, the trading desk might break up an order and patiently purchase small, incremental amounts over the course of one or more trading days. The traders, in consultation with the portfolio manager, might decide that the need for anonymity trumps the desirability of gaining a speedy execution.

In another case, a fund manager, acting on input from an investment research analyst, might want to quickly sell a substantial position in a stock out of concern that the company will suffer a sharp drop in earnings for the quarter that is coming to a close. Under these circumstances, the trading desk might decide to move quickly, accepting a less attractive price for the entire block of stock. The traders, in the interest of speed, would forego attempts to do better by selling the stock piecemeal over the course of the trading day.

To begin to understand how traders make these types of decisions, we'll need to start by studying the securities markets. We'll be zeroing in on the U.S. stock markets, returning to bond trading only at the end of the chapter.

THE EVOLUTION OF THE U.S. STOCK MARKETS

Stock trading in the United States has been radically transformed by technology in recent years. Innovations in computer systems and high speed data communications have led to a complete change in the way that larger investors buy and sell stocks. As a result of this new technology, trading has spread from traditional venues like the New York Stock Exchange to a variety of trading centers as securities markets have become more electronic. This radical change in market structure has taken place within the context of dramatically increasing trading activity. On the NYSE alone, average daily stock trading volume rose from 2.1 billion shares in 2005 to about 5.9 billion shares in the first part of 2009, a growth rate of almost 30 percent per year.[2]

In this section, we take a closer look at how the U.S. stock markets have evolved. We first describe the traditional market structure, centered on the NYSE and NASDAQ, and then turn to the new entrants. Finally, we examine how the old and the new are converging.

The Traditional Venues

Until very recently, there were two principal ways to trade stocks in the United States: on the floor of the New York Stock Exchange or *over the counter* on the NASDAQ exchange, both operating within the national market system.

New York Stock Exchange. For over a century, the NYSE (pronounced by spelling out each of its four letters) was synonymous with the financial business. Its location on Wall Street even gave the securities industry its nickname. Most major U.S. corporations *listed* on the NYSE, meaning that they made their stock available for trading there. In exchange for the privilege of inclusion on the exchange's roster, they agreed to adhere to certain standards regarding their financial condition and internal policies. In 2005, 85 percent of the trading in the shares of companies listed on the NYSE took place there.

Until very recently, trading on the NYSE took place literally on the floor of the exchange, in face-to-face dealings. A broker, on behalf of a customer wanting to buy stock, would seek another broker representing a customer wanting to sell the same stock. The broker would be paid a fee per share, called a *commission,* for this service.

Brokers for buyers and brokers for sellers would meet at the specialist's post. The *specialist* was an NYSE member assigned to a particular stock, such as ExxonMobil or IBM. What did specialist firms do?

- They served as *auctioneers*—soliciting offers to buy (called *bids*) and offers to sell (called *offers,* or *asks*) from brokers representing their customers in the trading crowd.
- They matched buyers and sellers who reached agreement on price and amount.
- They maintained a book of limit orders, which are bids and offers away from a stock's current market price and arranged for execution of the orders whenever the market price moved to the limit price.
- They used their own capital to reduce imbalances between buying and selling interest, by buying when others were selling and selling when others were buying.

"Making Your Best Offer" explains trading terminology.

NASDAQ exchange.[3] Beginning in the 1970s, at the advent of the computer era, a second major stock market emerged. Rather than granting a monopoly to a single firm to act as a specialist in a stock, NASDAQ (*Naz-dack*) allows all brokerage firms that meet certain requirements to *make a market* in any stock listed on the exchange by posting bids and offers.[4] Customers who want to trade a stock on NASDAQ buy or sell from one of these *market makers.* Trading that takes place in this way is said to occur in the *over the counter,* or OTC, market.

MAKING YOUR BEST OFFER

When a securities trader goes to buy a house, she makes a *bid,* not an *offer.* That's because traders are very particular about the language they use when making a purchase or sale. When traders want to buy a stock, they make a bid, which is a proposal to purchase a certain number of shares at a particular price. Similarly, they make an *offer,* or *ask,* when they propose to sell shares at a price.

Different traders will have different bids and offers. Let's see how this works in the hypothetical market for Netherfield stock. Three traders are interested in buying and selling. Table 8.1 shows their bids and offers.

TABLE 8.1   The Market for Netherfield Stock

Trader	Bid (per share for 100 shares)	Offer (per share for 100 shares)
Elizabeth	$23.00	$24.50
Jane	$23.50	$24.25
Charles	$23.25	$23.75

Jane is willing to pay the highest price to buy Netherfield shares. Therefore, her bid of $23.50 is the best bid. Charles, on the other hand, has the lowest sale, or offer, price of $23.75; this is the best offer, or best ask.

The difference between the best bid and the best offer is the *spread.* It is the cost of transacting immediately. For example, if Jane decides that she wants to buy 100 shares right now, she'll need to pay $23.75 or 25 cents per share more than the bid. The spread represents a profit to the specialist, or market maker, who supplies the liquidity to enable Jane to complete her trade. Spreads are generally bigger, or wider, for stocks that are riskier or less liquid; they are smaller, or narrower, for stocks that are actively traded or whose prices remain fairly stable.

An order to buy at the best offer or sell at the best bid is called a *market order.* Jane placed a market order when she decided to buy at $23.75. *Limit* orders are placed away from the best bid and offer. For example, Elizabeth has placed a limit order to sell 100 shares at $24.50, which is above the best offer of $23.75.

The computer-based nature of the NASDAQ market has appealed to many technology companies, which decided to make their shares available for trading on it rather than on the NYSE. Some of the world's largest companies, including Google and Microsoft, are listed on NASDAQ.

National market system. The national market system tied the NYSE and NASDAQ to each other, as well as to other smaller stock exchanges.[5] Congress called for the SEC to create the national market system in 1975 so it could advance, among other things:

- Efficient execution of trades
- Fair competition among broker-dealers and among markets
- Widespread public availability of current information on stock trades

Two of the key elements of the national market system are the *consolidated transaction reporting* and *consolidated quotation rules*. The first is often called the *consolidated tape* rule, after the ticker tape that was used in the telegraph era to record stock prices. It requires that the price and size of all stock trades—made on any exchange or trading center—be fed immediately into one consolidated, electronic reporting system and be made publicly available.

Similarly, the consolidated quotation rule requires that the price levels and amounts of bids and offers in stocks be fed into an electronic data processing system and that all market participants have access to these quotes.[6] The information is further consolidated to arrive at a *national best bid and offer,* or NBBO, for each stock.

One of the key features of both rules is that the data collected be made available to everyone—broker-dealers, specialists, market makers, and investors alike—enabling all market participants to make informed trading decisions. But note that the dissemination of the information has not been entirely symmetrical. Historically, specialists collected limit bids and offers from customers that they were not required to disclose. This gave them a more detailed view of the depth of the market for a particular stock—and, therefore, a potential trading advantage over the customers who supplied them with that information. The same has been true for firms that act as market makers and accept limit orders from their customers.

The New Entrants: Alternative Trading Systems

In the 1990s, advances in computer technology and high speed telecommunications paved the way for new competition to the NYSE and NASDAQ. Known as *alternative trading systems,* or ATS, these automated electronic trading platforms enable investors to trade anonymously with each other—allowing them to maintain control of information on their trading intentions, information that they formerly ceded to the specialists and market makers. Unlike the NYSE or NASDAQ, ATS don't enter into arrangements with issuers to list their stocks. Nevertheless, essentially all of the actively traded stocks listed on the NYSE or NASDAQ are now traded on at least one ATS.

The growth of ATS was given a tremendous boost when the SEC adopted the *trade through,* or *trade protection,* rule in 2005. In short, this rule requires a broker to send a customer's market order to the exchange or ATS that is quoting the highest bid or the lowest offer—as long as it has a fast market, meaning that it uses electronic trading. Once the rule came into effect, brokers could no longer automatically route customers' market orders for NYSE-listed stocks to the NYSE, as they often did in the past. The rule had a huge impact: it led the NYSE to try to keep up with NASDAQ and the ATS by dropping its historic floor-based trading model and developing a hybrid system that includes purely electronic trading. "Counting the Pennies" reviews another SEC regulation that also significantly changed stock trading.

COUNTING THE PENNIES

Another factor that has shaped the equity trading markets has been the change to decimal pricing of stocks. Historically, bids and offers would be in $1/8$s, equal to one-eighth of a dollar or 12.5 cents. For example, the national best bid and offer for a stock might be $10^1/_8$ bid and $10^1/_8$ offered, for a spread of $1/4$. That translated to \$10.125 and \$10.375, for a spread of 25 cents. One of the first things that new traders had to learn was the value of these fractions.

But as technology made the stock market more efficient, a spread of 12.5 cents—the lowest spread possible when pricing in $1/8$s—was just too high. So in 1997, pricing increments were reduced for some stocks to increments of one-sixteenth of a dollar or 6.25 cents, known to traders as *teenies*.

Finally, beginning in 2000, the SEC ordered that stock prices be quoted in dollars and cents, so that an actively traded issue today can be quoted at \$20.43 bid and \$20.45 offer, for a spread of just 2 cents.

The changes have led to lower spreads, which have fallen from an average of around 12.5 cents in the mid-1990s to about 2.5 cents shortly after decimalization was introduced.[7] That in turn has meant lower costs for investors—and much easier math for traders!

ATS have taken one of two forms: electronic communication networks and *dark pools*. Let's look at each in turn.

Electronic communication networks. An electronic communication network, or ECN, allows any of its subscribers—whether a market maker, broker, or investor—to post bids and offers for specific amounts of stock. The ECN automatically matches buy and sell orders that are input at the same price. That's a big cost advantage for investors, who no longer have to pay a spread to a market maker or a commission to a broker to get a trade done. Instead, investors just pay a fee for use of the network, which is much lower than a commission paid to a full service broker. Major ECNs include DirectEdge and BATS.[8]

ECNs address the information asymmetry that characterized traditional stock trading. In an ECN, subscribers are allowed to see the entire *book*—meaning all public bids and offers at all prices—so that they have the ability to evaluate the depth of the market for a particular stock for themselves. At the same time, participants don't have to publicly display their bids or offers—some or all can be held in reserve to be used only if a matching trade should be input. That makes it easier for larger investors to buy and sell blocks of stock without affecting the market price.

For example, a mutual fund might wish to buy 25,000 shares in Northanger stock, but does not wish to tip its hand to the market. The fund sends in an order for 25,000 shares at $10 per share, but designates that only 500 shares be displayed on the ECN and that the rest of its order be kept in reserve as a resting order. If a seller hits the fund's bid, by entering a sell order at $10 share, the ECN would automatically record a trade for 500 shares at $10 per share. It would then refresh the fund's bid, posting a buy order for another 500 shares. In this way, the fund can work its purchases over the course of the trading day while reducing the chances that its total order for 25,000 shares would become known to the market and thereby push the stock's price upward.

Dark pools. There is no single model for a dark pool. The term is broadly understood to describe any automated, electronic trading market that amasses *hidden liquidity*, in which participants do not disclose to one another the prices or amounts at which they are prepared to buy or sell and trades are completed in anonymity. Dark pools developed to respond to the special concerns of mutual funds and other large investors who worry about affecting a stock's price when trading in large volumes. Like ECNs, dark pools allow participants to trade directly with one another and thus avoid paying a spread to a dealer or a commission to a broker.[9]

The average size of trades arranged in these pools is around 50,000 shares, and some trades can take place in even larger blocks. The dark pool world is highly populated. In late 2009, there were about 32 dark pool platforms, accounting for 8 percent of total trading in U.S. stocks. Among the larger independent dark pools are Liquidnet, Matchpoint, Pipeline, and POSIT, and many of the major broker-dealer firms have developed significant dark pool trading platforms.

Each dark pool has its own set of rules. We look here at just two, Liquidnet and POSIT, to illustrate how each dark pool operates differently:

- *Liquidnet* brings together fund managers by electronically linking its system to the in-house trade order management systems—often called *trade blotters*—used by fund trading desks. Assume, for example, that the Wentworth Fund, in its trade blotter, wants to buy 250,000 shares of Kellynch stock and the Uppercross Fund wants to sell the same amount. Liquidnet will *scrape the blotters* of the two funds—that is, it will detect that Wentworth's and Uppercross's orders can be matched and send an automated a message to each fund's trading desk that a counterparty stands ready to trade Kellynch stock. The two trading desks can then anonymously communicate their respective bid and offer prices to each other and negotiate a price, all without having to tell the world at large that they're buying or selling.
- *POSIT*, in contrast, handles the negotiation and trade automatically; POSIT does not scrape blotters like Liquidnet. Instead, traders place buy and sell orders with quantities only—no prices—into the system. At scheduled times during the day—at 10 A.M., for example—POSIT automatically matches buy and sell orders at a price midway between the current national best bid and the national best offer as reported in the consolidated quotation system. If buy orders outnumber sell orders, or vice versa, POSIT randomly selects orders to match.

  Because the names of buyers and sellers are not disclosed, mutual funds and other larger investors can trade without tipping their hands as to their future intentions. So if the Avon Hill fund held 800,000 shares of a small cap stock, it could sell 20,000 on POSIT without generating fears that it was about to liquidate its entire position. On the negative side, trades entered into POSIT are not completed immediately, and the midpoint price might not be a favorable one when the trade is eventually executed.

ATS and the national market system. Where do alternative trading systems fit in to the national market system? While the ATS are included in the system, they are subject to a special SEC rule—known as Regulation

ATS—that imposes a lower level of regulation if trading volume on the alternative platform remains low.

- *Less than 5 percent of volume.* An ATS is basically free from regulation as long as no more than 5 percent of the total trading volume in a stock takes place on its platform.
- *More than 5 percent but less than 20 percent.* Once an ATS crosses the 5 percent threshold, it becomes subject to the consolidated tape rule; it also becomes subject to the consolidated quotation rule, but only if it displays bids and offers on its system. (To avoid this rule, dark pools solicit only *indications of interest* with no price attached.)
- *20 percent or more.* If trading in a stock reaches 20 percent or more of total volume, the ATS becomes subject to additional regulation, including a requirement that there be some access to the platform for all market participants.

The Convergence of the Old and the New

Both the NYSE and NASDAQ have transformed their own operations to respond to the competitive challenges posed by the ATS. NASDAQ acquired two major ECNs. The changes at the NYSE were even more dramatic: in 2007, it abandoned its monopoly specialist system and opened up trading to competing market makers. It acquired an ECN (renamed NYSE Arca) and now considers itself a hybrid market with a trading floor that operates alongside a fully electronic venue. And it merged with the company operating the Amsterdam, Brussels, and Paris exchanges and is now part of NYSE Euronext.

At the same time, some of the electronic venues are positioning themselves to compete head on with the traditional exchanges. The BATS ECN, for example, has registered with the SEC as an exchange, meaning that it is now fully subject to a wider set of rules. The upside is that BATS, as an exchange, gets a share of the fees paid by investors for access to the consolidated tape and consolidated quotes—a revenue stream not shared with ECNs. (While anyone can access the consolidated tape and consolidated quotes, there may be a fee for doing so.)

The intense competition among markets has led to a dispersion of trading among what are now called *market centers,* or *trading centers,* with no single one commanding a dominant position. In 2009, the three largest were NASDAQ, with 19.4 percent of total equity trading volume, the traditional NYSE with 14.7 percent and NYSE Arca, an exchange-registered ECN, with 13.2 percent. ECNs and dark pools combined, accounted for more than

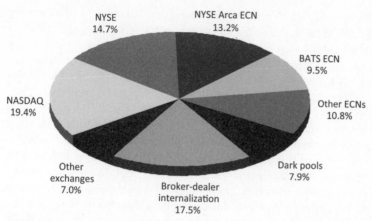

FIGURE 8.1 U.S. Stock Trading by Market Venue (September 2009)
Source: SEC, *Concept Release on Equity Market Structure,* January 2010.

40 percent of trading. Broker-dealer *internalization*—which occurs when a firm matches buy and sell orders from two different clients without using a trading center—accounted for 17.5 percent. (See Figure 8.1 for a breakdown.) Where a stock is listed no longer determines where it is traded; in 2009, only 20 percent of the volume of stocks listed on the NYSE traded on either the NYSE floor or on Arca.

In earlier years, the SEC was worried that this sort of fragmentation of the markets would result in less liquidity and wider spreads. But high speed data linkages among the markets have had quite the opposite effect. For example, market depth has increased significantly, meaning that more shares can be bought or sold near the national best bid and offer than in the past. By late 2009, investors could, on average, buy 80,000 shares of stocks in the S&P 500 within 6 cents of the national best bid and offer. That compares to only 15,000 shares just six years earlier.[10] Recognizing these developments, the SEC has abandoned the term *fragmentation* and now refers to the *dispersion* of trading among the market centers.

Trades are also being implemented at higher speeds (or, as it's known in industry jargon, *with lower latency*)—though the *flash crash* on May 6, 2010, suggested that it's not always a good thing. On that day, the Dow Jones Industrial Average dropped 1,000 points in a matter of minutes. Regulators and academics will be parsing the causes of that crash for some time to come, but the preliminary reading is that the plunge was caused by computer-programmed *stop-loss* orders—which are market orders to sell—that kicked in as stock prices dropped. At the same time, traders willing to buy had fled the market because their computerized trading activities had been programmed to shut down automatically in response to the sharp market drop. All of this happened in such a short amount of time that humans couldn't exercise judgment to intervene fast enough. Exchange-traded funds were particularly affected, as we discuss in Chapter 12.

To prevent a recurrence of a flash crash, in 2010 the SEC is testing new rules on a limited number of stocks and exchange-traded funds. The rules require that trading in an issue stop for five minutes if its price has fallen by 10 percent or more in the preceding five minutes. The trading halt acts as a *circuit breaker* that gives the system a chance to cool down when it is in danger of becoming overheated. These stock-by-stock circuit breakers are being added to a system of marketwide circuit breakers that impose a similar pause in trading when the market as a whole moves too far too fast.[11] If the tests are successful, the SEC may apply the stock-by-stock circuit breakers more broadly.

The new market structure has also raised serious concerns about fairness. It has created what some consider unreasonable advantages for a select few, those that benefit from *co-location* and *flash orders*.

- *Co-location*. In co-location, a market center allows very active traders, often hedge funds, to place their computer servers in close physical proximity to the market center's own computers, giving these traders a lower latency than other market participants. The speed advantage may be only a millisecond or two, but that can mean the difference between gains and losses. Critics of co-location are urging the SEC to adopt a rule that would prohibit this type of favoritism.
- *Flash orders*. Another issue of concern is the use of *flash orders* by hedge funds and other active traders. These are orders sent to a market center that are immediate-or-cancel orders. They take advantage of a loophole in the consolidated quote rule that allows certain immediate orders to be submitted without being displayed. The advantage that traders gain from flash orders? They are able to test the depth of the market for a stock, without having to follow all the rules that apply to other market participants. The SEC is considering revising the consolidated quote rule to require inclusion of flash orders as quotations.

More generally, the SEC is worried that an increasing lack of transparency in stock trading will make it easier for industry insiders to make profits at the expense of public investors. As we've seen, the alternative trading systems don't have to provide information to either the consolidated tape or quotation system unless volume exceeds certain levels. Nor do broker-dealers have to provide quotations for trades that are executed internally. That means that more than 25 percent of trading activity is not completely captured in the national reporting systems. The SEC is particularly concerned about the impact of this undisclosed trading on individual investors, although one academic study concludes that the lack of transparency imposes higher costs on everyone, including the sophisticated investors using dark pools.[12]

To ensure that the markets remain fair for all, the SEC has proposed that the threshold that triggers reporting of trades to the consolidated tape be lowered from 5 percent of nationwide volume to 0.25 percent, and it's evaluating whether indications of interest in dark pools should be treated as bids and offers that must be reported to the consolidated quotation system. It's also considering limits on internalization of orders within a brokerage firm. Mutual fund managers are generally not in favor of these proposals, since they would reduce the ability to trade anonymously—to the detriment of the individuals investing in the funds.

THE ROLE OF THE MUTUAL FUND TRADER

Executing a fund's buy and sell orders on the best terms possible in this very dynamic environment is the challenge facing the mutual fund trader. Trading desks are usually organized around the type of funds that they serve, so a fund manager will normally have a bond desk, a money market desk, and an equity desk. Within each desk, traders are often assigned to particular portfolio managers and develop expertise in a specific type of security, whether municipal bonds or small company stocks. Figure 8.2 shows how traders act as a bridge between portfolio managers and market centers.

We discuss in this section the responsibilities that traders have when executing buy and sell orders:

- Ensuring that the fund complies with all relevant rules
- Choosing a trading strategy that seeks to achieve *best execution*
- Selecting broker-dealers to execute trades
- Managing trading across multiple funds

After a trade is completed, the trading desk also works with investment operations to make sure that the settlement process goes smoothly. This is the *back office* aspect of a trade, when cash and securities actually change hands between buyer and seller. (Chapter 14 covers the process in detail.) We'll concentrate on stock trading in our discussion. Fixed income traders

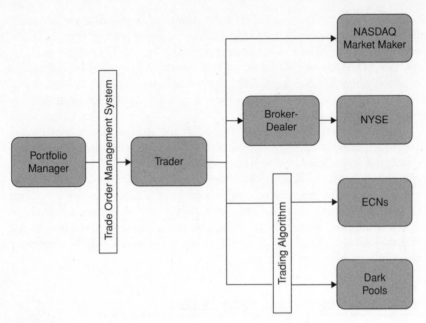

FIGURE 8.2   The Trader's Role

have similar responsibilities, although they typically do not use brokers to execute trades for the funds. See the "Career Track" box for a glimpse at an equity trader's typical day.

CAREER TRACK: MUTUAL FUND EQUITY TRADER

As an equity trader, a large part of your job involves communication— face to face, on the phone or by electronic means—with portfolio managers, broker-dealers, and the investment operations team. Let's consider the handling of a typical trade, a buy of 40,000 shares of Highbury stock, which is currently trading at $47.

8:30 A.M. Before the market opens, the portfolio manager sends the trade to the desk electronically, through the order management system.

9:00 A.M. The manager calls the trading desk and gives you additional instructions: "There may be more behind it, so only do that size if you don't have to push the price up too much."

9:15 A.M. Since the stock is very liquid, you decide to try to execute most of the trade through a broker-dealer. You send an electronic message to the broker you've selected, then follow up with a phone call to your contact there. You give the broker a $46.75 limit order to buy 30,000 shares. You send through the trading desk's electronic link to a dark pool an order to buy 10,000 shares at $46.80.

Morning. You monitor the progress of the order throughout the morning, talking with the broker periodically, but the broker has not found a counterparty prepared to sell at $46.75 or less. At noon, however, the dark pool has crossed buy and sell orders at $46.80 per share, resulting in the fund's purchase of 10,000 shares.

1:00 P.M. In the afternoon, the broker calls to let you know that 50,000 shares are available at $47. Since part of your role is keeping the portfolio managers abreast of the latest market intelligence, you call her to relay this information. The portfolio manager wants to buy the 50,000 shares at $47 and sends you an order for another 20,000 shares electronically. You, in turn, convey the new instructions to the broker. You also enter another bid at $46.60 for 10,000 shares in the dark pool.

1:10 P.M. The broker calls to confirm that 50,000 shares have been filled at a slightly better price of $46.95 and follows up with an electronic message. You call the portfolio manager with the good news.

1:15 P.M. You ensure that the fill has been correctly entered in the trade order management system, so that the fund's records will be properly updated.

2:00 P.M. The dark pool crosses buy and sell orders at $46.60, resulting in the fund's purchase of the last 10,000 shares of the revised order.

As you can see, the trader's job requires an attention to detail and good follow-up skills—in addition to an ability to read the markets.

Fund Compliance

Traders help to ensure that buy and sell orders comply with all the rules that are applicable to a particular fund, whether that's a limitation established in the prospectus, a government regulation, or an internal policy. This can be straightforward, such as making sure that a fund doesn't accidentally sell more stock than it owns. (Sounds simple, but when a fund complex holds thousands of positions, it can happen.) Special rules limit the amount of shares that a fund can purchase of any single company. Generally, a fund can acquire no more than 10 percent of a company's voting stock. And many fund complexes put additional limits on the aggregate ownership of all their funds in a single company, such as 15 percent across all funds. Fund traders help monitor these and other restrictions, and it's a critical role. If there's an error that requires a fund to sell shares that should not have been bought, the fund management company may be required to compensate the fund for any losses.

To help traders with this task, most larger fund managers have computer systems that prescreen proposed trades to determine whether they are in compliance. In these systems, portfolio managers enter trades that are automatically checked before being routed to the trading desk. But even with these tools, fund traders must still remain vigilant, especially when handling trades that involve unusual or particularly complex circumstances.

Trading Strategy

Once the trader has confirmed that a proposed buy or sell is appropriate for a particular fund, it's time to choose a trading strategy. The goal is simple: traders always seek the *best execution* possible for the fund—though there's never a guarantee that they can achieve it. See "Doing Your Best" for a discussion of the difficulty of even defining the term. The decision is complex, since it involves both a selection of a venue and choice of approach for submitting an order within a market center.

Some of the more common trading strategies are:

Working orders. For NYSE-listed stocks, traders might decide to retain a broker who will work the order throughout the day on the exchange floor, on ECNs or through market makers not based on the exchange floor and therefore often called *upstairs* market makers. The trader might keep part of the order to work directly, sending bids and offers to one or more ECNs or dark pools. Other times, the trader might not give the broker the entire order at once, but instead place only part of the order at first, perhaps with a limit ("Take 25,000 Northanger to buy with a $46.50 top"). If the trade is going well, the trader can increase the order until the entire amount is placed. If not, the trader has not revealed the entire order and can later either place it with another broker or take back control of the order, executing it using the trading desk's direct links to ECNs, dark pools, and other electronic trading centers. This multipronged approach is normally used for large or mid-size orders.

Basket trades. Another strategy is the *basket trade*, also known as a *program trade, portfolio trade,* or *list trade.* It's often used when a trader

DOING YOUR BEST

While *best execution* is simple in concept, it's been tough to define in practice. The normally precise SEC, for example, has not spelled out exactly what it means when it now refers to the term.

Seeking best execution entails balancing a number of factors. It's assessed over time and over many transactions, rather than trade by trade. Best execution is not just getting the best price and incurring the lowest trading commissions and fees, although those are both extremely important. It also considers the risk of not executing a trade if price and cost are the only considerations. The ability to remain anonymous often factors into an assessment of best execution, since the fund might get a worse price or maybe even not be able to complete an order at all if its intentions become public.

If defining best execution is difficult, measuring it is even harder. One common approach is to compare the trade price to the average price for other similar trades made that same day using a measure called the *volume-weighted average price,* or VWAP. Another technique, called *implementation shortfall,* is to estimate the expected cost of a trade based on the trading pattern of a stock, and then see how actual results stack up against the estimates. (Estimated costs will be higher for more volatile or less liquid stocks.) Specialized consulting firms collect and store market data and provide fund trading desks with extensive reports analyzing their trade results using one of these two approaches.

has a long list of orders; that may happen when a fund needs to buy or sell a slice of its entire portfolio to either invest or raise cash. The trader will show the entire list to a small group of broker-dealers who compete for the business. Sometimes the list does not name the stocks but simply gives other details, such as market caps and price volatility of the stocks in the basket. If a fund is the selling stocks in a basket trade, the firm that offers the best combination of price and fees buys the full set of stocks at a specified price from the fund. Because the risk of the entire group of stocks taken as a whole is typically less than the risk of any single stock, funds can normally get a better execution when they trade stocks as baskets rather than one by one.

Electronic trades. Working the order directly in electronic markets is the most common strategy for orders in NASDAQ stocks. That's a change from the recent past, when traders almost always went to the market maker displaying the best quotes. While that's still done today, it's no longer the dominant practice. Electronic markets also offer an efficient way for the desk to trade small orders.

Algorithmic trading. For very large orders, on the other hand, traders today often opt for algorithmic, or *algo*, trading, using mathematical models or algorithms that are programmed into the trading desk's computer systems. These models automatically submit a series of trading orders to an electronic network; the exact sequence depends on price movements in the stock or other factors. (Figure 8.3 gives a very simple example.) Algo trading allows the desk to easily break large orders into multiple, smaller orders, enabling the fund to maintain anonymity and reduce market impact.

Trading desks work closely with quantitative analysts to develop effective algorithms, and they track results to determine which work best in particular circumstances. They are constantly fine-tuning their approach, trying to gain even more of an edge.

Algo trading is a fairly new phenomenon linked to the rise of the alternative trading systems, but it has already had a profound effect on the markets. Because it breaks up large orders into small ones, algo trading has caused a dramatic decrease in average trade size.

Broker-Dealer Selection

A decision to work an order with a broker-dealer creates another decision point: which broker-dealer to choose? Again, seeking best execution takes precedence. The trader may choose a firm that has expertise in a particular sector or that has been active in the stock recently or that has demonstrated its ability to handle similar orders well in the past. Beyond best execution, traders may consider research services and must pay particular attention to the use of affiliated brokerage firms.

Soft dollar services. When selecting a broker, traders are permitted by law to consider not just how well the broker executes trades but also the research services that a broker supplies to help the portfolio managers make successful investment decisions. This research often consists of investment recommendations from the brokerage firm's own team, familiarly known as *Street research*. At other times, the research may come from third parties at the broker's expense. This third-party research may take the form of electronic data feeds and quotation services, such as Reuters or Bloomberg, rather than traditional investment analysis. That's possible because the SEC defines research quite broadly. Many of these services are essential to the operations of fund managers.

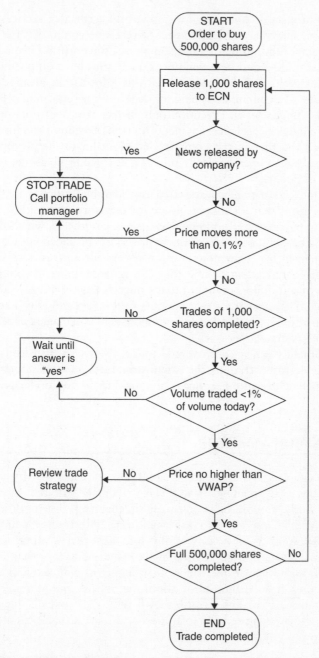

FIGURE 8.3 A Simplified Trading Algorithm

Many brokers do not charge for any of these research services in hard cash dollars. They may instead expect to receive a certain level of trading volume from a fund. In many fund complexes, the portfolio managers give input to the trading desk on which brokerage firms have supplied the most valuable research, and the traders keep this information in mind as they direct orders. The commissions paid for these trading services may be higher than those charged by an execution-only broker that does not supply any research. In industry parlance, payments for trade execution and for research are bundled together in the commission. More lingo: the portion of the commission that compensates for a broker for providing investment research is called *soft dollars*.[13]

Soft dollar research has attracted considerable criticism in the past. Detractors argue that it's inappropriate for investors to subsidize, through commission payments, a fund manager's research process, which they contend should be included as one of the basic services provided in exchange for the management fee. They note that the system encourages portfolio managers to do more trading so that they can generate more in commissions. Defenders of soft dollars point out that Congress has specifically sanctioned the practice. They also argue that banning soft dollars would be likely to reduce competition in the fund industry, since smaller managers depend more on soft dollars than larger ones.

The practice is less controversial today. That's partly because of the increase in electronic trading; the commission rates on these trades are very low and include execution services only, making the soft dollar pool much

INDEPENDENT MONITORS

As you can see, in some trading situations, the interests of the fund and of the fund's managers can diverge. To make sure that funds are treated fairly, the SEC has given the independent directors on fund boards special responsibility for monitoring both trading policy and trade execution. Fund boards of directors must review all trades that take place between funds advised by the same manager or that involve an affiliated broker-dealer. Independent directors will also look at the manager's soft dollar and trade allocation policies and practices. Nor do they neglect the big picture: they'll review the overall quality of trading, often using reports from one of the firms that evaluate best execution.

smaller. And SEC guidance on what can be paid for with soft dollars and how to design commission agreements has ended some of the most-criticized practices. "Independent Monitors" discusses the role of the board of directors in monitoring soft dollars and other trading issues.

Use of an affiliated brokerage firm. Traders working for larger financial services companies may need to consider one other factor in their choice of a brokerage firm. If their company also owns a broker-dealer, they must limit the fund's trading with that firm. Under the provisions of the 1940 Act, the affiliate may only act as an agent for the fund, helping it to arrange trades with other, unaffiliated buyers and sellers; it may not buy or sell securities directly from the fund. Because of the conflict of interest, some funds prohibit affiliates of the fund manager from acting as a broker or severely limit the use of their services. The SEC has also placed restrictions on the purchase of securities in a public offering if the affiliate is part of the group underwriting the offering.

Trading Across Multiple Funds

A mutual fund manager can easily oversee a number of funds, and they all come to the trading desk to buy and sell. Traders are responsible for ensuring that each fund is treated fairly. They get involved with multi-fund issues in three ways: fund cloning, trade allocation, and interfund trades.

Fund cloning. In many fund complexes, one portfolio manager may be in charge of multiple versions of the same portfolio. For example, he may manage a mutual fund sold to U.S. investors only, a mutual fund sold to non-U.S. investors, and an account for single large client—all using the same investment approach. To manage these different customers fairly and efficiently, the portfolios may be *cloned,* meaning that their holdings are as closely aligned as is practicable in terms of percentage weightings.

At some money managers, the trading desk is responsible for implementing the cloning. The portfolio manager often personally manages the largest of her funds; the traders then replicate any changes in that fund in the smaller accounts. This is not always as easy as it may sound, since the smaller accounts may have special constraints imposed by the particular client, or it may not be feasible to obtain exactly the same securities at the same price for all accounts. The traders must then make adjustments as appropriate.

Trade allocation. When trading for multiple funds, trading desks usually *bunch* orders for the same stock, executing them all at the same time. That approach ensures that all of the funds are treated exactly alike, eliminating any accusations of favoritism. It works particularly well when the desk is able to complete the trade on the same day.

But what happens if only part of the trade has been completed by the close of business? How are the shares allocated among the funds that participated in the order? Generally, traders will allocate the stock on a pro rata basis, filling the same percentage of the initial order for each fund. But if one portfolio manager had provided slightly different instructions, the desk might need to make a judgment call on how that affected the ultimate execution and adjust the allocation accordingly. Very small funds might get precedence in the allocation, since, if not for their larger cousins, they'd have easily completed their orders. And very small trade executions, not uncommon when purchasing hot initial public offerings, may be rotated among funds on a predetermined schedule.

Interfund trades. Traders must also manage situations in which one fund is buying and another is selling. This may happen because funds have different cash flows or because two portfolio managers have opposing views on the outlook for a particular investment. The trader must determine whether to *cross* the trade between the two funds, without placing an order in the market. This saves both funds the execution costs, but the trader must be certain that the proposed transaction is in the best interests of both funds. The price on an interfund trade is determined by SEC regulation; it's usually the last sale price for stocks and the average of the bid and the ask for other securities. All of these trades must be reviewed by the board of directors.

TRADING IN BOND FUNDS

While we have focused on transactions in stock funds, trading is arguably even more important in bond funds. Because returns on bonds are generally lower than stock returns, costs play a bigger role in determining fund rankings—and that includes the costs related to trading.

The sheer number of bond issues creates tremendous challenges. Because there are more bonds issued in a year than there are stocks trading, just tracking down the other side of a trade in a particular issue can be quite difficult. For example, bond fund managers might not be able to find a seller of a bond that they're interested in buying. They might be offered a similar issue instead, and they'll have to decide whether the substitution is consistent with their portfolio strategy. In other words, the line between trader and portfolio manager is much fuzzier in bond funds—sometimes the roles are even combined, especially in smaller firms.

The wide variety of types of bonds means that a trader must be familiar with many different submarkets. For example:

- U.S. Treasuries are extremely liquid and trade with very narrow spreads, so buying and selling them is only a challenge when extremely large blocks of securities—valued at billions of dollars—are involved.
- High-yield bonds are less liquid, and trading them can be quite complex. Their prices may be influenced by the issuer's earnings outlook and perhaps by moves in its stock price, and spreads will vary widely, depending on the size of the issue and its credit quality. A smaller, lower-quality high-yield bond issue might *trade by appointment only,* to use a favorite trading desk phrase, while a larger one rated BB might be readily available.
- Traders working with structured securities need to be familiar with the complex characteristics of those issues, to understand how they'll be affected by market factors, including economic news.

There's no one place to turn to trade all these different types of bonds. There aren't any bond exchanges like NASDAQ and the NYSE, which—despite their decreased market share—still have a significant place in stock trading. Instead, bond trading is widely dispersed.

Bonds can be bought and sold in one of two ways:

1. *New issues.* Bonds can be bought in the *primary market* when they are issued by a corporation or government. There is a steady flow of new issues, if only to replace the bonds that mature every year. The new issue market is particularly important in the municipal market. Traders must keep on top of the calendar of new offerings and make sure that the portfolio managers are aware of the timing of deals.

   Even in the new issue market, different types of bonds are handled differently. U.S. Treasuries can be bought directly from the government through a program called Treasury Direct or indirectly through a primary dealer. Other types of bonds will generally be marketed through broker-dealers.

2. *Dealer market.* After they are issued, bonds can then be bought and sold in the *secondary market.* The bond market is an over-the-counter or *dealer market,* which means that investors transact with a broker-dealer who is either acting as principal or agent. If the investor is selling and the broker-dealer is acting as a principal, the broker will buy the bond for its inventory. When the broker-dealer already has a client on

the other side of the trade, it will act as agent and simply trade the bonds from one party to the other—taking a small spread out of the price as compensation for its services.

In recent years, technology has started to bring more coordination to the bond market. For a long time, bond traders could get good pricing information only on government securities. Now, there are two separate systems providing consolidated trade price reporting. For corporate bond trades, the system is called TRACE, which stands for Trade Reporting and Compliance Engine, and it's run by FINRA. The equivalent in the municipal bond world is the Municipal Securities Rulemaking Board's Real Time Transaction Reporting or RTRS system. But unlike stock trades, which are automatically reported almost instantaneously, there is a lag time in the reporting of bond trades: dealers need only report trades within 15 minutes of execution. All of the trade information—and much more—is available on Bloomberg. (And, yes, it's related to the New York City mayor, who founded the company.) Virtually all professional bond traders have the Bloomberg information system on their desktop and use it constantly to access data about bonds.

Trade execution has also gone electronic in the bond world. TradeWeb is the largest electronic trading platform, and there are others, including BondDesk and MTS BondVision, that have developed a lead in specific niches. But there is a key difference between these systems and the ECNs in the stock arena: all of the bond platforms serve to connect investors to dealers. Direct trading between investors—each on an ECN or through a dark pool—is still only a minor component of bond trading.

CHAPTER SUMMARY

Trading can have a significant impact on fund performance. Because a fund buys and sells in large size, it can have a market impact, driving up the price of securities it's trying to buy and pushing down the price of securities it's trying to sell. Other investors may try to anticipate a fund's actions and try to earn a profit by front running them. Many mutual fund management companies have dedicated traders—working on trading desks—who focus on minimizing the cost of buying and selling investments.

Trading in U.S. stocks today is largely electronic and is widely dispersed among many market centers. The traditional stock exchanges—the New York Stock Exchange and NASDAQ—continue to play an important role in stock trading, although their market share has fallen dramatically in the past decade. In contrast, alternative trading systems have gained share. There are two types of alternative trading systems: electronic communication networks and dark pools, each operating with its own set of rules. Despite the diversity of their features, all of these systems allow investors to trade anonymously with each other without the involvement of a broker-dealer.

Mutual funds and other large investors have supported the development of alternative trading systems because they believe that trading through them creates less market impact. However, some industry observers are concerned that individual investors are worse off under the new system. That's because the alternative trading systems are not always required to publicly report trade information. Also, the new systems have not yet been fully tested in extreme market circumstances, as demonstrated by the flash crash of May 2010. Preliminary analysis suggested that automation played a key role in the market plunge.

The mutual fund trader is charged with seeking the best execution possible by selecting the trading venue and approach that will enable the fund to implement its investment decisions at the lowest possible cost, considering both opportunity cost (meaning the cost of not trading) as well as direct costs such as spreads and commissions. As part of this process, the trader may select brokerage firms that provide important investment research in addition to trade execution services. The trading desk also plays a key role in helping a fund comply with all the relevant rules, including regulations on trading with affiliated firms, trade allocation, and interfund trading. All of these activities of the trading desk are overseen by the independent directors of the funds.

Because of the large number of bond issues, fixed income trading is arguably even more complex than equity trading. There are no central exchanges for bonds, with the result that trading is highly dispersed. Investors can buy bonds from the issuer in the primary market or through a dealer in the secondary market, often through an electronic network. Unlike stock investors, however, bond investors rarely trade with each other.

CHAPTER 9

Mutual Funds as Institutional Investors

Because of their extensive stock ownership, mutual funds can play a key role influencing the leadership of public companies.[1] They can have significant say on whether a company moves forward with a proposed merger or whether a particular slate of candidates is elected to a company's board. Whether mutual funds use that potential influence effectively is the subject of debate among regulators, academics, corporate executives, and fund managers themselves.

In this chapter, we focus on a mutual fund's investments in the stock of other companies—ownership that comes with both rights and responsibilities. As we discussed in Chapter 2, mutual funds themselves have shareholders—the investors in the fund. While those investors enjoy ownership rights in the fund, they are not the topic of discussion in this chapter. When we use the terms *stockholder* and *shareholder* throughout this chapter, we refer to the owners of the stock of operating companies and not to holders of mutual fund shares.

This chapter reviews:

- The powers of stockholders in the governance of corporations
- How mutual funds exercise those powers
- The role of shareholder activism
- The role that social issues play in mutual fund investment and proxy voting decisions
- The challenges facing mutual funds in exercising their shareholder rights outside the United States

MUTUAL FUNDS AS STOCKHOLDERS AND THE PROXY VOTING PROCESS

The largest owners of stock in the United States are now *institutional investors,* a term that refers to large investors who are usually managing money for others, who are often individual investors. The percentage of outstanding stock controlled by institutional investors has been growing, as Figure 9.1 illustrates.

Mutual funds, taken as a group, are the largest holders of stock among institutional investors. Figure 9.2 shows the breakdown of assets among the various types of institutional investors.

If institutional investors are the predominant owners of stock, and mutual funds are the largest U.S. stockholders among institutional investors, funds are then necessarily the most important owners of stock in the United States. Several mutual fund management companies almost always rank among the top 10 holders of any major U.S. corporation. That substantial ownership stake gives funds considerable influence in corporate policymaking.

The Role of Stockholders

Mutual funds exercise this influence within the context of a balance of power that is commonly referred to as *corporate governance.* Legally, stockholders are the owners of a company; they elect a board of directors to represent their interests. The typical corporate board is composed of 8 to 12 individuals

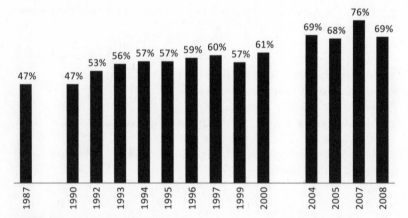

FIGURE 9.1 Institutional Ownership of the Top 1,000 Corporations
Source: The Conference Board, *2009 Institutional Investment Report.*

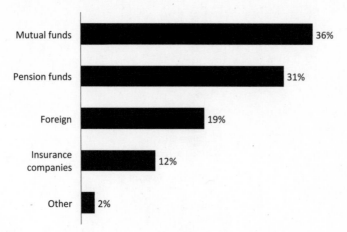

FIGURE 9.2   U.S. Holdings of Stocks by Institutional Investor Type[2]
Source: SIFMA, *Fact Book 2009.*

serving either one- or three-year terms. Neither shareholders nor the board of directors manage the business directly. Instead, the board appoints a chief executive officer to manage day-to-day operations. Directors take a big-picture role, overseeing the work of the management team and helping guide the company on strategic initiatives.

In addition to electing the board of directors, stockholders vote on other matters that might have a significant impact on a company's direction. For example, shareholder approval is usually required before a significant merger can be completed or before compensation plans involving company stock can be adopted. Figure 9.3 diagrams the interaction of shareholders, the board, and the CEO.

The exact balance of power among a company's executive management team, directors, and stockholders is largely determined by the interplay among state law, stock exchange rules, federal regulations, and the company's charter and by-laws.

- State law has historically been the primary regulator of corporate governance matters, establishing the minimum powers guaranteed to stockholders of all public companies incorporated in that state.
- Stock markets, such as the New York Stock Exchange, may impose additional requirements on their listed companies. They may mandate stockholder approval of substantial stock issuance or of stock compensation plans.

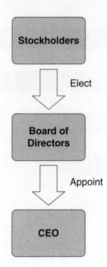

FIGURE 9.3   Indirect Stockholder Control

- Certain federal laws may also affect stockholder rights, particularly with regard to what information must be publicly disclosed to all stockholders.
- Finally, the company's charter and bylaws outline the specific powers of its executive management team, directors, and stockholders, operating within the framework of all state, federal, and stock market regulations. The charter may make some shareholders more equal than others, as "Exercising Control" explains.

EXERCISING CONTROL

Shareholder democracy is not always "one share–one vote." Some companies, like Google, have a class of *control shares* that carry a majority of the voting rights. This *supervoting* class is usually owned solely by the company's founders or management. In other cases, shareholders may all have the same voting rights, but because only a minority of the shares has been sold to the public, the bulk of shares are in the hands of small group—again usually founder and management—that retains all the power. For these controlled companies, the public stockholders generally do not have any significant ability to influence the company's management.

Given this complex web of requirements, it can sometimes be very difficult to clearly determine exactly what rights stockholders have in a particular company.

The Proxy Voting Process: Stockholder Meetings

Under state corporate law, companies are required to hold a meeting of stockholders at least once a year.[3] During these meetings, stockholders are asked to vote on a variety of proposals that could have an impact on the current or future financial value of the company. Exactly which issues must be voted on is again determined by the interplay of state, federal, and stock exchange rules.

Under federal securities laws, companies must send stockholders detailed information about each proposal submitted for a vote. This information is contained in a document called the *proxy* or *proxy statement.* The company must deliver the proxy to stockholders far enough in advance of the meeting to give them adequate time to consider the information and cast their votes. Most companies send out proxies four or five weeks before the meeting. Few stockholders physically attend meetings to vote their shares. Rather, they complete ballots—most large investors do this electronically—that direct management to vote for or against the proposals contained within the proxy statement. This process is commonly referred to as *voting proxies* or *proxy voting.* A link to a sample proxy statement is included on this book's web site.

The majority of proposals in the proxy statement are submitted by the company's management. The most common type of management proposal presents a slate of director candidates, who must be elected by stockholders. Other items typically submitted by management include the ratification of corporate auditors and the approval of the stock compensation plans that the company will use to pay its executives. Depending on the type of proposal and the applicable corporate governance rules, management must get a certain level of shareholder approval before it can implement the proposals. While a simple majority of votes cast is usually sufficient, in some cases a supermajority— which is defined in the company's bylaws as, for example, two-thirds of the shares outstanding—may be needed.

Stockholders may also submit proposals in the company's proxy statement for other stockholders to vote upon. These submissions must comply with specific SEC requirements. For example, a stockholder wanting to put a proposal in the proxy must first provide evidence that he has continuously held the company's stock for at least one year and that the holdings were worth at least $2,000 or accounted for at least 1 percent of the company's shares. The SEC also places limits on the length of the proposal and

TABLE 9.1 Typical Shareholder Proposals

Category	Typical Proposals
Corporate governance	Implement different voting procedures for director elections.
Executive compensation	Limit company payments to top executives upon termination of their employment.
Environmental and social	Increase disclosure regarding greenhouse gas emissions.

specifies deadlines for submission. With regard to content, the proposal cannot suggest that the company act contrary to any laws nor can it deal with a matter relating to the company's *ordinary business,* a term that lacks a clear definition and is often the subject of much debate.

Stockholder proposals are generally written in the form of recommendations and don't mandate a particular course of action by the company. This is because most state laws vest the directors—not shareholders—with the discretionary power to manage the company.[4] As a result, a company is not obligated to implement most stockholder proposals, even if the proposal receives support from a majority of stockholders. For example, shareholders at one company have approved a proposal requiring annual elections of all of its directors in each of the past six years, but the company's board has continued to elect only one-third of its directors each year.

Despite the procedural challenges—not to mention the often discouraging outcomes—many stockholders submit proposals that make it into the proxy statement for a vote at annual meetings. Stockholder proposals generally fall into one of three categories, outlined in Table 9.1. We discuss each of these types of stockholder proposals in greater detail later in this chapter.

In addition to annual stockholder meetings, companies must hold special or extraordinary stockholder meetings if certain events occur during the year. That is most likely to happen if a company's executive management team and board of directors has negotiated an agreement to merge with another company, and the deal requires stockholder approval. A special meeting may usually be called by shareholders with more than a specified percentage of the company's outstanding shares.

PROXY VOTING BY MUTUAL FUNDS

As with many aspects of mutual fund operations, a fund's proxy voting is regulated by the SEC. Before 2003, mutual funds had no specific restrictions or obligations with respect to proxy voting activities, other than to advance the interests of fund investors. Some fund industry critics, however, believed that fund managers were not aggressive enough in voting their proxies and sided with company management too often. Others felt that fund investors wanted to know how fund managers were voting their proxies in specific cases. While there was little academic evidence to support these critics, the SEC decided to encourage fund managers to become more involved in proxy matters by requiring them to publicly disclose:

- Their proxy voting policies and procedures
- The actual votes cast throughout the year
- How they manage any potential, material conflict of interest with regard to voting proxies

Note that these disclosure requirements apply only to mutual funds and not to proxy voting by other types of institutional investors—with one exception. The Dodd-Frank financial reform legislation requires that all institutional investment managers annually disclose votes on certain executive compensation issues. (We talk more about these issues later in this chapter.)

Since these regulations were enacted, funds with an informal approach to proxy voting have codified their policies and procedures. And all fund management companies post information about their proxy voting on their web sites.

Proxy Voting Policies

Most mutual fund proxy voting policies contain the same key elements. They begin with a statement of principle: virtually all funds cast votes based on what they believe is in the best, long-term economic interest of fund investors. That's often defined as increasing company profitability or boosting shareholder value—which many investors believe is best measured by the stock price over the long term. Since there's much debate over exactly what actions are in the best interest of investors, different mutual funds and other shareholders—all acting on the same general principle—may cast different votes on the same ballot items.

The proxy policy will then outline how the fund will vote on the proposals that are submitted most often to publicly traded companies. Two types of proposals are almost always covered: director elections and executive compensation.

Director elections are the most common proposal in the proxy statement. They are also arguably the most important, since the board has tremendous influence on the management of the company. A mutual fund's proxy voting policies will explain when the fund will support particular director candidates. For example, a fund may vote only for candidates that have attended at least 75 percent of the previous year's board meetings. Directors may also need to be independent if they are to serve on a key committee of the board. Independent directors do not receive any compensation from the company, directly or indirectly, other than fees paid for their service as directors.

Executive compensation is another issue that appears often in proxies and, therefore, in proxy voting policies. Company managements often propose plans that award shares of stock to executives as part of their compensation. Since these awards decrease or dilute a fund's ownership of the company, proxy policies generally set a limit on the plan size. For example, a fund may not approve a plan that involves more than 10 percent of a company's outstanding shares.

While the proxy policy will be specific about the approach to voting on common proposals, it will then explain that votes on other ballot questions will be determined on a case-by-case approach, and it may describe the general principles that it applies when evaluating particular types of proposals. In the case of proposed mergers, for example, a policy may explain that a mutual fund will support the deal if the investment team concludes that it will provide significant opportunities for generating incremental revenues or for cost savings as a result of economies of scale.

Proxy Decision Making

As we have noted, mutual funds and other institutional investors may disagree over what—precisely—is in the best, long-term economic interest of fund investors. Proxy voting is often a judgment call, but fund managers can draw on a wide variety of resources to help them make their voting decisions.

Academic research. Corporate governance is a very popular topic for academic studies at both law and business schools. This research can provide evidence that certain corporate governance practices tend to increase shareholder value or improve company performance. For example, there's a body of research that establishes a negative link between certain anti-takeover devices and stock returns. (We come back to anti-takeover devices shortly.) Unfortunately, much of this research does not generate conclusive results, so fund managers must turn to other sources.

Proxy advisory firms. Most mutual funds subscribe to a proxy advisory service that provides reports and recommendations on all proxy proposals. These firms produce in-depth research and analysis on issues and make recommendations on how investors should vote. Their opinion can have a substantial impact on vote outcomes—which means that they are not always popular with corporate managements. (We review their pros and cons in "Is Too Much Advice a Bad Thing?")

IS TOO MUCH ADVICE A BAD THING?

The leading proxy advisory firms in the United States are RiskMetrics Group and Glass Lewis, and most institutional investors at least consider their vote recommendations when deciding how to cast their ballots. While the extent of their influence over vote outcomes is the subject of much debate, it's clear that they play an important role in the proxy voting process—and that doesn't sit well with the management of some companies. Some managements contend that the advice provided these firms:

- Takes an unreasonable check-the-box approach, when a more thoughtful, case-by-case analysis is needed.
- Is not independent, because some advisory firms may be hired as a consultant by some corporations to help them design proxy proposals that are likely to get a positive recommendation. Others may be unduly influenced by their parent companies.
- Is not realistic enough, because the advisory firms aren't stockholders themselves.

Proxy advisory firms maintain that they provide investors with valuable, independent, and thoughtful research on proxy voting issues worldwide. Their defenders are quick to point out that the advisory firms often advocate votes against management proposals, which may be why they are unpopular with some corporate executives.

Engagement. Mutual funds will also get information and opinions about proxy issues from the company managements proposing them. Public companies often employ investor relations professionals and proxy solicitation firms. These advisors identify large stockholders, provide them with information about the proposal, and lobby them for their support. This *stockholder engagement,* as it's known, has become increasingly popular over the past few years and is often used after a company receives an unfavorable recommendation from a proxy advisory firm.

Fund boards of directors. Mutual fund boards of directors also play a role in proxy voting. All boards approve the voting policies for their funds and review them annually in light of the issues that have arisen recently or are likely to arise in the coming year. While most delegate the actual voting of proxies to the investment advisers, some boards weigh in on specific votes, such as those involving a contentious merger.

Proxy Voting Results

So with all this information, how do mutual funds and other shareholders generally vote on common proxy items? Based on a recent study by the Investment Company Institute, mutual funds supported management proposals more than 96 percent of the time.[5] In this regard, mutual funds behave like other stockholders, given that most management proposals contained in the proxy statement obtain majority support.

This high level of consensus between stockholders and management is not surprising—at least for actively managed mutual funds. That's because owning a company's stock ordinarily indicates a belief in the ability of a company's management. As a result, active portfolio managers are inclined to vote with management's recommendation. Moreover, if active managers become dissatisfied with management, they can simply sell the stock, a course of action commonly referred to as the *Wall Street walk*. It's viewed as an efficient and low-cost way to send a message to management that stockholders are unhappy. Because significant selling can lead to a declining stock price, it's a signal that management can't afford to ignore, since a falling stock price can hurt a company's ability to raise additional capital, make certain acquisitions, and retain top talent through stock grants.

However, there are many occasions when mutual funds and other stockholders *do* vote against management on a particular proposal. Stockholders may vote against a compensation plan because the size is too large or against a director due to independence concerns. Despite opposition from company management, certain types of shareholder proposals average at least majority support from other shareholders, as shown in Table 9.2. In 2009, for example, shareholder proposals to repeal a classified board averaged almost 66 percent support and proposals to reduce supermajority vote requirements averaged almost 70 percent support. (We discuss the intent of both proposals in the next section.)

ACTIVISM AND MUTUAL FUNDS

The strong support for certain shareholder proposals reflects an increasing willingness on the part of institutional investors to actively use proxy

TABLE 9.2 2009 Proxy Season Scorecard (December 15, 2009)

	Number of Results Available (2009)	Average Support (2009)*
Governance Shareholder Proposals—Executive Pay Issues		
Advisory vote on compensation	76	45.6%
Vote on golden parachute	5	33.2%**
Anti-gross-ups policy	2	50.2%
Vote on executive death benefits	13	39.6%
Retention period for stock awards	14	26.1%
Establish bonus banks	4	26.6%
Governance Shareholder Proposals—Board Issues		
Independent board chairman	34	36.9%
Allow for cumulative voting	32	34.2%
Require majority vote to elect directors	49	58.0%
Governance Shareholder Proposals—Takeover Defenses/Other		
Right to call special meeting	61	50.8%
End or reduce supermajority vote requirement	17	69.7%
Repeal classified board	63	65.6%
Reincorporate in North Dakota	16	7.4%

*Support as percentage of shares voted for and against, abstentions excluded. Results may be preliminary.
**The average is skewed by a vote at Ingles Markets, where CEO Robert P. Ingle controls 86 percent of voting power.
Source: RiskMetrics Group. Reproduced by permission of RiskMetrics Group, Inc. ©2009. RiskMetrics Group, Inc. All rights reserved.

voting to enhance shareholder value. This represents a dramatic change in approach, because for most of the twentieth century, corporate annual meetings were sleepy affairs at which stockholders regularly approved all management proposals with very little comment or dissent.

In the 1980s, however, corporate raiders and leveraged buyout specialists like Carl Icahn demonstrated how stockholders could use their rights to take over a company without the consent of management. They'd buy a large block of stock in a company they thought was undervalued and then propose an entirely new board of directors. With the help of other investors, they'd garner a majority of shares to vote in their candidates—who would promptly toss out management and complete the takeover—paying stockholders a premium price for their shares.

While the corporate raiders were popular with investors who were happy to get more cash in their pockets, they were not at all well liked by the company managements who objected to the raiders' aggressive tactics and to the damage that their cost cutting did to companies after acquisitions were completed. (Raiders responded that managements were more worried about their jobs than their companies.)

To protect themselves against these acquirers and thwart these unwanted bids, known as *hostile takeovers*, many companies added anti-takeover provisions to their charter and bylaws. Companies were often able to implement these anti-takeover devices without seeking stockholder approval. The most common of them are:

- *Stockholder rights plans.* A shareholder rights plan, commonly known as a *poison pill*, is triggered if a single investor acquires more than a certain amount of the company's stock—usually 15 percent or 20 percent. Under those circumstances, the other stockholders of the company receive the right to acquire a large number of company shares at a severely discounted price, such as one cent per share. Since most current shareholders would act on this generous offer, the potential buyer's interest would be significantly diluted, meaning that it would become a very small percentage of the outstanding shares. In the process, a potential acquirer would not only lose a lot of economic value (because the value of her holdings would fall), but would also find it extremely difficult to get a majority vote from shareholders to complete the takeover.

- *Staggered, or classified, boards.* Some companies don't elect all directors annually. Instead, they elect directors for multiyear terms and then stagger those terms, so that only a portion of the directors are on the ballot every year, creating what are called classified boards. It is much harder to pull off a hostile takeover of a company with a classified board and a poison pill, because the potential buyer can't propose an entirely new set of directors at one time. Instead, the buyer would have to win two annual elections to obtain a majority of the board seats and redeem the pill.

- *Supermajority voting.* Companies may require that a very high percentage of outstanding shares approve any takeover proposal or related merger, a percentage that is high enough to discourage any potential acquirer. Sometimes, a group of controlling shareholders will have enough of an ownership stake to block any takeover proposal that it doesn't like.

- *Control share statutes. Control share* statutes are state laws that deny shares their voting rights once their owner has acquired more than a certain percentage of the stock of the company, unless the purchase has been approved by the company's board. Many states have adopted a 15 or 20 percent threshold. Again, this is a device that makes it almost impossible for an unwanted acquirer to complete a merger.

■ *Stakeholder constituency statutes.* Some states have adopted *stakeholder constituency* statutes, usually as political responses to the hostile takeovers of the 1980s that often led to plant closings and layoffs. These statutes permit—but do not require—boards of directors to take into account constituencies beyond the company's stockholders—such as employees, customers, and local communities—when evaluating whether to accept a proposed takeover. In other words, these laws provide liability protection for boards that want to reject an offer from an acquirer, even if it will result in substantial gains for shareholders.

Stockholder Activism

Serious concern over anti-takeover devices contributed to the rise of a new type of stockholder—the activist. To be activist investors, shareholders must do more than diligently read proxies and regularly vote shares. Activists might nominate an alternative slate of directors, publicly express dissatisfaction with management in the media, submit shareholder proposals, or lobby against management's recommendation on proxy matters.

One of the pioneers of activist investing was Robert Monks. He founded the first proxy advisory firm, Institutional Stockholder Services, which is now part of RiskMetrics Group. He and other early activists developed ways to deal with the regulatory framework governing takeover bids, the filing of stockholder resolutions, and the submission of alternative slates of directors. They paved the way for the institutional activist investors that were to follow in their footsteps.

Today, some state and union pension funds have become prominent activists. Many of these funds have a substantial proportion of their assets invested in stock index funds. That means that they can't simply sell a stock when they're unhappy with management, since a passively managed fund must hold all the stocks in the index. If index fund investors want to express dissatisfaction with a company, they must do so more directly.

These pension plans may openly criticize corporate managements and encourage other investors to become more active in investigating proxy issues. For example, the California Public Employees' Retirement System publishes an annual focus list of underperforming companies with poor corporate governance practices that CalPERS would like to see change, and it has a web site devoted to corporate governance at www.calpers-governance.org. These activities—at CalPERS and other pension plans—have been controversial. While the activist funds contend that they are advancing the interest of all shareholders, critics have argued that their motivations are more often parochial or political.

Hedge funds have proven quite willing to increase shareholder value through activism, often serving as the catalyst for proxy fights and other battles for corporate control. Briefly, a hedge fund is a commingled investment vehicle that is not registered with the SEC and that uses aggressive investment strategies. (Hedge funds are covered in depth in Chapter 12.) Here, too, critics have alleged that hedge funds are not building shareholder value over the long term; they're just looking to make a quick profit by selling the company to the highest bidder. Whatever their motivations, hedge funds generally take much more concentrated stock positions than mutual funds in certain public companies and then aggressively use their rights and resources to agitate for change.

Actively Managed Mutual Funds and Activism

Actively managed mutual funds do not typically engage in shareholder activism. They rarely initiate proxy fights, submit shareholder proposals, or take any of their issues with management to the media. Does this make them poor stewards of their stock holdings?

Many activist investors would answer yes. They argue that mutual funds are generally too passive when it comes to being responsible owners and holding management accountable. Funds vote against management far less often than do activist investors. And while mutual funds may vote to support some shareholder proposals, they don't usually expend the resources to submit any proposals themselves. Some critics of the industry claim that fund managers avoid activism because they do not want to disrupt any business relationships with the company's management. For example, a mutual fund may be earning a large advisory fee for managing a company's 401(k) plan and might therefore be reluctant to vote against management on proxy matters.

In response, mutual fund managers maintain that their first line of defense against poorly performing management is selling the stock. They argue that the costs of preparing shareholder proposals and waging expensive proxy fights outweigh the potential benefits to their funds, which rarely hold more than 10 percent of a company's common stock. Instead, most of the benefits would accrue to other shareholders who would be free riders on their efforts. As a result, mutual fund managers who do have issues with management often prefer to express their concerns behind closed doors, believing that this quiet approach may be more effective than statements made through the media. There are many instances where mutual fund managers have had a key influence on corporate decision making. "Which Side Are You On?" describes one example.

WHICH SIDE ARE YOU ON?

The fight for over Laureate Education's proposed transaction in 2007 was a great example of how management, directors, and stockholders can all use their powers to attempt to influence the direction of a company.[6]

The Buyout Deal. In January of 2007, the board of directors at Laureate Education announced a deal that would transition the company from a publicly held company to a private one. (This type of transaction is also known as a *leveraged buyout,* or *going private.*) Laureate—formerly Sylvan Learning Systems—owns and operates campus-based and online universities around the world. A syndicate of buyers had agreed to purchase all of the company's shares for $60.50 per share, an 11 percent premium to the price of the stock at the time. The syndicate of buyers would consist of various private equity firms and would be led by the company's then-current chairman and CEO.

Shareholders Weigh In. A majority of shareholders had to approve the deal at a special shareholder meeting to be held later that year. But before the company even distributed proxy materials—and after failing in an attempt to discuss the matter privately with company management—mutual fund manager T. Rowe Price stated publicly that it opposed the deal. It felt that the Laureate was worth considerably more than the proposed price, and—as the second-largest shareholder, with about 8 percent of the outstanding shares, its opinion carried weight.

The Conflict. T. Rowe Price noted that the deal didn't just undervalue the company, it also involved a very significant conflict of interest. Specifically, the chairman and CEO had conflicting loyalties. As leader of the purchasing group, he had a vested interest in getting the lowest price for the potential buyers, since that would increase their—and his—future profits on the deal. But as the senior executive of the company, he had an obligation to get the highest price for the company's shareholders. While the company was quick to point out that the transaction had been approved by the entire board of directors—not just the chairman and CEO—the perception of bias remained.

The Role of Proxy Advisory Firms. T. Rowe Price encouraged the proxy advisory service, Institutional Shareholder Services (later to merge with RiskMetrics), to recommend that shareholders vote against the deal. A negative vote recommendation could swing the opinion of any shareholders who were on the fence.

A Win for Shareholders? In June 2007, before the vote could take place, the buying group agreed to raise the price by $1.50 a share, an increase of 2.5 percent from its original offer. But in an unusual move, the board changed the structure of the deal to a tender offer—which would not require a shareholder meeting and vote. In a tender offer, shareholders sell, or *tender,* their shares to the buyer. If more than 50 percent of shares are tendered in this way, the deal is completed. Since Institutional Shareholder Services does not provide recommendations on tender offers, this change took the proxy advisory service out of the picture. Ultimately, 59 percent of the shares were tendered and the deal was approved.

Current Issues in Proxy Voting

In the wake of the recent credit crisis, there has been no shortage of proposals to reform and improve the corporate governance system. The more popular ones have focused on the company's board of directors and on executive compensation practices.

Board of directors. Stockholders have recently raised some serious concerns over the validity of the director election process.

- *Plurality voting.* While stockholders can elect directors, they can't easily turn them out of office. In most corporate elections, stockholders can either cast their votes in favor of a director, or they can withhold their votes for that director. The latter is the legal equivalent of not voting at all, because the number of votes withheld has no effect on the outcome of the election. As long as at least one share is voted in favor of a director, he is legally elected to the board. This system is called *plurality voting,* and it's the default standard under the corporate laws of most states, including Delaware, where most large U.S. companies are chartered. Many shareholders claim that this voting structure does not provide shareholders with an adequate ability to fire directors that they believe are underperforming. Companies defend the practice because it avoids a failed election that could leave the company without enough directors to oversee the company.

  More and more large public companies have adopted procedures requiring that directors submit their resignations if they don't receive a majority of votes cast at an election. And other companies have begun to respond to the shareholder discontent behind withheld votes. A recent study suggests that large numbers of withheld votes—often the result of a campaign by a shareholder activist—can prompt boards to take actions that enhance shareholder value, such as firing a CEO who is performing poorly.[7]

- *Proxy access.* Until recently, shareholders didn't have much choice when it came to director candidates. Only the candidates nominated by the current board of directors appeared on the company's proxy statement. If stockholders wanted to see their own candidates on the board, they had to create their own proxy statement, which had to be published and distributed at their own expense. Since presenting a competing slate through a mailing to all shareholders can cost millions of dollars, it was not a common occurrence. For example, when Microsoft considered proposing its own slate of directors as part of its attempt to acquire Yahoo, it estimated the cost of a proxy battle at $40 million. One alternative that has been proposed would allow shareholders to solicit votes directly from large shareholders but then use the Internet to communicate with the remainder—a suggestion that's in step with the SEC's interest in increasing Internet solicitation of proxies.

But all of this is changing because of the passage of the Dodd-Frank financial reform legislation in 2010. With the backing of the new law, the SEC has adopted rules which allow shareholders to place their own nominees on the company's proxy ballot, a new right known as *proxy access*. To qualify for proxy access, shareholders must have owned at least 3 percent of a company's shares for at least 3 years continuously and cannot be seeking to take over the company.

Executive compensation. Certain executive compensation practices have been blamed for the credit crisis of 2008. Industry observers contend that large bonus awards were structured in a way that encouraged executives to produce great short-term results—but that those short-term gains were generated at the expense of long-term value. In some cases, the practices used to reap the fabulous pay packages even decreased long-term value—and in a few cases even destroyed the company altogether.

As a result of these problems, activist investors have suggested greater shareholder involvement in setting executive pay. In the past, compensation for specific executives was set by the board of directors without shareholder input. Directors inform stockholders of the pay packages after the fact, providing detailed information on the compensation of the top five executives along with a discussion of the principles that the board used in deciding on the amounts. Stockholders would be called upon only to approve the size of a company's total stock compensation program, but not any cash payments or the amounts of stock allocated to specific individuals.

As a result of the Dodd-Frank financial reform legislation of 2010, shareholders will have an opportunity to weigh in on a company's compensation practices at least once every three years, through a vote commonly referred to as "Say on Pay." Although the vote will be advisory only, rather than binding, similar advisory votes in other countries have been effective in curbing egregious instances of excessive executive pay. Shareholders will also have an opportunity to cast an advisory vote on severance packages for executives—commonly referred to as *golden parachutes*—that could be triggered by a merger or acquisition already the subject of a shareholder vote.

MUTUAL FUNDS AND SOCIAL CHANGE

A minority of shareholders have also used the proxy voting process to advocate for social change. Unlike activist investors, their goal wasn't necessarily to make money. They believed instead that what they were doing was right from a moral perspective. Over the years, however, a growing group of investors has come to conclude that taking a stance on certain social issues can be important from a financial perspective. We take a look here at how the thinking about proxy voting has evolved and the role mutual funds have played in movements for social change.

Socially Responsible Investing

A subset of mutual funds, known as *socially responsible investing*, or SRI, funds, appeal to investors who would like to effect societal change as well as seek a financial return. They are only a small part of the fund industry, making up less than 1 percent of assets in 2007, but they are growing rapidly.[8] Major SRI firms in the United States include Calvert Investments, Domini Social Investments, and Pax World.

These funds invest only in companies that meet criteria outlined in the prospectus—criteria that align with the environmental, religious, or social views of their investors. For example, an SRI fund focused on the environment may forego investing in a high-performing oil company if it believes that the company is not doing enough to limit its greenhouse gas emissions. Similarly, a fund with a religious or social tilt may choose not to invest in companies that are doing business in or with Sudan. SRI funds don't just eliminate companies from consideration for what they consider unacceptable policies and procedures. They may actively seek out companies that have adopted practices that they they'd like to encourage, such as firms that been successful at bringing diversity into their boardrooms.

SRI funds often use their rights as stockholders to try to change policies at the companies in which they invest. For example, they may submit stockholder proposals requesting that the company reduce its greenhouse gas emissions by a certain percentage by a certain time. Or they may ask for more extensive disclosure on a company's hiring practices. Because of their dual objectives of seeking both financial return and social return, SRI funds ordinarily submit and vote for these types of proposals at a much higher rate than traditional mutual funds.

Responsible Investing

As SRI funds have sought a broader impact, their experience has raised questions about the approach used by more traditional funds. Mutual funds have historically maintained that social issues are best addressed by regulatory or legislative bodies and are not a proper subject on which stockholders should voice their opinion.

However, the arguments for SRI investments have evolved from concerns about morality to concerns about financial impact. For example, does the emission of greenhouse gases pose a potential financial risk to the company as governments move forward on carbon caps? Does a company doing business with organizations tied to the Sudanese government expose the company to significant public relations risk? Raising these types of questions has led to an increased awareness by traditional mutual funds of the potential financial impact of social issues.

THE UN PRINCIPLES FOR RESPONSIBLE INVESTMENT

Signatories to the UN Principles for Responsible Investment agree to:

1. Incorporate environmental, social, and governance or ESG issues into investment analysis and decision making.
2. Be active owners.
3. Seek appropriate disclosure on ESG issues.
4. Promote acceptance and implementation of the UN PRI within the investment industry.
5. Work with other signatories to enhance the effectiveness of the UN PRI.
6. Report on activities and progress toward implementing the UN PRI.

More information on these principles is available at www.unpri.org.

As a result, many investment managers now incorporate consideration of environmental, social, and governance, or ESG, issues into their investment analysis, in an approach called *responsible investing,* or *sustainable investing.* Responsible investing thus links ESG issues to traditional stock analysis, which evaluates how various nonfinancial as well as financial factors are likely to affect a stock's future price movements.

To emphasize their support of this approach, a growing number of managers are signing on to ESG principles. See "The UN Principles for Responsible Investing" for information on one influential set of guidelines. Since they were developed in 2006, the UN Principles have garnered more than 700 signatories, among them more than 400 investment managers. These include not just the socially responsible investment firms, but traditional mutual fund complexes as well.

PROXY VOTING OUTSIDE THE UNITED STATES

Over the past few decades, U.S. mutual fund complexes have increased their investments in non-U.S. equities. In 2009, stock mutual funds with an international or global mandate had more than $1.3 trillion in assets, close to one-third of assets in all types of stock funds. Fund managers investing outside the United States must deal with a different set of corporate governance challenges. This discussion that follows is not intended to be comprehensive; we focus instead on illustrative examples from a few countries. We discuss other challenges related to international investing in Chapter 16.

Dominant Stockholders

Dominant stockholders may seek to preserve their influence by frustrating the exercise of rights by minority stockholders, often through special voting structures. That's true everywhere in the world, including the United States. We've already seen how a company's founders might establish a *supervoting* class of shares that allow them to maintain control of company.

What's different at many foreign companies is that the dominant stockholder is often the government. France, for example, has a strong tradition of state involvement in the economy. In many of the industries that the government has partially privatized—such as the energy, telecommunications, and banking sectors—the state retains a *golden share* with greater voting power in the company than it should have based on its stock position.

Dominant shareholder groups have played a particularly important role in Japan, through the prevalence of *keiretsu,* which are groups of interrelated firms, usually affiliated with a commercial bank or insurance company. Keiretsu members generally have large positions in each other's stock in an interlocking system of cross-holdings. The keiretsu system was touted during the 1980s as an effective way of ensuring management accountability, because the large stockholders in the system have the knowledge and power to monitor management's decisions. Its reputation fell during the 1990s, however, when it was seen as impeding needed reforms by preventing takeovers and making restructuring more difficult. The system is now on the decline, as many Japanese companies are selling their cross-holdings and moving toward a more open system of corporate governance.

Legal Relationship between the Company's Board and Stockholders

The legal relationship between a foreign company's board and its stockholders may limit the rights of minority stockholders. In general, under U.S. state corporate law, a company's directors owe a fiduciary-type duty to all of its stockholders and to the company. By contrast, in many non-U.S. legal systems, the board may be required to take into account the interests of other stakeholders in the enterprise, including the company's labor unions and suppliers, as well as community groups and local governments. The interests of these groups may, on occasion, conflict with the interests of minority stockholders.

For example, under French law, while the board of directors represents the company and must act in its best interest, French courts have ruled that the best interests of the company go beyond and are distinct from the interests of stockholders. Similarly, Japanese law doesn't require the company's board of directors to represent the interests of stockholders. Courts there have ruled that directors have only an indirect duty to stockholders as the ultimate owners of the company. However, Japanese stock exchanges do provide limited oversight of the treatment of minority shareholders by the companies listed on those exchanges.

The structure and composition of company boards may make their directors particularly unlikely to protect the interests of minority stockholders. In France, for example, boards of directors often include a significant number of government officials. In Japan, the size of the board can be quite large, numbering over 20 individuals, and the vast majority of Japanese directors may be affiliated with the company.

Disclosure and Operational Issues

The quality of proxy information provided to stockholders in most other countries is generally much less comprehensive than in the United States.

In many countries, companies provide only the most basic information describing the proposals to be voted upon by stockholders, and little or nothing on executive compensation. In Brazil, the names of director candidates are not even publicly disclosed in certain cases!

In many countries, proxy information may be disseminated just in local newspapers or financial publications only a few days before a meeting and may not be translated into English. Even with the help of a proxy advisory firm, many U.S. investors find it quite difficult to receive timely information to make informed voting decisions.

Besides these informational disadvantages, U.S. stockholders with foreign holdings face a variety of operational challenges that can frustrate the exercise of stockholder rights. For example, some markets, such as Japan's, require physical delivery of proxy ballots, rather than electronic ballots. Other markets require a signed power of attorney to vote electronically and obtaining one can be a very cumbersome and time-consuming process. Certain markets practice *share blocking*, which means that they generally prohibit the sale of shares from the time a proxy vote is cast until shortly after the shareholders' meeting. Forced to choose between the ability to sell the stock and the ability to vote the stock, fund managers often conclude that retaining the flexibility to sell is more important. Share blocking is becoming less common, thanks to the passage of a recent European Union directive, but many major markets outside the European Union, including Switzerland, continue this practice.

CHAPTER SUMMARY

Mutual funds are large holders of stock and, as such, can play a key role in the management of public companies. Together with other shareholders, they elect the members of a company's board of directors. Stockholder approval is required before a company's management can take certain actions, such as launching a stock-based compensation program. Companies hold shareholder meetings at least annually—and more often if certain extraordinary events occur. Before the vote is held, they prepare a proxy statement describing the items on the ballot. While most of those items are included at the request of management, some are proposals submitted by shareholders.

The independent directors of mutual funds approve policies that govern their proxy voting of the funds. These policies generally state that the fund will vote in the best long-term interests of fund investors. They include specific guidelines for voting on the most common proxy proposals—usually director elections, executive compensation, and anti-takeover proposals. Funds may decide how to vote on other issues on a case-by-case-basis, using academic research and the recommendations from proxy advisory services among other inputs. The SEC requires that funds disclose both their proxy voting policies and the actual votes they cast during the year.

Some investors, known as activists, use the proxy voting process to initiate change at companies, by nominating an alternative slate of directors, publicly expressing dissatisfaction with management decisions, or submitting shareholder proposals to the proxy statement. Mutual funds are generally not activist investors, even though they often vote against certain types of management proposals in the proxy statement. Instead, fund managers normally express dissatisfaction with a company by selling its shares.

Other investors encourage companies to pay more attention to social issues, if only because failure to do so might have a negative financial impact in the future. An increasing number of mutual funds now consider the potential effects on stock prices of environmental, social, and governance factors.

Mutual funds that buy non-U.S. stocks may face additional challenges in exercising their rights as shareholders. Decisions may be made by a dominant shareholder—possibly the government—or a shareholder group that is not particularly concerned with the rights of minority shareholders—and may even be legally required to consider the interests of constituencies other than shareholders when making policy. Information about proposals in non-U.S. proxy statements may be hard to obtain, and investors may be blocked from selling shares around the time of a proxy vote.

Three

Selling Investment Funds

The U.S. mutual fund industry has been phenomenally successful. According to the Investment Company Institute, at the end of 2009, there were more than 7,600 funds—almost seven times the number offered in 1984. The increase in fund assets was no less spectacular, with the dollar value of fund investments rising from $370 billion to $11.1 trillion over that same 25-year period.

Expanded distribution of mutual funds was a key driver of this growth. Very simply put, fund management companies sold more funds to a larger group of people using a wider variety of sales methods.

Distribution of mutual funds takes place through three main channels:

1. In the *intermediary* channel, consumers purchase funds through brokerage firms, banks, insurance companies, or registered investment advisers. These firms act as intermediaries between fund sponsors and investors.
2. In the *direct* channel, a consumer buys shares directly from the fund or through a fund supermarket.
3. The *retirement* channel encompasses 401(k) plans and other employer-sponsored retirement plans known as *defined contribution plans*.

This section examines the three channels and the trends in each. It also takes a look at exchange-traded funds and hedge funds, investment vehicles that have become the toughest competitors faced by traditional mutual funds. It has three chapters:

Chapter 10 discusses retail sales of mutual funds. It begins with a review of the factors that drive sales of funds. It surveys the intermediary channel, reviewing the different types of intermediaries—broker-dealers, banks, insurance companies, and registered investment advisers—and discussing how they are paid. It then looks at the no-load fund complexes and fund supermarkets that compose the direct channel. The chapter concludes with a review of trends affecting all the distribution channels, specifically open architecture, the increasing demand for advice, and the development of needs-based products.

Chapter 11 focuses on retirement plans and the role that mutual funds play in them. It begins with a summary of the benefits of tax-deferred retirement investing. The chapter then goes on to examine the two most popular retirement plans: employer-sponsored 401(k) plans and individual retirement accounts. It summarizes the historical development of their features and reviews the principal regulations that govern them. The final section discusses recent trends in retirement planning in the United States, including the increasing focus on distribution planning, on making retirement plans simpler and on ensuring retirement security for all.

Chapter 12 examines exchange-traded funds and hedge funds, which have become tough competition for traditional mutual funds. The first half looks at the growth in exchange-traded funds, examining their advantages and disadvantages, and their unique structure and operations as well as the investment strategies they use. It also discusses current trends in the use of exchange-traded funds. The second half discusses the advantages and disadvantages of hedge funds and reviews the investment strategies they use. The chapter concludes with a description of hedge fund investors and a summary of hedge fund regulation.

CHAPTER 10

Retail Sales

Individual investors are by far the biggest purchasers of mutual fund shares. By the end of 2009, more than 75 percent of industry assets had been bought for individual accounts, according to the Investment Company Institute.[1] Therefore, we begin our survey of mutual fund sales with a look at the retail channels that distribute funds to individual investors.

Consumers can buy fund shares through three different avenues.

1. They can invest through intermediaries, using professional advisers to interact with the fund management company. These advisers usually provide personalized investment advice in addition to transaction processing. This is the *intermediary channel*.
2. They can purchase shares directly from the fund sponsor.
3. They can open a brokerage account at a mutual fund supermarket and purchases fund shares through that account.

Together, purchases made directly from a fund complex or through a supermarket constitute the *direct channel*.

This chapter reviews:

- The factors that drive sales of mutual fund shares
- The characteristics of the intermediary channel, consisting of broker-dealers, banks, insurance companies, and registered investment advisers
- The characteristics of the direct channel
- Trends affecting all of the distribution channels

WHAT SELLS MUTUAL FUNDS?

Before we take a detailed look at the distribution channels, we need to answer a very basic question: What sells mutual funds?

One surefire route to growth of fund assets has always been outstanding investment returns.[2] Although every fund advertisement warns that "past performance is no guarantee of future results," investors chase funds with hot short-term performance. During the Internet bubble of the late 1990s, aggressive growth funds with lots of exposure to the popular technology sector posted dazzling returns. Investors responded by funneling assets into these areas almost exclusively. Similarly, they poured into emerging market equity funds in 2005 and 2006 when countries in the developing world experienced strong economic growth, and their stock markets soared.

Unfortunately, the strategy of buying funds with exceptional past performance is rarely successful. Investors in the technology stocks and emerging market equities in our examples suffered substantial losses during subsequent market collapses. But poor experience with the approach has not dimmed its appeal to some investors.

While many prospective buyers favor funds with the highest positive returns, others focus on particular aspects of performance, as we discussed in Chapter 4. For example, many investors gravitate toward funds with high Morningstar ratings, which measure risk-adjusted performance. One study calculated that funds with an initial five-star rating experienced sales that were 53 percent above average.[3] Others prefer funds that generate a high yield from interest income, especially when they're considering bond funds. And a third group looks for a low cost of owning a fund. Most notably, many investors will not pay a front-end load when they buy shares.[4]

Advertising also appears to affect sales. According to one study, funds that advertise in national newspapers or magazines have greater inflows than those that do not advertise.[5] Little wonder, then, that fund advertising has become a multimillion-dollar business. Fund sponsors selling through both the intermediary and direct channels use TV, radio, Internet, and print ads to build their brand image. They also heavily advertise specific funds emphasizing the performance factors that most appeal to prospective investors, so that fund ads are full of star ratings, performance rankings, and impressive return figures.

But there's a third factor at work: investors often buy a particular fund because a financial adviser has recommended it. An Investment Company Institute survey found that close to three out of four fund investors consulted with a financial adviser before they made their fund purchase; of those, 60 percent said that advisers were the most important source of information on the fund they ended up owning. (In contrast, only 34 percent looked at the prospectus before making their investment.) Of those who talked with an adviser about a purchase, almost one-third allowed him or her to take the lead on the final decision, while one-half said they made the decision jointly with the adviser.[6] In short, financial adviser opinion has a huge influence on fund selection. Most of these advisers work within the intermediary channel, the first stop on our tour of mutual funds sales channels.

THE INTERMEDIARY CHANNEL

Advice is the key selling proposition of the intermediary channel. Almost all of the firms in this channel work through representatives—financial advisers, insurance agents, or trust officers—who provide investment advice to clients as part of an ongoing relationship. The adviser may recommend a mutual fund to help the client implement that advice. For the past 15 years, the majority of household mutual fund assets were purchased with the help of professional financial advisers, as you can see in Figure 10.1.

The industry divides the intermediary channel into four segments:

1. *Broker-dealers.* Broker-dealers, or B/Ds, or brokerage firms, advise their clients on the purchase of all types of securities, not just mutual funds. Their sales representatives were traditionally called brokers, though today they are usually referred to as financial advisers, or FAs, financial consultants, or account executives.

   The best-known broker-dealers are the *wirehouses,* so-called because they were early adopters of the telegraph wire as a means of communication with branch offices. Because of industry consolidation, there are only four major wirehouses left today: Merrill Lynch (which is now owned by Bank of America), the Morgan Stanley Smith Barney

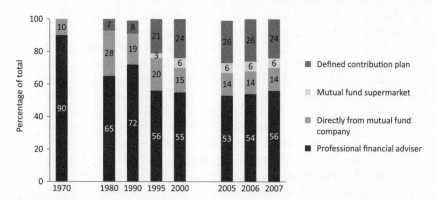

FIGURE 10.1 Household Mutual Fund Assets by Purchase Source (Percent)[7]
Source: Investment Company Institute, "Ownership of Mutual Funds Through Professional Financial Advisers, 2007." Components may not add to 100 percent because of rounding.

joint venture, UBS Financial Services, and Wells Fargo Advisers. They operate as an integrated network of national offices, providing a high level of both guidance and support services to their financial advisers, including—true to their name—the latest technology.

At the opposite end of the size spectrum are the independent broker-dealers. These are typically small shops staffed by a few professionals, often former wirehouse employees, who left larger firms in search of greater flexibility and an ownership stake.

In-between are firms that try to combine the support services of the wirehouses and the flexibility of the independents, sometimes by acting as a network for independent broker-dealers. In industry rankings, they are often combined together as regional broker-dealers. A major firm in this category is Edward Jones.

2. *Banks.* Banks make up the second segment of the intermediary channel. They distribute mutual funds to the general public through their bank branch networks and to wealthier individuals through their trust departments. Technically, they do this through subsidiaries registered as broker-dealers.

Note that all four of the big wirehouses are owned by banking giants, so that there is a growing overlap between the broker-dealer and bank segments. When we refer to the bank segment throughout this chapter, however, we exclude these wirehouses.

3. *Insurance companies.* Insurance companies are a third segment. While they make some sales directly to the public (again, through broker-dealer subsidiaries), they're more likely to sell funds through insurance agents as part of variable annuities, an investment vehicle we discuss in detail shortly.

4. *Registered investment advisers.* Finally, registered investment advisers usually recommend funds as part of a comprehensive package of asset management and financial planning services. One of the distinguishing features of RIAs is their fee structure: they often charge clients a percentage of account assets for their services. Like independent broker-dealers, most RIAs are smaller shops, and many RIAs are former wirehouse employees. (The term *RIA* applies to both the firms and the professionals working in them.[8]) Also like independent broker-dealers, they may participate in a network that provides support services. LPL Financial is a prominent firm providing centralized services to this group as well as to independent brokerage firms.

While we've talked how independent broker-dealers and registered investment advisers are alike, there is a clear legal distinction between them. "Shades of Advice" explains.

SHADES OF ADVICE

What's the difference between a financial adviser and a registered investment adviser? To the individual investor, it sometimes seems as if the only thing distinguishing them is what they call themselves. Certainly they both provide investment advice to individuals, usually as part of an ongoing relationship.

But to the SEC, there's a significant distinction. FAs work for broker-dealers, which are regulated under the provisions of the Securities Exchange Act of 1934. RIAs fall under the provisions of the Investment Advisers Act of 1940. As a result, FAs and RIAs take different licensing exams.[9] This differing oversight has three practical effects on clients:

Fee structure. Only FAs may receive commissions from the trading of securities, while only RIAs may receive fees based on the assets in an account. While this might seem any easy way to tell FAs and RIAs apart, many advisers—and the firms they work for—hold both types of licenses. This dual registration allows them to charge both types of fees, with the choice in a particular instance determined by the type of service provided.

Brochure. RIAs—but not FAs—are required to give their clients a brochure describing their services in detail. (This requirement is commonly referred to as the *brochure rule.*) The brochure must include information on fees, types of clients served, investment approach, the education and business background of key staff, affiliated companies, financial interest in transactions made for clients and compensation paid to third parties—everything included in Part II of Form ADV, which is the form that RIAs file when they register with the SEC. In fact, many RIAs simply send the form to their clients to satisfy the brochure rule.

Standard of care. RIAs owe a fiduciary-type duty to their clients; this is a high standard of care, generally requiring them to place client interests ahead of their own. In contrast, FAs must understand a client's financial situation and recommend investments that are suitable—but not necessarily the best—under those circumstances. This is often referred to as the suitability standard. The difference in the standard of care is the most important distinction between the two types of advisers—but it's one that will be narrowed soon. The Dodd-Frank financial reform legislation requires that the SEC study this issue and figure out a practical way to apply a fiduciary-type standard to FAs.[10]

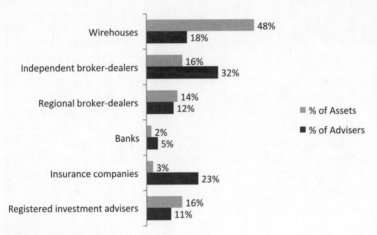

FIGURE 10.2   Advisers and Assets (2008)
Source: Cerulli Associates.

Broker-Dealers

Broker-dealers were among the first purveyors of mutual funds, and they remain a distribution powerhouse today. As Figure 10.2 shows, the three categories of broker-dealers—wirehouses, independents, and regionals—together account for 62 percent of the advisers and 78 percent of the assets in the intermediary channel.

The broker-dealer sales and service model is based on personal relationships between financial advisers and their clients. In the simplest form, the sales process starts with a meeting between the client and the financial adviser during which the two parties discuss the client's financial status and goals.[11] The FA uses the information gathered, often together with analysis software provided by her firm, to develop investment recommendations tailored to the client that generally can be implemented using the services of the brokerage firm. This advice may involve many other types of investments and services in addition to mutual funds. The FA maintains an ongoing relationship with the client, monitoring existing investments, and suggesting changes as appropriate.

FAs normally can—and often do—recommend mutual funds from many different fund managers. They are not limited to funds sponsored by their brokerage firm, which are called *proprietary funds*. Thirty years ago, these proprietary funds were a significant factor in the industry, mainly because FAs were offered financial incentives to sell proprietary funds rather than competing offerings. Today, however, that kind of favoritism is prohibited by regulation, and the importance of proprietary funds has dropped dramatically in all categories except money market funds. As a result, some broker-dealers have exited the fund management business altogether. For example, funds formerly sponsored by wirehouse Merrill Lynch are now run by the BlackRock fund management company.

Today, FAs can present clients with fund choices from many independent, or nonproprietary, fund firms under a concept known as *open architecture*. (This is a concept that we'll refer to many times throughout this chapter.) Among the largest providers of nonproprietary funds are American Funds, BlackRock, Federated Investments, Franklin Templeton, and PIMCO. These firms are not affiliated with a retail broker-dealer or a commercial bank.

When recommending funds to clients, FAs look for above-average performance, although FAs may put greater emphasis on long-term consistency of results than the individual investors typically do. But FAs also look for funds that have a visible and well-established presence at the brokerage firm.

Fund management companies are continually battling for the FA's attention—the fund industry's equivalent of shelf space. They generally try to increase the visibility of their funds in one of two ways: by selling directly to the FAs through a wholesaling force and by participating in wrap programs:

- *Wholesaling.* Fund wholesalers are in the front lines of the battle for shelf space. They are normally employees of the fund manager who are paid to interact directly with FAs and provide them with marketing materials and sales strategies. They may help an FA locate performance information on the fund manager's web site or organize a client seminar, maybe providing speakers for that event. Most fund managers believe there's a direct correlation between the size of their wholesaling team and sales volume. Most firms that are preparing a marketing push, therefore, start by hiring more wholesalers. See the "Career Track" box to learn more about the wholesaler's job.
- *Wrap programs.* Brokerage firms offer mutual fund *wrap programs* to help their FAs and clients sort through the more than 7,600 funds available to investors. In these programs, the brokerage firm uses a rigorous process to select high quality funds that it believes will provide superior returns. The brokerage firm may even interview portfolio managers as part of its due diligence, a process we discuss in more detail later in this chapter. The funds chosen will span a wide range of assets types, investment objectives, and portfolio strategies.

CAREER TRACK: MUTUAL FUND WHOLESALER

As a mutual fund wholesaler, you'll promote your company's funds to financial advisers to increase the likelihood that they'll recommend them to their clients.

External wholesalers. If you're an external wholesaler, you'll talk with FAs face to face, making presentations at office meetings and maybe even speaking at client seminars. That means that excellent interpersonal and presentation skills are a must for this position. You'll also need a lot of stamina since you'll be traveling constantly—maybe four days out of five—to brokerage firm branch offices in a specific geographic territory.

Internal wholesalers. As an internal wholesaler, you'll remain in the home office, contacting FAs mainly by telephone, traveling only occasionally. You'll likely be assigned to brokerage firms and to FAs who generate a lower volume of sales; those who are bigger producers are more likely to get face time with the external wholesaler.

Hybrid wholesalers. To make sure there are no gaps in sales coverage, firms often team up an external wholesaler and internal wholesaler in an approach known as hybrid wholesaling. The two work together to maintain a cost-effective presence with all the FAs in a territory.

FAs then work with their clients to select specific funds from within this group, based on the customer's financial planning goals and risk tolerance. Clients pay an annual fee to the brokerage firm for this service—calculated as a percent of assets in the program—a fee that is in addition to the funds' annual expenses. As an offset to these higher annual costs, investors don't pay a sales load when they buy funds through a wrap program.

Fund management companies work hard to get their funds included in these programs for a simple reason: Wrap accounts have become a significant factor in the intermediary channel. According to Cerulli Associates, these programs had estimated assets of $465 billion at the end of 2009, having more than quadrupled in size over a 10-year period.

Note that these mutual fund wrap programs are distinct from separately managed accounts, which are also often referred to as *wrap accounts.* (Turn back to Chapter 2 if you need a refresher on SMA programs.) However, mutual fund wraps and SMAs are sometimes combined in a *unified management account.* See "A Unifying Force" for more.

A UNIFYING FORCE

Problem: You'd like professional management of your investment assets, but you don't want to be limited to either mutual funds or individual securities.

Solution: The unified management account or UMA.

Developed by broker-dealers in the late 1990s, UMAs enable investors to combine mutual funds with separately managed stock and bond accounts in another form of open architecture. Each is placed in what is called an investment *sleeve.* The unified format makes it easier to see the interaction among the sleeves and ensure consistency across them.

UMAs are geared for investors with substantial assets. The account minimum is usually $100,000 and average account size is substantially more.

Banks

With only a 2 percent share of fund assets under management, banks appear to be small players in the mutual fund world. However, unlike many broker-dealers, banks continue to manage funds as well as sell them—and have increased their presence as fund managers through acquisitions. Bank of New York Mellon helped launch this trend when it acquired the managers of both the Dreyfus fund family and of the Founders Funds in the 1990s. More recently, the manager of the Evergreen funds was bought by the holding company which included Wachovia bank—which was itself later acquired by Wells Fargo. While some portion of the sales of these funds in these complexes comes from the banks' own trust offices or branch networks, most are operated as independent firms selling primarily through the other three intermediary channels.

Involvement in the fund management business has largely been the province of the national banks. Smaller regional banks have often lacked the resources to obtain key investment talent and maintain compensation structures to compete with the major fund complexes. As a result, many regional banks are refocusing their fund management efforts—continuing to manage municipal funds focused on their own state but often turning to outside fund managers for other investment needs.

Insurance Companies

Insurance companies account for only 3 percent of mutual fund assets. Most of these sales are made through variable annuities or VAs, which can be offered only by insurers. (See "Variable Options" for a detailed

---

VARIABLE OPTIONS

Many investors who want to save on taxes while saving for retirement have turned to variable annuities issued by an insurance company. In contrast to a *fixed annuity*—which pays out a specific monthly amount in retirement—the payout from a *variable annuity* depends on the investment performance of a professionally managed portfolio of securities.

Variable annuity owners determine the asset allocation in their account by choosing from a full range of investment options, which are almost always mutual funds. The average VA offers 49 investment choices, called *subaccounts*.[13] Because of this high degree of flexibility, VAs are often referred to as an investment with an insurance *wrapper*.

VAs offer significant tax benefits. Assets within a VA grow tax free until they are distributed—and there are no limits on contributions to VAs. That's a big advantage versus many other tax-deferred vehicles, which are subject to laws that limit the size of contributions or the income of the contributor. (We discuss some of these tax-advantaged accounts in the next chapter.)

On the negative side, contributions to VAs must be made from after-tax income. (In many other retirement savings vehicles, contributions can be deducted from income before taxes are paid.) Profits withdrawn from a VA are taxed at ordinary income rates, even if they are the result of capital gains, which would be taxed at a lower rate if realized in the investor's brokerage account. Finally, VA investors may pay substantial fees.

On the other hand, these fees cover more than just access to an investment vehicle—they also include some insurance coverage. Almost all VAs protect against a decline in account value below the amount of the initial contribution. Many now allow investors to lock in their gains on specified dates, while some even provide guaranteed minimum rates of return. VAs can also include insurance that pays off in the event of death and disability of the investor before retirement.[14]

description of this vehicle.) Insurance companies began to use mutual funds as investment options within VAs in the 1980s.[12]

Sales of variable annuities have been steady in the decade ending in 2009, varying between $110 billion and $180 billion per year. Almost all of these sales—a full 98 percent in 2009—were made through the intermediary channel. This complex product is not usually sold without a professional adviser's help.

However, a significant portion of recent VA sales have been transfers from one VA to another. These exchanges were so prevalent that from 2005 to 2009, net sales after adjusting for these exchanges were only 17 percent of total VA sales, and this trend seems likely to continue. They are called *Section 1035 exchanges* after the provision of the Internal Revenue Code that allows investors to make these swaps without incurring any income tax liability. Product innovation drives these exchanges, because most are made to take advantage of new features, such as larger death benefits, more diverse payout options, a larger number of investment choices, or lower costs.

Like banks, many insurance companies are major fund managers. For example, the Oppenheimer Funds, John Hancock, and Prudential fund complexes are owned by insurance companies. Most of these insurance company fund management units were developed internally as an outgrowth of insurers' efforts to manage their own assets, though some were acquired.

Registered Investment Advisers

Compared to broker-dealers, the registered investment adviser segment is tiny. But the RIA segment is growing rapidly—and it has made an impact on the mutual fund industry that's all out of proportion to its size.

The appeal of RIAs: their fees are based on the level of client assets rather than number of transactions, meaning that RIAs have no incentive to buy and sell investments that are not in a client's best interests. And they don't sell their own proprietary funds. In other words, RIAs use a business model that helps ensure that they act as independent advocates of client welfare. RIAs often provide investment advice as part of comprehensive financial planning services (but see "Everyone's a Financial Planner" to understand the malleability of that particular term). Many of these innovations have been mimicked in the broker-dealer segment—which now puts more emphasis on fee-based wrap programs and financial planning—and less on stock trading.

While growth in the RIA segment was partly a result of the appeal of its model, it was also a function of the advent of fund supermarkets. We'll return to this innovation shortly.

EVERYONE'S A FINANCIAL PLANNER

What exactly is a financial planner? It's hard to say. Broadly speaking, planners help clients develop a strategy for meeting longer-term financial goals. They look beyond the choice of specific investments and consider all the factors affecting a client's financial health, including income levels, savings rates, tax status, retirement goals, and estate plans.

It's otherwise hard to generalize about financial planners. A financial planner might impose a fee based on assets, charge a flat fee for developing a financial plan, receive commissions for selling investments to clients—or get paid in all of those ways. She might be a financial adviser or a registered investment adviser—or an accountant or a lawyer.

Some financial planners have earned the Certified Financial Planner or CFP designation, a program sponsored by the Certified Financial Planner Board of Standards. CFPs must meet an education requirement, pass a rigorous exam, have experience in the industry, and agree to abide by a code of ethics. (See www.cfp.net for more information.) But other financial planners may have no qualifications whatsoever.

In fact, anyone can call himself a financial planner—because the term has no legal definition. That may soon change, however. A provision in the Dodd-Frank financial reform legislation calls for the Comptroller General of the United States to study how financial planners market their services to individuals and recommend additional regulation based on its findings.

Compensation for Selling Fund Shares

Intermediaries are paid for selling mutual fund shares and providing advice in three ways: through fees paid directly by the client, through fees imposed by the fund, or through fees paid by the fund management company.

Direct client charges. As we discussed, brokerage wrap programs and registered investment advisers often charge fees that equal a percentage of the client assets in an account. A variable annuity will charge fees in addition to those related to the mutual fund investment options. These fees are paid by shareholders directly to the intermediary; they are usually deducted from the account.

Fees imposed by the mutual fund. Clients pay fees to the mutual fund, which are relayed to the intermediary. There are three types of sales-related fees imposed by funds: front-end loads, back-end loads, and 12b-1 fees. These fees vary by fund and by share class (which we define in a moment), and not all funds charge these fees.

- *Front-end loads.* When buying a fund through an intermediary, investors may be required to pay a sales commission—known as a front-end sales load, or sales charge. This amount is deducted directly from the shareholder's account. Funds sold with a load have both a NAV and an offering price that reflects the impact of the load. To illustrate: a fund with a 4 percent load and a NAV of $9.60 has an offering price of $10.00. That means that $9.60 of an investor's $10.00 purchase goes to buy one share of the fund, while the remaining $0.40 pays the load. The $0.40 load equals 4 percent of the total investment.

  The maximum sales load on stock funds averaged 5.3 percent in 2009, though many investors pay less.[15] That's because funds often charge lower loads for purchases exceeding a specified dollar amount, in what is called *breakpoint* pricing. (See "Volume Discounts" for details.) They may reduce loads for certain types of investors, such as military personnel. Finally, they may waive loads altogether for other classes of investors, such as retirement plans or trust accounts. As a result of breakpoints and waivers, the sales load actually paid by investors in 2009 was 1.0 percent on average.

VOLUME DISCOUNTS

Continually patronize the same bookstore and get a discount for being a frequent shopper—buy more shares from a fund family and get a reduced front-end load. Like any company, mutual funds want to win consumer loyalty and increase sales. One way they encourage repeat buying is by offering price concessions to investors who concentrate their assets within their fund family. In the case of mutual funds, this usually means lower front-end loads (in percentage terms) for amounts that exceed specified *breakpoints*.

For example, a fund may have the following schedule for its front-end load:

- 5.75 percent for amounts under $50,000
- 4.5 percent for amounts from $50,000 to $99,999
- 3.5 percent for amounts from $100,000 to $249,999
- 2.5 percent for amounts from $250,000 to $499,999
- 2.0 percent for amounts from $500,000 to $999,999
- No load for amounts of $1,000,000 and up

All monies invested within the fund family are combined to determine the discount level, and the amount may be accumulated over time. The discounted load may be applied prospectively, if the investor signs a letter of intent agreeing to purchase a certain amount within a specified time, usually about a year. Or it may be applied retroactively, under a feature known as *rights of accumulation.*

If a fund offers breakpoint pricing, the intermediaries selling the fund must disclose the availability of the discount to prospective buyers, and they must be careful not to sell fund shares in an amount just below the breakpoint so as to gain a higher commission. Both features act to reduce sales compensation, so perhaps it's not surprising that some intermediaries did not pay enough attention to these two obligations.

When securities regulators examined sales practices in 2003, they found that there were often problems with the way intermediaries handled the administration of breakpoints. Many brokerage firms paid fines and agreed to compensate affected investors as a result of these findings. Funds enhanced their disclosures on breakpoints, while intermediaries and fund managers agreed to better coordinate account information to ensure that the rules were applied correctly.

- *Back-end loads or CDSCs.* As some investors pay front-end loads when they purchase shares, others may pay back-end loads when they redeem. Back-end loads are normally imposed only when the shareholder has owned the fund for less than a certain minimum holding period, and they typically decline the longer a shareholder stays invested. For example, a shareholder might pay a 5 percent load after one year, a 4 percent load after two years, and so on, with no back-end load at all after six years. Such declining back-end loads are also called CDSCs, which stands for *contingent deferred sales charges*. Back-end loads are charged on the lesser of either the initial investment or the value of the shares at the time of redemption. They are deducted from the value of the shareholder's account.

■ *12b-1 fees*. Funds may also charge shareholders an annual fee to support the cost of distributing its shares; these fees are called *12b-1 fees* after the SEC rule that allowed them. Many funds charge a 12b-1 servicing fee of 25 basis points, designed to compensate intermediaries for providing ongoing service to shareholders, by monitoring their positions, and contacting them regularly with updates and advice. Some funds may impose an additional asset-based sales charge of 25 to 75 bp, often as a replacement for front-end sales loads. In total, annual 12b-1 fees are limited to 1 percent of assets. They must be approved annually by the fund's independent directors and listed separately in the fee table in the prospectus.

Unlike loads, however, which are paid directly from the shareholder's account, 12b-1 fees are paid by the fund—making them quite controversial. Critics contend that funds should not be allowed to use their assets to increase sales, an activity that primarily benefits the management company.[16] Supporters of the charges counter that 12b-1 fees are just a way to pay for distribution on an installment basis rather than in an upfront lump sum. The SEC has recently proposed changes to the regulations covering 12b-1 fees which we discuss in more detail shortly.

Loads and 12b-1 fees are paid to the fund's distributor, which is usually a subsidiary of the fund management company. (Smaller fund complexes may outsource this function to a third party.) The distributor must be registered as a broker-dealer for it to accept these payments.

However, the distributor does not hang on to the money it receives for very long. Most of the loads and some 12b-1 fees are passed through, or reallowed, to the intermediaries that sell the fund's shares to the public. Most distributors reallow 5.0 percent—or even all—of a 5.5 percent load. Distributors will generally reallow 45 bp (or all) of a 50 bp 12b-1 fee, though they may retain a larger portion of higher 12b-1 fees if they have previously paid upfront commission to intermediaries, as we'll discuss.

The intermediary firms, in turn, pass a portion of the reallowance on to the individual advisers responsible for the investor account. The percentage the adviser receives is called the *payout*. Payouts tend to be higher at independent broker-dealers—often because the adviser is an owner of the firm—which helps to explain why many advisers migrate from wirehouses to the independents.

Today, most funds offer several share classes that allow investors in the same fund to pay different combinations of loads and 12b-1 fees.

- Each share class owns its proportional amount of underlying fund assets.
- Each share class may charge a different front-end load, if it charges a load at all.
- Each share class may charge a different contingent deferred sales charge, if any.
- The 12b-1 fee may vary by class.
- The transfer agent or shareholder service fee will usually be different for each class. That's because transfer agent fees are often based on the number of shareholder accounts, which can vary by class. See Chapter 13 for more on these fees.
- Other fees—such as management and custodian fees—are generally applied at the same percentage rate across all classes of shares.

See Figure 10.3 for a quick view of how the class structure works.

The different share classes are designed to appeal to distinct groups of investors. Table 10.1 shows the share classes for a typical intermediary-sold stock fund.

- *Class A shares* are traditional load shares. They have a high front-end load—reduced through breakpoints—and a low 12b-1 fee. Class A

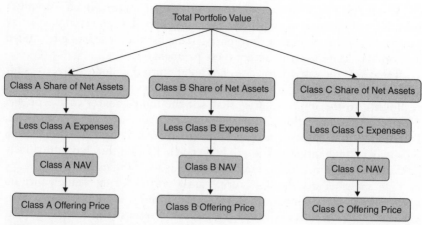

FIGURE 10.3 The Share Class Structure at a Glance

TABLE 10.1 Shares Classes for a Typical Intermediary-Sold Stock Fund

Share Class	Front-End Load	Back-End Load (CDSC)	12b-1 Fees	Class Name
Class A	5.75% with breakpoints	None	0.25%	Load shares
Class B	None	5% in first year, declining 1% per year thereafter	1.00%	Spread load
Class C	None	1% per year for two years	1.00%	Level load
Class I	None	None	None	Institutional
Class R	None	None	0.50%	Retirement

shares are often most appropriate for investors who qualify for a reduced load or for those planning to hold fund shares for a long time, giving them more opportunity to earn back the load with higher investment returns.

- *Class B shares* replace the front-end load with a high 12b-1 fee—at least that's how it appears from the investor's perspective. But this class of shares is particularly complex, because the intermediary is often paid as if these were Class A shares. In other words, the intermediary is paid a sales commission at the time the shares are sold that's equivalent to a front-end load. The fund distributor then relies on the receipt of the 12b-1 fee over a number of years to recoup this upfront payment. In this case, most of the 12b-1 fee is retained by the fund distributor and not reallowed to the intermediary—which has already received a sales commission. If the shareholder redeems from the fund before the distributor expected to be repaid, a contingent deferred sales charge is imposed as an offset to the lost 12b-1 revenue.

  One more complication: after a specified number of years—which roughly approximate the time it takes for the distributor to recoup the sales commission paid to the intermediary—most Class B shares are converted to Class A shares. While popular in the late 1980s and early 1990s, Class B shares have fallen into disfavor lately. Quite a few funds no longer offer them.[17]

- *Class C shares* are sometimes described as level load shares, because they combine a high 12b-1 fee with a modest CDSC for one or two years. Class C typically imposes no front-end load, although the fund sponsor usually advances a small commission to the intermediary. The SEC's proposed regulations on 12b-1 fees would require that C shares eventually convert to Class A shares. See "12b-1: The Sequel" for more information.

12B-1: THE SEQUEL

In the summer of 2010—after much study—the SEC staff proposed replacing Rule 12b-1 with a new regulation named, not surprisingly, Rule 12b-2. The proposed rule has four main provisions:

1. *New name.* Shareholders would no longer read about 12b-1 fees in a fund's prospectus and annual report; they'd see *marketing and service fees* and *ongoing sales charges* described instead. Marketing and distribution charges would be limited to 25 basis points per year, while ongoing sales charges could not exceed 75 bp per year. Class A shares would have a marketing and service fee but not an ongoing sales charge.

2. *Lifetime cap on ongoing sales charge.* The total ongoing sales charge paid by a fund shareholder—for the entire period that she owns fund shares—cannot exceed the maximum front-end load imposed by the Class A shares. Once she has paid the maximum amount, her shares must be converted to Class A shares. Let's assume that the Avon Hill Bond Fund has Class A shares with a 3.0 percent front-end load and Class C shares with a 75 bp ongoing sales charge. After four years, her position in the fund will convert from Class C shares to Class A shares.

3. *No director approval.* The independent directors on the fund board would not have to review and authorize 12b-2 charges annually, as they are required to do now with 12b-1 fees. The proposal requires, however, that they determine whether the ongoing sales charges are fair and reasonable.

4. *Non-standard pricing.* Under the proposed Rule 12b-2 a fund could create a class of shares that allows intermediaries to determine the front-end load to be paid by its customers—and each intermediary could charge a different front-end load. That's a radical departure from current practice. Today, each shareholder in the same class of fund shares has paid fees based on the same schedule. Under 12b-2, a customer of the Silas Deane brokerage firm might pay a different load than the customer of the Arch Street brokerage.

The fund management companies are preparing comments on the new legislation. The proposal for non-standard pricing is likely to be the most controversial element. The SEC hopes that allowing intermediaries to determine the fees paid by consumers will lead to greater competition and, eventually, lower costs to shareholders. Critics of the proposal aren't so sure that it will work that way. They suggest that, because comparison shopping for fees will be more difficult, consumers may actually end up paying more as a result of the new rule.

- *Class I shares*—sometimes called Y or K shares and referred to as institutional shares—charge no loads or 12b-1 fees at all. They're designed for sizable investment programs, including larger retirement plans and brokerage wrap programs.
- *Class R shares* are for use in retirement plans. They charge a moderate 12b-1 fee that may be used to defray recordkeeping costs.[18]

Fees paid by the management company. There is one other source of income for intermediaries who sell mutual fund shares—fees paid by the fund management company, in the form of *revenue sharing,* or *subtransfer agent,* fees.

- *Revenue sharing.* Revenue sharing, or marketing support, payments are made by the fund sponsor out of its own profits to compensate the intermediary for the costs of maintaining their distribution system. These payments are called *revenue sharing* because fund sponsors are effectively sharing part of their management fee with the intermediary. Fund complexes that would like to do a large amount of business with a particular intermediary will ordinarily enter into a revenue-sharing agreement with it. Funds must disclose these revenue-sharing arrangements in their prospectuses.

  In a typical agreement, a fund sponsor will pay 25 bp on new sales and 5 bp on fund assets held by the intermediary. For a $20,000 sale, that's $50 upfront and $10 per year. In addition, sponsors may pay fees to make a presentation or set up an exhibit booth at a conference hosted by the intermediary.

  Intermediaries take steps to ensure that the payments do not influence recommendations made by their associates. Financial advisers don't receive a payout on revenue sharing receipts. In addition, fund sponsors that haven't signed a revenue sharing agreement are still allowed access to branch offices, and financial advisers may still recommend their funds to clients. Intermediaries must disclose these arrangements to their clients; information is usually available on their web sites.

- *Subtransfer agent fees.* Intermediaries may also be paid for maintaining shareholder records if they combine individual accounts into a single omnibus account at the fund. Not every intermediary uses omnibus accounts, although they are becoming more common. As compensation for taking over this recordkeeping work—which otherwise would have to be done by the fund itself—the intermediary receives a *subtransfer agent,* or *sub-TA,* fee. We say more about transfer agents and omnibus accounts in Chapter 13.

   Sub-TA fees may be paid by the transfer agent out of its fees, or they may be paid directly by the fund—which then usually reduces the fee it pays to the transfer agent. Since the transfer agent is often a subsidiary of the management company, sub-TA fees generally lower the management company's revenues and profits.

Before we move on to the direct channel, it's worth noting that selling fund shares can be a very profitable business. Much of the balance of power struggles within the industry occur because intermediaries are looking to increase their profitability at the expense of the fund managers—and vice versa, of course. This may also explain why a number of larger fund complexes have developed a distribution arm for selling funds alongside their traditional business of managing funds.

THE DIRECT CHANNEL: NO-LOAD FIRMS AND FUND SUPERMARKETS

The second retail channel is the direct channel, and no-load fund complexes are the largest segment within it. Because funds sold directly to consumers generally do not impose a front-end load, the terms *no-load fund group* and *direct marketer* are often used interchangeably. "Taking the Load Off" delves into the fees charged by direct marketers.

   The direct distribution model first became popular in the 1970s with the advent of money market funds, which were often advertised and sold directly to investors without any sales loads. While money funds ruled the roost, the market share of direct-sold funds soared. In 1980, they accounted for more than one-quarter of funds assets. (Go back to Figure 10.1 to see the trend.)

   When the bull market for stocks and bonds began in the 1980s, these direct marketers began to offer other types of funds as well, again without the front-end loads that characterized the traditional mutual fund offerings at the time. No-load funds appealed to do-it-yourself investors who didn't need the advice from a financial adviser that a sales load subsidized. To

TAKING THE LOAD OFF

Under FINRA rules, a fund may call itself *no-load* if it meets two tests: It can't impose a sales load—front-end or back-end—and it can't charge a 12b-1 fee greater than 25 bp.

Today, many directly marketed funds have two share classes:

1. *Class I shares* are *pure no-load,* meaning that they charge no sales loads or 12b-1 fees at all. This class of shares usually has a high minimum investment, although one fund family makes them available to investors with smaller accounts who have held shares for at least 10 years.
2. *Class N shares*, which have no loads, but do charge a 12b-1 fee (which can't exceed 25 basis points). This class requires a much lower minimum investment than Class I shares.

attract this market segment, no-load fund complexes promoted their lower costs and the convenience of their services. At the time, that meant keeping their telephone service centers open 24/7. They still try to stay in the forefront of customer service trends, which today means providing easy web access to information and online transaction processing.

Directly sold funds are less of a factor today, accounting for a steady 15 percent of assets over the past decade. The three largest direct marketers are Fidelity, Vanguard, and T. Rowe Price. While no-load funds continue to be popular with do-it-yourself types, more and more investors are looking for personalized advice to help them choose funds—not a traditional strength of the direct marketers. They've turned to professional financial advisers—buying fund shares through their firms or using their advice to invest through a mutual fund supermarket. (We return to fund supermarkets in a second.)

Despite the high level of customer service, the direct-sold model has some inherent inconveniences. No-load accounts were limited to positions in mutual funds, even though many investors wanted a broader array of options, including the ability to trade individual stocks and bonds, all in one account. At the same time, moving investments between no-load fund managers is a cumbersome process. For example, a no-load investor wanting to sell shares of the Avon Hill Equity Fund to buy the Arch Street Equity Fund would have to contact Avon Hill to make the sale, wait for the proceeds to arrive, and then call Arch Street to make the purchase. An investor using an intermediary, by contrast, could take care of the entire transaction with one call to his adviser.

Enter the mutual fund supermarket. Few other innovations have made as big an impact on the fund industry. Today's version was introduced in the early 1990s, and it has since transformed the way investors buy and sell funds. Like supermarkets for food shopping, fund supermarkets bring together a variety of similar products from different suppliers, allowing consumers to put them all in one grocery bag—in this case, a single brokerage account. They have soared in popularity because they provide convenient access to a broad range of investments along with information that allows consumers to compare choices easily. While many financial services firms have launched supermarkets, this segment is dominated by two platforms: Charles Schwab One Source brokerage accounts and Fidelity Investments' Funds Network Program, which is distinct from the Fidelity mutual fund family.

The mechanics are straightforward. Investors who want to invest through the supermarket open a brokerage account with the supermarket operator—which is always a broker-dealer. Investors can then buy shares of any fund in the supermarket, typically without a load or other transaction fees.[19] They can also use the account to buy other investments, which can include individual stocks and bonds, exchange-traded funds, or other mutual funds that are not participating in the program. (Purchases of these other investments may involve additional fees.) All of the customer's holdings are combined in one integrated statement.

The Internet is integral to the operations of the mutual fund supermarket. Operators provide online and wireless trading tools that allow investors to purchase, sell, or exchange funds and other securities in their portfolios at any time. They deliver fund disclosure documents, such as prospectuses and annual reports, to fund investors through their web sites using hyperlinks—saving mailing costs. Finally, supermarket web sites are full of factual information about the funds, providing historical investment performance as well as ratings and rankings from multiple sources. Supermarket operators usually offer interactive web-based fund screeners that enable investors to sort through thousands of funds quickly and efficiently.

Supermarket operators receive fees for providing these services from mutual funds and fund management companies. They receive a reallowance of the 12b-1 fee from the fund distributor. And since fund supermarkets use omnibus accounts, they earn subtransfer agent fees. They may also receive revenue sharing or other marketing support payments from fund management companies. In total, annual fees for participation in a fund supermarket usually equal 25 to 45 basis points of assets held at that supermarket. The fund management company may also pay fees for cooperative marketing arrangements highlighting a particular fund. These might include print or online ads, direct mailings, space in an investment newsletter, or an opportunity to make a presentation to investors.

Fund supermarket programs have had a tremendous impact on the structure of the mutual fund industry, in three key ways:

1. *Growth of registered investment adviser segment.* They have enabled the growth of the registered investment adviser segment of the intermediary channel. A large proportion of RIAs keep client assets in fund supermarket brokerage accounts and make recommendations from the options available within it. Professionally advised accounts are a significant portion of supermarket assets, and supermarkets actively encourage independent broker-dealers and RIAs to use their networks by providing dedicated support services. (See www.schwabadvisorcenter.com for an example.)

2. *Opportunity for boutique firms.* They allow smaller fund managers, often called boutique firms, to market to a niche audience in a cost-effective way. Using a supermarket gives these firms broad distribution—including sales support and customer service—without having to make a substantial upfront investment in building their own sales and service facilities.

THE COMPETITIVE THREAT

The appeal of the fund supermarket has been its simplicity and flexibility. It's one-stop shopping for investors who are considering purchasing funds from different fund managers. For at least a decade, fund supermarkets have been the only place to get this broad access without paying front-end loads or asset-based fees.

But a competitive threat looms on the horizon: exchange-traded funds also allow investors to buy professionally managed portfolios through any brokerage account. The price of entry is usually just an initial trading commission. It's not certain whether ETF investing will directly challenge supermarket programs for assets, but they represent a formidable challenge to the status quo—especially given the recent drop in commissions on ETF trading. We talk about ETFs in detail in Chapter 12.

3. *Load/no-load convergence.* While at first the only participants in fund supermarkets were no-load funds, many load funds are now available as well. This cross-selling has helped to blur the lines between load and no-load funds. We discuss this trend more in a moment.

But fund supermarkets will need to continue to innovate if they want to remain a premier resource for fund investors. "The Competitive Threat" discusses one cloud on the horizon.

CROSS-CHANNEL TRENDS

Investors today are better informed and more engaged than ever. It's now easy to compare fund returns, fees, and services on the Internet and then just as easy to buy and sell fund shares based on this information. As a result, customer expectations are changing rapidly. Investors have been moving away from accepting anything that resembles a one-size-fits-all approach—since that's so readily available—and demanding products and services tailored to their particular needs. This section explores how the fund industry is innovating with new funds, new fund features, and new marketing strategies to meet investor needs.

We focus here on three themes. We look first at open architecture and how it has pushed fund sponsors to develop new ways of bolstering customer loyalty. Then we examine investment advice and how it is now being delivered through a range of platforms to different types of investors. Finally, we discuss needs-based marketing, which seeks to meet specific consumer goals with targeted products and services.

Open Architecture

In the computer world, open architecture allows users to easily add, upgrade, or swap system components. In the fund world, open architecture achieves a similar end: it gives investors centralized access to funds from many different sponsors and even to different types of professionally managed accounts. It has become one of the most powerful forces in the mutual fund industry, shaping every distribution channel. In this chapter alone, we've talked about five instances of open architecture:

1. Brokerage firms offering funds managed by many different firms, not just proprietary funds, to their clients
2. Brokerage wrap programs

3. Unified management accounts
4. Variable annuities
5. Mutual fund supermarkets

Open architecture has increased competition in investment management. It has blurred the line between load and no-load funds, which in the past were the exclusive provinces of the intermediary and direct channels, respectively. Today, in contrast, a brokerage fund wrap program might well include no-load funds, while fund supermarkets sell load funds on a no-transaction-fee basis. In fact, it's not unusual for the same fund—sometimes in slightly different forms—to be sold in multiple distribution channels.

DOING DUE DILIGENCE

Some open architecture platforms also have open access—they'll include any fund that meets some minimum standards and that pays the relevant fees. Mutual fund supermarkets generally fall into this category.

But other platforms are quite exclusive, with space for only a limited number of funds. As we've seen, a variable annuity will, on average, include just 49 funds as investment options, while a brokerage wrap program might have only a few hundred slots available. That may seem like a lot, but it's small potatoes in a universe of thousands of funds.

Fund management companies work hard to get their funds included on these platforms. A specialized sales team—often called a key accounts group—becomes familiar with the standards that the various platforms use to choose funds. The selection process—called a due diligence process—is usually quite rigorous. The platform operator will pore over data on a fund's past performance and risk. The portfolio manager will need to provide a detailed description of the investment process and maybe even make an in-person presentation.

If a fund makes it onto the platform, there's no time for celebrating—the real work is about to begin. The fund sponsor must persuade investors and their advisers to choose that fund out of all the others available. To help make that possible, the key account group will coordinate marketing efforts with the intermediary's home office team and its own wholesaling force.

Open architecture has created marketing challenges for fund management companies, which can no longer rely on proprietary access to a distribution channel to drive fund sales. For example, they must spend more time promoting placement of their funds in open architecture platforms. "Doing Due Diligence" explains the process.

In a world with open architecture, management companies must also work harder to distinguish themselves in investors' minds. As part of that effort, fund managers have become major advertisers, both in print and electronic media—despite the strict regulations that apply to fund ads. (See Chapter 3 for an overview of these rules.) Fund ads tend to fall into one of seven categories:

1. *Performance.* Because fund performance is a powerful driver of fund sales, many ads focus on past results. Fund portfolio managers may appear as spokespeople in these ads.

2. *Investment category.* Investment category ads are close cousins to performance ads. They promote a group of similar funds, usually ones that have done well recently or that have been written up in the press. For example, a firm may promote natural resources funds after oil prices have rallied, or international funds if the foreign markets have surged ahead. These advertisements are often very dense, since they must include a description of the investment category together with complete performance and fee information.

3. *Retirement themes.* Fund sponsors emphasize their tax-deferred retirement savings vehicles during tax season, which runs from January 1 through April 15 each year. We talk more about these vehicles in the next chapter.

4. *Costs.* No-load fund groups and index-fund providers often emphasize the low cost of owning their funds—and explain how lower fees can translate into substantially higher returns over the long hauls. These ads are often placed in publications and media outlets that cater to the high net worth investors who are most likely to consider fees in their decision making.

5. *Brand.* Brand advertising helps establish a firm's reputation for qualities such as trustworthiness, reliability, and experience. Spending on brand ads tends to drop during times of market weakness, as fund firms focus on performance ads, which are more likely to have an immediate impact on sales. However, fund management companies will still try to convey a consistent brand image in all their ads.

6. *Investment advice.* Ads may explain how fund management companies or their affiliates can help investors with their financial planning. We talk about some of the tools that fund companies provide a little later on.

7. *Online trading and account access.* Fund families that sell directly to consumers may appeal to the web savvy with ads describing their online trading capabilities and online access to account information.

Whether they advertise their online services or not, all fund firms—both those that are directly marketed and those sold by intermediaries—are using technology to improve customer service. The goal is to provide both convenience and the customization that consumers demand. Firms are introducing features like:

- *Account aggregation.* Account aggregation allows investors to view all their financial data—from all providers—together on one web site. For example, in an ideal account aggregation, an investor would be able to see holdings in accounts at several different fund firms, in a brokerage account, in a 401(k) plan, and in a variable annuity—all in one report. Investors like account aggregation because it simplifies portfolio monitoring and financial planning by gathering and integrating portfolio information. Financial services firms like account aggregation because it allows them to see a customer's entire financial situation, making it easier for them to match marketing appeals to investor needs.

   Technically, account aggregation is simple to implement: investors provide user IDs and passwords for online access to the accounts they'd like to aggregate, and the web site does the rest, using one of two techniques. Some account aggregation sites use *screen scraping.* They send out bots to the customer's other online accounts that scrape them for the relevant data and then bring it back to the aggregator's site. Other sites use direct feeds from participating financial firms. While this latter approach is harder to set up initially, it can collect data more quickly. It's often used to gather information from the largest firms
- *Interactive web presence.* Fund managers are following the lead of technology companies in using the Web for real-time interactions with customers. Some firms now allow customers to enter into instant messaging sessions with client service representatives, rather than forcing them to call in by telephone to resolve problems. Firms may soon have video capabilities that allow investors to both see and talk with a representative while using the firm's web site.
- *Blogging and social media.* Fund management companies are also dipping their toes into blogging and social media. Many firms now blog on their own web site, microblog on Twitter, or maintain pages on Facebook, LinkedIn, and other social media sites. But remember that almost all postings are considered advertising and must be filed with

FINRA. Compliance with these advertising regulations make it challenging for fund firms to use social media on a real-time basis.

- *Wireless communications.* Finally, fund managers are rapidly moving into providing services through cell phones, PDAs, iPhones, iPads, and Blackberrys. They have designed special versions of their web sites that can be easily viewed on these devices so that investors can access account information and trade online without a computer. Some firms have even developed account management and trading apps for the iPhone.

Advice

More funds, more distribution channels, more share classes, more platforms, more ads, more planning tools. No wonder that many investors—especially those with relatively little experience in the financial markets—feel overwhelmed by all the options. They know that their choices can have a significant effect on their lives in the future, and they're worried about making a mistake, especially as they approach retirement—which they're doing in increasing numbers as the baby boom ages. These investors prefer to consult with a financial professional—if for no other reason than to validate their own conclusions. The result has been a large and growing demand for investment advice and guidance.

To meet this demand, fund management companies—including even the no-load companies—have developed new services for their investors. They have generally developed separate sets of services for the two distinct segments of their customer base: high net worth investors and the mass affluent.

- *High net worth investors.* Because high net worth investors—which are generally defined as individuals with $1 million or more in investable financial assets excluding their homes—have the capacity to buy a lot of funds, they are highly desirable clients, and their accounts tend to be the most profitable. While a significant number of high net worth investors are do-it-yourself types who are comfortable making their own investment decisions using no-load funds, the majority look for personalized advice, which has traditionally been provided by the firms in the intermediary channel. These firms continually develop new investment programs to meet the evolving needs of this segment. Wrap accounts, separately managed accounts, and unified management accounts are specifically designed for the high net worth investor.

  The major no-load fund groups would like to increase their market share in this profitable segment, so they have begun linking their funds to advice. Vanguard now provides personalized advice through a telephone consultation for a fixed fee. Fidelity and T. Rowe Price have taken a different approach and now sell funds through intermediaries as well as directly to consumers.

▪ *Mass affluent.* Investors with less substantial assets—sometimes called the *mass affluent*—are clamoring for advice and guidance as well. For fund sponsors, however, this group presents substantial challenges. Because these investors have smaller account balances, it's not cost-effective for fund sponsors to offer high levels of personal service. They have created instead a wide range of hybrid funds that allow investors to delegate asset allocation decision making to an investment manager. These funds have become very popular, especially in retirement plans. Chapter 4 provides an overview of hybrid funds.

At the same time, they have also built web-based tools that provide a recommended asset allocation—sometimes including suggestions on specific fund choices—based on information that investors provide regarding their investment goals and preferences. An investor creates a personal profile that includes information such as date of birth, planned retirement date, savings goals, time horizon, and current asset allocation. These tools also try to assess risk tolerance, often by asking questions about how an investor would react in a particular situation. A typical question along this line would ask how the investor would respond to a sharp drop in stock prices. The investor who selects "I would buy more" is probably a better fit for an aggressive stock fund than one who selects "I would sell." We include links to some of these tools on this book's web site.

Needs-Based Products

Needs-based investment products are designed to address a particular investor requirement. We talk here about two: college planning and charitable gift accounts.

College planning. As college tuitions have soared over the past 25 years, families with children are increasingly focused on setting aside money for college tuition—and mutual fund sponsors are there to help them.

The traditional vehicle for college savings is a custodial account established under the Uniform Transfers to Minors Act or Uniform Gifts to Minors Act.[20] These accounts are available at mutual fund companies. A donor establishes an UTMA or UGMA account on behalf of a child, appointing a custodian—who is usually a parent—charged with managing the assets for the child, who is the actual owner of the account. The child may take full control of the account when she reaches age 18 or 21 (the exact age varies by state). Although the account is owned by the child, income that exceeds certain limits is taxed at the parents' rate, while income below those limits is taxed at the child's—normally lower—rate. As a result, UTMA/UGMA accounts are most appropriate for saving small amounts.

A second option for college savings—also available using mutual funds—is the Coverdell Educational Savings Accounts, opened on behalf of a child. It's more attractive than an UTMA/UGMA account because contributions to it grow tax-free within the account until the child reaches age 18. Withdrawals from the account can also be tax-free if used to pay for tuition expenses at a qualified higher education institution. Unfortunately, while their structure is attractive, contributions to Coverdell accounts are capped at relatively low amounts and are limited to taxpayers earning below a certain level of income.

Given the drawbacks of UTMA/UGMA and Coverdell accounts, college savers and fund managers alike have welcomed the introduction of Section 529 plans, named after the provision of the Internal Revenue Code that authorizes them. Section 529 plans have the same tax advantages as Coverdell accounts, but have much higher limits on contributions and place no restrictions on the income of the donor. They have become a popular way to prefund a child or grandchild's education.

Section 529 plans are sponsored by the states which, in turn, have often tapped large mutual fund managers to both administer the programs and provide the investment options, which are usually mutual funds. Those options may be quite limited; in fact, some plans do not even permit a contributor to select the investment vehicle, instead assigning a portfolio to a child based on his age. This portfolio is invested in a mix of stocks and bonds that becomes less risky as the child approaches college age. At the end of 2009, Section 529 plans had $111.1 billion in assets. Figure 10.4 shows their growth over the past 12 years.

Donor-advised funds. With the increase in investor wealth over the past 20 years, fund sponsors are positioning themselves not only to help investors increase their assets, but also to help investors transfer their wealth to others. They're using a vehicle technically known as a *donor-advised fund* but that's often referred to as a *charitable gift trust*. Individuals make irrevocable contributions to their account in the trust, taking a tax deduction in the year of the gift. At any later time, donors can recommend that any portion of the assets in their account be given to a qualified charitable organization that meets standards set by the trust. Donor-advised funds have long been available to wealthy individuals through community foundations, faith-based organizations, and educational institutions.

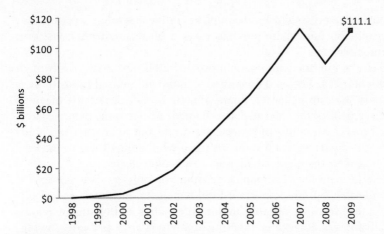

FIGURE 10.4 Section 529 Plan Assets
Source: Investment Company Institute, *2010 Investment Company Fact Book.*

Mutual fund management companies have made donor-advised funds an attractive philanthropic option for the less well-heeled. Individuals can make gifts of as little as $5,000 to an account in their name at these mutual fund–based trusts. Donors then choose how their accounts should be invested, selecting from an array of mutual fund options. They can later choose to make donations from their accounts to charities they select—subject to a potential veto by the trustees.[21]

The Fidelity Charitable Gift Fund is the oldest and largest of the donor-advised funds sponsored by a mutual fund management company. Other large mutual fund-based programs are the Schwab Charitable Fund and the Vanguard Charitable Endowment Program. Combined, they are an extremely significant source of philanthropy. For example, the Fidelity program alone has made more than $9.5 billion in grants to over 130,000 nonprofit organizations since its inception. According to the National Philanthropic Trust, national donor-advised funds—which includes the mutual fund–related programs—had over $11 billion in assets at the end of 2008.

CHAPTER SUMMARY

Individual, or retail, investors are the largest purchasers of mutual fund shares. Mutual fund sponsors sell shares to individuals through two channels: the intermediary channel and the direct channel.

Investors are often interested in buying shares of funds with strong past performance, even though this approach has often not generated good future returns. Advertising by fund complexes influences sales. Investors also make decisions on fund share purchases based on recommendations from professional advisers.

Firms in the intermediary channel provide advice to investors through their representatives. These advisers may recommend mutual funds to their clients as part of a comprehensive financial plan. Broker-dealers are the most important segment of the intermediary channel. At one time, many broker-dealers had their own family of proprietary funds, but today they sell funds from many third parties. Fund sponsors use a wholesaling force to increase their presence with the financial advisers at a broker-dealer.

Banks and insurance companies account for only a small portion of mutual fund sales, but are important fund managers. Insurance agents primarily sell funds through variable annuities, which is an investment vehicle with tax advantages. Registered investment advisers are a fast-growing segment of the intermediary channel. They are unusual because they charge clients a fee based on assets under management rather than on the number of transactions.

Intermediaries are paid for fund sales in three ways. First, they may charge asset-based fees directly to clients. Second, they may receive a portion of fees charged by the fund. Funds charge front-end loads and back-end loads directly to investors and pay 12b-1 fees out of fund assets. Third, intermediaries may be paid revenue sharing fees from the management company or subtransfer agent fees for providing shareholder recordkeeping.

The direct channel has two segments. No-load fund companies, also known as direct marketers, sell funds directly to shareholders. Fund supermarkets allow investors to buy funds from many fund complexes in a single brokerage account with no transaction fees.

Open architecture has become a significant factor in the fund industry. Under open architecture, investors have easy access to funds from many different fund families. Fund management companies must work hard to place their funds in platforms that provide this open access. While convenient for consumers, open architecture creates marketing challenges for fund companies. They have increased advertising and try to stay one step ahead of their competitors with innovative customer service.

More and more investors are looking for help making fund decisions; financial intermediaries and fund sponsors must respond to this increased need for advice. Financial intermediaries offer personalized advice to high net worth investors, while fund sponsors provide online tools and asset allocation funds to the mass affluent. Management companies are also providing investment programs that help investors reach specific financial goals. Two examples are 529 plans for college saving and charitable gift trusts.

CHAPTER 11

Retirement Plans and Mutual Funds

Employer-sponsored retirement plans—retirement savings programs that are available to individuals through their workplace—are the third major distribution channel for mutual funds, in addition to the intermediary and direct channels. Selling fund shares through an employer-sponsored plan is a multistep process:

- First, a plan administrator, often a fund manager, works with an employer to establish a plan for its workforce.
- The employer, perhaps with the help of a plan administrator, financial adviser, or independent consultant, chooses funds to include as investment options in the plan.
- The plan administrator provides employees with information on the benefits of the plan and encourages them to participate.
- Only then do the employees who have enrolled in the plan choose one or more of the mutual funds or other investment options available in the plan.

So, an employer-sponsored plan involves sales to at least two parties—the employer and the employee—and maybe to some third-party advisers—such as an administrator, financial adviser, or consultant.

We take a close look in this chapter at the structure of the most popular of the employer-sponsored plans—the 401(k) plan—and the key role that mutual funds play in their operations. We also examine another type of retirement savings vehicle—the individual retirement account, or IRA (spelled out or spoken like the man's name). IRAs are technically not considered part of the retirement channel. As their name suggests, IRAs are purchased by individuals and are, therefore, distributed through the two retail channels—the intermediary and direct channels—that were discussed in the last chapter. However, because 401(k) plans and IRAs have similar tax-deferral features and because money often flows from one to the other in the form of a rollover, we review IRAs here.

Retirement savings play a key role in the mutual fund industry. Together, defined contribution plans and individual retirement accounts made up more than one-third of fund assets at the end of 2009. Conversely, mutual funds play a critical role in the U.S. retirement savings system. Of the $16 trillion in assets in all types of retirement plans at the end of 2009, more than one-quarter were invested in mutual funds. The fund industry had an even higher share—about 50 percent—of the assets invested in 401(k) plans and IRAs, the two fastest-growing segments of the retirement market.[1]

We examine in this chapter both the overall structure of the U.S. retirement savings system and the role that mutual funds play within it. Specifically, this chapter reviews:

- The benefits of tax-deferred retirement savings plans in general
- The growth, structure, and operations of the most popular employer-sponsored retirement plan, the 401(k) plan
- Individual retirement accounts and the growing importance of rollovers to those accounts
- The future of retirement saving plans in the United States

THE TAX BENEFITS OF QUALIFIED RETIREMENT PLANS

We start by taking a step back from mutual funds to look at the value of retirement plans in general. Their advantages come largely from tax savings. The Internal Revenue Code provides tax incentives that encourage both corporations and individuals to set money aside today to finance retirement income needed in the future. To qualify for these tax benefits, savings must be placed in special retirement accounts that adhere to certain restrictions. Let's take a closer look at how this works in both employer-sponsored plans and IRAs.

Employer-Sponsored Retirement Plans

If an employer-sponsored retirement plan meets certain IRS requirements, it becomes a *qualified* plan that enjoys several tax advantages. Subject to some limitations, which we discuss further on, these benefits are:

- The employer's contributions to the plan are deductible for income tax purposes.

- Employees who enroll in the plan—dubbed *participants* once they do so—don't realize any taxable income when their employer makes contributions to the plan on their behalf.
- Participants who contribute some of their own compensation to the plan don't pay taxes on that income before it goes into the plan.
- Earnings on contributions to the plan, from both the employer and participants, accumulate tax-free within the plan.
- Participants realize taxable income only when they actually receive their retirement benefits.[2]

In short, employers and employees enjoy tax benefits at the same time. The employer making a contribution to a qualified plan on behalf of an employee takes an immediate tax deduction, while the employee can defer paying taxes on both contributions and the income earned on them until making withdrawals from the account in retirement.

Nonqualified retirement savings accounts don't receive this favorable treatment. An employer can't take a tax deduction for a contribution to a nonqualified plan until it becomes taxable income to the employee. That's usually when the employee earns the right to withdraw the contribution from the plan or—in retirement lingo—when the contribution *vests*. Another disadvantage to nonqualified plans: investment income from unvested contributions is taxable to the employer each year as it is earned and does not accumulate tax-free. In short, nonqualified plans incur taxes on a current basis, with little tax deferral.

The value of this tax deferral compounds over time—and since retirement planning takes place over decades, its lifetime dollar value can be very large indeed, as Figure 11.1 illustrates. This hypothetical example assumes a $3,000 annual contribution to an account that earns 6 percent per year.

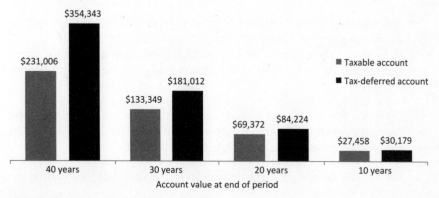

FIGURE 11.1   The Value of Tax Deferral to Employees

It also assumes that in the taxable account, the investor pays taxes at a 28 percent rate every year on both the contribution and the annual earnings. In the tax-deferred account, no taxes are incurred until the end of the period, when 28 percent is paid on the accumulated value. The advantages of the tax deferral are apparent even over a 10-year period, and they are quite substantial over 30 or 40 years—not an unreasonably long period of time for retirement planning.

But the tax benefits of qualified plans come with restrictions. Congress insists that qualified plan coverage extend as broadly as possible and that benefits be distributed fairly. More specifically, qualified plans must:

- Cover all employees who meet minimum age and length of service standards
- Provide benefits that do not favor highly paid employees
- Cap the level of contributions and benefits per employee
- Vest employee rights to benefits within a specified period
- Provide benefits for the employee's spouse under certain circumstances

In other words, the tax benefits of qualified plans may not inure to just a small group of privileged executives. Their benefits must be spread among a large group of workers, so that qualified plans become part of a larger social safety net that helps most employed Americans meet their income needs in retirement.

Individual Retirement Accounts

But many people work for an employer who does not offer a qualified plan, so Congress created the individual retirement account to make tax-deferred savings account available to all. The tax benefits of IRAs are very similar to those of qualified plans, namely:

- Individuals are able to deduct contributions to IRAs from their taxable income in the year those contributions are made.
- Earnings on the contributions to the IRA accumulate tax-free.
- Individuals pay taxes only when they actually receive their retirement benefits.

These are the benefits of a traditional IRA. There is also a newer type of IRA that operates a bit differently—a Roth IRA, named after the U.S. senator who proposed the law creating them.

- Individuals do *not* get a tax deduction in the year that they contribute to the Roth IRA.

- As in traditional IRAs, earnings on contributions to the IRA are accumulated tax free.
- Here's the big difference: distributions from a Roth IRA—including investment earnings—are entirely tax-free, if they are made after the account holder has reached age $59\frac{1}{2}$ and more than five years after the IRA was established.

To summarize: in traditional deductible IRAs, contributions are not taxed, while withdrawals are taxed; the opposite is true for Roth IRAs. Which is better? The answer is that it depends—on the number of years that earnings accumulate, on investment returns, and on the tax rates applied to both contributions and withdrawals. For example, a Roth IRA may be preferable for workers who expect their income tax rate in retirement to be higher than it is now. This might be the case for younger workers who are far from their peak earnings years.

Note that a worker can make an after-tax contribution to a traditional IRA, which higher-income workers may choose to do if they cannot make a contribution to a Roth IRA or a deductible contribution to an IRA. (We talk about the limits on those contributions in a moment.) As in a Roth IRA, the earnings on a non-deductible contribution grow tax-free, and the contribution itself can be withdrawn without taxation in retirement. Unlike a Roth, earnings are taxed when withdrawn. Even with this drawback, however, a non-deductible contribution can make economic sense because of the tax-deferred accumulation of earnings.

Congress has set tight limits on access to the tax benefits of IRAs. These limits are:

- *Roth contributions.* Contributions to Roth IRAs are limited to workers with incomes below a specified amount.
- *Deductible IRA contributions.* Deductible contributions to traditional IRAs are limited to workers with incomes below a specified amount. These limits do not apply, however, if neither the worker—nor the worker's spouse—is covered by a retirement plan at work.
- *Overall limit.* In 2010, contributions to a Roth IRA, deductible contributions to a traditional IRA and non-deductible contributions to a traditional IRA cannot total more than $5,000 for younger workers and $6,000 for those aged 50 and older. As we'll see, this overall limit is much lower than the annual contribution limits for employer-sponsored plans. That's deliberate—to encourage employers to create and maintain plans for their workers, rather than just let them save on their own through IRAs.

401(k) PLANS

With that background, let's take a close look at one type of employer-sponsored plan—the 401(k) plan—named after the section of the Internal Revenue Code that made them possible. These plans have become the predominant retirement plan offered by corporate employers. They're extremely important to the mutual fund industry, because mutual funds are the most popular investment option within them. We'll take a quick look at the history and growth of 401(k) plans. Then we'll zero in on the features of these plans: the limits on contributions, their investment options, and the complexity of plan administration. We'll also talk about why mutual funds are the leading investment choice in 401(k) plans.

History and Growth

Even though 401(k) plans did not exist before 1982, they now dominate new contributions to employer-sponsored retirement plans. In less than 30 years, assets in 401(k)s have grown to more than $2.7 trillion, representing 17 percent of U.S. retirement plan assets, according to the Investment Company Institute. Figure 11.2 shows the growth trajectory.

When Section 401(k) was added to the Internal Revenue Code, no one expected that it would transform the U.S. retirement system. It was a technical provision, intended to formalize the tax treatment of a burgeoning number of deferred bonus programs. But clever employers and their tax advisers soon discovered that Section 401(k) allowed employees to defer payment of their regular salaries—not just bonuses—and to allow them to

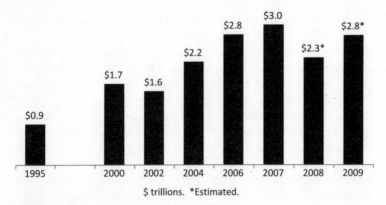

FIGURE 11.2   401(k) Plan Assets
Source: Investment Company Institute, *2010 Investment Company Fact Book.*

accumulate on a tax-favored basis. At first, 401(k) plans were envisioned as modest supplements to traditional pension plans. But beginning in the late 1980s, they began to completely replace pension plans as workers' primary retirement savings vehicles.

To understand this trend, we need to examine the differences between traditional pension plans, technically known as *defined benefit,* or DB, plans, and 401(k) plans, one of several types of *defined contribution,* or DC, plans. Other types of DC plans include 403(b) plans for educational institutions and 457 plans for state and local governments. These two types of retirement plans predate 401(k) plans and were originally quite different from them, but legislative changes over the past 20 years have made them very similar to 401(k) plans. We focus on 401(k) plans in this chapter. See this book's web site for more on 403(b) and 457 plans and how they compare to 401(k) plans.

In DB plans, retirement benefits are typically determined by the number of years a participant has worked and his average salary in the years immediately before retirement. These amounts are fixed—determined by a schedule—hence the term *defined benefit.* To finance these benefits, an employer makes regular contributions to an account dedicated to the DB plan.[3] The employer—or, more likely, its investment manager—chooses the investments for the assets in the plan, and employees have no say in how they are invested. These plans have pluses and minuses for workers.

- *Employer bears risks in DB plan.* On the plus side, in a defined benefit plan, the employer bears all the responsibility for making sure that there's enough money available to pay benefits. If the contributions to the DB plan and the investment performance of DB assets together aren't enough to pay the scheduled benefits, the employer must make up the shortfall by making higher contributions to the plan. On the other hand, if investment performance is better than expected, benefits remain the same and the employer's future contributions to the plan are lowered.

  Accordingly, participants are highly dependent on the employer's continuing ability to make contributions. That raises a concern: if the employer sponsoring a DB plan goes bankrupt, and its DB plan is not fully funded, meaning that assets in the plan are not sufficient to pay benefits—as is usually the case when a firm goes bankrupt—participants will probably not get the retirement income they expected.[4] They are guaranteed some benefits by a federal insurance plan administered by the Pension Benefit Guaranty Corporation, a program established by law under ERISA, though these benefits could well be below the income they were promised by their employer's plan. ("Landmark Legislation" gives a quick overview of ERISA.)

LANDMARK LEGISLATION

The single most important piece of legislation governing retirement plans is the Employee Retirement Income Security Act, better known as ERISA ("er-*iss*-a").[5] It was enacted in 1974 to broaden coverage under employer-sponsored plans to ensure that benefits are distributed fairly among those who are covered by retirement plans and to protect the rights of participants and their beneficiaries to those benefits. The Department of Labor has responsibility for issuing ERISA regulations and enforcing them.

- *Lack of portability for DB plans.* Another negative for defined benefit plans: employees who change jobs generally can't take their DB plans with them to their new firm. Instead, workers must typically wait until age 65 to receive benefits from those DB plans. And even if their new employer offers its own DB plan, workers might still find that their pension benefits are less for the two plans combined than they would be if they had stayed at one employer and in one DB plan for their entire careers. That's because benefits from a DB plan are based on both years of service and final pay. For workers in the United States today—who change jobs every 4.1 years, on average—lack of DB pension portability makes it difficult to accumulate enough savings for retirement through these plans.[6]

An employer sponsoring a 401(k) plan, in contrast, is not obligated to provide a defined level of retirement benefits. In fact, employers have no obligations at all other than to provide access to the plan. Workers decide whether they want to participate (or not) by contributing part of their compensation to the plan through a salary reduction program. The employer may (or may not) match some or all of those participant contributions or make other nonelective contributions. In 401(k) plans, employers select the array of investment alternatives that will be available in the plan, but it's the participants who choose the investments for their own accounts from that menu. Retirement benefits are determined by the amount of contributions and the performance of the investment alternatives chosen by the participants—hence the name *defined contribution* for these types of retirement plans. They have two key features:

1. *Employee bears risks in DC plans.* Note that, in stark contrast to defined benefit plans, employees are the ones who bear the risks in defined contribution plans. If the retirement benefits of the employee are lower than desired either because contributions have been too low or because the plan investments did not perform well, the employee must either make do with those benefits or make higher contributions. At the same time, if the investments perform better than expected, it's the employee who reaps the reward.
2. *Portability of DC plans.* Workers who change jobs frequently are often better off with a defined contribution plan than with a traditional pension plan. Employees can easily transfer their vested account balances to a new employer's plan or to an IRA—or they can even withdraw them as a lump sum in cash if they're willing to pay taxes on the income at the time they make the withdrawal.

Defined contribution plans have become very popular. While defined benefit plans were the preferred type of retirement plan just 30 years ago, today private sector employees are much more likely to be saving for retirement through a DC plan. At the end of 2008, 55 percent of workers at medium and large private employers participated in a DC plan, while only 33 percent were covered by a DB plan. That's a dramatic change from 1980, when 84 percent of workers were included in a DB plan and 401(k) plans were nonexistent. (Table 11.1 shows the trends in coverage for different types of employers.)

Employers who are starting up a new plan are likely to choose to establish a defined contribution plan. At the same time, many sponsors of

TABLE 11.1 Percentage of Employees Participating: Defined Benefit versus Defined Contribution

	1980		1990		2008	
Employer type	DB	DC	DB	DC	DB	DC
Medium and large private establishments	84%	–	59%*	48%*	33%	55%
Small private establishments	n/a	n/a	20%	31%	9%	33%
State and local governments	n/a	n/a	90%	9%	79%	18%

*Figures for 1991.
Source: Employee Benefits Research Institute, *EBRI Databook.*

defined benefit plans have terminated those plans. In fact, in 1993, there were roughly 84,000 defined benefit plans. During the following 14 years, that number fell by more than a third, to 49,000 by 2007.[7]

The shift has occurred for three main reasons. We've already talked about two of the three: employers don't like bearing investment risk, which they are required to do in DB plans, and employees like the portability of DC plans. But there was another factor at work. Changes in federal laws and regulations, beginning with the enactment of ERISA—have added to the cost and complexity of sponsoring DB plans. Companies must pay high premiums to the Pension Benefit Guaranty Corporation, which provides some protection for workers' pensions in the event the employer goes bust. And employers are under pressure to fully fund their plans by setting aside enough in assets to cover all expected benefit payments. If they don't, stringent accounting rules require that they show these funding gaps as liabilities on their balance sheets—a disclosure that can have a negative impact on their stock prices.

One final note: while this shift from defined benefit to defined contribution plans has been most dramatic among private employers, state and local governments have not been immune from it. Although still largely a DB world, there has been some movement to DC plans in the public sector, particularly as states grapple with significant budget deficits. See "Retirement in the Public Sector" for more information.

RETIREMENT IN THE PUBLIC SECTOR

The retirement systems maintained by state and local governments continue to be dominated by defined benefit plans—but these plans are facing a looming crisis. That's because the assets in these plans are $1 trillion less than needed to support the retirement benefits promised to public sector employees.[8]

As a result, states are following the lead of corporations and moving—though very slowly—toward defined contribution plans. As of September 2009, 13 states and the District of Columbia were offering participation in a DC retirement plan to at least some of their employees; a few have even closed their DB plans to new employees.[9] This shift is being met with stiff resistance from the unions representing public workers, who fear that a transition to DC plans will adversely affect the retirement security of their members. In their view, public workers accepted lower salaries in exchange for better pension benefits.

Contributions

Now that we have an overview of the advantages and disadvantages of 401(k) plans, let's take a closer look at how they operate day to day. We start with the contributions that can be made into a 401(k) plan. There are three principal types:

1. *Elective.* Contributions made by employees, usually in the form of salary reduction.
2. *Matching.* Employer contributions that match employee elective contributions up to a flat dollar amount or a specified percentage of salary (often 3 percent of annual salary).
3. *Nonelective.* Other contributions made by the employer to all participants, which may include profit-sharing contributions.

Congress has established annual limits on contributions. Participants can elect to contribute up to $16,500 per year. (This is the limit in 2010. This and other dollar figures in this section are adjusted annually to reflect changes in the cost of living.) Employees over age 50 can add another $5,500 to the annual limit. These *catch-up contributions,* as they're called, are designed to let older workers make up for any past savings shortfalls, when their priorities might have been setting aside money for the down payment on a house or for a child's education, rather than for retirement. Employer matching and nonelective contributions can bring the total contribution per employee to $49,000 per year—significantly higher than the limits on contributions to individual retirement accounts. However, many workers don't take full advantage of the flexibility that these high limits provide, as we discuss in "Decisions by Default."

These limits apply only if there is broad participation throughout a company in its 401(k) plan. The IRS has issued complicated antidiscrimination rules that prevent *highly compensated employees,* or HCEs—those earning more than $110,000 per year—from contributing disproportionately more than other employees.[11] The antidiscrimination rules ensure that a plan serves a broad social purpose—helping all employees save for retirement—and is not just a means for senior executives to avoid paying taxes on their income.

If the plan does not comply with the antidiscrimination test in any given year, a portion of the contributions made by HCEs must be returned to them at the end of the year. Failing the test can be costly from both an administrative and employee relations point of view. Plan sponsors therefore go to great lengths to encourage all employees to contribute at as high a rate as possible—through matching contributions and communications programs.

DECISIONS BY DEFAULT

Retirement saving has been fertile ground for economists specializing in behavioral finance. They have confirmed what many in the fund industry had already suspected: that many workers did not act rationally when it came to saving in their retirement plans. Economists observed that:

- Some workers who could participate in a 401(k) plans did not.
- Many who did participate didn't contribute enough to get the full benefit of employer matching contributions, essentially passing up on free money.
- Younger workers often heavily weighted money market funds and other conservative investments in their portfolios, even though their long time horizon made stocks—with their higher potential returns—more appropriate investments for them.
- Many 401(k) participants failed to increase their contributions as their income rose.

The net result of all of these mistakes: Many workers were likely to find themselves with insufficient savings at retirement.

To help employees reach their retirement income goals, behavioral economists have suggested that 401(k) plans should offer the rational choices as a default option, so the workers who wanted to save less than optimally would have to make an active decision to do so. They proposed, for example, that employees should automatically be enrolled in a plan on the day they become eligible to participate without having to hand in a form first. Only those workers who didn't want to contribute would have to take action by filling out paperwork. Put another way, workers would have to opt out rather than opt in.

When companies actually tried out *automatic enrollment,* as it has been named, the empirical results bore out the theories. These programs boosted 401(k) participation significantly, particularly among lower-income workers.[10] Congress endorsed the theories of the behavioral economists when it passed the Pension Protection Act of 2006, which included provisions that allow 401(k) plans to include automatic enrollment and a number of other default options.

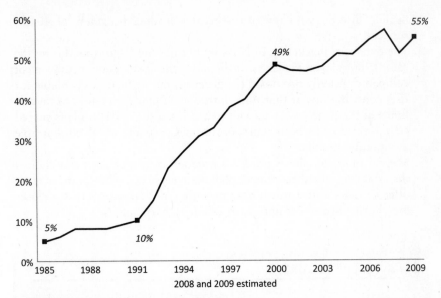

FIGURE 11.3 Mutual Fund Share of 401(k) Assets
Source: Investment Company Institute.

Mutual Funds in 401(k)s

The surge in popularity of 401(k) plans has been a key factor fueling the growth of the mutual fund industry. Before 401(k)s arrived on the scene, banks and insurance companies dominated the business of managing retirement plan assets—which were almost entirely in defined benefit plans. During the 1990s, however, mutual funds rapidly gained market share, as plan sponsors turned to fund managers to help them establish new 401(k) plans. By the end of 2009, about 55 percent of 401(k) assets were invested in mutual funds. (See Figure 11.3 for an illustration of mutual funds' increasing market share.) In recent years, banks have been fighting to recapture some of the share they have lost—see "Back to the Future" for more.

Why did plan sponsors choose mutual fund complexes to manage their 401(k) programs? For three main reasons:

1. Mutual fund complexes were better prepared to handle the retail aspects of 401(k)s, maintaining account records for hundreds or thousands of individual plan participants and communicating with them about their investment options. Ability to provide daily NAVs was another distinguishing capability. Perhaps not surprisingly, Fidelity, T. Rowe Price, and Vanguard—all no-load complexes accustomed to

dealing directly with investors—became leading providers of 401(k) services.

2. The extensive marketing of IRAs by mutual fund sponsors during the early 1980s played a role. As we discuss in the next section, management companies heavily promoted the generous tax deductions available for IRA contributions at that time, introducing many investors to mutual funds in the process. As a result, when interest in 401(k) plans surged later in the decade, both plan sponsors and participants felt comfortable using mutual funds.

3. Mutual fund complexes offered a broader array of investment choices than did traditional retirement plan managers, and plan sponsors must offer a range of investment options within a 401(k). Let's take a closer look at the investment options available to participants.

BACK TO THE FUTURE

After having lost ground to mutual funds in the battle for the nation's retirement funds, banks are back in the thick of the fray. Their weapon is an old one: the bank *collective trust fund*. CTFs, like mutual funds, allow multiple investors to combine their money to invest in a pool of diversified assets.[12]

What distinguishes CTFs from mutual funds? They do not have to register with the SEC as long as they are offered only to employer-sponsored retirement plans, which include 401(k) plans. As a consequence, CTFs do not have to prepare prospectuses, have boards of directors, charge every investor the same fee, or even value and redeem shares daily. Instead, they can decide which services they would like to offer. (Most do provide daily NAVs.)

Note that CTFs are still subject to regulation—just not SEC regulation. The bank offering a CTF is a fiduciary for ERISA purposes and must comply with the complex rules of that law.[13] CTFs are also reviewed by the relevant banking regulator.

Even so, CTF regulation is generally seen as more flexible—and therefore lower cost—than mutual fund regulation. As a result, CTFs appeal to large plan sponsors that are focused on reducing expenses, and many fund management companies have formed trust companies to offer CTFs in response to demand from major clients. Cerulli Associates estimates that there were more than $1 trillion in assets held by CTFs in mid-2009.

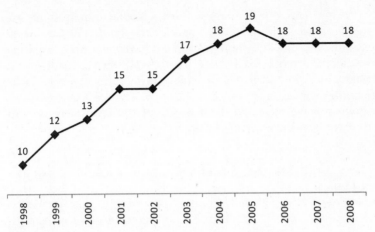

FIGURE 11.4 Number of Investment Options in 401(k) Plans
Source: Profit Sharing/401k Council of America, *PSCA's 52nd Annual Survey of Profit Sharing and 401(k) Plans.*

401(k) Plan Investment Options

As we've discussed, the employer selects the investment options available within a 401(k). Almost all employers include at least three options in their plans, so that they sail into the safe harbor of Section 404(c) of ERISA—which protects them from liability for the investment choices made by their employees, no matter how bad the results of those choices are. To come within the safe harbor, the three investment alternatives must have materially different risk-and-return characteristics—a typical range of offerings is a money market fund or other low-risk option, an income alternative such as a government or corporate bond fund, and a broad stock fund. Each of the options must be well diversified within their asset class, and the plan sponsor must also provide sufficient information about them to participants.

But most plans have many more than three investment options. These usually include several stock funds, one or more bond funds and a money market fund or other stable value investment. Public companies often include their own stock as yet another choice. In fact, according to the Profit Sharing/401k Council of America, the average plan had 18 investment options at the end of 2008. The number of options has gradually increased over the past decade, as shown in Figure 11.4.

How participants allocate their assets to these options tends to vary by age. Table 11.2 shows the average asset allocation at the end of 2008 for investors in their twenties and for those in their sixties. Equity funds are the most popular choice for both groups. *Stable value funds* and *guaranteed investment contracts,* or GICs, rank second for investors in their sixties. Both of these options pay a fixed rate of return—adjusted annually—that can be attractive to those in or near retirement. Younger investors make target date funds their second choice.

Plan sponsors have increased the diversity of the investment options available to participants in a number of ways:

- Many have added different types of funds, such as international funds or sector funds.
- Large employers have included offerings from multiple fund complexes, another example of open architecture. (See Chapter 10 for a full discussion of open architecture.)
- They eliminated policies mandating that employer contributions be invested in company stock. Many firms were pressured to change these policies after high-profile bankruptcies—notably the collapse of Enron in 2001—wiped out the retirement savings of a large number of workers. As a result, company stock accounted for only 10 percent of the assets of all age groups in 2008—a significant decline from its 19 percent weighting in 1996.[14]
- Many plans have made nonfund investments available to 401(k) participants. These include low-risk offerings such as stable value funds and guaranteed investment contracts.[15] They might also add self-directed brokerage accounts that allow participants to buy individual stocks or other securities.

TABLE 11.2 Average 401(k) Plan Asset Allocation (2008)

Investment Option	Participants in their 20s	Participants in their 60s
Stable value funds and GICs	8%	23%
Money funds	6	9
Bond funds	9	15
Target date funds	15	6
Balanced funds	13	8
Equity funds	38	28
Company stock	8	8
Other funds	3	3

Source: Investment Company Institute, *2010 Investment Company Fact Book.*

This increasing variety of 401(k) plan offerings has led to charges that they have become too complicated for any but the most financially sophisticated participants. These concerns, in turn, have resulted in two somewhat contradictory, but not mutually exclusive, trends.

> *Simplification.* First, many employers have tried to simplify the options within their 401(k). They've limited the number of choices to straightforward funds that provide broad exposure to an asset class. At the same time, they've eliminated more specialized funds such as sector funds. As part of this trend, more and more plans have begun to include *target date* funds as core offerings, often designating them as the default investment option if the employee doesn't make an active choice of fund. Target date funds are like one-stop shopping for participants who would rather not worry about allocating their assets among different types of funds. See "Gliding Along" for more on these funds.

GLIDING ALONG

Among the newest investment options for 401(k) plans are *target date* funds, also known as *life cycle* funds. While virtually nonexistent at the beginning of the decade, these funds had $256 billion in assets at the end of 2009, according to the Investment Company Institute.

A target date fund is an asset allocation fund that invests in a broad range of asset classes—from cash to aggressive stocks—often through buying shares of other mutual funds within the same complex as a *fund of funds*. Participants find them attractive because they make it possible to make an investment decision once and then forget about it.

The distinguishing feature of target date funds is that they gradually change their allocations as they approach a specific target date that's roughly equal to the date that investors in the fund plan to retire. For example, a fund designed for workers who are age 35 in 2010 and planning to retire 30 years later would have a target date of 2040. A fund complex offers a series of target date funds to cover the entire population of workers. The target dates of the fund series are usually 10 years—but occasionally 5 years—apart. The fund family periodically adds new target date funds to cover the latest entrants to the workforce.

Because most investors become more sensitive to losses the closer they get to retirement, the asset allocation of a target date fund gets steadily more conservative over time. A possible baseline allocation is portrayed in Figure 11.5. Because the allocation to stocks steadily declines over time—hopefully creating a smooth landing for the investor—the asset allocation pattern for target date funds is referred to as the *glide path*. (Projected retirement is at Year 0 in the x-axis on this chart.)

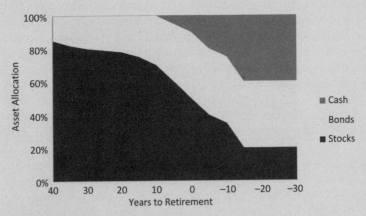

FIGURE 11.5   Sample Target Date Fund Glide Path

This is, however, only a hypothetical glide path. In actuality, funds with the same target year—but offered by different fund complexes—can have vastly different asset allocations. Their performance can vary widely as a result—as highlighted in the market turmoil of 2008. Target date funds with a heavier exposure to stocks fared less well during the credit crisis than those with a more conservative positioning.

Many target date investors were surprised by the losses they suffered in 2008. Some learned too late that their fund had more exposure to the plunging stock market than they expected. Others mistakenly believed that a target date fund fully protected their savings in the last five years before retirement. To help investors better understand how these funds fit into a personal financial plan, the SEC has proposed that target date fund managers provide more information about glide paths.

Advice. The second trend takes almost the opposite approach. It doesn't try to change the number or complexity of the investment options; it seeks instead to provide more advice to participants who would like some help deciding on a retirement portfolio. Of course, 401(k) participants who would like this type of advice could always hire an outside investment adviser—if they knew where to find a good one and had the money to pay for that assistance. Most don't, so many workers look to their employers or plan manager for low-cost personalized advice.

Unfortunately, both plan sponsors and plan providers shy away from providing individualized investment recommendations. Plan sponsors are concerned about potential liability if they give out advice that eventually goes sour, while ERISA generally prohibits plan providers from giving opinions on their own investment products. The most that providers can do under current Department of Labor regulations is publish model portfolios, with different combinations of investment options that are suitable for a variety of investment objectives and risk appetites. While the Pension Protection Act of 2006 allows providers to give advice generated by a computer model if verified by an independent firm, the Department of Labor has yet to issue final regulations that make it possible for providers to understand exactly how to comply with the law. Until then, plan participants are typically on their own. To provide truly personal advice, plan providers must hire an independent adviser—at a cost.

Before we leave the topic of investment options, what about the expenses on the mutual fund options in a 401(k) plan? Retirement plans almost never pay sales loads, and plan sponsors are often very sensitive to the level of annual fees. As we learned in Chapter 10, many funds have established a separate class of shares, usually called Class R, for use in most retirement plans with no loads and a modest 12b-1 fee. Very large retirement plans may even qualify for Class I, or institutional, shares which are even less expensive, since they impose no distribution charges at all—neither sales loads nor 12b-1 fees.

Plan Administration

To conclude our discussion of 401(k)s, let's take a brief look at the administrative services that these plans require. In a nutshell, 401(k)-related operations are extremely complex—largely as a result of the intricate tax rules that govern qualified plans. Administrators of defined contribution plans must be able to:

- Accept three types of contributions—elective, matching, and nonelective —for large numbers of employees and keep track of each separately. Administrators generally process contributions by building automated links to payroll systems.
- Handle different types of distributions. Some of these may be taxable and some not. For example, a voluntary withdrawal from a 401(k) before age $59\frac{1}{2}$ is usually taxable, unless the money is used for certain purposes approved by the IRS, such as the first-time purchase of a home. The plan administrator must provide accurate tax reports.
- Calculate *required minimum distributions,* or RMDs. The tax rules require that participants begin withdrawing money from their accounts once they reach age $70\frac{1}{2}$. The RMD varies from year to year based on the value in the account and the age of the participant—and on the political weather in Washington. Congress eliminated the RMD in 2009—for one year only—in response to the credit crisis.
- Keep records of beneficiary provisions, which designate the new owner of plan assets upon the death of the participant.
- Process loans. Many plans allow participants to borrow money from their accounts. Administrators must keep track of the loans and repayments.
- Provide reports to plan sponsors. Plan sponsors are interested in asset balances at the plan level. In addition, administrators typically provide other services, such as tax reporting and antidiscrimination testing.
- Accommodate non–mutual fund options such as company stock and stable value funds. To do this, plans must *unitize* the investments, setting them up in what are effectively mini-mutual funds.

All of this is in addition to the basic services that funds supply to all their investors: daily calculation of NAV, regular reporting of account balances to plan participants, and customer service support facilities to answer questions or resolve problems.

Plan administrators must also set up systems for communicating with plan participants about both the provisions of the plan and the investment options available. As we've seen, such a communications system is critical for two reasons: it helps plans meet antidiscrimination requirements by encouraging non–highly compensated employees to contribute, and it protects employers from liability under the safe harbor of Section 404(c). Plan sponsors have increasingly been demanding that these communications use the latest technology. Virtually every 401(k) provider today offers extensive online sites for plan participants, often incorporating video and other features.

Who does all of this administrative work? Some mutual fund management companies are full service 401(k) plan providers that handle administration along with investment management. They get paid a separate fee for their administrative services. This fee is usually paid by plan participants, in the form of a per-account charge, although some plan sponsors assume responsibility for all or part of these costs. Other investment-only fund groups just manage the investment options within the plan, leaving administration to another fund company or a third party administrator, or TPA. This approach is sometimes referred to as *DCIO,* for *defined contribution investment only.* These two options aren't mutually exclusive; full service providers often promote their funds as DCIO options in plans they don't administer.

INDIVIDUAL RETIREMENT ACCOUNTS

If the growth in defined contribution plans has been amazing, the growth in individual retirement accounts has been staggering. By the end of 2009, assets in IRAs totaled about $4.2 trillion. That's more than the assets in either defined contribution plans or nongovernment defined benefit plans, making IRAs the largest component of the private pension system. These accounts have become a basic component of household financial planning. By 2009, more than 46 million U.S. households, representing almost 40 percent of all households, owned an IRA. Figure 11.6 shows the growth in IRA assets over the past two decades.

As we reviewed in the first section of this chapter, IRAs are very similar to 401(k)s in terms of their tax-deferral features. They are simpler in some ways: because each IRA holder has an individual account, there's no need for reporting at the plan level—and no antidiscrimination testing. But the administrators of IRA accounts—called *custodians*—must still keep track of beneficiary provisions, compute required minimum distributions, determine the tax status of withdrawals, and comply with all the other rules that make IRAs eligible for tax deferral. Many custodians charge IRA account holders an annual fee for these services.

Mutual funds are the most common investment choice in IRAs for the same reasons that they dominate 401(k) plans. At the end of 2009, 46 percent of all IRA assets in 2009 were invested in mutual funds, more

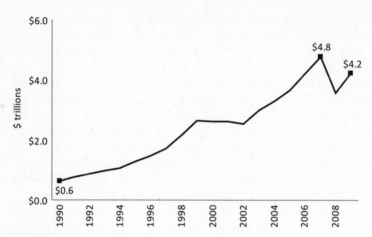

FIGURE 11.6   Individual Retirement Account Assets
Source: Investment Company Institute, *2010 Investment Company Fact Book.*

than double their 22 percent share in 1990. Banks deposits in particular have lost significant market share to mutual funds. (See Figure 11.7 for a breakdown of IRA assets by type of investment.)

IRAs have been around for quite a bit longer than 401(k) plans. They came into being in 1974 as part of the ERISA legislation; they were

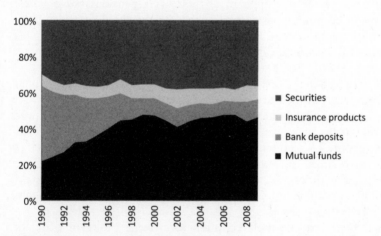

FIGURE 11.7   Individual Retirement Account Assets by Type of Investment
Source: Investment Company Institute, *2010 Investment Company Fact Book.*

included in that law as a means for taxpayers not covered by traditional pension plans to save for their retirement. But IRAs were little noticed until 1981, when Congress dramatically enhanced their appeal by allowing all taxpayers—including those covered by an employer-sponsored plan—to make tax-deductible contributions to them. Mutual fund managers and other financial institutions actively promoted the value of these universal IRAs. Not surprisingly, contributions soared, although they were to level off after 1986, when Congress again tightened the eligibility for tax deductions. (The back and forth on the tax deductibility of IRAs is not unusual. It has varied considerably over the years, as Congress continually tries to balance promotion of retirement savings with budget deficit concerns.)

In fact, Congress often makes adjustments in the individual retirement account program to encourage retirement savings. The 1990s saw two innovations in IRAs:

1. *SIMPLE IRAs.* In 1996, Congress encouraged small employers to offer retirement plans by creating the Savings Incentive Match Plan for Employees, or SIMPLE, plan. While large employers have generally provided some type of retirement plan to the workers, smaller employers typically have been scared away by their cost and the administrative burden. The SIMPLE IRA, for firms with no more than 100 workers, was designed to make it—dare we say it?—simple to sponsor a retirement plan.[16]

    SIMPLE plan participants can contribute up to $11,500 per year to their account, less than the limit for 401(k) plans. Older workers may contribute an additional $2,500 as a catch-up contribution. (Again, these are figures for 2010—contribution limits are adjusted annually for inflation.)

    Plan sponsors must make a contribution on their employee's behalf: they may either match employee elective contributions up to 3 percent of annual salary or make a nonelective contribution for everyone of 2 percent of annual salary. The trade-off for the lower limit and the mandatory employer contributions is that SIMPLE plans are free from the antidiscrimination tests that apply to 401(k) plans.

    The simplicity of these plans has led to a modest level of acceptance among small employers. According to the Investment Company Institute, well over two million workers participated in SIMPLE IRA plans by the end of 2008. These plans held $46 billion in assets, of which $35 billion, or more than 75 percent, were invested in mutual funds, according to the Investment Company Institute.

2. *Roth IRAs.* In 1997, Congress created the Roth IRA, and the Investment Company Institute reports that by year-end 2009 some 15 percent of U.S. households held a Roth IRA. Unfortunately, Roth IRAs have not been a major factor in increasing retirement savings; rather, they seem to have cannibalized the appetite for traditional IRAs, partly through conversions. "Convertible Option" has an explanation.

CONVERTIBLE OPTION

When Congress passed the legislation that created Roth IRAs, it included a provision that allowed holders of traditional IRAs to convert them to the new Roth IRAs. To make the conversion, the IRA holder pays income tax now on the full value of the account.

Why take this tax hit? Because the future tax benefits of the Roth IRA may be worth it. Remember that the big benefit of Roth IRAs is that the money can be withdrawn from them tax-free. These distributions are tax-free even if made to your descendants after your death, making Roth IRAs an excellent estate planning tool. And Roth IRAs do not have to make required minimum distributions, meaning that an IRA holder who doesn't need additional income can continue to let investment earnings accumulate within the account tax-free.

The details of the conversion can be quite complicated. For example, should you pay the taxes from the Roth IRA itself, or should you fund them from your taxable accounts? To maximize the tax deferral, advisers recommend that you leave the assets in the IRA alone and pay the taxes from your other income—though that only works if you have enough spare cash lying about to meet the IRS bill. And a Roth IRA conversion may not make much sense for estate planning purposes if you believe that your assets will be subject to the estate tax. That's why financial planners recommend that anyone considering a Roth conversion should prepare a detailed analysis of how long it will take them to break even on the transaction.

Got the calculation wrong? No worries—the IRS allows you to reverse a Roth IRA conversion, up until the time you file your taxes in the following year. This undo is called a recharacterization.

An extremely important trend in the IRA market is the increasing use of *rollover IRAs* that hold assets that have been transferred from, or rolled over,

TABLE 11.3 Individual Retirement Account Contributions, Rollovers, and Withdrawals ($ billions)

	Contributions	Rollovers	Withdrawals
1996	$14.1	$114.0	$ 45.5
1997	15.0	121.5	55.2
1998	11.9	160.0	74.1
1999	10.3	199.9	87.1
2000	10.0	225.6	99.0
2001	9.2	187.8	94.3
2002	12.4	204.4	88.2
2003	12.3e	205.0e	88.3
2004	12.6	214.9	101.7
2005	13.6e	246.5e	112.3
2006	14.4p	282.1p	124.7
2007	14.4p	323.1p	148.0

eEstimated.
pProjected.
Source: Investment Company Institute, "The U.S. Retirement Market, 2009."

from an employer-sponsored retirement plan. With a rollover, workers can easily transfer assets from one tax-deferred account to another. Rollovers totaled $323 billion in 2007—more than 20 times the $14 billion in new contributions to IRAs from other sources in that same year. (Table 11.3 shows recent trends in flows in and out of IRAs.)

Congress has actively encouraged rollovers. In fact, they have created a significant penalty for outright withdrawals from 401(k)s. Plan administrators must withhold 20 percent of those withdrawals for the IRS, unless they go directly into a rollover account. Employers must also automatically roll over small 401(k) distributions—the distributions that are least likely to be voluntarily transferred to an IRA.

Rollovers are only expected to increase, as baby boomers begin to retire and become eligible to remove what are now quite substantial savings from their retirement plans—a fact that has caught the attention of mutual fund management companies. Fund managers actively market to near-retirees, hoping to capture their rollover dollars when the time comes. This is a particularly critical strategy for fund firms that administer 401(k) plans; they have access to plan participants and risk experiencing asset declines. Let's take a closer look at *distribution planning,* as it's called, and other trends in retirement planning.

THE FUTURE OF RETIREMENT PLANNING IN THE UNITED STATES

The U.S. retirement savings market is maturing, largely as a result of demographics. The first wave of the baby boom is now in its sixties and has begun to retire in significant numbers. As a result, the percentage of the U.S. population over age 65 is now increasing steadily and will not level off for almost 30 years. Over the next decade, these demographics will lead to a greater emphasis on distribution planning, a renewed focus on making retirement plans simpler, and an increased interest in ensuring retirement income security for all workers.

Distribution Planning

While retirement plans have been in an accumulation phase—meaning that assets in the plans have been steadily growing—in the coming years, the marketplace will move into a distribution, or withdrawal, phase, when more money will be coming out of retirement plans than will be going in. That's because the baby boomers will begin to retire and, rather than putting more money into their retirement accounts as they've been doing several decades, they'll start tapping them to support their retirement income needs. The withdrawal column in Table 11.3 shows that this is already starting to happen.

As a result, distribution planning—figuring out how much to take out of a retirement account, how to minimize the taxes on those withdrawals and how to incorporate the distributions into an estate plan—will become as important as the investment planning that helped grow the balances in those accounts.

More and more, investors will look for investment strategies that help them balance the need for income today with the need to continue to grow assets and protect against a loss of purchasing power through inflation—both of which are critical for financing withdrawals tomorrow. They'll also be looking for ways to hedge their longevity risk, which is the risk that they'll outlive their savings—a very real risk, since the combination of the trend toward earlier retirement and the reality of increased life expectancies means that retirement income must cover a longer time span.

Aging investors will need access to specialized technical tools and expertise, including:

- Information on the complex rules governing required minimum distributions
- Advice on integrating beneficiary provisions into an overall estate plan

■ Tools that allow investors to look at all their sources of retirement income—whether from a defined benefit plan, defined contribution plan, an individual retirement account, a variable annuity, or Social Security—in a single financial plan

Mutual fund sponsors may need to redesign their offerings to meet these needs. They may offer a combination of fixed and variable annuities to retirees who are contemplating a withdrawal from their tax-deferred savings accounts. Fixed annuities—issued by an insurance company—provide a regular payment for the annuitant's lifetime, helping reduce *longevity risk*, which is the risk of retirees outliving their savings. And variable annuities might be promoted as a way to invest distributions from retirement accounts while continuing to accrue income on a tax-deferred basis. Fund management companies have also introduced *managed payout funds* that seek to generate a regular monthly income from assets, though this income stream is not guaranteed.

Making Plans Simpler

As we've seen, both plan sponsors and legislators—prodded by research from behavioral economists—have warmed to the need for greater simplicity in the design and administration of defined contribution plans. This has become especially critical because 401(k) plans are no long just a nice side dish, with defined benefit plans continuing to be the main meal. For most workers, 401(k) plans are their sole retirement program other than Social Security—and in many instances their primary source of personal savings as well. Encouraging them to use these plans has become a public priority.

Many plans now incorporate several default options. In addition to automatically enrolling participants, they may direct contributions to a target date fund—rather than a low-yielding money market fund—and they may increase contributions as a participant's income grows—unless a participant specifically opts out, of course. All of these defaults ensure that participants aren't missing out on important opportunities to save and invest simply because of inertia.

But many participants are still overwhelmed by the decisions related to their retirement plans. Take the issue of investment allocation—the average participant has to choose from among 18 different options when deciding how to invest their 401(k) assets. Students of plan design suggest that most participants would find it easier to arrive at an appropriate asset allocation if plan sponsors winnowed down the options. The most radical advocates of simplification argue that there's no good reason to offer anything but a series of target date or asset allocation funds in 401(k) plans. More moderate reformers suggest trimming the number of choices and eliminating some of the riskier ones, such as company stock.

Managing withdrawals from retirement plans is another daunting challenge for many participants. Just figuring out how much to withdraw every year while leaving enough in the account to fund future income requires a complex calculation. This involves estimates of investment returns, tax rates, and life expectancy that can too easily turn out to be wrong—leaving a retiree very short of money late in life. Default options might play a role here, as well. Perhaps a portion of retirement distributions would automatically be applied to vehicles that aimed to supply a regular monthly income, such as a fixed annuity or a managed payout fund. As with all defaults, plan participants would be free to choose another path, but only if they took active steps to do so.

Ensuring Retirement Income Security for All

Perhaps the greatest problem confronting the private pension system in the United States is its lack of anything approaching universal coverage. In fact, at any given time, no more than 50 percent of the workforce has access to a private pension plan, whether a defined benefit plan or a defined contribution plan.[17] Lower-income workers are least likely to be covered, for three reasons:

1. They are more likely to be seasonal or part-time workers who, under ERISA, need not be included in a plan.[18]
2. They are also more likely to work for smaller employers, and, as we've seen, these employers are much less likely to have a retirement plan.
3. They are less likely to elect to participate in 401(k) plans even when one is available, simply because they cannot afford to so.

A few small steps have been taken to address this problem. We've discussed two of these measures already: SIMPLE IRAs made it much easier for smaller employers to offer retirement plans, and automatic enrollment features increase participation rates. Congress has also introduced a Saver's Credit, which gives lower-income workers a tax credit of up to 50 percent of their 401(k) contributions, with a maximum credit of $1,000 per year.[19] But none of these steps have really made a significant dent in the problem.

One proposal that has gained favor with policymakers, called the Automatic IRA, would require all employers with more than 10 or 20 employees to offer them a payroll deduction retirement plan. Default options would encourage employees to participate—though, again, they could choose to opt out. Employers wouldn't have to make a contribution to these plans;

they would just have to connect their payroll each quarter to a financial institution providing individual retirement accounts with enough investment options to come within the safe harbor we described earlier. The financial institutions would handle all the administrative functions and tax reporting for employers with Automatic IRAs.

Despite the challenges, finding a way to incorporate all workers into private retirement plans is critical given the strained finances of the public Social Security system (discussed in "The Third Leg of the Retirement Stool"). The shortfall will grow only worse with time as the baby boomers start drawing on both the private and public systems for income in their golden years. The clock is ticking.

THE THIRD LEG OF THE RETIREMENT STOOL

After employer-sponsored retirement plans and personal savings, Social Security is the third leg of the retirement stool. It is by far the most important because it covers all workers and provides them with lifelong retirement income. In contrast, private pension plans are voluntary, do not cover everyone, and provide income benefits for only as long as the money lasts. Social Security is also an extremely important source of income for many elderly Americans. In 2005, it provided the majority of income for two-thirds of retirees and accounted for almost all the income of one-third.[20]

Unfortunately, Social Security has been funded in a way that makes it very vulnerable to demographic changes. It's essentially a pay-as-you-go system, in which current taxes pay for current retirees. (In contrast, defined benefit and defined contribution plans are largely pre-funded, meaning that money is set aside today to support retirement income in the future.) Pay-as-you-go works well when the retired generation is supported by a younger working generation sufficiently large enough to pay for the Social Security benefits of retirees.

But the prospective retirement of the baby boom generation challenges the basic premise of pay-as-you-go. The statistics are alarming: in 1950, there were 16.5 workers to support each retiree; by 2030, there will be only 2.0 workers to support each retiree. Therefore, the payroll taxes collected each year will be less than the Social Security benefits paid out from 2016 onward. Economists predict that sometime around 2038, Social Security will be effectively bankrupt—meaning that it will be able to pay out less than three-fourths of the currently scheduled benefits to retirees.

Congress will ultimately have to make a difficult decision. The math is simple. It can:

- Reduce the Social Security benefits for future retirees, possibly by raising the retirement age further or making the benefit schedule less favorable for higher-income retirees
- Increase Social Security payroll taxes, by raising the tax rate or the maximum salary subject to the tax
- Divert general tax revenues from other programs to fund Social Security benefits, probably leading to cuts in those other programs

With none of these alternatives having any political appeal, Congress has been reluctant to confront the funding problem squarely. And any type of Social Security reform would have to be phased in slowly over many years. In this situation, the private retirement system becomes even more important.

CHAPTER SUMMARY

Qualified retirement plans provide significant tax benefits to investors who wish to save for retirement. For most plans, contributions are tax-deductible, while investment income grows tax-free within the plan; withdrawals are fully taxable. However, Roth plans provide a different set of tax benefits. Contributions to these plans are made on an after-tax basis, but withdrawals are then tax-free.

The most popular type of employer-sponsored qualified plan is now the 401(k) plan. In the past, the most popular plan was a traditional pension plan. These plans, also known as defined benefit plans, promised workers a retirement income based on their income while working. Employers bear investment risk in a defined benefit plans. In a 401(k) plan, which is a type of defined contribution plan, the employee bears the investment risk. Employees who participate in a 401(k) plan make contributions to their personal account; an employer sponsoring the plan may make contributions as well, though these are not required. Participants decide how to invest assets in their account, choosing from a menu of investment options selected by the employer. Retirement income is determined by the level of assets in a participant's account, which in turn is determined by the level of contributions and investment performance.

Mutual funds are the most common investment option in 401(k) plans, although plans may include other options such as collective trust funds and company stock. Target date mutual funds have been growing in popularity in 401(k) plans, but disappointed many plan participants in the market crash of 2008. These funds gradually reduce their asset allocation to stocks as the fund nears a target date, which approximates the expected retirement date of fund investors.

The regulations for 401(k) plans are very complex. Plan administrators must be able to keep track of different types of contributions, the tax status of withdrawals, required minimum distributions, beneficiary provisions, and plan loans. They must also help employers comply with complex antidiscrimination rules, which require that a plan be used broadly throughout a company and not just by senior executives.

Individual retirement accounts are the most common type of private retirement savings vehicle, and mutual funds are the most common investment within them. Under certain circumstances, investors may transfer assets from a 401(k) plan into an IRA. These rollover transactions are increasing as more baby boomers reach retirement age. As more investors start tapping into their retirement accounts for income, they will look for help with distribution planning.

Many policymakers believe that universal participation in private pension plans should be a public policy priority, in light of the financial difficulties that Social Security is expected to face in the near future. To increase participation by workers covered by a private retirement plan, legislators have allowed the use of a greater number of default options that automatically include workers in plans unless they act to opt out. However, many lower-income workers are still not covered by any type of private retirement plan.

CHAPTER 12

The Competition from Exchange-Traded Funds and Hedge Funds

We looked in the last two chapters at how funds are distributed to investors through the intermediary, direct, and retirement channels. Now we turn our attention to two of the toughest competitors faced by traditional mutual funds: exchange-traded funds—commonly called ETFs—and hedge funds. Both have been growing rapidly. We take a closer look in this chapter at how they are structured and why they have had so much appeal for investors.

This chapter reviews:

- Exchange-traded funds: their advantages and disadvantages, structure, operations, investment approach, and future
- Hedge funds: their advantages and disadvantages, strategies, investors, and regulation

EXCHANGE-TRADED FUNDS

Exchange-traded funds are hot! They're the smart, new apps of the fund world. Need a low-cost fund based on the S&P 500? There are several ETFs that will work for you. Want to win big if the Dow Jones Industrial Average goes down? There are ETFs that will serve your purpose. How about an investment in bonds? Or are you interested in owning commodities like platinum, gold, and oil? Yes and yes. There are ETFs that match all your investment objectives, whether conservative or aggressive. And it seems as if new ETFs are being launched every day.

The recent growth of ETFs has been eye-catching, especially when compared to the overall growth in the fund industry. That hasn't always been the case. The ETF industry grew slowly in the dozen years after the launch of the first ETF in 1992. (See "Of SuperTrusts, SPDRs, and WEBS" for more about the earliest ETFs.) At the end of 2004, there were only 152 ETFs from a handful of sponsors with just $228 billion in assets. In the mid-2000s, however, ETFs hit a tipping point, and growth took off. By the end of 2009, the industry had grown to more than $775 billion in assets with close to 800 funds from approximately 30 sponsors.[1] Over a five-year time frame, ETFs had a compound annual growth rate of more than 27 percent. Growth in the mutual fund industry overall was only 7 percent in that same period.

OF SUPERTRUSTS, SPDRs, AND WEBS

Q: What was the first ETF in the United States?

Some students of industry history argue that it was the SuperTrust, which began trading on the American Stock Exchange in 1992. Developed by the principals of California investment firm Leland O'Brien Rubinstein, the SuperTrust responded to the need for an S&P 500 Index fund that traded on an exchange.[2] It was a complex product designed for institutional investors, that never developed much of a following and was eventually liquidated.

That's why most historians award the claim of "first" to another S&P 500 Index-based ETF—the Standard & Poor's Depositary Receipts, abbreviated as SPDRs and pronounced like *spiders*. A streamlined version of the SuperTrust, the SPDRs trust was launched by the American Stock Exchange in 1993, and its underlying portfolio remains the largest ETF today. SPDRs is structured as a unit investment trust.

Looking for the first mutual fund–based ETFs? (We review the difference between the unit investment trust and mutual fund forms shortly.) Those are the WEBS—an appropriate complement to SPDRs—which were developed by former Leland O'Brien Rubinstein staff for Barclays Global Investors and Morgan Stanley in 1996. The Barclays WEBS grew into the largest family of ETFs in the world, now under the BlackRock iShares brand.

As you can see from Table 12.1, much of the growth in ETFs appears to have come at the expense of traditional index mutual funds. ETFs—which are usually passively managed themselves—are direct competitors for index funds. In 1998, index funds comprised $264 billion of fund industry assets,

TABLE 12.1 ETF and Mutual Fund Assets by Fund Type ($ billions)

Year	Exchange-Traded Funds (excludes commodity ETFs)		Long-Term Mutual Funds (excludes money market funds)	
	Index	Active	Index	Active
1998	$ 16		$264	$3,910
1999	34		387	4,847
2000	66		384	4,736
2001	83		371	4,319
2002	102		328	3,791
2003	151		455	4,907
2004	226		556	5,638
2005	296		621	6,244
2006	408		750	7,309
2007	580		857	8,058
2008	496		603	5,167
2009	702	$1	837	6,968

Source: Investment Company Institute, *2010 Investment Company Fact Book.*

versus just $16 billion for passively managed ETFs. Even as late as 2005, index funds still had more than twice the assets of ETFs. But by the end of 2009, the $703 billion in index ETFs—which excludes $75 billion in commodity ETFs—was not far behind the $837 billion in index mutual funds. (Note that both ETFs and index funds captured share from actively managed funds, as we discussed in Chapter 4.) And now that actively managed ETFs have been introduced, as we'll discuss shortly, some ETF advocates have begun to suggest that they may become more popular than traditional mutual funds over time.

Advantages and Disadvantages of Exchange-Traded Funds

Exchange-traded funds are similar to mutual funds in many ways, but they have a unique feature that sets them apart from mutual funds: their shares trade on a stock exchange or other market center. So, ETFs match mutual funds in providing investors an easy way to own a diversified basket of securities. But ETFs offer advantages compared to traditional mutual funds, specifically:

- *Exchange-traded.* Unlike mutual funds—whose shares are generally sold or redeemed only once a day after the close of business on the New York

Stock Exchange—ETF shares can be bought and sold throughout the trading day.

- *No investment minimum.* ETFs can be bought in quantities as small as one share, while most mutual funds require a minimum investment of several thousand dollars to open an account.
- *Lower expense structure.* Since most ETFs are index funds, they have naturally lower management expenses. Also, because they are exchange-traded, their shareholder servicing costs are lower. As a result, many ETFs have lower expense ratios than mutual funds with comparable investment strategies.
- *Broader set of investments.* Some ETFs allow investors to have exposure to commodities and currencies, which traditional mutual funds are generally not permitted to own.
- *Tax efficiency.* ETFs are considered to be more tax-efficient than many mutual funds, meaning that they generate fewer taxable capital gains. We explain why this is the case later in this section.

On the other hand, traditional mutual funds have their advantages, too:

- *Daily redemption at NAV.* Mutual fund investors can go directly to the fund at the end of every business day to redeem their shares for the NAV. ETF investors must sell their shares on the stock exchange at the prevailing price—which can be different from NAV. While ETFs have mechanisms that keep prices and NAVs in line, they have not always been effective, as we'll see.
- *No trading commissions.* While ETFs often have lower fund expenses than traditional mutual funds, investors in ETFs must normally pay brokerage commissions whenever they buy or sell shares—a cost that mutual fund owners do not incur.[3]
- *Broader array of actively managed strategies.* Most ETFs are passive index funds; actively managed ETFs are just beginning to be developed. As we'll see shortly, many fund managers believe that ETFs are an inappropriate format for active strategies, so traditional funds may continue to be preferred by active managers.

So, What Is an Exchange-Traded Fund, Really?

The term *exchange-traded fund* has come to apply to a spectrum of exchange-traded instruments whose price depends on the value of an underlying investment portfolio. There are essentially three main types of ETFs, summarized in Table 12.2.

TABLE 12.2 Comparison of ETF Models

	Investment Company ETF		Commodity ETF		
	Mutual Fund–Based	UIT Based	Partnership or Investment Trust	Grantor Trust	ETN
Investment approach	Active or passive	Passive only	Passive only	Static basket of securities	Return based on index
Replication or sampling?	Either	Replication only	Either	Static basket of securities	n/a
1940 Act registered?	X	X	No	No	No
Independent board of directors?	X	No	No	No	No
Pass-through tax status?	X	X	Varies[1]	Yes[2]	No[3]
Issuer credit risk exposure?	No	No	No	No	No
Examples	iShares	Original SPDRs	GLD, GSG	HOLDRs	iPath

[1] Commodity and currency ETFs have varying tax treatments, generally passing through income, gains, and losses. Income from gold is not eligible for capital gains rate.

[2] Investors considered holders of underlying securities.

[3] Tax status under review. The IRS is considering whether to require that capital gains be accrued during term of note. (They are currently taxed only upon sale.)

Type 1: Investment company ETFs. Most ETFs invest in securities such as stocks and bonds and are generally structured as open-end mutual funds or unit investment trusts. They are, therefore, regulated under the 1940 Act—though ETFs must ask the SEC for exemptions from some of the rules that apply to traditional funds. (See "Mother, May I?" for details.) As we've mentioned, most of these ETFs use index strategies, though actively managed ETFs were introduced in 2008.

MOTHER, MAY I?

Exemptive application and *exemptive order* are two terms that touch the very heart of exchange-traded funds. As we've learned, the 1940 Act contains detailed provisions regarding the structure, governance, and operations of funds—but ETFs don't square well with these. Even some of the basics are challenges for ETFs under the 1940 Act. For example, as we've mentioned, shareholders of an ETF can't redeem at NAV at the end of every business day.

To get relief from these ill-fitting regulations, an ETF and its sponsors must file an exemptive application with the SEC. After review and public comment—and, sometimes, even a public hearing on the merits of the application—the SEC issues a final exemptive order that spells out alternate rules for that ETF. The original ETF exemptive order took more than three years to negotiate, and while the process has gotten much faster, it still takes 12 to 18 months for a new ETF to get exemptive relief. (Compare that to just three to six months to set up a traditional mutual fund.) Why does it take so long? Because each exemptive order is individually negotiated. To speed things up, the SEC in 2008 proposed standardized rules that would eliminate the need for exemptive relief for many new ETFs. It's not clear when or even if these rules will be adopted.

Type 2: Commodity ETFs. A small but growing number of ETFs own commodities, real estate, or currencies either directly or through the use of derivatives. These ETFs emerged in the mid-2000s and have blossomed along with interest in commodities, particularly precious metals such as gold. At the end of 2009, commodity ETFs accounted for 10 percent of total ETF assets, up from only 3.5 percent just two years earlier, according to the Investment Company Institute. Examples of commodity ETFs are the SPDR Gold Shares (ticker symbol GLD) and the iShares S&P GSCI Commodity Index Trust (ticker symbol GSG).

Because commodities, real property, and derivatives are legally difficult for 1940 Act funds to buy in any quantity, these ETFs are typically organized as partnerships, investment trusts, or grantor trusts that are not subject to the 1940 Act. As a result, commodity ETFs lack some of the investor protections enjoyed by mutual fund investors, including investors in traditional ETFs. For example, commodity ETFs do not usually have an independent board of directors watching out for shareholder interests. These ETFs, however, are still securities that must be registered with the SEC.

Type 3: Exchange-traded notes. Exchange-traded notes, or ETNs, are not funds at all. Rather, they are bonds, normally issued by a bank, with an investment return that's tied to the performance of an index or basket of securities, commodities, or currencies.[4] For example, the iPath EUR/USD Exchange Rate ETN pays a return based on changes in the exchange rate between the euro and the U.S. dollar. ETNs are a small but quickly growing part of the ETF market. Their assets totaled only $4.9 billion in April 2009 but had risen to over $11 billion at the end of April 2010, although that's still just a tiny fraction of the ETF market in total.[5]

As with commodity ETFs, ETNs must register with the SEC but are not governed by the 1940 Act—meaning that owners do not enjoy the investor protections provided by that legislation. And ETNs involve an additional—and quite substantial—risk: the risk that the issuer goes bankrupt and is unable to make payments to ETN investors, known as *credit risk*.

How Do Exchange-Traded Funds Operate?

Let's explore how ETFs operate from day to day. We'll look at how ETFs create and redeem shares and how they manage subsequent market trading of their shares, focusing on investment company ETFs.

Creation and redemption of ETF shares. ETFs use a complex process to create and redeem their shares. As we've learned, in a traditional mutual fund, new shares are created whenever a shareholder makes an investment in the fund by buying fund shares in exchange for cash. Shareholders in traditional funds can reverse the process at any time, selling fund shares to receive cash equal to the NAV. In contrast, ETFs don't deal directly with their shareholders; they instead create and redeem shares through an *authorized participant,* or AP, who is usually a large investor—often a hedge fund, market maker, or a broker-dealer—which has signed an agreement with the ETF. Creating ETF shares and distributing them in the market is a three-step process, illustrated in Figure 12.1:

- *Step 1.* The authorized participant assembles a *creation basket,* a portfolio of securities that exactly matches the portfolio of securities held

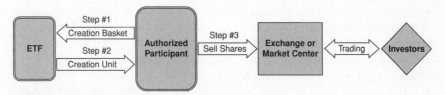

FIGURE 12.1 The Creation Process for ETF Shares

by the ETF. To assist the AP, the ETF publishes a *portfolio composition file* that discloses the ETF's holdings, at least once a day.

- *Step 2.* The AP delivers the creation basket to the ETF. In exchange, it receives a *creation unit,* which is a large batch of shares of the ETF—usually either 50,000 or 100,000 shares—based on the ETF's NAV.
- *Step 3.* The AP breaks the creation unit down into smaller sets of shares and sells them in the public market, or the AP may decide to hold on to some or all of these shares.

Once the shares are on the market, they continue to trade between investors like any other stock.

The redemption process works like the creation process in reverse:

- The authorized participant assembles shares of the ETF, enough shares to equal a creation unit. Again, that's usually either 50,000 or 100,000 shares.
- The AP delivers these shares—now known as a *redemption unit*—to the ETF. It receives in exchange a *redemption basket* of securities that reflects the portfolio composition file of the ETF.[6]

The creation and redemption process is a key advantage of the ETF model as compared to the traditional mutual fund structure. It allows ETFs to keep their trading costs very low, since it's the authorized participant that does most of the buying and selling of portfolio securities.

The in-kind nature of the process helps ETFs minimize the capital gains that it passes through to its shareholders. An ETF need never sell its holdings to meet its obligations to redeeming shareholders; it simply transfers securities instead—together with any capital gains—to the AP, which may be a tax-exempt pension fund or an investor that has the ability to offset the gains with other transactions. Sound like a good deal? Some observers think that it's too good a deal—and have urged changing the tax laws to put ETFs on the same tax footing as traditional mutual funds. Another potential cloud on the horizon is that it's unclear whether APs will continue to be able to absorb all gains as the asset base continues to grow.

Exchange trading and the arbitrage process. As we've just learned, once ETF shares are created, they can trade freely on the stock exchange or in another market center. That means an investor can buy and sell them like regular stocks any time the markets are open. They'll most likely trade on NYSE Arca, which dominates ETF exchange listings, having acquired the original home of ETF trading—the American Stock Exchange—in 2008.

The price of the ETF on the exchange will normally track very closely to the ETF's NAV. That's because arbitrageurs will create or redeem units if the ETF share price and its NAV get too far out of line. For example, if ETF shares are trading at a discount to or below its NAV, the arbitrageur will buy the ETF shares in the market to assemble a redemption unit, and then exchange the redemption unit for a basket of securities with a value equal to the ETF's NAV. Since the NAV is higher than the ETF share price, the arbitrageur can make a quick profit by selling the securities. By automating both the monitoring and the creation-and-redemption process, arbitrageurs can take advantage of even small pricing discrepancies. Arbitrageurs are usually authorized participants because they have the inside track on the creation and redemption process.

It's this arbitrage feature that distinguishes ETFs from closed-end funds. As we discussed in Chapter 2, both ETFs and closed-end funds trade on exchanges. But closed-end funds frequently trade at substantial discounts to NAV. That's because they have a fixed number of shares, and there's no mechanism to keep their market prices aligned with their NAVs. Only ETFs have the creation and redemption feature that helps to minimize premiums and discounts.

Because ETFs want their share price to closely track their asset value, they actively encourage this arbitrage by providing extensive information about portfolio holdings and their value. As we've noted, ETFs issue a portfolio composition file daily. The listing exchange also publishes an *intraday indicative value,* or IIV, at 15-second intervals throughout the trading day. The IIV is an estimated NAV that applies current market prices to the published portfolio.

Overall, the arbitrage system has worked fairly well at keeping ETF share prices and NAVs in line—but it's not perfect. As you can see from Table 12.3, close to 60 percent of ETFs traded within 25 basis points of

TABLE 12.3 ETF Pricing (September 2009)

Percentage Discount or Premium versus NAV	Number of ETFS	Percent of Total	Cumulative Percent
≤0.25% discount	38	5%	5%
0.26% – 0.50% discount	47	6%	10%
0.11% – 0.25% discount	108	14%	25%
0.10% discount – 0.10% premium	251	33%	59%
0.11% – 0.25% premium	85	11%	70%
0.26% – 0.50% premium	93	12%	82%
> 0.50% premium	135	18%	100%

Source: Cerulli Associates, *The Cerulli Report: Exchange-Traded Funds: Threat or Threatened?* (2009).

their NAV in September 2009—though one-quarter of ETFs experienced a meaningful discount. Discounts and premiums have been widening. And the arbitrage system has only just begun to be tested by market turmoil. (You can learn about a recent problem in "Gone in a Flash.")

GONE IN A FLASH

Exchange-traded funds were particularly hard hit in the "flash crash" in the U.S. equities markets on May 6, 2010, when the Dow Jones Industrial Average fell by 1,000 points in just a few minutes. More than 70 percent of the problematic trades that day were in ETFs. (These were trades that resulted in price declines of 60 percent or more during the very brief duration of the crash and that were to be subsequently canceled.) Some ETF prices collapsed to almost zero—almost certainly well below their estimated intraday NAVs.

What happened? At least three factors came into play after a fund manager electronically submitted a large sell order.[7] First, investors tried to use ETFs to offset falling stock prices, either by selling an index ETF or buying an *inverse* ETF that rises in price when the market falls. Second, the rapid collapse in prices may have interfered with the arbitrage process, making it difficult to keep ETF prices and NAVs in line. Finally, communications among some market centers were suspended during the flash crash. Liquidity on NYSE Arca—the exchange on which most ETFs trade—appears to have been most affected by the communication cut-off.

How Do Exchange-Traded Funds Invest?

When determining their investment strategy, exchange-traded funds have a very important initial decision to make: whether to be index-based or actively managed.

Index ETFs. Most ETFs are passively managed, basing their portfolio composition on an index. The original ETFs were based on widely recognized indexes such as the S&P 500, the Dow Jones Industrial Average, or the Wilshire 5000. As ETFs have become more specialized, they have begun to focus on certain sectors, sometimes using custom indexes developed just for the ETF.

Index ETFs must decide what process they will use to track the target index. As we discussed in Chapter 5, index funds can use one of two portfolio management techniques: replication or sampling. In replication, a fund buys exactly the same securities as the index in exactly the same proportion. In sampling, a fund buys only a carefully selected subset of the index stocks, perhaps in conjunction with derivative securities.

Not all ETFs have a choice of technique, however. ETFs that are structured as unit investment trusts must use replication, while grantor trusts must hold an unchanging basket of securities. So it is that SPDRs—organized as a unit trust—must own all the stocks in the S&P 500, while its main competitor, the iShares S&P 500 Index Fund—organized as a mutual fund—can use sampling if it chooses. Sampling can introduce divergences from index performance known as tracking error. As a result of this and other factors, some ETFs have struggled to successfully track their index, as explained in "Whoops! I Missed the Target."

WHOOPS! I MISSED THE TARGET

Tracking error: It's an expression that can send chills down a portfolio manager's spine. As we discussed in Chapter 5, minimizing tracking error is one of the major challenges of managing passive investment strategies. It's becoming quite an issue for exchange-traded funds. A recent Morgan Stanley study found that the average index ETF deviated from its benchmark by a substantial 1.25 percent in 2009; most funds lagged their benchmark returns.[8]

The increased use of specialized indexes—covering narrow or less liquid segments of the market—has made it more challenging for many ETF managers to hit their targets for four reasons:

1. *Fees and expenses.* The higher the ETF's fees and expenses, the higher its tracking error—since the benchmark normally includes no allowance for costs at all. And the specialized ETFs that have been launched recently have tended to have higher fees than those based on broader indexes.
2. *Diversification requirements.* Narrow indexes are often highly concentrated in a few holdings, which can make them very tough to replicate while still complying with regulatory requirements regarding diversification.
3. *Sampling.* If an ETF can't replicate its index exactly, it must use sampling. And with sampling, unanticipated factors such as distortions in the pricing of derivatives or changes in the correlations

of index components can generate tracking error. These are most likely during periods of high market volatility.

4. *Cash management.* ETF managers risk expanded tracking errors if they don't manage their cash flows effectively. This is especially problematic when there are a lot of creations or redemptions.

Moreover, leveraged and inverse ETFs face particular challenges when it comes to tracking error, as we'll see later in this section.

Since ETFs are exchange-traded, it can be argued that tracking errors are less important than market prices. But remember that market prices should reflect underlying NAVs. As tracking errors increase, they make NAVs less reliable and introduce greater unpredictability into the calculus of investors and arbitrageurs. And tracking errors don't necessarily need to be negative: in 2009, a Vanguard Telecom Services ETF bested its target index by 17 percent!

Tracking errors: something investors and portfolio managers need to keep track of.

While passive management sounds very conservative, some ETFs have used it to take a very aggressive approach to investing. These are the inverse, or short, ETFs and the leveraged ETFs that work their magic by buying and selling derivatives. Inverse ETFs enable investors to profit from declines in the market—so that if the S&P 500 were to fall 10 percent one day, an inverse ETF on the S&P would be expected to gain 10 percent. Leveraged ETFs give investors a chance to multiply their gains—or their losses. For example, investors who owned shares in an ETF that provides exposure to the S&P 500 leveraged three times would expect a 30 percent profit when the S&P gains 10 percent. When the S&P loses 10 percent, that same ETF would be expected to decline 30 percent. Inverse and leveraged ETFs can be combined. An investor who was convinced that the S&P 500 was going to fall would want to buy a leveraged, inverse ETF on that index.

Note that the inverse ETFs target their indexes daily, which means that their returns can deviate from the index quite significantly over the long term. Let's look at the hypothetical Windy Corner 2x Leveraged ETF that's leveraged two to one to an index. Let's say that the index rises by 20 percent on the first day, then falls 10 percent on the second, for a total two-day return of 8 percent. The ETF would move twice as much as the index on each day, so it would rise 40 percent on the first day and fall 20 percent on the second. That's a two-day return of 12 percent, which is only 1.5 times

TABLE 12.4 Windy Corner 2x Leveraged ETF

	Index value	ETF NAV
Day 0	$100	$100
Day 1	$120 = $100 + 20%)	$140 = $100 + 40%
Day 2	$108 = $120 − 10%	$112 = $112 − 20%
Two-day return	+8% = $8 gain / $100	+12% = $12 gain / $100

the index return. (Table 12.4 summarizes these numbers; we're ignoring expenses.)

These supercharged ETFs—and, specifically, their performance during the credit crisis—have drawn very negative attention in the press and a lot of scrutiny from the regulators. For example, one inverse ETF—leveraged two times to its index—fell 48 percent during a period when its underlying index fell 39 percent—a time when investors would expect strong positive returns from this investment. Some investors who experienced losses have taken their grievances to court.

Both the SEC and FINRA have taken steps to improve disclosure about how these funds work and imposed limits on investors borrowing to buy shares of such ETFs. In March 2010, the SEC announced that it will defer review of exemptive applications for new ETFs that plan to use derivatives extensively until it can develop rules to improve disclosure and regulation for these funds. In the meantime, some brokerage firms have restricted sales of these ETFs by their financial advisers.

Another set of index ETFs use enhanced index investment approaches that seek to improve on the performance of an index using a quantitative security selection techniques. The formulas for these enhancement strategies are disclosed so that portfolio composition is predictable. As a result, while these ETFs involve an element of active portfolio decision making, they do not raise the concerns that have attached to fully actively managed ETFs, as we'll see in a moment.

Actively managed ETFs. Fund sponsors have long viewed actively managed ETFs as the Holy Grail, the portfolio approach that would put ETFs on an equal footing with traditional mutual funds. Still, active ETFs have been very slow to launch, largely because portfolio managers fear that they could be vulnerable to front running. As we've seen ETFs depend on arbitrage to keep their NAV and their share price in line; to make the arbitrage process work, ETFs must be completely transparent, publishing their holdings data at least once a day.

Active managers generally don't like operating in that kind of spotlight; in fact, as we saw when we reviewed securities trading in Chapter 8, they go to considerable lengths to keep their activities out of the public eye. They don't want other traders anticipating their actions and placing trades in front of them, a strategy known as *front running*. In the eyes of many active managers, the portfolio composition files published daily by ETFs—which may include information on trades that have been started but not yet completed—are nothing more than a license for this front running.

No surprise then that the first active ETFs were fixed income funds that focused on U.S. Treasury and money market securities. Their sponsors apparently felt that disclosing the portfolio compositions of these funds would not seriously impair their investment strategies given the depth of the markets for the portfolios' fixed income securities.

The actively managed equity ETFs that have been subsequently introduced have triggered more of a debate in the fund industry on whether the risks of front running outweigh the other benefits of ETFs. Advocates of active ETFs argue that they provide a benefit because they allow mutual fund managers to sponsor funds specifically for active traders and market timers, accommodating such investors without potential harm to the long-term buy-and-hold investors in their regular mutual funds. Some ETF sponsors have recently proposed active ETFs that would disclose details on only a portion of their portfolio, providing only summary statistics on the balance. They believe that this compromise would prevent front running but still allow for efficient arbitrage. The SEC is still mulling over these proposals.

Despite the front-running concerns, active ETFs continue to gain adherents. By year-end 2009, there were 22 actively managed ETFs managing about $1 billion, a small, but growing, portion of the market, according to the Investment Company Institute.

What Does the Future Hold for Exchange-Traded Funds?

The fuss about actively managed exchange-traded funds is important because—if ETFs are to challenge traditional mutual funds—they must dramatically expand their investor base. To date, ETFs have appealed largely to wealthier individuals and institutional investors. On average, households owning ETFs have $120,000 in annual income and $350,000 in assets; that compares to $80,000 in income and $150,000 for the average mutual fund–owning household. More than 90 percent of the retail owners of ETFs have investments in stocks. ETFs are also popular with institutional investors, including mutual funds, who may use ETFs in lieu of derivatives to manage their exposure to the market.[9]

On the flip side, only 5 percent of the households that own funds have positions in ETFs. The new vehicles have failed to penetrate some of the core markets for traditional mutual funds. As we've seen, there are still very few actively managed ETFs—while active funds account for more than 80 percent of traditional fund assets. According to Cerulli Associates, ETFs make up only 5 percent of financial advisers' product mix, even though these advisers are involved in the majority of mutual fund sales. And ETFs have little presence yet in the defined-contribution retirement plans that account for one-quarter of mutual fund assets. Like company stock, ETFs must be *unitized* to be held in a 401(k) or other defined contribution plan, which imposes additional costs. (See Chapter 11 for more on these plans.) Also, many of these plans would not be comfortable paying brokerage commissions to acquire ETF shares.

Still, the interest in ETFs is high, and their outlook is bright. Amazon.com offers more than 200 books and articles relating to ETFs. Its top-selling item, *The ETF Book,* has six chapters—over 70 pages—of advice on structuring investment portfolios using just ETFs.[10] Many believe that with their perceived lower internal costs and more efficient operating structure, ETFs are well poised to grab market share from traditional funds. Others question whether ETFs will lose their advantages as they become more and more like traditional mutual funds, paying the same fees for active management or access to distribution through wrap accounts and other packaged products.

HEDGE FUNDS

The pros and cons of hedge funds have become a topic of discussion not just in the media, but at cocktail parties. In 1969, 20 years after the launch of the first hedge fund, the SEC estimated that there were 200 hedge funds with a total of $1.5 billion in assets under management. According to HedgeFund.net, by the end of 2009, the numbers had grown to almost 5,000 hedge funds with $2.2 trillion in assets, a compound growth rate in assets of close to 20 percent per year. What are these vehicles that have attracted so much interest?

The term *hedge fund,* while not defined in any law or court case, refers to pooled investment vehicles that share certain investment and regulatory characteristics. On the investment side, hedge funds seek to generate consistently positive returns in all kinds of markets, with low volatility and low correlation to the returns of other asset classes. To generate these returns, hedge funds employ diverse investment strategies—strategies that mutual funds generally find difficult to implement.

On the regulatory side, hedge funds and their advisers are exempt from many of the regulations governing mutual funds and their advisers. As a result of those exemptions, hedge funds can:

- Invest in a wide variety of assets, including large positions in illiquid assets that can be difficult to sell
- Require investors to remain in funds for months or years at a time
- Use large amounts of borrowed money—or *leverage*—to try to enhance investment returns
- Engage extensively in short sales
- Charge performance fees based on gains, in addition to management fees based on assets

CAREER TRACK: HEDGE FUND MANAGER

What's involved in running a hedge fund? The big surprise in store for many start-up hedge fund managers is that the hedge fund business involves substantially more than investment acumen. Running a hedge fund involves all of the chores and headaches of running any small business—in addition to the day-to-day challenges of investing.

That means you'll spend a lot of your time marketing—rounding up new investors and holding on to existing ones—and most of these investors will want to talk with you personally. It's a critical function since new investment capital is the lifeblood of hedge funds, and no hedge fund has ever grown to significant scale based on investment returns alone. You'll also routinely get involved in personnel decisions, fund operations, space planning, compliance issues, and technology implementation.

And you'll make some investment decisions as well. You probably started your career as an investment professional at a bank or investment adviser where you developed an investment approach. Running your own hedge fund gives you a chance to express your investment views on a relatively open canvas with relatively few restrictions. And if you make the right decisions, there's the promise of a large payoff. But for every hedge fund manager who's a billionaire, there are more than a few would-be investing stars struggling to pay the rent and payroll, imploring investors not to redeem, and staying up at night reading annual reports and sell-side research.

Importantly, it is the right to do these things, not the fact of doing them, that qualifies a fund as a hedge fund. That is, a hedge fund is not a hedge fund because it actually uses leverage to invest in illiquid assets and engages short sales. Rather, it's a hedge fund because it has the legal right to engage in these activities, or more precisely, because it's exempt from laws that prohibit engaging in these activities. More than anything else, hedge funds are defined by what they are not—namely, regulated.

But as they say on Wall Street and in Greenwich, Connecticut, where many of the best-known hedge fund managers are based, there's no such thing as a free lunch. And so it is with hedge funds: as a price for their regulatory exemptions, Congress and the SEC have imposed limits on who may invest in hedge funds and how hedge fund managers may market their products. Generally, only investors that own at least $5 million in investments—excluding their homes—may participate in hedge funds. And hedge fund managers may not market themselves or their funds through any of the retail channels typically used by mutual funds, such as television, newspapers, magazines, radio, or Internet. The "Career Track" box talks about the life of a hedge fund manager.

Advantages and Disadvantages of Hedge Funds

Hedge funds offer certain investment and risk-mitigation advantages. But those advantages can be offset by disadvantages relating to fees, illiquidity, lack of transparency, and other matters.

Institutions, high net worth individuals, and others invest in hedge funds for seven primary reasons:

1. *Alpha, or above-market, returns.* Investors in hedge funds believe that their managers can generate returns with positive *alpha,* meaning returns that are higher than the market return. Alpha reflects the value added by a hedge fund manager's skill.
2. *Absolute returns.* Hedge funds are intended to provide absolute returns—positive returns in any market environment over any reasonable measurement period. By contrast, most mutual funds are intended to provide relative returns, that is, returns that are measured by reference to a benchmark. For example, if the market goes down, most mutual funds are supposed to go down less than the market, but most hedge funds are supposed to go up. Hence the saying in the hedge fund world: "You can't eat relative returns."
3. *Lower volatility.* Hedge funds are intended to provide lower volatility, or variations in returns, than mutual funds. Hedge funds try to do

this by taking offsetting positions in similar investments with different prospects. For example, if a hedge fund purchased shares of Exxon Mobil stock, it can limit its losses by also selling Royal Dutch Shell stock short. "Selling Short Yourself" describes the strategy in more detail.

SELLING SHORT YOURSELF

What exactly is *short selling?* It's a way of making a profit when the price of a stock declines—by selling stock that you don't own. To do this, you borrow shares of stock from another investor—with the help of a broker-dealer who arranges this *securities lending*—and then sell the borrowed shares.[11] To close the *short position,* you buy shares in the market, then give them to the broker-dealer to repay the loan. If the price at which you sell the stock is higher than the price at which you buy it back, you will make money on the short sale.

Why would anyone lend stock to help another investor who wants its price to decline? Because you can make a profit doing it. *The shorts*—as short sellers are fondly (or not-so-fondly) called—must pay interest on the stock loan. And, in most circumstances, the risk of lending is limited. That's because short sellers must set aside other high quality securities as collateral to guarantee that they will eventually return the stock; if they fail to do so, the lender gets to keep the collateral. (Securities lending did generate losses during the credit crisis of 2008. We discuss these problems in Chapter 14.)

Short selling is controversial. The shorts have often been blamed for large declines in the market, such as in 1929 and 2008, and for attacking companies in the media to see their stock prices decline. On the other hand, some of these attacks were well founded. Short sellers have been credited with exposing fraud and other irregularities, as they did in the cases of Enron and Lehman Brothers.

4. *Low correlation.* The returns of hedge funds are designed to be relatively uncorrelated with the returns of traditional asset classes because their portfolios are structured so that they are affected by different market events than are the returns of stocks and bonds—or affected to a different degree by the same market events. Accordingly, hedge funds have the potential to diversify an investment portfolio and thus reduce its risk.

5. *Unique strategies and assets.* Unlike mutual funds, hedge funds are exempt from regulatory restrictions on investments and, therefore, can invest in any asset—at least in theory. In practice, hedge funds are limited to the strategy stated in their private placement memoranda, which is the hedge fund analogue of a mutual fund prospectus.

Given this freedom, hedge funds don't just invest in traditional asset classes like publicly traded stocks or Treasury securities; they often invest in quite illiquid assets like real estate, shares of private companies, and securities of companies in bankruptcy. (Remember that the liquidity of an asset refers to how difficult or easy it is to sell the asset.) These assets can offer some of the most interesting investment opportunities. Because the market for illiquid assets is frequently inefficient, they can often be purchased at a discount to their true value. Moreover, hedge fund managers can take actions that increase the value of illiquid assets, such as hiring a new management company to oversee a real estate investment. ("Looking at the Alternatives" explains the terminology used for these investments.)

LOOKING AT THE ALTERNATIVES

Assets other than publicly traded stocks and bonds are often referred to as *alternative investments*. There's no official definition of this term, but it's loosely used to refer to investments in commodities, real estate, derivatives, and private equity, which are investments in non-public companies, and venture capital, which are investments in firms that are just starting up.

The term is loosely applied to funds or managers that invest in these assets as well. So, hedge funds and hedge fund managers are often called *alternative investments* and *alternative investment managers*, respectively.

6. *Star management talent.* The high compensation at hedge funds and relatively unfettered investment discretion allowed hedge fund managers is thought to attract high-caliber investment management talent.
7. *Manager co-investment.* Hedge fund managers often invest substantial personal assets in their own funds. Such hedge fund manager investments are believed to align the incentives of managers and fund investors.

Critics express five main concerns with the hedge fund business model:

1. *Advantages reconsidered.* Perhaps most importantly, detractors question whether hedge funds have actually delivered on the promises they have made to investors, a critique that has only gained visibility after the credit crisis. During that turmoil, many hedge funds failed to deliver alpha, with some hedge funds declining further and faster than the market. Similarly, many hedge funds actually fell in value and thus did not provide positive absolute return. As a group, hedge funds were quite volatile and had negative, correlated returns.

   To compound the case against hedge funds, mutual funds are starting to incorporate some of the investment advantages previously only available in hedge funds, such as absolute return strategies and volatility management techniques. And it's not clear that hedge fund managers—many of whom started their careers in mutual fund management—have any greater skill than their counterparts running more traditional funds.

2. *High fees.* Hedge funds are often criticized for their high fee structure. They generally pay their managers two types of fees: a management fee and a performance allocation, also known as the *carry,* or *carried interest.* The management fee is calculated as a percentage of assets under management, while the performance allocation is calculated as a percentage of realized capital gains. Traditionally, the management fee has been 2 percent, and the carried interest has been 20 percent, a fee structure referred to in the industry as "2 and 20," although the management fees of sought-after hedge funds have often been higher. Contrast that to an average management fee of less than 1 percent for a stock mutual fund—which may not charge a performance fee unless it prevents a penalty for losses as well as a reward for gains. (Chapter 15 has more on mutual fund performance fees.)

   The management fee is taxed as ordinary income, and historically, carried interest was taxed as long term capital gains. However, Congress is seriously considering legislation to increase the tax rate applicable to carried interest. Although hedge fund managers will not earn less than the base fee—even when performance is poor—the performance allocation is generally subject to a *high water mark.* This means that a hedge fund manager will not earn a performance fee unless the value of the hedge fund at the end of a given year is higher than its value at the end of any previous year. "Getting Out from Under Water" has an example of a hedge fund fee calculation.

GETTING OUT FROM UNDER HIGH WATER

Let's look at how a high water mark provision works in practice. Let's assume that the Avon Hill Fund has a 2 and 20 fee structure and $1.0 billion in assets under management at the start of Year 1. As shown in Table 12.3, if returns were positive during that first year and the value of the fund rose to $1.1 billion, the fund would pay its manager management fees of $22 million—equal to 2 percent of the $1.1 billion fund value—and a performance allocation of $20 million—equal to 20 percent of the gain in fund value from $1.0 billion to $1.1 billion. (We're assuming in this example that all gains were realized through the sale of the fund's portfolio holdings.) The $1.1 billion account value now becomes the high water mark.

Let's now assume that returns were negative in Year 2, causing the fund value to drop to $0.9 billion. The fund would still pay a 2 percent management fee of $18 million, but it would not pay a performance allocation since the fund value fell below the high water mark of $1.1 billion. Even if the fund then regained some ground in Year 3, it would still be under its high water mark and therefore would again not pay a performance allocation. It would take another gain in Year 4 before the fund would exceed its high water mark. If the fund value were $1.2 billion at the end of that year, the fund would pay a performance allocation of $20 million, which is 20 percent of the difference between the new fund value and the high water mark of $1.1 billion. The value of $1.2 billion now becomes the new high water mark. Table 12.5 has a summary.

TABLE 12.5 Avon Hill Hedge Fund Fee Calculation

	Fund Value ($ billions)	Management Fee	Performance Allocation
Start of Year 1	$1.0		
End of Year 1	$1.1	$22 million	$20 million
End of Year 2	$0.9	$18 million	$0
End of Year 3	$1.0	$20 million	$0
End of Year 4	$1.2	$24 million	$20 million

3. *Lack of liquidity.* Hedge fund investors are not able to redeem their investments on a daily basis as are mutual fund investors. Most hedge funds offer investors the right to redeem only quarterly, semiannually, or even annually, and some newer hedge funds have longer *lock-ups,* often for a period of two years. Hedge funds that invest in illiquid investments often have special provisions such as *gates, side pockets,* or *redemption suspension* rights that keep investors in the fund for long periods; that's to avoid having to sell those assets at fire sale prices to raise cash to pay redeeming investors. (See "Hedging Vocabulary" at the end of this section for a glossary of hedge fund terminology.)

4. *Transparency.* Investors frequently complain that hedge fund managers don't give them enough data—neither often enough nor in enough detail—to enable them to monitor their investments effectively. In other words, hedge funds are not transparent, allowing investors a clear view of their inner workings. As we saw in Chapter 3, disclosure in the mutual fund world is determined by government regulation—which requires that funds regularly publish lists of holdings and reviews about performance. For hedge funds, in contrast, the release of information is governed by their contract with investors.

   Those contracts may favor larger investors. Unlike the mutual fund world, where large investors may get slightly reduced sales loads or qualify for a lower-cost class of shares but otherwise get the same deal as smaller investors, in the hedge fund world, different investors in the same fund may have dramatically different rights. Large investors may negotiate for daily reports on fund positions and may receive special redemption rights and may be charged lower fees. Hedge fund managers effectuate these special deals with large investors through two methods: *side letters* and *managed accounts.* (See "Hedging Vocabulary" for definitions.)

5. *Overstatement of performance results.* Academic studies have found that average hedge fund returns as reported in the media are overstated—by more than 2 percent per year—creating an unduly rosy picture of their investment prowess.[12] That's because the central databases suffer from considerable *backfill bias* and *survivorship bias.* Backfill bias results when managers report only favorable past returns. For example, a hedge fund may open up in Year 0 but not start reporting results to the databases until the end of Year 2—and then only if the numbers for the two years of its existence look good. As backfill bias relates to the startup of a hedge fund, survivorship bias occurs when it shuts down—most often because its performance has been poor. Once the fund closes, its entire track record is deleted from the database, adding another upward bias to the average numbers. Since starting up and shutting down a hedge fund is relatively easy to do, the average life

span of a hedge fund is quite short—only three to four years—so there is ample opportunity for both types of bias to come into play.

In contrast, opening and closing a mutual fund is much more difficult and costly, which means that backfill and survivorship bias play much less of a role—though they don't disappear altogether. Fund management companies sometimes close poorly performing funds—usually by merging them into another fund—to eliminate their track record. Much less frequently, a sponsor may sell a mutual fund to a relatively small number of investors in a public offering and later start selling it to the world at large only if it amasses a positive performance record. But the overall effect of the two types of bias is much lower than in the hedge fund world.[13]

Hedge Fund Strategies

Given the flexibility of the hedge fund format, hedge funds can pursue a wide variety of investment strategies. Some of the more common hedge fund investment strategies include:

- *Equity long-short.* Equity long-short was the strategy used by A.W. Jones & Co., the first hedge fund, and remains the most popular hedge fund strategy today; approximately 30 percent of all hedge fund assets globally are allocated to this strategy or a variation of it. Long-short involves buying stocks long and selling stocks short at the same time. Hedge funds usually buy stocks they consider undervalued and short stocks they consider overvalued. (Chapter 5 gives a brief description of the long-short strategy.)
- *Relative value or arbitrage.* Relative value is a long-short strategy involving specific types of securities or assets other than stocks. One of the oldest hedge fund strategies is merger arbitrage; hedge funds using this strategy buy shares of a company that is in the process of being acquired and short the shares of the acquirer. Relative value managers will look at past relationships among different securities issued by the same company and look to profit when they vary from historical norms. One variant on this strategy is convertible arbitrage, which involves buying a convertible security and selling short the underlying stock. Intercredit strategies look at relative value relationships between different types of fixed income securities, such as corporate bonds versus government bonds.
- *Distressed.* A distressed strategy involves purchasing the securities or other assets of a company in or near bankruptcy.
- *Shareholder activism.* Activist hedge funds seek major changes in the way a company is managed. (Chapter 9 discusses shareholder activism.)

- *Global macro.* This strategy involves taking a view on macroeconomic events such as changes in interest rates, the relative value of currencies, or the global supply and demand for natural resources. Probably the most famous global macro trade was George Soros's short sale of the British pound in 1992, which earned Soros the sobriquet "The man who broke the Bank of England."
- *Managed futures.* Also known as commodity trading advisers, managed futures hedge funds invest in futures contracts on various types of commodities—including energy, metals, and grains—and on the financial markets.
- *Multistrategy.* As the name implies, these hedge funds invest across all the foregoing strategies and others besides. Multistrategy funds have fallen out of favor for two related reasons. First, investors do not want to wind up overweighted in a particular strategy, as they can if a multistrategy fund drifts toward the strategy of another hedge fund in the investor's portfolio. Second, investors want managers to stick to core investment competencies and to strategies with which they have proven track records.
- *Leverage.* Leverage is a critical underlying strategy of many hedge funds, used together with any of the previously listed strategies. As we discussed when we reviewed leveraged exchange-traded funds, leverage allows funds to increase the impact of their investment decisions. Funds can increase leverage in one of two ways: they can either use derivatives that have a potential for a large payoff on a small investment, or they can borrow money, hoping to earn the spread on the return on their investments and the cost of the loan. Leverage allows hedge funds to earn spectacular returns on the upside when they make good investment decisions—and to fail equally spectacularly when they don't.

In theory, the hedge fund strategies we've just described are not limited to hedge funds. An individual investor is free to pursue a global macro strategy, for example, and an equity long-short approach would fit well with the investment goals of many mutual funds. But for practical and regulatory reasons, these strategies have been much more heavily used by hedge funds than other types of investors. Individual investors may not be able to own many illiquid assets; purchases of these investments are often restricted to institutional buyers. And the 1940 Act places limits on short selling and leverage by mutual funds. Remember from Chapter 2 that a mutual fund's borrowings can't exceed one-third of the value of its assets; short sales, which involve borrowing stock, are included in this limit. In contrast, borrowings at hedge funds often equal 80 percent of assets.

Despite the difficulties, a few mutual funds have begun to use these strategies to the maximum extent permissible. They are said to use *hedge strategies* or *alternative strategies* to achieve the same ends as hedge funds themselves—higher returns and lower volatility.

Hedge Fund Investors

There are three main types of investors in hedge funds:

1. *Institutional investors*. Institutional investors, particularly traditional pension funds, account for a significant and growing proportion of assets under management of hedge funds globally.
2. *Individual investors*. Individuals have been another noteworthy category of hedge fund investors; they are particularly important for start-up managers who are often staked by friends and family. As we'll discuss shortly, investors in hedge funds are usually quite well off; most funds require that they have at least $5 million in investments.
3. *Fund of funds*. But the largest investors in hedge funds are other hedge funds; these are the hedge "fund of funds" that allocate assets to multiple hedge fund managers. Institutional investors (such as pension funds, endowments, and foundations) invest in funds of funds for their presumably superior expertise in selecting underlying hedge fund managers. Fund of funds managers stress their careful due diligence, or research, into potential hedge fund investments and their ongoing monitoring of positions.

    The fund of funds model has come under serious criticism, however, for providing returns that only equal or even underperform their benchmark indexes, while adding another layer of fees—often a 1 percent base fee plus a 10 percent performance fee—on top of the fees charged by underlying managers.[14] Also, a number of hedge fund of funds were heavily invested in the Madoff Ponzi scheme, calling into question the value of their due diligence process.

Hedge Fund Regulation

As we talked about in the introduction to this section, hedge funds in the United States are exempt from many of the laws and regulations that govern mutual funds. Let's look closely at how this works in practice.

At the fund level, hedge funds are structured so that they do not fall within the definition of *investment company* under the 1940 Act, and therefore do not have to register with the SEC. No registration equals no limits on leverage, short sales, or illiquid investments, no rules on the types of fees that can be charged, no required disclosure, and no need for an independent board of directors.

Hedge funds avoid registration in two ways. First, many incorporate in low-tax countries outside the United States, like the Cayman Islands; these offshore hedge funds fall outside the jurisdiction of the 1940 Act. Hedge funds also avoid making a public offering to U.S. investors, because investments that are publicly offered in the United States, such as mutual funds, must be registered with the SEC—even if offered by an offshore fund.

Instead, hedge funds make sure that their marketing activities fall under the definition of *private offering*. They do not market themselves or their funds through conventional retail channels such as television, newspapers, magazines, radio, or Internet. They also limit the type and number of investors in the fund. They may accept a maximum of only 100 accredited investors who are individuals who have a net worth of at least $1 million after excluding the value of their primary resident or who had an income of at least $200,000 in each of the past two years. (The 2010 Dodd-Frank financial reform legislation requires that this amount be adjusted for inflation at least every five years.) Alternatively, hedge funds can accept up to 499 investors if they require all those investors to have at least $5 million in investments. Most hedge funds rely on this latter provision and often ensure compliance with it by requiring a $5 million minimum investment.[15]

In sum, hedge funds are exempt from many of the more onerous laws and regulations governing registered investment funds. As a price for those exemptions, hedge funds are limited in the people and entities from whom they may accept investments, and hedge fund managers are limited in their ability to market their wares. However, the price may not be so high in practice, because the structure and strategies of hedge funds do not lend themselves to retail investing in the first place. In particular, the illiquidity of many hedge funds does not fit the cash flow needs of many retail investors. For example, most people wouldn't want their child's college money to get stuck behind a hedge fund gate.

There are three chief arguments in favor of these exemptions from regulation, namely:

1. *Knowledgeable investors.* Defenders of light regulation for hedge funds note that only investors with considerable assets can own hedge funds, and these investors can fend for themselves without regulatory protection. Proponents of more regulation counter that size and financial wherewithal do not necessarily translate into sophistication, as recently highlighted in the SEC's lawsuit against Goldman Sachs for its structuring and marketing of credit derivatives to European banks.
2. *Little systemic risk.* Hedge fund advocates suggest that, because of their comparatively low level of assets under management and the diverse strategies used, hedge funds do not pose a systemic risk to the financial

system. In other words, problems at a single hedge fund or even at many hedge funds, would not do significant damage to the U.S. financial system. But critics point out that while hedge funds are small relative to mutual funds or banks, hedge funds' ability to use leverage and derivatives can dramatically enhance their collective exposure. Small size didn't prevent a hedge fund called Long-Term Capital Management from causing widespread panic in the financial system in 1998.[16]

3. *Self-regulation.* Self-regulation by knowledgeable hedge fund investors, creditors, and counterparties serves as a workable proxy for government-imposed regulation. (Creditors lend money to hedge funds, while counterparties engage in other transactions with hedge funds—such as securities lending and derivatives trades—which involve credit risk.) But it's not clear that these parties can be relied upon to regulate others when they themselves pose significant risk to the financial system. Most notably, before its demise, Lehman Brothers was a significant hedge fund creditor and counterparty, but employed significantly more leverage than any of its hedge fund counterparties or borrowers.

In the wake of the credit crisis, the advocates of tighter regulation have gathered strength, and new legislation in both the United States and Europe have led to increased supervision of hedge fund managers. In the European Union, where hedge funds and hedge fund managers are already subject to regulatory oversight in several countries, the Alternative Investment Fund Managers directive will require that all EU countries impose a stricter regulatory regime on hedge fund managers. Furthermore, hedge fund managers from countries outside the European Union will not be allowed to raise funds in the EU unless those non-EU countries meet certain standards in regulating hedge fund managers.

In the United States, within one year of the mid-2010 enactment of the Dodd-Frank financial reform legislation, U.S. hedge managers will be required to register with the SEC as investment advisers, as long as they have at least $150 million in assets under management; previously, they were exempt from this registration requirement.[17] As a result, hedge fund managers must appoint a chief compliance officer, must have and enforce a code of ethics, must maintain and file specified reports, and must distribute a brochure to the clients every year with information about their firm. Moreover, hedge fund managers registered as investment advisers will be subject to periodic inspections by SEC staff. However, these managers will still be allowed to charge wealthy investors performance fees based on realized gains (not offset by losses) and to adopt any investment strategy with any amount of leverage they please. Moreover, despite the new oversight of hedge fund managers, hedge funds themselves will remain largely unregulated.

HEDGING VOCABULARY

Like any industry, the hedge fund industry has many unique terms and concepts. Here are the definitions of the terms we used in this section:

Gate. A hedge fund provision that prevents a large percentage of investors from redeeming at once. Specifically, if more than a certain percentage of investors—usually 10 to 30 percent—want to redeem at the same time, the manager only has to satisfy redemptions representing that 10 to 30 percent of assets and can carry the remainder forward to the next scheduled redemption date. Managers include gates to prevent fire sales of assets and to ensure that remaining investors don't end up with a very illiquid portfolio after a manager sells the more liquid assets to raise cash to pay redemptions.

Lock-up. The period an investor can't redeem from a hedge fund. For example, in a two-year lock-up, an investor must remain in the fund for two years from the date of investment. Following that lock-up, the investor may have the right to redeem annually, semiannually, or monthly.

Managed account. A mini–hedge fund for one investor. This structure provides complete transparency on holdings and activity, but only for that one investor.

Redemption suspension. The right of a hedge fund manager, often included in hedge fund governing documents, to refuse to satisfy redemption requests from investors in specified circumstances. These circumstances may include a determination by the manager that selling assets to raise the cash required to pay redemptions would adversely affect the value of the fund.

Side letter. A special agreement with a large investor in a hedge fund. For example, a side letter may grant a certain investor preferential redemption rights or additional access to portfolio data.

Side pocket. A separate account within a hedge fund that is set up by the manager to hold illiquid assets. After a hedge fund manager transfers an asset from a hedge fund to a side pocket, investors redeeming from that hedge fund do not get the value of their pro rata interest in the side-pocketed asset. Rather, they only get their interest when the asset is sold, which can be years after they redeem from the hedge fund.

CHAPTER SUMMARY

Exchanged-traded funds, or ETFs, and hedge funds are fast-growing competitors to traditional mutual funds.

ETFs are similar to mutual funds, but have shares that trade on a stock exchange. They allow investors to buy shares throughout the day with no minimum investment, though buyers must pay a brokerage commission to execute the transaction. Most ETFs are organized as mutual funds or unit investment trusts. However, other ETFs take advantage of structures that enable them to invest in commodities, real estate, or currency—investments that are difficult for traditional mutual funds to invest in extensively.

While traditional mutual funds issue shares directly to investors, ETFs create or redeem shares through an authorized participant that has signed an agreement with the ETF. To create shares, the authorized participant buys a basket of securities that matches the portfolio held by the ETF, and then exchanges that basket for ETF shares. This unique creation and redemption process helps ETFs minimize capital gains. Arbitrageurs—who are usually Authorized Participants—use the creation and redemption process to keep the ETF's share price in line with its NAV. While this system has generally worked well, significant differences between share price and NAV have at times occurred.

Most ETFs are index funds that use a passive investment strategy. However, some index ETFs use leverage and have a very aggressive approach as a result; these ETFs have been quite controversial. A few actively managed ETFs have been launched recently, despite concerns that they are vulnerable to front running because they have to disclose their portfolio holdings at least daily.

Hedge funds are unregulated pooled investment vehicles. Investors choose to put their money in hedge funds because they believe they will provide high returns in any market environment and that those returns will have a low correlation with the returns of traditional investments. Hedge funds have the freedom to invest in a wide range of assets. Hedge fund managers frequently place a large percentage of their own assets in the fund alongside investors.

Critics of hedge funds point out that these vehicles have often failed to deliver their expected returns and that their average returns are overstated. Hedge funds also charge high fees. They frequently place restrictions on investor redemptions, and they provide little information about their activities, at least to smaller investors.

Hedge funds use a variety of investment strategies. Many of these strategies involve short selling—to profit from a decline in the value of an investment—and leverage, which increases the impact of decisions. The largest investors in hedge funds are funds of funds, which allocate assets to multiple hedge fund managers.

To avoid regulation in the United States, hedge funds must limit the number of investors, and those investors must meet certain minimum standards for net worth. Regulation of hedge fund managers is increasing in both Europe and the United States. Recent U.S. legislation requires that the managers of hedge funds register with the SEC as investment advisers, although the funds themselves do not have to be registered.

Four

Operations and Finance

We go in this section behind the scenes at a mutual fund complex. We look beyond the front office investment and sales functions to see how the back office provides critical support for fund investors. A fund's transfer agent keeps records of shareholder accounts and provides customer service, not an easy task given the volume of records and transactions and the complexity of the fund itself. The fund accounting, custody, investment operations, and audit teams maintain fund records. Each plays a critical role in calculating a fund's NAV at the end of every business day, an intricate procedure that requires tight coordination among the many parties involved. The valuation of portfolio holdings is a critical component of this process.

We end this section with a review of the financial dynamics of the fund management industry. Funds charge a variety of fees, and each has a differing impact on management company profitability. The overall level of that profitability—and whether there is sufficient competition within the fund industry to restrain it—is the subject of considerable controversy. Many diversified financial firms outside the fund industry have entered the business—usually by buying a fund management company—to try to capture some of those profits. However, the three largest mutual fund managers have concentrated on investment management and have grown organically rather than through acquisition.

This section has three chapters:

Chapter 13 reviews how mutual funds provide shareholder service. It discusses the responsibilities of the transfer agent and reviews the sophisticated technology that supports the service function. The final section discusses the organization of shareholder service operations and the structuring of transfer agency fees by independent directors.

Chapter 14 reviews fund recordkeeping and portfolio valuation. It begins by describing the daily process for NAV calculation, which is coordinated by the fund accountant. Its next section explains the complexities involved in valuing a fund's portfolio of investments. The chapter ends by discussing the roles of the custodian, the investment operations team, and the independent auditors.

Chapter 15 reviews the financial dynamics of the mutual fund industry and the management companies within it. It summarizes the expenses incurred by mutual fund shareholders and discusses how they relate to management company profitability. It describes the controversy over management fees and the level of competition within the industry. The chapter concludes with a review of mergers and acquisitions in the industry over the past decade.

CHAPTER 13

Customer Service

Mutual funds pride themselves on the high quality of their customer service. Given the complexity of the funds themselves, the diversity of their customer base, the multiplicity of distribution channels and the high level of regulation—not to mention the sheer volume of transactions—providing top-notch service is no mean feat. It's done by a specialized service provider—called the *transfer agent*.[1] In 2009, transfer agents kept records for more than 270 million distinct mutual fund accounts, employing in the process some 55,000 people—representing more than one-third of the jobs in the fund industry as a whole.[2]

This chapter reviews:

- The many responsibilities of the transfer agent
- The technology that supports mutual fund shareholder service
- The economics of the transfer agent function

THE ROLE OF THE TRANSFER AGENT

Transfer agents are generally responsible for maintaining records of shareholder accounts and providing customer service. Specifically, they:

- Process transactions
- Provide reports to shareholders on their fund holdings
- Respond to customer inquiries
- Help funds comply with the numerous regulations that govern their operations

We take a look at each function in turn.

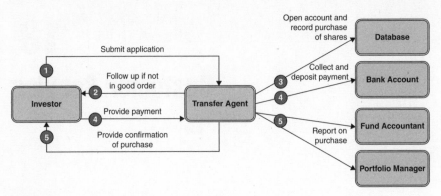

FIGURE 13.1 The Mutual Fund Share Purchase Process

Processing Fund Transactions

Transfer agents process four basic types of transactions: purchases, redemptions, exchanges, and distributions. To get a sense of a transfer agent's daily operations, let's walk through the steps involved in processing a new investment in fund shares. They're diagrammed in Figure 13.1. We'll pick up the transaction as soon as a prospective customer has decided to make the purchase.

Step 1: Application. As a first step, the customer completes a company's application for opening a new account and returns it to the transfer agent. While some investors now open accounts entirely through the Internet, most still complete a paper form and mail it or fax it back.[3] They may be asked to do this to confirm instructions initially given in a phone call. We've posted an example of an account application on this book's web site. Customers buying fund shares in a brokerage or retirement account can usually skip this step, since they've already supplied their vital statistics as a part of opening that account.

Step 2: Transfer Agent Review. The transfer agent then reviews the application to make sure that it is in good order, meaning that all the required information has been included. Under the provisions of the USA Patriot Act, the transfer agent must verify customer identity by collecting name, date of birth, and a physical address—which can't be a post office box. It must obtain a taxpayer identification number for reporting to the IRS. (For U.S. citizens, this is their Social Security number.) The transfer agent will also make sure that the proposed purchase complies with all the relevant fund rules. For example, it will confirm that the amount being purchased is at least the minimum account size specified in the prospectus.

Step 3: Open Account and Record Purchase of Shares. If the application is, in fact, in good order, the transfer agent will open an account in the name specified; this could be for an individual—either solo or as a joint account—or for a corporation, partnership, or trust. If, on the other hand, there are problems with the application, the transfer agent will delay opening the account until all issues can be resolved with the customer. After the account is set up, the purchase of a specific number of fund shares is recorded in it.

Step 4: Collect Payment. The transfer agent is responsible for collecting payment for share purchases and arranging for its deposit into the fund's bank account. Today, most payments are made by check, by electronic transfer from a brokerage or retirement account or as the result of an exchange from another fund in the same complex. (More on exchanges in a moment.) Funds do not accept cash.

A brief word on the timing of all this: purchases of fund shares are entered throughout the day, but the price paid is not determined until the end of the business day, when the fund NAV is calculated. The electronic transfers of funds occur during the night, so that the money is in the fund's bank account ready to invest first thing the next morning. The collection of checks takes somewhat longer, though advances in check processing in recent years have expedited the clearance process substantially. And what if a check bounces? The purchaser remains legally obligated to buy shares at the original purchase price.

Step 5: Reporting. After the purchase has been processed, the transfer agent sends a confirmation to the buyer with all the details. Also, both the fund accountant and the portfolio manager are informed that money has come in. (We provide a detailed description of the role of the fund accountant in the next chapter.)

When a shareholder decides to reduce his position in a fund, the processing of the *redemption* of fund shares follows steps 3, 4, and 5, with the obvious difference that money flows out of the fund rather than into it. Proceeds are credited to the shareholder's brokerage or retirement account if he's invested through one. Individuals who own shares directly with the fund can receive their money through their choice of check, electronic funds transfer, or wire transfer, though the last method may entail an additional fee.

Process the application, open an account, register the purchase of shares, collect the payment, inform everyone: described this way, shareholder recordkeeping in mutual funds sounds like a snap.

On the contrary, making sure that transaction processing is handled accurately at lightning speed is an amazingly intricate business. Part of the complexity arises from the sheer number of accounts and transactions. A simple change in the telephone area code or zip code for a neighborhood can involve updating thousands of records.

Take the case of a correction in a fund's NAV. On rare occasions, a fund's NAV per share can be miscalculated, because a securities trade or price has been entered incorrectly. If the error is more than 1¢ per share, the transfer agent may need to reprocess some purchases and redemptions that occurred while the NAV was misstated. For a popular fund, that might mean account adjustments that require reissuing confirmations to thousands of shareholders. The transfer agent itself can make mistakes that involve a complex correction process, as we discuss in "As-Of Trades."

AS-OF TRADES

When processing so many transactions, mistakes are bound to happen, and transfer agents have developed detailed procedures for handling them. The industry has developed a term for the corrections, calling them *as-of trades* because they are entered using the fund price *as of* a previous date.

Take the hypothetical case of two buy orders that Jane faxes in on April 1. The transfer agent processes the first one correctly, but completely misses the second. Jane phones in again a week later to find out why she has received a confirmation for one of her purchases, but not the other. This triggers a research process at the transfer agent to find out exactly what should have happened. After reviewing the facts, the transfer agent will enter Jane's purchase as of April 1st using the NAV on that day.

As-of transactions have a financial impact on the fund, because the as-of NAV is usually different from the NAV on the date that the correction is made. In this case, Jane submitted the order for 1,000 shares when NAV was $10.00, but her purchase was recorded when NAV is $10.02. When she sent in the order, the total cost of a purchase of 1,000 shares was $10,000 (using the $10.00 NAV), and that's the price that Jane still pays after the correction is made. But that same purchase at the time of the correction would cost $10,020 (equal to 1,000 shares times the current $10.02 NAV). Who compensates the fund for the $20 difference? Most transfer agents track the cumulative effect of as-of transactions and reimburse the fund when the total NAV impact of the mistakes is greater than 1¢ per share.

Yet while volume is a factor, the real challenge comes from the many features that funds have added in recent years—and the detailed rules governing them. Exchange privileges are a perfect case in point. Fund sponsors allow shareholders to redeem shares in one fund and use the proceeds to buy shares in another one in the same fund family, in a transaction called an *exchange*. The benefit: shareholders who paid a sales load to invest in a fund generally do not have to pay a second sales load when they make an exchange. In all other respects, however, an exchange is an unrelated redemption and purchase. In the eyes of the IRS, for example, an exchange is a taxable event.

But exchanges entail additional work. To correctly process an exchange, the transfer agent must be able to:

- Recognize that the proposed transaction is an exchange, rather than a redemption with a subsequent purchase. This might entail redesigning forms or creating special computer programming to flag these orders.
- Determine whether the proposed transaction qualifies for a waiver of the sales charge. If a shareholder is exchanging from a money market fund—which has no front-end load—to an equity fund with a load, the shareholder will be required to pay the load upon purchase of the equity fund—that is, unless the investor had initially bought an equity fund, paying a load in the process, and then exchanged into the money market fund. In that case, the waiver still applies.
- Keep track of the total time that the shareholder has been invested in the fund family. Holding periods for all funds—except money market funds—are added together for certain purposes, such as computing the contingent deferred sales charge if the shareholder redeems altogether.

In other words, to handle one seemingly simple feature, the transfer agent must design a system to track a shareholder's entire history with the fund family.

But exchange transactions are not unique in the challenges they pose. Many fund features involve similar complexity. For example:

- *Breakpoints.* As we've seen, most funds allow shareholders to reduce the sales loads they pay by taking advantage of volume, or *breakpoint,* discounts. Some investors qualify by making a series of purchases over time; they can either claim the reduced sales charge up front, by signing a letter of intent, or retroactively, under a feature called *rights of accumulation*. It's the transfer agent who has the responsibility of monitoring actual purchase activity to make sure that shareholders are treated fairly. (Refer back to Chapter 10 for more detail on sales charges.)
- *Short-term trading.* What if the fund imposes a limit on short-term trading—meaning that it prohibits multiple purchases and sales of fund shares within a specified time period? The transfer agent is the one who enforces it, by blocking purchases from investors who are moving

money in and out of the fund more frequently than is permitted by its
board of directors.
- *Systematic withdrawal plans.* If shareholders are enrolled in a systematic
  withdrawal plan that allows them to receive a steady flow of income,
  the transfer agent must sell a portion of their fund shares at regular
  intervals. It must also keep track of whether the shareholder would
  prefer to receive a specified dollar amount, to sell a specific number of
  shares, to redeem a fixed percentage of their account value, or to base
  their withdrawals on their life expectancy.

One final fund transaction managed by the transfer agent: the processing
of distributions of income earned and capital gains realized by the fund. (As
discussed in Chapter 2, funds must pay out almost all of this income at
least annually.) Again, the transfer agent must ensure that the cash from
the distribution is properly credited to shareholder accounts. If an investor
elects to reinvest distributions in fund shares—as most do—the transfer agent
must calculate and record the number of additional shares purchased. For
fixed income funds that accrue dividends daily, the transfer agent must also
calculate and pay out the accrued amount when a shareholder completely
redeems a position.

While most fund distributions are routine, funds must occasionally make
a special distribution as the result of a settlement of a lawsuit or a regulatory
inquiry. These settlements are often designed to compensate investors who
held shares between specific dates or who meet other detailed tests. Determining who exactly is entitled to receive a payment and in what amount
requires careful sifting through ownership records.

Account Information and Fund Reports

The transfer agent must provide fund shareholders with information about
their accounts on a regular schedule.

Daily. We've already mentioned that funds provide immediate confirmations of purchase and redemption transactions.[4] Most fund complexes
send out confirmations of changes to nonfinancial information, including
address, account ownership, and certain account features, such as systematic withdrawal plans. First-time buyers must also be given a copy of the
fund's prospectus or summary prospectus.

Quarterly. Shareholders normally receive quarterly account statements
detailing their positions in the fund. Most fund sponsors have made account
statements user-friendly by consolidating all of a shareholder's holdings
of funds within a complex into a single statement. (Funds generally don't
provide statements for positions held in a brokerage account or retirement

plan. Information on those holdings usually comes from the brokerage or retirement plan sponsor directly.)

Semi-Annually. As we learned in Chapter 3, funds must provide shareholders with reports on performance and positioning at least twice a year. Transfer agents oversee the dissemination of these reports to the funds' investors.

Annually. To help shareholders with tax planning, transfer agents supply estimates of fund distributions toward the end of each calendar year. Early in the next year, they send out Form 1099-DIV, which provides the exact amounts that investors will need to include in their tax returns. This form breaks down fund distributions into taxable ordinary income, tax-exempt income, long-term capital gains, short-term capital gains, and return of capital, and it's sent to the IRS as well as the shareholder. Beginning in 2012, funds will have to provide additional information on any capital gains and losses generated by the redemption of fund shares. (See the "Q&A on Cost-Basis Reporting" for more information.) About every year, the transfer agent usually sends each fund shareholder an updated prospectus.

Q&A ON COST BASIS REPORTING

In 2008, Congress made significant changes in the tax information that mutual funds and brokerage firms must supply to investors and to the IRS.

Q: What are the requirements of the new law?

A: Funds and brokerage firms must provide, on Form 1099B, the gain or loss that results when an investor sells a position. That's a big change. Up until now, many investors had to calculate gains or losses themselves. Starting in 2012, transfer agents will do the calculation for them, using a methodology that the shareholder can select.[5]

Note that this rule applies only to redemptions of mutual fund shares by the fund investor. It does not apply to the sale of securities within the fund. Funds are already required to distribute the net capital gains from these sales and report on them to shareholders.

Q: Why did Congress pass this law?

A: For the same reason it passes most technical tax legislation: to close loopholes and increase tax revenue. The U.S. General Accountability office estimated that underreporting of capital gains by taxpayers costs the U.S. Treasury $11 billion in lost tax revenue every year. That's the figure for all types of securities: stock, bonds, mutual funds, and so forth. Ironically, mutual fund investors often pay too much in taxes when they sell their holdings. That's because fund holders who reinvest their distributions in fund shares sometimes forget to deduct the distribution amounts from the sale proceeds when computing their gain. (They've already paid taxes on these amounts.) As a result, they pay taxes on their distributions twice: once when the distributions are made and then again when they sell their fund shares.

Q: *How are fund firms preparing for the change?*

A: Once again, transfer agents are preparing for complexity. Many funds already provide some cost basis information to shareholders on a voluntary basis, but these calculations don't include all the soon-to-be-required information, such as cost basis information on shares transferred between two different brokerage accounts. And they don't reflect some of the trickier tax rules, such as the wash sale rules, that prevent investors from taking a tax loss on shares they've sold, but bought back within 30 days of the sale. To comply with these new requirements, transfer agents are programming their computer systems to capture all the data needed, and they're training their customer service representatives to field the shareholder questions that will start to come in once the law takes effect.

Periodically. When the fund holds a shareholder vote, the transfer agent will coordinate the mailing of a proxy statement. See Chapter 3 for more on the proxy statement.

To save both money and the environment, most fund complexes now offer fund shareholders the option of receiving all of these reports online. They'll also mail only one hard copy of documents to all the shareholders at the same address, though investors can opt out of *householding,* as it's known, if they prefer to receive separate mailings.

Customer Inquiries and Problem Resolution

Probably the most challenging service function is responding to inquiries from customers—broadly defined to include both the investors in fund shares as well the financial intermediaries advising them. To respond to questions and problems, fund complexes have customer service centers staffed with representatives trained to field requests related to a broad range of subjects—from address changes to foreign stock prices to estate taxes. "A Customer Inquiry" provides an example of a typical dialogue.

A CUSTOMER INQUIRY

As part of their training, new customer service representatives practice answering the most common questions from customers. Here's a typical dialogue between a representative and a fund investor:

Representative: Thank you for calling Avon Hill Investments, this is Leah Jones. How may I help you?

Investor: Good morning. I have an account with Avon Hill and I'd like to set one up with you for my two-year-old daughter, Jenny. Can I do that over the phone?

Representative: I can help you with that. May I have your name and account number before we get started?

Investor: Yes, it's Michael Smith, account number 123456789.

Representative: Thanks, Mr. Smith. Because Jenny is a minor, you'll need to establish a Uniform Transfers to Minors Act account, or UTMA. An adult will need to serve as custodian on her account until she reaches the age of majority, which for your state is 21. We'll need the signature of the custodian to set up the account, so we'll have to do this in writing rather than over the phone. Will you be listing yourself as custodian for Jenny on the account, Mr. Smith?

Investor: I'm not sure. I'll need to discuss it with my wife. What does the custodian have to do?

Representative: The custodian is the only one with authority to act on the account, such as requesting transactions or making changes to the account. However, since the assets in a UTMA account belong to the minor, any money withdrawn from the account must be used for the benefit of the minor.

Investor: Can you send us the paperwork?

Representative: Absolutely. I can e-mail or mail the account application to you if you'd like or you can download it from our web site.

Investor: E-mail would be great. My e-mail address is msmith @zdomain.com.

Representative: Thanks Mr. Smith. [Representative reads back e-mail address.] You should be receiving that in the next few minutes. Our mailing address is listed in the upper right-hand corner of the form. The minimum investment amount for this type of account is $1,000, but if you set up a systematic investment through your bank for $100 a month or more, we'll waive the investment minimum. Do you think you'd like to set up a systematic investment for this account?

Investor: Yes, I think we will.

Representative: Okay. In that case, please be sure to complete section four and include a voided check or deposit slip with your application so that we can add your bank information to the account.

Investor: Okay. Thanks very much for all of your help.

Representative: You're welcome, Mr. Smith. Is there anything else I can help with today?

Investor: No, that's it, Leah. You've been a big help.

Representative: It was my pleasure. Thank you for calling today, and please call back if you have any other questions.

Source: NQR, Inc. Used with the permission of NQR, Inc.

To ensure that neither rain nor snow nor any other weather condition interferes with service, most fund complexes can draw upon two or more customer service centers located in different regions of the country. They also have detailed disaster recovery plans that they test regularly. And many fund firms now enable a significant percentage of their customer service representatives to work from home, so that a problem affecting a single building won't interrupt service. Sophisticated telecommunications systems route customer calls to the appropriate location based on the current availability of representatives with the right expertise to handle the inquiry.

Staffing a mutual fund service center is a major undertaking in and of itself. Large fund groups can have hundreds of representatives ready to answer customer inquiries at any time. Consequently, most centers have invested in sizable human resource departments that manage recruiting and training. They reach out to local colleges, offering positions to new graduates. Many of the entry-level openings at fund management companies arise in the transfer agent. See the "Career Track" box to learn more about a customer service representative's job.

Scheduling phone coverage alone presents a huge human resources challenge, since the volume of inquiries can vary dramatically with the ups and downs of the stock market and the season of the year. Call volume soars during the January 1 to April 15 tax season, for example. Some firms rely on temporary employees to meet expected spikes in volume, while others adjust internally, borrowing staff from other areas and extending staff hours during crunch times.

Service centers monitor labor markets around the globe and will often open new facilities in areas where there is a well-educated workforce but

CAREER TRACK: CUSTOMER SERVICE REPRESENTATIVE

As a customer service representative for a fund complex, you'll be working in a dynamic and fast-paced environment. You'll be asked to get up to speed quickly: Extensive training begins the day you walk in the door. You'll start with a 6-to-12-week course that will cover the basics of the mutual fund industry, details about the firm's products, in-depth systems training, and grounding in customer service skills. This course may also include preparation for licensing exams administered by FINRA that require you to demonstrate your knowledge of the securities markets.

Training is essential because you'll field many types of customer inquiries. You'll process transactions and resolve problems, and you may even talk with customers about potential investments. The diversity of the job makes it interesting, but that does mean that there's a high potential for burnout. Dealing with customer problems all day can be exhausting—and some service centers are now open around the clock. As a result, it's not unusual for a service center to experience upward of 40 percent staff turnover each year, meaning that the typical employee stays for only two to three years.

On the other hand, because of their extensive training and experience handling customer requests, customer service representatives are prime candidates for jobs in other parts of the fund management company, such as sales, compliance, and fund accounting. In effect, transfer agents often act as hiring agents for the company as a whole. As a result, a position as a customer service representative is a common entry point for a career in mutual funds.

not enough jobs. Generally, transfer agents service their U.S. clients with call centers based in either the United States or Canada. But for non-customer-facing functions, transfer agents are willing to cope with the challenges of multiple time zones and cultures. Many have opened technology support operations in India, for example.

Compliance

Transfer agents also have substantial responsibilities when it comes to making sure that the fund complies with all applicable laws and regulations and with the fund's own policies and procedures. Among the issues that the transfer agent monitors are:

- *Prospectus compliance.* Transfer agents must make sure that all the transactions they process comply with the requirements set out in the prospectus. As we've discussed, they check to confirm that purchases exceed the required minimum amounts, that frequent trading limits are applied accurately and that any account and transaction-related fees are calculated and collected correctly.
- *Privacy protection.* Transfer agents must ensure that personal identifying information is protected. (See "Protecting PII" for a definition of the term.) The increased collection of personal information by businesses in recent years—combined with some highly visible failures to safeguard that information—have raised consumer awareness of privacy issues. In response to this heightened sensitivity, both the federal government and many of the states have passed legislation designed to protect against identity theft and other misuse of personal information. To comply with these rules, funds now send shareholders an annual privacy notice explaining how they will use information and giving investors a chance to stop their information from being shared with third parties, if that's under consideration. More importantly, transfer agents frequently

PROTECTING PII

In recent years, most transfer agents have reviewed their operations to ensure that they're doing everything they can to protect the security of PII, or *personal identifying information.*

What exactly is PII? While there's no universally accepted standard, the Commonwealth of Massachusetts has defined it as name and address combined with Social Security, driver's license, credit card, or bank account number. Give thieves this package of information, and they might just find a way to finance that Caribbean vacation at your expense.

To keep criminals from enjoying the good life, transfer agents have tried to reduce the amount of information they collect and keep, limited use of mobile devices, controlled the flow of paper documents, and tightened computer password requirements and data access controls. And most now have an information security officer who keeps an eye on all of this.

review their processes to ensure that their customers' personal information remains confidential.

- *Anti–money laundering.* Funds must take steps to avoid providing a laundry service for criminals with dirty money. As mentioned earlier, transfer agents must verify a customer's identity when they open an account for someone. And they must file Suspicious Activity Reports with the U.S. Department of the Treasury if they have concerns that a share purchase has been made with funds earned through illegal activities.
- *Backup tax withholding.* Mutual funds are required to withhold taxes on fund distributions and on redemption proceeds if the investor has not provided a valid taxpayer identification number. The transfer agent forwards the money it collects to the IRS.
- *"Blue Sky."* Transfer agents are responsible for complying with state requirements by filing notice of shares sold in the state and ensuring that the appropriate fees are paid. Many transfer agents outsource this function to specialized service providers. The term *Blue Sky* refers to state securities laws—which were enacted to prevent unscrupulous securities promoters from selling unsuspecting consumers investments with no more substance than the blue sky. (We review the role of the states in fund regulation in Chapter 1.)
- *Escheatment.* Funds must comply with state laws regarding *escheatment,* which is the handling of unclaimed property. While it may be surprising that anyone would lose track of one's money, it actually happens quite often, usually after a shareholder moves or passes away. State laws require that funds take certain steps to locate the legitimate owner. Here, too, transfer agents often hire a firm that specializes in this work to handle the process for them.

TECHNOLOGY AND SHAREHOLDER SERVICING

To process a high volume of transactions subject to a complex set of demanding rules—all at a reasonable cost—transfer agents must make extensive use of automation. Technology pervades every aspect of transfer agent operations, and transfer agents are major purchasers of hardware and software.

Technology Behind the Scenes

The automation often begins even before a transaction arrives at the service center. Orders from other financial institutions, including brokerage firms and banks, are transmitted electronically through Fund/SERV. This system has standardized and centralized trade processing and money movement among financial intermediaries and fund complexes. Before Fund/SERV was established, each fund sponsor would go through the costly and inefficient process of establishing an individual relationship with each intermediary that sold its shares. (This is the system that still predominates in Europe and Asia.) Funds now only make one wire transfer per day to settle the purchase and redemption activity; Fund/SERV takes care of allocating it to brokerage firms and other distributors of fund shares.

A second industrywide platform, called Networking, enables funds to provide information about existing account positions to the intermediaries that sold mutual funds to their clients. This system also coordinates the payment of income and capital gains distributions as well as the dissemination of the related tax information. The Networking system allows the intermediary to control the degree of direct interaction between their investor clients and the fund sponsor by selecting a particular service level. Under Networking Level 4, for example, the intermediary can process purchase and sale orders, but the fund sponsor otherwise handles all client service. In Level 3, the reverse is true: the intermediary maintains the client relationships. The fund complex has no direct connection with shareholders and usually does not even know their names. See "The Vaults of Wall Street" to learn about the owner of both Fund/SERV and Networking.

THE VAULTS OF WALL STREET

Both Fund/SERV and Networking were developed and are operated by the Depository Trust & Clearing Corporation, or DTCC, through its subsidiary, the National Securities Clearing Corporation, or NSCC.

DTCC plays a special role in the securities industry: it processes virtually every stock, corporate bond, and municipal bond transaction in the United States, standing between the buyer and the seller each time. It keeps ownership records in its computer system, based on the trade information reported to it. As a depository, it actually holds many of those securities, represented by paper certificates stored in DTCC's vaults or by uncertificated electronic records. DTCC is owned by the principal users of its services.

Within the service center, everything at the transfer agent revolves around the database system, which stores information about funds, investors, intermediaries, and transactions. These systems embody millions of lines of code and would cost hundreds of millions of dollars to build from scratch. Service center staff access and enter information into the database through intelligent workstations with a graphical user interface.

Transfer agents today rely heavily on document imaging systems that scan incoming mail and then automatically route the images to the appropriate area for processing. This makes documents available to the staff using them to set up new accounts or enter trades and to the customer service representatives who might later need to review an account's history with a caller—all without having to rummage through dusty files. While e-mail correspondence has become increasingly common, especially about account issues, transfer agents still handle a lot of paper, especially for issues involving legal authorizations.

Other systems that transfer agents commonly use to run their operations include:

- *Workflow management* systems to track the status of all items as they make their way through the service center and to sound alarms if there are any problems or delays
- *Case management* systems to maintain records of the contacts that shareholders and their advisers have with the service center
- *Computer Output to Laser Disk, or COLD,* systems to allow representatives to see images of the printed statements that have been mailed to shareholders
- *Fulfillment* systems to capture orders for hard copies of literature such as prospectuses and to transmit them to the mail house
- *Correspondence* systems to help service representatives generate letters and e-mails, by providing templates with text that address the most commonly encountered situations

Customer-Facing Technology

Technology is a critical element in the center's customer contacts, beginning with phone answering. An automatic call distributor routes calls to a service center based on the workload among representatives and the area code from which the call was placed. The number that was dialed factors in as well: shareholders with large amounts invested might be given a special number, while the phone number to request literature may be different from that for account inquiries. In addition to routing calls, the distributor tracks call volumes, wait times, queue lengths, and abandoned call rates.

A voice response unit or VRU is usually the next point of contact. While notorious with consumers—and a favorite source of inspiration for stand-up comics—VRUs are essential for efficient service. By steering callers to the representative with the specialized expertise to handle their inquiry, they reduce the number of hand-offs or callbacks. If the systems capture identifying information, either through caller ID or consumer entry of account information, they can get basic account data onto the representative's computer through a *screen pop* even before the call begins.

Mutual fund service centers record all the calls made by their representatives. If there should later be a dispute about the content of a call, the service center can resolve it by reviewing the recording. State laws generally require that customers be informed that a call is being taped. To that end, before the representative picks up, callers hear an automatic announcement along the lines of, "For training or quality assurance, this call may be recorded." Sometimes, the caller will hear a recurring beep on the call indicating that she is being recorded.

Shareholders still generally phone in to the customer service center to correct account errors or for answers to more complex questions, such as those involving fund taxation. To increase the odds that issues can be resolved within a single call, transfer agents have invested in powerful workstations that allow representatives to pull up extensive background information quickly.

But for routine inquiries, more and more customers are skipping the call center altogether and getting the answers they need over the Web. Both investors and their advisers have found the Internet to be an easy way to check fund prices and account balances or to get background information.

This shouldn't be surprising since mutual fund owners are a web-savvy bunch. According to a survey conducted by the Investment Company Institute, 90 percent of fund-owning households had Internet access in 2009, and more than three-quarters of these went online at least once a day. As you can see in Figure 13.2, this same group was very likely to look up financial information on the Web, with direct-market channel buyers most inclined to turn to the Internet for this purpose.

While investors have become very comfortable looking up financial information online, they have been more reluctant to use the Internet to effect transactions. The same ICI study found that only 23 percent of the households that both owned funds and had Internet access bought or sold investments through the Web in the previous year.

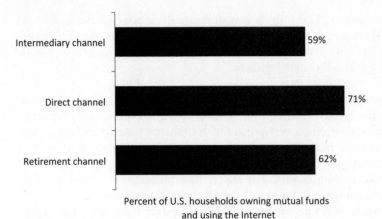

Percent of U.S. households owning mutual funds
and using the Internet

FIGURE 13.2 Mutual Fund Owners Accessing Financial Information through the
Web (2008)
Source: Investment Company Institute, "Ownership of Mutual Funds, Shareholder
Sentiment and Use of the Internet, 2009."

Investors have been particularly slow to use the Web to buy and sell
mutual fund shares—in sharp contrast to stock trading, in which online
transactions are common. There are, however, key differences between the
two activities:

- *Pricing.* Brokerage firms offer significantly lower prices to customers
  who buy and sell stocks through the Web. In contrast, mutual fund
  buyers generally don't save anything by buying online instead of by fax
  or phone.
- *Activity levels.* There are many stock traders who buy and sell often and
  therefore value the convenience and flexibility of Internet trading. Fund
  investors normally transact only a few times per year—in fact, most
  funds close their doors to investors who trade their shares frequently.
  As a result, fund shareholders may feel that it's not worth the trouble
  to establish an online account for the occasional trade.
- *Speed.* Mutual fund buys and sells are executed all at once at the end
  of the day, so it doesn't much matter if a phone call takes longer than
  an Internet order. Stock traders, on the other hand, may be very sensitive to the time it takes to process an order, especially if they're trying to buy at the low or sell at the high when the market is moving
  rapidly.

- *Intermediaries.* Many stock investors are do-it-yourself investors who enter their own transactions. Mutual fund investors, on the other hand, are most likely to purchase funds through financial advisers who handle the buy and sell orders for them.

Still, willingness to both open new accounts and make purchases and sales over the Internet has been increasing steadily, especially in the direct channel or within employer-sponsored retirement plans. One major no-load firm reports that three-quarters of its new accounts are now opened online without paper applications. And despite the obstacles, mutual fund management companies anticipate that online transaction volumes will only increase and continue to build web-based processing capabilities.

In short, transfer agents must regularly update their systems, keeping them current with latest technology. It's a massive investment, which means that there are large economies of scale in the transfer agency business.

TRANSFER AGENTS AS AN INDUSTRY

Given the extensive technology required, fewer and fewer mutual fund complexes run completely independent transfer agency operations. Instead, most outsource at least some functions to third-party providers who capture enough volume from multiple clients to benefit from the economies of scale. Let's take a look at the models that fund firms can use when it comes to organizing their transfer agency operations:

Model 1: Fully internal. Fund management companies can decide to go it alone, handling all data processing and answering all customer inquiries themselves. While this used to be the most common model, the rising capital investment required has made this option less and less popular. Today, only one in five fund complexes has a fully internal, or *captive,* transfer agent, down from almost one in three 10 years ago. (See Table 13.1 for the industry statistics.) The two largest firms, Fidelity and Vanguard, manage shareholder services themselves.

Model 2: Fully External. Funds can outsource all shareholder servicing functions to a specialist provider. The smallest fund complexes almost always choose this option.

Model 3: Remote. In this model, firms contract with a third-party vendor for use of their data processing system, but retain all other functions. This option avoids the expense of building and maintaining a shareholder recordkeeping database.

Model 4: Hybrid. The increasingly popular customized solution. Fund management companies decide exactly which functions they'd like to handle

TABLE 13.1 Types of Mutual Fund Transfer Agents

Type	2007	1999
Fully internal	20%	30%
Hybrid	33%	25%
Fully external	18%	12%
Remote	29%	33%
Total	*100%*	*100%*

Source: Investment Company Institute, *Mutual Fund Transfer Agents—Trends and Billing Practices 1999 and 2007.*

themselves, and then outsource the others. For example, many firms continue to answer calls from financial advisers, but hire a third party to manage all other transfer agency functions. Mid-size fund firms are likely to go this route.

Where do fund firms turn when they decide to go external? As you can see from Table 13.2, which lists the largest full-service external transfer agents, they will likely use a provider affiliated with a bank. The only firms on this list that are not at least partly bank-owned are ALPS Fund Services and DST Systems. (Boston Financial Data Services is 50 percent owned by the financial group that includes State Street Bank and Trust Company.)

TABLE 13.2 Largest Full-Service External Providers of Transfer Agent Services (2009)

Service Provider	Number of Accounts (thousands)	Number of Clients
Boston Financial Data Services/DST	33,300	176
BNY Mellon Asset Servicing	12,081	160
U.S. Bancorp Fund Services	2,225	123
Citi	947	224
ALPS Fund Services	550	21
Northern Trust	421	169
J.P. Morgan	354	93
UMB Fund Services	265	46

Source: Source Media, *The 2010 Mutual Fund Service Guide.* Used with the permission of Source Media.

Two of these providers dwarf the others: DST/Boston Financial Data Services and BNY Mellon Asset Servicing.[6] The former is technically two separate firms, although DST provides the technology to BFDS and owns the other 50 percent of its shares. These firms together serviced close to 17 percent of the 271 million fund shareholder accounts in the United States as of December 31, 2009, according to Source Media. That's up from about a 10 percent share in 1999, illustrating that there are economies of scale in certain aspects of transfer agency operations.

Use of Omnibus Accounts

It's not just the cost of technology that's driving the consolidation in transfer agents: the shift toward omnibus accounts has also played an important role. Brokerage firms and retirement plans are using these accounts more and more often.

Let's take the example of a fund purchase made through the hypothetical Silas Deane OneNetwork fund supermarket. The Silas Deane brokerage firm sets up only a single omnibus account at the fund's transfer agent. It is used for all the holdings in that particular fund of all the investors who have OneNetwork accounts. The fund's transfer agent only knows the total number of shares held by all the accounts in the supermarket. It doesn't know the names of the specific investors or the size of their individual holdings—Silas Deane keeps track of that information. Every business day, Silas Deane adds together all of the purchases and redemptions of the fund made through the supermarket and reports only the net change to the transfer agent.

Silas Deane may set up separate omnibus accounts for the OneNetwork holdings for wrap programs it sponsors or for positions in brokerage accounts. Or it may combine holdings from more than one of these programs into a single account. Similarly, the administrator for retirement plans might create separate accounts for each plan it oversees or combine them all into a single omnibus account.

Omnibus accounts have three main advantages for financial intermediaries selling mutual funds:

1. *Account minimums.* Using an omnibus account makes it easier to comply with a fund's account size minimums. This is important for retirement plans and wrap programs, since the amount that a plan or program participant may put in a single fund can be quite small. Assume, for example, that a brokerage firm wrap program allocates 10 percent of assets to an emerging market fund. If the program used individual accounts,

an investor with $20,000 in the program could find that her emerging market position is below the $3,000 account minimum imposed by the fund. But if the $20 million program uses an omnibus account, the $2 million total allocation easily meets the requirement.

2. *Customer control.* Intermediaries like omnibus accounts because they can maintain greater control over the customer's account. The fund can't contact a shareholder directly about another investment—maybe a fund purchase that won't involve the intermediary—because the fund doesn't know the shareholder's identity. This makes marketing much more difficult for fund sponsors, since they don't have direct personal contact with their customers. They must learn about their shareholders indirectly—through the intermediaries—and communicate with them through advertising instead.

   It also makes it harder for funds to enforce certain prospectus rules, most notably the restrictions on frequent trading. To help funds discharge their duties in this regard, SEC Rule 22c-2 requires that intermediaries provide detailed information on transactions within an omnibus account whenever the fund asks for it, disclosing the taxpayer identification number but not the customer name. Even so, funds can't follow up directly on any violations they detect; they must rely on the intermediary to impose trading restrictions on the offenders.

3. *Fees.* Intermediaries also like omnibus accounts because they get paid for administering them. They're handling many shareholder service functions that the transfer agent would otherwise perform, such as paying out distributions, calculating cost basis, issuing tax forms, and answering shareholder questions—so it makes sense that they would get paid for the work.

   These fee arrangements are called *subtransfer agent,* or sub-TA, contracts. Sub-TA fees may be paid by the transfer agent out of its fees, or they may be paid directly by the fund—which then usually reduces the fee it pays to the transfer agent. As a result, while these fee arrangements are popular with intermediaries, they create business challenges for fund transfer agents who watch their fee income decline as accounts are consolidated. The resulting cost pressure has accelerated the trend toward use of external transfer agents.

Pricing and Service Quality

The transfer agent usually signs a separate contract with the fund, which is approved by the board of directors and reviewed at least annually. Transfer agent contracts use a variety of fee structures. The most common approaches are:

- A flat fee per account
- Flat fee plus per transaction charges, along the lines of $3.00 per representative-assisted phone call and $.50 per automated call
- A variable flat fee that declines as the number of shareholder accounts or net assets increase
- An allocated fee that allows the transfer agent to earn a specified profit margin over costs
- A basis point fee computed as a percentage of assets
- An asset and account fee that combines a relatively low flat fee per account plus a charge based on assets

Boards of director generally use the same fee structure for all funds within a complex. Table 13.3 provides a breakdown of the usage of these different structures.

When they're negotiating fees, both the board of directors and the transfer agent are trying to develop a fee schedule that's related to costs. Since transfer agents must provide services to every account—regardless of its level of assets—most fee schedules incorporate a per-account charge. The contract may make adjustments in the flat fee to more precisely reflect underlying expenses. For example, the variable structure adjusts the flat fee downward as volumes increase, while flat-plus fees provide extra compensation for particularly costly activities.

But even with adjustments, per-account fees can be burdensome to a small fund, especially one with a low average account size. So the board may consider a transfer agent fee that's based on assets under management.

TABLE 13.3 Transfer Agent Fee Structures (2007)

Fee structure	Percentage of funds
Flat fee	34%
Flat fee plus	13
Variable flat fee	13
Allocated fee	15
Basis point fee	10
Asset and account fee	14
Other	1

Source: Investment Company Institute, *Mutual Fund Transfer Agents: Trends and Billing Practices 2007.*

TABLE 13.4 Transfer Agent Charges (2007)

Fund type	Charge per account	Basis point charge
Money market	$25.74	16
Bond	$23.95	14
Stock	$23.81	20

Source: Investment Company Institute, *Mutual Fund Transfer Agents: Trends and Billing Practices 2007.*

That might save money when a fund is small, although it could allow the transfer agent to make significant profits if the fund should grow.

In addition, directors may authorize transfer agents to levy extra transactional fees for holders who request special services, such as wire transfers. Other funds may impose an annual maintenance fee on very small accounts.

How much does transfer agency service cost? In 2007, it averaged about $24 for each open account. Per-account charges were highest for money market funds because they are the most service intensive; many shareholders use money funds as checking accounts. When viewed in basis point terms—relative to the amount in the account—stock funds have the highest transfer agency costs. That's because stock funds generally have the smallest average account size. Table 13.4 has details.

To make sure that they get their money's worth from the transfer agent, fund boards establish procedures for monitoring the quality of the service provided. The transfer agent helps by collecting data on all aspects of their operations. Some of the statistics they might provide include:

- Average wait time for a caller
- Abandoned call rate (percentage of callers who hang up before their call is answered, presumably because they have grown tired of waiting)
- Call center quality
- Transaction processing accuracy
- Average number of days to respond to customer inquiries

Funds also routinely survey shareholders on their satisfaction with the service they received. Today, survey efforts are continual, with funds asking random callers or Web visitors to provide their opinions on their experience. To maintain objectivity, firms usually hire independent firms to conduct these surveys and evaluate their results. "Checking In" gives an example of the type of information that a fund collects in this process.

CHECKING IN

Here's an excerpt of a telephone survey being conducted between an interviewer and a financial adviser, who frequently recommends Arch Street mutual funds to her clients. The adviser calls the Arch Street customer service center regularly about client accounts.

Interviewer: Hello Ms. Green, my name is Samantha Smith, and I am calling on behalf of Arch Street Funds. I am conducting a telephone interview concerning your satisfaction with the quality of services provided by Arch Street Funds during the past 12 months. The ideas and opinions you discuss during this interview will be used in Arch Street Funds' efforts to continuously improve its services. Can you please take approximately 5 to 10 minutes to answer a few questions concerning your satisfaction with Arch Street Funds' services?

Financial Adviser: Yes, I have time now.

Interviewer: Thank you. I am going to ask you to rate your satisfaction with the quality of several services provided by Arch Street Funds. Please use a scale from 1 to 5, with 5 representing Very Satisfied, and 1 representing Very Dissatisfied. We would welcome any feedback you can provide to us as we move through each set of questions. Are you ready to begin?

Financial Adviser: Yes.

Interviewer: On a scale from 1 to 5, how would you rate your satisfaction with the overall quality of telephone customer service? And please feel free to provide comments.

Financial Adviser: I'd give them a 5. They seem very knowledgeable and responsive whenever I call. They're very prompt in giving me information. Occasionally, there's a new person who is not as knowledgeable as others, but for the most part they're able to give me the information I need and are really willing to help.

Interviewer: How would you rate your satisfaction with the Arch Street Funds' problem resolution abilities? And please feel free to provide comments.

Financial Adviser: I'm satisfied, so I'd rate that 4. Problems, unfortunately, do occur from time to time, yet we feel these are always resolved expeditiously and efficiently. There was a service question that I had once. There was an issue on achieving breakpoints for a client at the $500,000 level that I went through a vast number of people (probably about four different people) to get to the right calculation. That was just one issue that was not good.

[The interviewer asks several other questions.]

Interviewer: On a 1 to 5 scale, how would you rate the overall quality of service you receive from Arch Street Funds.

Financial Adviser: I've been very satisfied. 4.

Interviewer: And finally, if asked, would you recommend Arch Street Funds to another financial adviser?

Financial Adviser: Oh yes, I definitely would. I've been doing business with Arch Street Funds for 10 years and have always found their service to be great.

Interviewer: That concludes our survey. Thank you so much for your time, Ms. Green. We appreciate your participation in this survey. Your comments will be very valuable to Arch Street Funds and will allow them to address your specific issues with you.

Source: NQR, Inc. Used with the permission of NQR, Inc.

Management company executives understand that consistently providing high quality customer service is critical to building and retaining customer loyalty. As a result, transfer agents play a critical role in helping firms build their brand identity.

CHAPTER SUMMARY

Transfer agents provide fund shareholders with a broad array of services. This is a major task given the large number of shareholder accounts and the complexity of fund features. More than one-third of the jobs in the fund industry are at the transfer agent. Transfer agents maintain records of shareholder accounts and process purchases, redemptions, exchanges, and distributions. They also provide regular reports to shareholders on their holdings as well as on the tax status of distributions and sales of fund shares. Fund complexes establish customer service centers staffed with representatives trained to respond to customer inquiries. These centers have sizable human resource departments to manage recruiting and training.

Transfer agents have substantial compliance responsibilities. They must ensure that they process all transactions in accordance with prospectus requirements, while protecting the privacy of shareholders' personal information and preventing money laundering. They are required to withhold taxes on fund distributions in specified circumstances. In addition, they must comply with state laws regarding notice filings and abandoned property.

Technology plays a critical role in transfer agent operations. The Fund/SERV and Networking systems have automated communications between the transfer agent and the distributors of fund shares. The work within the service center revolves around a sophisticated database system. Service centers also use technology extensively to manage workflow and route information to customer service representatives. Most customer inquiries come to the service center by telephone, and fund complexes have specialized technology to route and record these calls. However, customer use of the Internet is increasingly steadily, and fund complexes are investing heavily in online capabilities.

Given the extensive technology investment required to deliver transfer agency services, more and more fund complexes are outsourcing at least some functions to third parties. Intermediaries are also assuming more shareholder recordkeeping duties by establishing omnibus accounts, which combine holdings for many clients in a single account at the transfer agent. Intermediaries get paid by the fund for maintaining these omnibus accounts.

Transfer agents provide services to the fund under a separate contract. While these contracts use a wide variety of fee structures, most include a flat fee per account plus extra charges for providing specialized services. The board of directors negotiates the contract with the transfer agent and monitors the quality of service provided.

CHAPTER 14

Portfolio Recordkeeping and Valuation

There is a drama that unfolds every business day at mutual fund companies. Each afternoon, funds must calculate their NAV with a deadline of 5:50 P.M. Eastern Time—only 110 minutes after the U.S. stock exchanges post their closing prices for the day. Computing the NAV is an intricate procedure that involves verifying all the holdings in the portfolio, recording any liabilities, and valuing each security that requires tight coordination among the many parties involved. The fund accountant plays the leading role in this daily production, with the custodian, investment operations, independent auditor, and many other service providers all making critical contributions.

Although we discuss specific responsibilities in depth later in the chapter, let's start with an overview of the key players:

- *Fund accounting* is responsible for determining the daily NAV and maintaining all the fund records needed to support the NAV calculation. The fund accountant also prepares the fund's financial statements and tax returns for review by the management company, the auditors, and the fund's board of directors.
- The *custodian* holds the funds' securities in safekeeping, maintains an accurate inventory of portfolio securities, and manages cash payments and receipts.
- *Investment operations* oversees trade settlement, which is the actual exchange of cash and securities that occurs after a trade has been executed. This group also works closely with the investment managers and traders to ensure that portfolio reports are accurate and that funds comply with all the relevant rules.
- The *independent auditor* works behind the scenes to help ensure the integrity of the fund's financial data. Auditors review financial records and

confirm that all the parties contributing to them are using appropriate procedures to generate information.

These parties are constantly exchanging and comparing information—with each other, with the transfer agent, with brokers who execute transactions in the fund portfolios and with DTCC, the central securities depository. Reconciling differences in their records—they each usually keep a separate set—is a major part of their work. To make this process as efficient as possible, they work through industry associations to set standards for the automated transfer of data. Both mutual fund industry associations—the Investment Company Institute and NICSA—play an important role in this effort.

This chapter reviews:

- The daily work of fund accountants, especially their role in calculating the daily NAV
- The valuation of portfolio securities
- The role of the custodian in the safekeeping of holdings
- The role of the investment operations team in trade settlement and portfolio recordkeeping
- The role of the independent auditor in financial statement review and internal control assessment

A DAY IN THE LIFE OF THE FUND ACCOUNTANT

The fund accountant has responsibility for calculating the daily NAV. As we discussed in Chapter 2, funds must calculate their NAV each day that the New York Stock Exchange is open. The work must be completed by 5:50 P.M. Eastern Time, which is the deadline for getting NAVs to NASDAQ for dissemination the next day. For mutual funds, NASDAQ is more than just a place to buy and sell certain securities. The NASDAQ quote system is the central repository for records of fund NAVs.

If a fund's NAV does not reach NASDAQ by 5:50 P.M., it will appear in the database as *n/a,* for *not available.* The consequence is that shareholders may not be able to look up the value of their fund through quote services the following day. Even more importantly, it means that transfer agents and subtransfer agents will need to manually input NAVs to complete the transactions that they have already booked. As a result, everyone works hard to complete the NAV calculation on time whenever possible.

But it's a very tight deadline. That's because extremely important information—the valuation of the fund's securities—is not available until the New York Stock Exchange closes at 4 P.M. Eastern Time. Therefore fund accountants spend much of the day preparing to *strike* the NAV in late afternoon. They gather key information from other participants, post activity to the fund's books, and resolve *exceptions,* which is accountant-speak for *problems.* Figure 14.1 depicts the timeline of the NAV calculation

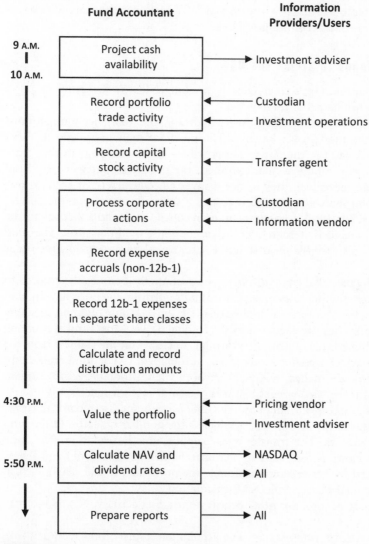

FIGURE 14.1 NAV Calculation Time Line

process as well as the parties that contribute to each step. Follow along with this chart as we walk through a fund accountant's day.

A brief word on where all this work takes place. Some fund managers prefer to retain control over portfolio servicing and handle these functions themselves. For example, Fidelity, Franklin Templeton, and Vanguard all maintain internal service provider organizations. Other fund complexes out-source fund accounting to a third party—usually a bank—that specializes in the work. State Street, J.P. Morgan, and BNY Mellon are the largest external providers of fund accounting services.

Getting Ready to Strike the NAV

The fund accountant's day starts by looking back at the previous day's trading. Morning activities include:

Project cash availability. Every morning the fund accountant must calculate the fund's cash balance. The portfolio manager needs an exact number—as early in the day in the possible—to be able to plan that day's trades. If cash is higher than expected, the portfolio manager may need to purchase more securities to get it invested; conversely, if cash is low, the portfolio manager may need to make sales. To determine the correct cash figure, the fund accountant must reconcile the fund's records to the custodian's records, researching any exceptions, or differences. The fund accountant also adjusts the cash number for transactions scheduled to occur that day.

Record portfolio trade activity. The accountant updates the records to reflect purchases and sales made in the fund's portfolio the prior day. In fund accounting lingo, trades are booked on *T+1*, or *trade date plus one*, meaning one day after they are executed by the trading desk.[1] Most fund accounting systems obtain trade information through an electronic file transfer from the custodian, which updates fund records automatically. The fund accountant resolves any anomalies, talking with both the custodian and investment operations if there's any missing information or inconsistencies.

Record capital stock activity. The fund accountant also records the prior day's change in the capital stock, which is the number of shares of the fund held by investors. The transfer agent supplies this information. The daily cap stock figure is increased by net shareholder purchases of fund shares and reduced by net redemptions made the prior day. It will play a critical role in the final phase of the NAV calculation.

The fund accountant now records nontrading activity. Next steps may include:

Process corporate actions. The accountant adjusts fund records to re-flect any corporate actions that become effective that day; notification of corporate actions comes from the custodian. ("Taking Action" provides a definition of the term.) Some corporate actions are extremely complex—making it very easy to make a mistake when processing them. To keep errors to a minimum, custodians and fund firms often hire specialist firms to provide them with information on the details of corporate actions and use automated systems to record them. The fund accountant will double- and triple-check to make sure that corporate actions are entered correctly.

TAKING ACTION

The term *corporate action* has a very specific meaning in the investment world. It's an event—usually initiated by the board of directors—that changes the terms of the securities issued by the corporation. Common corporate actions include:

- Mergers between two companies that replace existing securities with new ones issued by the combined company
- Spin-offs—the opposite of mergers—when companies divide their once-combined operations into separate corporations that each issue their own shares of stock
- Stock splits, when companies issue additional shares to current investors and decrease the share price at the same time
- Rights issues, when companies give existing shareholders the right to purchase additional shares at advantageous terms

Record non-12b-1 expense accruals. Expenses come next. The fund accountant records a daily accrual of expenses. As we've discussed, the fund pays the management company, the transfer agent, and many other parties for their services to the fund. (The fund also pays the distributor a 12b-1 fee; we come back to that fee in a moment.) Most of these fees are calculated as a percentage of assets, though the transfer agent fee is often based on the number of shareholder accounts. The accrual amount is based on a prepared schedule, but the calculation can be complicated when management companies cap, or subsidize, expenses. While these fees are accrued daily, they are paid in cash only periodically. The fund accountant also authorizes cash payment of expenses at scheduled times. NAV is reduced when the expense is accrued; the cash payment has no effect on NAV.

Record 12b-1 expenses in separate share classes. The fund accountant maintains the records of all of the share classes. In Chapter 10, we explained that many funds have multiple share classes, each with a unique combination of sales loads and 12b-1 charges. On a daily basis, that means applying the correct 12b-1 fee to each class. As with other expenses, the accountant accrues a small amount daily and initiates cash payment periodically.

Calculate and record distribution amounts. The fund's accountant also keeps track of interest income, dividends received, and capital gains realized from the sale of securities. As we discussed in Chapter 2, funds must distribute almost all of this income to shareholders—after deducting expenses—at least annually for it to qualify for pass-through tax status. Each fund has its own schedule for paying out this income, which might be annually, quarterly, monthly, or even daily. When a distribution is due to be paid, the fund accountant computes the distribution per share by adding the interest, dividend, and capital gain income for the period, subtracting expenses, then dividing by the capital stock figure. This per-share amount is then communicated to the transfer agent, who handles the actual distribution to shareholder accounts. The payment of the distribution reduces NAV. Again, while distribution payments are often made only periodically, the fund accountant keeps track of income daily.

Striking the NAV

At 4 P.M. Eastern Time, the final phase of NAV calculation begins. As mentioned, all work must be completed by 5:50 P.M., so it's an extremely busy time of day for the fund accountant. The choreography must be perfect for the NAV to be struck on time.

The next step is to price the securities held in the portfolio at their 4 P.M. values. While 4 P.M. is the closing time for U.S. stock exchanges (and closing prices on those exchanges are used for those securities), the same time is used for valuing all securities, including bonds and non-U.S. stocks. Valuation is a complex process that we'll discuss in detail in the next section.

Once each security in the fund's portfolio has been priced—and most accounting systems will not move on until this step has been completed—the system totals the value of the securities, adds in cash and any other assets and then subtracts liabilities. The resulting number is divided by the capital stock figure to produce the NAV.

Time for a double check: if the NAV has changed by more than a prespecified amount, the fund accountant will go over the entire calculation to make sure that the movement is not the result of an input error. A supervisor will review and sign off before the NAV is finalized—and senior management may even get involved if there's a significant change.

Seems simple, doesn't it? Some days it is, but on other days—usually when market activity is at a peak—any number of problems can hold things up: systems can slow down at the worst possible times, pricing vendors may have trouble valuing securities in a sector that has been particularly active, or there may be so many significant swings in prices that research into exceptions takes much longer than usual.

Before we discuss valuation, an important note: fund accountants do more than just calculate the NAV each day. They play a key role in preparing many required reports. For example, fund accountants produce drafts of the financial statements that form part of the annual and semiannual shareholder reports and of the tax returns that funds file with the IRS every year. These drafts are reviewed by the fund management company, the auditors, and the board of directors. The "Career Track" box talks more about the key attributes of a fund accountant.

CAREER TRACK: FUND ACCOUNTANT

What does it take to be a fund accountant? Here are a few of the skills required, according to recent job postings from several firms with major fund accounting operations:

> *"ability to work in a challenging and changing environment"*
> *"ability to meet tight deadlines and work under pressure"*
> *"ability to recognize potential problems and escalate them to a supervisor"*
> *"strong aptitude for numbers"*
> *"detail orientation"*
> *"team player with the ability to work productively within a group and maintain a high degree of independence"*
> *"good organization skills"*
> *"analytical, prioritization, organizational, and time management skills"*

It's a demanding job, requiring both the ability to work under pressure with both accuracy and speed.

VALUATION OF PORTFOLIO HOLDINGS

As we've seen, one of the key final steps in the calculation of NAV is the valuation of the fund's portfolio holdings. For the NAV to be a good representation of the worth of a fund share, the prices used must reflect the securities' current market value.

A fund's board of directors has ultimate authority for the determination of its NAV. The board reviews and adopts pricing policies—which are disclosed in the fund's statement of additional information—and authorizes any exceptions to those policies. To address the valuation issues that do arise, most boards establish a *pricing, valuation, or fair valuation* committee that is available at the end of every business day. These committees are generally made up of experts from the management company (though not portfolio managers). In some fund complexes, directors serve on these committees as well. Pricing committees have access to the investment staff—who can brief them on the circumstances that have created the valuation issue—and the authority to establish valuations when use of the standard policies is not appropriate. The board of directors regularly reviews the committee's decisions.

Valuation Procedures

Funds use different valuation methodologies for each type of security:

- Stocks are easiest, especially actively traded stocks in developed countries. They're almost always valued at the price of the last trade made on that day. With U.S. stocks, that's the last transaction reported on the consolidated tape. (Chapter 8 discusses the consolidated reporting system.)
- Money market securities are normally priced at their amortized cost, as we explained in Chapter 7.
- Most bonds are valued using matrix pricing. To oversimplify, *matrix pricing* backs into a bond's price by estimating its yield spread over the Treasury curve and over the yields of other bonds in the same sector, based on its historical yield spread and the impact of option features, if any. (The appendix to Chapter 6 describes yield spreads.) Why does this work? Because most of the daily movement in the value of these bonds is determined by changes in interest rates, as measured by shifts in Treasury yields. The yield spread remains much more stable, reflecting the generally slow-to-develop trends in underlying credit quality.
- For less frequently traded investments, the average of the bid and the offer from one or more market makers may be used.

- And whenever a fund's board of directors believes that none of these methods truly reflect the price that position would receive in a current sale, those securities may be priced at fair value. Fair value is the fund manager's best estimate of how much the security could be sold for in an orderly market, rather than its price in a distressed sale or forced transaction. Fair valuation can apply to a single security—or even to an entire portfolio, as we'll see in a moment.

Today, many funds get valuations—especially for fixed income securities—from specialized pricing vendors. These services examine historical data and trends to estimate the spreads used in matrix pricing. They've identified reliable market makers to supply quotations. They use sophisticated analytical programs to validate all their valuations and reduce the possibility of error, double checking all changes in security valuations that exceed specified thresholds to make sure that they reflect market reality rather than oversight.

Since some pricing vendors specialize in the pricing of certain types of securities, it's not unusual for a fund complex to use multiple pricing vendors to cover the full range of investments. Some funds use a back-up vendor's quotes as a second opinion to make sure that valuations are correct.

In the annual report, funds must give shareholders an overview of how they actually applied these procedures when calculating NAV. As part of this reporting process, fund accountants sort holdings into three categories according to the valuation methodology used. These categories were established by the Financial Accounting Standards Board.[2] They are:

1. *Level 1* for identical securities trading in active markets with quoted prices. Treasury securities and most stocks fall into this category.
2. *Level 2* for securities that trade less often but that can still be valued using observable market inputs, such as quoted prices on similar securities or interest rates. Securities valued by market-maker quotes and matrix-priced bonds are included in this category.
3. *Level 3* for securities for which there are no observable inputs. For these holdings, funds must make their own analysis of current financial information for them to arrive at a valuation. Securities in Level 3 trade infrequently, often because the issuer is in financial distress.

The fund accountant will talk with auditors, analysts, and market experts about the assignment of a security into a particular level and then calculate the dollar value of the securities in each level. These dollar amounts must be included in the annual report.

The NAV Calculation and Fair Valuation

Let's take a closer look at the timing of the valuation of securities and the NAV calculation. Mutual funds use *forward pricing,* which means that investors who want to buy or sell fund shares always get the next available NAV. As we've learned, a mutual fund's NAV is established once per day using prices determined as of the close of the New York Stock Exchange at 4 P.M. Eastern Time. Investors who place an order to buy or redeem fund shares before that time will receive the NAV that is calculated later that same day. But if the order comes in at 4:01 P.M. or later, the shareholder's order won't be completed until the next business day—at the NAV computed at the end of the next business day. Forward pricing ensures that no one can use superior knowledge to take advantage of other shareholders.

Contrast forward pricing with the backward-pricing system that mutual funds used before 1968. Under backward pricing, purchases and sales of fund shares were made at the most recent prior NAV. In this system, investors who waited until the end of the day to place an order had an advantage. For example, if stock prices moved higher during the day, investors who placed an order to buy a stock mutual fund at the end of the day would be able to lock in a profit. That's because they received the NAV from the preceding day, a NAV that was too low because it reflected the prior day's lower stock prices. Investors buying shares earned this profit at the expense of existing shareholders—who effectively sold some of their shares at too low a price. Backward pricing made trading fund shares such a sure thing that it was actively promoted by fund managers as way to increase sales.

Forward pricing eliminates this ability to game the system—or does it? The current NAV calculation timing was developed for funds that invested primarily in U.S. securities. It works well because valuations for U.S. securities are established at the end of the trading day at exactly the same time that the NAV is calculated—and at the same time that purchases and redemptions are cut off for the day.

But when mutual funds began investing in non-U.S. securities, life got a lot more complicated. Valuations for foreign securities are established when their local markets close—and because of time zones they may close long before the U.S. market even opens. Yet investors in funds investing in those countries can continue to make purchases and sales of fund shares until 4 P.M. Eastern Time—which may be 12 or more hours after the local market has closed. (See Table 14.1 for the opening and closing times of major stock markets.)

In effect, funds that own a lot of foreign securities use backward pricing—giving investors the opportunity to game the system by watching the performance of the U.S. market. Since the United States is such

TABLE 14.1 Stock Market Hours (Eastern Time)

Stock market	Opens	Closes
Australia	7 P.M.	1 A.M.
Tokyo	7 P.M.	1 A.M.
China	8:30 P.M.	2 A.M.
Hong Kong	9 P.M.	3 A.M.
Bombay	10:30 P.M.	5 A.M.
Russia	3 A.M.	10 A.M.
Frankfurt	3 A.M.	2 P.M.
London	3 A.M.	11:30 A.M.
Paris	3 A.M.	11:30 A.M.
Brazil	9 A.M.	4 P.M.
New York	9 A.M.	4 P.M.

an important driver of the world economy, movement in the U.S. stock market tends to predict movements in other stock markets the following day. So if the U.S. market goes up on Tuesday, the Asian and European stock markets are likely to be up on Wednesday. Yet, because of the timing of the NAV calculation, investors can still buy shares of a fund investing in the Asian and European markets at a NAV that reflects Tuesday's closing prices, giving them a very good chance of earning a short-term profit.

To prevent investors from taking advantage of the time zone gap, fund boards of directors may adjust the prices of non-U.S. securities to reflect movements in U.S. stock prices or other significant events that occur after the foreign markets close. This adjustment is known as *fair valuation*. Funds with substantial holdings in foreign securities almost always have written policies and procedures that require use of fair valuation if market movements exceed a specified trigger, or threshold.

For example, a U.S. fund investing mainly in Japanese stocks might monitor the price of the U.S. Nikkei 225 futures contract. While this contract is traded in Chicago, it's based on an index measuring the performance of stocks on the Tokyo exchange. The pricing committee compares the price of this U.S. futures contract at 4 P.M. Eastern Time to the value of the Nikkei index at the close of the Tokyo Stock Exchange—which was 15 hours earlier. If the price of the futures is higher than the index value by more than a specified percentage—say 2 percent—the fund will use fair valuation. It will raise the valuation of its Japanese holdings by the percentage increase in the price of the futures contract. This higher valuation is an estimate of the value of the Japanese holdings at the close of the U.S.

exchanges and their expected price when the Tokyo markets open three hours later.

Fair valuation can be applied at other times as well. For example, a fund's policies might require fair valuation if trading is suspended in a security—or an entire market—or if there has been a natural disaster overseas that occurred after the close of the local market but before the close of the New York Stock Exchange.

The SEC requires that fund directors review the appropriateness and accuracy of the methods used in fair valuations at least annually, though most boards are continually working with fund managers to refine these procedures. As part of this process, the board may look at *back tests,* which compare the fair valuations used to the next available market price over a period of time. Good fair valuation procedures will minimize the difference between the two.

While fund boards are now focused on getting valuations right for all shareholders, less than a decade ago, the fund industry was shaken by a scandal involving preferential treatment for short-term traders—to the detriment of long-term investors—as explained in "The Favored Few."

THE FAVORED FEW

While regulators demand that all fund shareholders—regardless of the size of their investment—receive equal treatment, at times less scrupulous fund management companies were willing to bend the rules for favored shareholders. This happened in the late 1990s and early 2000s, when many fund complexes allowed some institutions and wealthy individuals to engage in late trading or market timing:

- *Late trading.* Some investors were regularly allowed to enter buy and sell orders in fund shares after 4 P.M.—in some instances as late as 9 P.M. With late trading privileges, these investors could profit from news—such as major company earnings announcements—released after the market close at the expense of other fund investors in the fund. Late trading is illegal.

- *Market timing.* Other investors were allowed to engage in *market timing,* which is the rapid purchase and sale of fund shares. While market timing is not illegal, most fund prospectuses specifically prohibit the practice because, like late trading, market timing imposes costs on the fund shareholders who don't participate in it.

To accommodate market timers, funds have to buy and sell securities more often, leading to increased transaction costs. More importantly, market timers are able to take advantage of the backward pricing in international funds to make short-term profits.

Some fund sponsors had direct knowledge of these practices—a few even required that investors pay for their privileges, usually by agreeing to invest in high-fee funds that generated additional revenue for the management company. Other fund complexes wanted to stop the activity but found that they couldn't. The suspicious trades often came through omnibus accounts maintained by intermediaries, and the fund firms didn't receive enough information to be able to block future purchases by the offenders. (Chapter 13 explains these accounts.) And still other fund management companies simply chose to overlook the suspicious trading.

A scandal broke in 2003 when then–New York Attorney General Eliot Spitzer exposed these practices. Several large fund sponsors were involved; most settled with Spitzer's office and the SEC, agreeing both to pay compensation to affected shareholders and to lower their management fees. Because the problems were so widespread—even a few fund portfolio managers personally engaged in market timing—the reputation of the fund industry was significantly tarnished by the revelations. Many of the affected firms saw assets in their funds decline as investors took their dollars elsewhere.

In response to the scandal:

- The SEC strengthened the regulations governing late trading and market timing, giving fund managers the ability to track these activities even when they occurred through an intermediary.

- Funds were required to appoint a chief compliance officer reporting directly to the board of directors to monitor adherence to these—and all other—laws and regulations.

- Fund managers improved their procedures for detecting the problematic practices.

- More funds imposed hefty redemption fees on short-term trading.

- Most fund boards began using fair valuation procedures—especially for funds investing outside the United States—to eliminate the opportunity to game the system.[3]

KEEPING TRACK OF PORTFOLIO SECURITIES: THE CUSTODIAN

While fund accountants play the lead role in the daily fund NAV calculation, they are not solo performers. One of the key members of the supporting cast is the fund custodian. The 1940 Act requires all funds to protect securities held in the fund's portfolios from mismanagement by hiring an independent custodian that is registered with the SEC. This custodian assumes responsibility for:

- The safekeeping of securities held in the fund's portfolio (see "Safety in Procedures" for a definition)
- Maintaining an accurate inventory of securities
- Processing activity associated with portfolio securities
- Initiating cash movements and monitoring cash balances
- Providing information to the fund accountant for the NAV calculation

In short, the custodian maintains the official list of all the assets held by the fund. The choice of custodian must be approved by the fund's board of directors, and the custodian's fee is usually paid directly by the fund.

SAFETY IN PROCEDURES

Q: What do we mean when we say that a primary role of the custodian is the safekeeping of securities in a mutual fund portfolio?

A: The dictionary defines *safekeeping* as "the process of preserving in safety from harm or loss." A custodian protects the assets in a fund by holding them in a segregated account that is separate from its own assets. The custodian must be financially stable, have a well-trained and appropriately supervised staff, provide adequate technology support for its operations, and comply with written policies and procedures. Finally, a safe operating environment requires knowledge of and strict adherence to securities laws.

A U.S. mutual fund always has a custodian based in the United States. If it invests outside the United States, it will also usually have a local *sub-custodian* in each foreign country it invests in. (See Chapter 16 for more on global custody networks.) Most fund complexes use one of a small number of large banks to manage this global network of custodians. These

TABLE 14.2 Largest Custody Providers (2009)

	Custody Assets ($ trillions)	
	Total	1940 Act Funds Only
BNY Mellon Asset Servicing[4]	$23.0	$2.2
J.P. Morgan	14.9	2.7
State Street Corporation	13.7	4.6
Citi	12.1	1.5
Northern Trust	3.7	0.2
Brown Brothers Harriman	2.3	0.8
U.S. Bancorp Fund Services	1.5	0.5

Source: Source Media, *The 2010 Mutual Fund Service Guide.* Used with the permission of Source Media.

organizations have made substantial investments in technology that streamline the transfer of information and movement of cash among issuers of securities, depositories, funds, and custodians. The pricing of custodian services is highly competitive, so profit margins are thin, which means that reaching critical mass to create economies of scale is essential in this business. Table 14.2 provides a list of the largest custodians.

To boost their profitability, most custodians offer higher-margin ancillary services to complement basic custody. For example, most custody banks can provide fund accounting services, and many fund complexes take advantage of their capabilities here, since combining fund accounting and custody further simplifies the flow of information required for the NAV calculation.

Custodians can provide a series of securities processing services, including:

- *Corporate action processing.* As we saw, the custodian passes on corporate action notifications to the fund accountant. The custodian may also provide research on the specific terms of the corporate action and automated systems for processing them.
- *Income collection.* In addition to keeping track of dividend and interest income due and received, the custodian may provide an income collection service by pursuing past-due payments from issuers.
- *Tax services.* The tax department of the custodian may research any tax issues related to income received by the fund. These can be complex for non-U.S. investments, where taxes may be owed to foreign governments, and for investments other than stocks and bonds.

- *Proxy services.* The custodian, usually through a third-party provider, informs the investment manager when companies in which the fund has invested are holding proxy votes.

Fund managers frequently look to their custodians for cash management services as well. The most common of these include:

- *Cash sweeps.* The custodian can automatically sweep any cash left at the end of the day into a money market fund or other short-term investment fund—often abbreviated as STIF (and pronounced like the slang for a dead body). These services ensure that all the money in a fund has the potential to earn a return.
- *Lines of credit.* The flip side of a fund occasionally having too much cash at the end of the day: unexpected transactions, such as unusually large shareholder redemptions, can result in a negative cash balance. To make sure that they have enough cash to make payments when they come due, funds will normally establish a committed line of credit with their custodian for a fee. Under these arrangements, the custodian will lend money to the fund to cover short-term cash needs.
- *Securities lending.* As we learned in Chapter 12, funds can earn extra income by lending securities to other investors, frequently hedge funds, who want to profit on a price decline through a short sale or use them in other trading strategies. The custodian will work with the fund manager to identify securities that can reasonably be made available for lending and arrange the transaction with the borrower. The custodian also collects collateral from the borrower—money that is given back when the securities are returned—and invests that collateral in short-term investments through a STIF.

    While securities lending is generally seen as a low-risk way for funds to earn additional income, the credit crisis showed that it is not 100 percent safe. Borrowers can go bankrupt, making it difficult to reclaim, or *recall,* the securities that have been loaned. And STIFs are not guaranteed, even though they are generally managed by banks. Many of these funds were heavily invested in asset-backed securities that plunged in value in 2008. While prices of some of these securities eventually rebounded as credit markets stabilized, others—such as those back by subprime mortgages—suffered permanent losses. Some STIFs also had investments in Lehman Brothers, which went bankrupt. In response to these problems, most fund custodians upgraded the quality of short-term securities that could be held by their STIFs.

A CRITICAL LINK: INVESTMENT OPERATIONS

A key role in portfolio processing is played by the investment operations area—also known as the *investment back office*—which handles all the operation support for a portfolio management team. Investment operations professionals must deal with a high level of complexity in three ways:

1. They are responsible for many different types of accounts. A portfolio team may oversee separately managed accounts, collective trust funds, hedge funds, single client accounts, and offshore funds, such as European UCITS funds—all in addition to 1940 Act mutual funds. Each type of account is governed by different regulations, and each individual fund will have its own set of investment policies and restrictions.
2. Investment operations will keep track of many different types of securities, some with complex features. Derivatives pose particular challenges. Funds using derivatives may have to post collateral or to make or receive payments based on market movements during the term of the contract. Many of these instruments are customized to the particular needs of a fund, and investment operations must stay on top of all their unique features. Because the complexity of the derivatives market increased the strain on the financial system during the credit crisis, the Dodd-Frank financial reform legislation passed in 2010 encourages greater use of standardized derivatives—which might help reduce the stress on investment operations professionals as well.
3. Finally, investment operations must interact with many different parties, including the trading desk, fund accounting, the custodian, and the broker-dealers who execute transactions for the fund. If the fund uses derivatives extensively, it may also have a prime broker, which is a broker-dealer that centralizes settlement and collateral for those instruments. Investment operations will help to coordinate the work of all these service providers and serves as a critical link among them.

Investment operations has historically been part of the portfolio management organization, but fund managers have increasingly been choosing to outsource this work, either to their custodians or to other specialized service providers. The track record of these outsourced arrangements is mixed. Many fund managers have built costly systems tailored to the unique requirements of the funds they advise. This high degree of customization can make it challenging to transition to the common platform of a third party provider.

The investment operations area plays a critical role in trade settlement, the exchange of money and securities that takes place after a trade has been completed. The investment back office is also in charge of portfolio recordkeeping.

Trade Settlement: Completing Buy and Sell Transactions

Investment operations works closely with the fund manager's trading desk to ensure that trades are settled properly. As we saw in Chapter 8, the trading desk is responsible for executing portfolio buys and sells upon instructions from the portfolio manager. Once the trading desk has done its job, the investment back office takes over, arranging for the actual exchange of cash and securities in a process known as *trade settlement*.

Today, trades in U.S. stocks are finalized in three days. The transaction takes place on the trade date, or $T+0$ or just T. Trades are settled, and money and stocks change hands, three days later on $T+3$, or *trade date plus three*. Between $T+0$ and $T+3$, all the parties involved in the transaction exchange information and resolve any discrepancies. This process is displayed graphically in Figure 14.2. Let's take a closer look at the communication flow.

Trade date (T+0). On the day of the trade, the market center starts the settlement process by determining whether all the details of the trade submitted by the broker on the buy side of the trade are the same as those submitted by the broker on the sell side. If they are, the market center considers the trade *matched* and sends a record of it to the National Securities Clearing Corporation or NSCC, which is a subsidiary of DTCC. (Remember from Chapter 13 that DTCC is a central depository that keeps the records of most of the securities held in the United States.)

T+1 and T+2. Over the next two days, the various parties exchange information. Investment operations gives the broker-dealer delivery details: the exact fund or funds that have bought the shares, the price that each fund paid and the name of the custodian. This same information is given to the custodian.

Once the broker-dealer receives the delivery details, it sends these to NSCC in the form of a confirmation or *confirm*, for short. NSCC then routes this confirmation to the investment back office, the custodian, and the broker-dealer. The confirm says, in effect, "This is what we at NSCC believe all of you have agreed upon regarding this trade." Both the buyer and the seller must *affirm* this confirmation before settlement can occur.

Occasionally, one of the parties to a trade will not recognize the trade order and will *DK* (don't know) the trade. Usually, this is a problem with

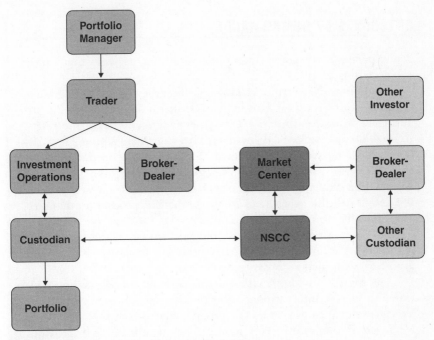

FIGURE 14.2 Parties Involved in Trade Settlement

missing information, although there could be a more serious mistake with the trade itself. If the problem is not resolved in a timely fashion, the trade will fail and will be *unwound,* or reversed. To reduce the number of fails, the securities industry is working to increase the automation of the settlement process. See "Untouched by Human Hands" for more.

T+3. Settlement date! NSCC transfers ownership of the securities, and the custodian for the buyer makes payment to the seller.

Settlement of trades in other securities involves a similar process, though often under a different time frame. Derivatives generally have settlement procedures that are unique to each instrument.

Portfolio Recordkeeping

In addition to trade settlement, the investment operations group is responsible for maintaining portfolio records and producing reports on holdings and trading activity. Portfolio managers use these reports for making investment decisions.

UNTOUCHED BY HUMAN HANDS

Many parties involved in trade settlement = many ways that things can go wrong.

To minimize the errors—and the risk that they'll have to reimburse clients for those errors—firms in the securities industry are working to automate the trade affirmation and settlement process to create *straight through processing,* or STP, for all types of securities. When STP works as designed, the two trade desks on each side of the transaction send out trade details in a specified format. For global equities, this is a Financial Information eXchange protocol or FIX message. If the parties agree on the details, all the other steps in the settlement process are handled electronically. Only exceptions require human intervention.

Not surprisingly, STP is technology-intensive. Many investment managers have turned to third party vendors for platforms that integrate STP with their recordkeeping systems.

The topic is so complex that there's an industry association dedicated to it—the International Securities Association for Institutional Trade Communication, or ISITC (pronounced "ee-*sit*-zee"). The Asset Managers Forum is also very involved in this effort. AMF provides a forum for investment managers, broker-dealers, and custodians to discuss operations issues. It's affiliated with SIFMA—the Securities Industry and Financial Markets Association—which is the primary trade association for broker-dealers. More information about these organizations is available at www.isitc.org, www.assetmanager.com, and www.sifma.org.

- *Portfolio accounting.* The investment operations team ensures that trades and corporate actions are properly reflected in the internal portfolio accounting system, by reconciling these holdings data in the fund manager's internal system to the custodian's records. Since many fund managers work with more than one custodian, this can be a massive job—one that can be difficult to automate completely.

   Why not just use the custodian's records for making investment decisions? One reason is that the custodian only enters trades on the day after they occur or $T+1$—while portfolio managers need more up-to-date information when they enter buy and sell orders. Trades are entered into portfolio accounting systems on the trade date, or $T+0$.

Portfolio managers may also need reports combining positions from funds held at multiple custodians.

■ *Data management.* The investment back office maintains detailed information on all fund positions in what is known as the *securities master file*. The record for each security will include, at the very least, the security type (such as stock or bond), issuer, country, and industry. For fixed income securities, the securities master will also—at a minimum—contain coupon rate, maturity date, and par value. The data in the master file are used to create portfolio-positioning reports.

■ *Portfolio compliance systems.* Investment operations play a key role in helping to ensure that funds comply with securities regulations and prospectus policies. Most fund managers have two compliance monitoring systems—a *pre-trade* compliance system that reviews proposed trades before they even reach the trade desk and a *post-trade* system that periodically reviews portfolio positions.

For example, if a bond fund's prospectus limits holdings of bonds rated BB or lower to 20 percent of assets, a pre-trade compliance system will reject a proposed purchase that would push total holdings of these lower-rated bonds above 20 percent. If the value of these holdings is above 20 percent of assets for any reason, this will be detected by post-trade compliance monitoring. The compliance team then determines the reason why the position is above the limit. It might be the result of changes in market prices, perhaps because lower-rated bonds in general are doing relatively well. No further action is needed in those circumstances—other than highlighting the weighting to the portfolio manager and the chief investment officer. But the position could be the result of an error—maybe the wrong credit rating was entered for a bond bought recently, so that pre-trade compliance did not block the purchase. In these circumstances, the trade may need to be reversed. See "When Compliance Monitoring Fails" for more.

Good compliance monitoring requires good data management. In this example, to monitor the percentage invested in lower-rated bonds, the compliance system must contain accurate market values and the most recent credit ratings for all the securities portfolios. The investment operations area is charged with locating sources for all the required information and for ensuring that it remains current. Since the compliance system must often monitor compliance for multiple limits for dozens of portfolios and thousands of securities, the data updates must be automated as much as possible.

WHEN COMPLIANCE MONITORING FAILS

What happens when compliance monitoring fails, and a fund invests in something it shouldn't?

Step 1: The fund manager must put the fund back in compliance by selling the problematic security.

Step 2: The fund manager must inform the fund's board of directors of errors above a certain size. (The board determines the reporting threshold.) The fund manager will explain why the error occurred and what steps it has taken to prevent a recurrence.

Step 3: If the security was sold at a loss, the fund manager will normally reimburse the fund for that loss.[5] For a large fund, the payment can be quite substantial. And if the error resulted in the gain? The fund usually gets to keep the profit.

Since compliance errors can only cost money, fund managers work hard to prevent them through pre-trade compliance or catch them quickly in post-trade review.

- *Client reporting.* The investment back office prepares an extensive package of reports for fund boards of directors and other clients. These reports provide detailed information on a fund's investment positioning, activities, and results.
- *Collateral management.* Collateral management also falls within the purview of investment operations. Funds that sell stock short or that engage in certain transactions using derivatives may need to set aside, or *post*, securities in the portfolio as collateral to ensure that they fulfill their obligations in these transactions. At the same time, funds may require that the counterparty on the other side of a repurchase agreement, stock loan, or other derivatives transaction post collateral that protects them. The investment back office handles the extensive paperwork related to these collateral arrangements and then ensures that collateral is actually posted in accordance with their terms. Many fund managers outsource this complex function to their custodians.

BEHIND THE SCENES: THE INDEPENDENT AUDITOR

The independent auditor is not an active player in all of this activity, but still plays an important role behind the scenes. The auditor reviews the financial statements and confirms that all of the fund's service providers are using appropriate procedures to produce the information that is used in them.

Financial Statement Review

The independent auditor provides an opinion on the accuracy of a fund's financial statements. The auditor is hired by the board of directors. Most boards select one of the major accounting firms as the auditor.

The audit opinion is published in the annual report in a letter to shareholders called—not surprisingly—an *opinion letter*. A fund always seeks an *unqualified* opinion, which means that its auditor believes that the financial statements accurately represent the assets of the fund and that procedures for calculating NAV are adequate. A *qualified* opinion can mean big trouble—forcing a fund to stop the sale of its shares. As a result, service providers work hard to anticipate auditor requirements and thereby earn an unqualified opinion.

The content of the opinion letter is the output of the annual audit, which involves a rigorous examination of a fund's records and procedures. The audit looks at five major areas:

1. *Investments.* The audit firm begins with a review of the securities holdings included in the financial statements. This auditor confirms that this list—which includes trades that have been executed but not yet settled—exactly matches the custodian's records. The SEC also requires that the auditor verify securities valuations by independently obtaining prices for all holdings and comparing these to prices used by the fund accountant in the NAV calculation. Finally, the auditor reviews the fund manager's compliance procedures to determine whether they are adequate to ensure that the fund adheres to all regulatory and prospectus restrictions.
2. *Income and gains.* After investments, income: the auditor checks to see whether interest income, dividend income, and realized capital gains have been recorded properly in the fund's financial records.
3. *Accruals and expenses.* Next, the auditor looks at expense records to determine if they have been charged to the fund—and allocated to share classes—in accordance with the investment advisory agreement and prospectus. The auditor also confirms that these payments conform to the terms of the contracts that the board of directors has signed with service providers.
4. *Taxes.* The auditor confirms that the fund has passed all of the IRS tests that allow it qualify for pass-through status. (Turn back to Chapter 2 if you need a refresher on these tests, which relate to ownership of voting

securities, diversification, distribution of income earned, and qualifying income.)

5. *Shareholders' equity.* Finally, the audit firm checks to see whether the fund's transfer agent has used the correct NAV when processing purchases and sales of fund shares.

Service Organization Reporting

As part of the annual audit, the auditor confirms that the service providers have internal controls that allow the fund to have confidence in the work they do. ("Control Environment" provides an introduction to internal controls.) Today, to help make this part of the audit easier, most service providers hire an audit firm to review their controls and express an opinion on their adequacy. The service provider's auditor does this as part of a standardized report that the service provider then sends to its clients. Before these standardized reports became widely accepted, each fund would have to do its own assessment of each service provider.

Auditors prepare one of two standardized reports.

1. Service providers working solely in the United States generally complete a Statement on Standards for Attestation Engagements 16 or SSAE 16
2. Service providers with a global presence may choose an Internal Standard on Assurance Engagement 3402 or ISAE 3402

Both replace the Statement on Auditing Standards 70, or SAS 70, which is being phased out after mid-2011. There are two types of each report: *Type A* looks only at the service provider's controls, while *Type B* also reviews past transactions to determine whether controls have actually been followed.

These service organization reports include:

- A description of the service provider's controls
- The auditor's opinion on whether the controls are suitably designed to achieve the results desired
- A summary of the testing that the auditor did to confirm the effectiveness of the controls (for Type B reports)
- A description of the risks that might prevent the service provider from discharging its duties as expected
- A written attestation from management providing a formal confirmation of its responsibility for the controls

Fund boards of directors can use these reports to evaluate the reliability of a service provider that it considers hiring to perform work for the fund.

CONTROL ENVIRONMENT

When auditors talk about *internal controls,* they're referring to processes that are designed to ensure that an organization is able to:

- Operate efficiently and effectively
- Produce reliable financial reports
- Comply with relevant laws and regulations

Internal controls may put in place by the board of directors, management, or other personnel.

According to COSO—the Committee of Sponsoring Organizations of the Treadway Commission—which is the thought leader on these issues, internal controls have five components:

1. *Control environment.* The control environment is the overall tone of an organization. In a control-conscious organization, everyone—starting with the members of the board of directors—is concerned with integrity and ethical values.
2. *Risk assessment.* The organization has identified and analyzed the factors that might prevent it from achieving its objectives.
3. *Control activities.* Throughout the organization, there are policies and procedures in place to ensure that management directives are carried out.
4. *Information and communication.* Important information is captured and communicated to the individuals who need it to carry out their responsibilities. Everyone within the organization is aware of his role in the system of internal controls.
5. *Monitoring.* The organization evaluates the effectiveness of its control system. Serious deficiencies are reported to top management and the board.

For more on internal controls, see www.coso.org.

CHAPTER SUMMARY

Maintaining accurate fund portfolio records is a complicated process that involves many parties—who must regularly exchange information with one another. The fund accountant is responsible for calculating the NAV. In the early part of the day, the fund accountant records the prior day's trading activity, accruals for expenses, and receipt of income in the fund's books. After the New York Stock Exchange closes at 4 P.M. Eastern Time, the valuation of fund securities is completed. The fund accountant then finalizes the calculation of the NAV and reports it to NASDAQ. This process is normally completed by 5:50 P.M.

The fund's board of directors establishes policies for the valuation of fund holdings. Each type of security is valued using a different methodology. When a fund's board believes that none of the standard methods reflects the true value of the position, it may elect to apply fair valuation—using an estimate of the security's value. Mutual funds use forward pricing, which means that investors who want to buy or sell fund shares always get the next available NAV. When funds don't use forward pricing—and use backward pricing instead—investors who are watching the latest market movements may profit at the expense of long-term shareholders in the fund. In 2003, a scandal erupted in the mutual fund industry when it was discovered that certain investors were profiting from late trading or market timing—sometimes with the support of fund management companies. To prevent similar problems in the future, funds now routinely use fair valuation, especially for overseas holdings, and enforce strict rules against frequent purchases and redemptions of fund shares.

The custodian is responsible for the safekeeping of the fund's portfolio holdings and maintains the official record of positions. Custodians often provide other services to funds, such as securities processing services and cash management services. Custodians also arrange for the lending of securities in fund portfolios to investors effecting short sales and other trading strategies.

Investment operations provides support to the portfolio management team—handling many different types of accounts and securities—and provides a critical link among other service providers. Investment operations works closely with the fund manager's trading desk to ensure that trades are settled properly. Trades in U.S. stocks settle in three days. Between trade date and settlement date, all the parties to the transaction involve compare information and resolve discrepancies. The investment operations area is also responsible for maintaining the data used by portfolio managers for making investment decisions. These same data are used in the systems that ensure that all investments are made in compliance with relevant rules and regulations.

The independent auditor reviews the fund's financial statements in an annual audit and provides an opinion on their accuracy. Auditors also assess the adequacy of the controls of service provider organizations and report on them in a standardized format.

CHAPTER 15

The Financial Dynamics of the Fund Management Industry

In all of the preceding chapters, we have looked mainly at mutual funds themselves: their basic features, how their investments are managed, how they are sold, and the services they provide to shareholders. In this chapter, we turn our attention to the management companies responsible for day-to-day fund investments and operations, examining the financial dynamics of both the individual firms and the industry they operate in.

As a prelude, let's review the difference between a mutual fund and a fund management company, by looking at the diagram of a fund's structure from Chapter 2 presented here again as Figure 15.1. You'll recall that mutual funds are unusual corporations because they generally have no employees. Rather than have a large staff, a fund gets its work done by signing contracts with service providers; the primary role of a fund's board of directors is to negotiate these contracts and monitor service provider performance under them.

The most significant contract the board signs is with the management company, the firm that usually lends its brand name to the fund and has often provided the seed capital at its creation. The management company is responsible for investment management, normally using the expertise of its own investment adviser, although it may at times hire a third party, called an *investment subadviser,* to handle all or part of this function. It arranges for distribution of shares of the fund, either directly to investors or working with intermediaries. Finally, it coordinates other needed services, such as shareholder servicing through the transfer agent. When legally permitted, some management companies will handle these services themselves, though they are just as likely to outsource them to specialized providers. Profits are derived from the fees earned for providing each of these services, with the management fee being the most important driver of profitability.

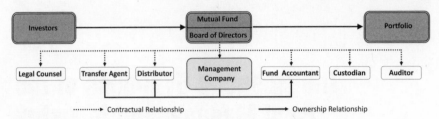

FIGURE 15.1 Typical Mutual Fund Service Provider Relationships

Managing mutual funds has historically been a quite profitable business. In the five years ending 2009, the nine publicly traded mutual fund sponsors with market capitalizations over $2 billion earned a net profit margin of 14 percent on average, despite substantial losses incurred by two of the companies during the credit crisis. Return on equity during this period was even higher, at 19 percent.[1]

No wonder, then, that many firms are interested in entering the mutual fund business—either by starting up new fund families or, more often, by acquiring existing managers. This has led to a rapidly changing composition of firms within the asset management industry.

This chapter reviews:

- The expenses incurred by mutual fund shareholders and their relationship to management company profitability
- The controversy over the level of management fees and the level of competition within the industry
- Mergers and acquisitions in the fund industry over the last decade

EXPENSES FOR FUND INVESTORS

Shareholders pay various charges when they invest through a mutual fund. We've explained most of these fees in detail in our earlier chapters, but let's summarize them here and review their impact on the management company's revenue. Table 15.1 provides an overview of these expenses, listing the type of expense, whether it is paid directly from the shareholder's account or indirectly through the fund, and which entity receives the fee.

The last column in the table indicates whether an item is included in the expense ratio, a statistic that funds are required to disclose in their prospectuses and shareholder reports. (Turn back to Chapter 3 for a refresher on these documents.) To compute this ratio, funds add together the expenses indicated in the chart, then divide by average net assets to arrive at a

TABLE 15.1 Expenses Incurred by Fund Investors

Expense Type	Paid by	Paid to	Expense Ratio?
Distribution charges (optional)			
Front-end sales load	Shareholder	Distributor; reallowed to intermediaries	No
Back-end sales load or contingent deferred sales charge	Shareholder	Distributor	No
12b-1 fee	Fund	Distributor; part may be reallowed to intermediaries	Yes
Securities transaction fees			
Commissions; ECN and SEC fees	Fund	Broker-dealer	No
Shareholder transaction fees (optional)			
Purchase and redemption fees	Shareholder	Fund	No
Service fees (IRA custody, small accounts, wire transfers)	Shareholder or Fund	Transfer agent	No
Fund services charges			
Transfer agency fee*	Fund	Transfer agent and subtransfer agents	Yes
Shareholder communication expenses* (printing, postage, proxy solicitation)	Fund	Service provider	Yes
Administrative services*	Fund	Fund administrator	Yes
Registration fees*	Fund	SEC, states	Yes
Professional services fees (audit, legal)*	Fund	Service provider	Yes
Custodian fee*	Fund	Custodian	Yes
Board of directors fees and expenses*	Fund	Directors	Yes
Management fee			
Management fee	Fund	Management company	Yes

*May be incorporated into an all-inclusive management fee.

percentage figure. Because the SEC requires that every fund calculate the expense ratio in exactly the same way, investors can easily compare costs across funds.

Fund expenses fall into five categories: distribution charges, securities transaction costs, shareholder transaction fees, fund services charges, and the management fee. We look at each in turn.

Distribution charges. Investors may pay sales loads when they buy or sell fund shares; they may also pay annual 12b-1 fees that cover ongoing service or distribution costs. These charges are used in different combinations to create a choice of share classes. Investors pay sales loads directly and 12b-1 fees indirectly as part of fund expenses.

Distribution fees can be substantial for a fund sold through intermediaries, but they're not a significant source of profit to fund management companies. That's largely because these fees are used to compensate the intermediary that has made the sale. In fact, the bulk of front-end sales loads are immediately passed on or *reallowed* to the intermediary. For most classes of shares, all or almost all of 12b-1 fees are also reallowed. (The notable exception is Class B shares: the fund's distributor retains a significant portion of the 12b-1 fees for this class so it can recoup the upfront commission payments made to the intermediary at the time of the sale.) The distributor does keep any back-end contingent deferred sales charges received, not just for Class B but for all classes of shares. These charges are in place to ensure that the distributor's recovers its upfront sales costs even if the investor redeems after holding shares for only a short period. (See Chapter 10 for more on share classes and intermediary compensation.)

Another reason why distribution fees are not an important source of revenues to the management company: sales loads have been declining over time. The maximum allowable front-end load dropped from 7.9 percent in 1980 to 5.3 percent in 2009. The decline in *actual* sales loads paid has been even more dramatic, falling from 5.3 percent to only 1.0 percent over the same period. In fact, according to Strategic Insight, sales charges were waived on almost 70 percent of the sales of mutual funds imposing front-end loads in 2008 and 2009. Intermediaries are now more likely to charge clients a separate asset-based fee that does not involve the fund manager.

If a fund is sold directly to shareholders, the management company does retain all of the distribution fees. But the dollars involved here are usually quite small, since funds sold in the direct channel generally do not impose sales loads, while the 12b-1 fees for these funds are low—or even nonexistent. Moreover, these 12b-1 fees are much less than the cost of building and maintaining a direct distribution system.

In sum, distribution is not a key driver of profitability for mutual fund managers. In fact, when all the costs of marketing are considered, distribution is usually a cost center for fund management companies. It's only a means of increasing assets under management and, therefore, management fee revenue. As we discussed in Chapter 10, distribution can be quite profitable for third parties that sell funds from many different sponsors along with other investment vehicles. But fund management companies generally do not view distribution as a source of profit.

Securities transaction fees. Funds may pay transaction fees whenever they buy or sell securities. These include:

- Commissions paid to brokers for executing trades in stocks (if a broker is used)
- Fees paid to electronic communication networks
- SEC fees imposed by the exchanges on each transaction

These fees are deducted from the value of the fund's investments and do not appear in the income statement as an expense. While these fees are paid directly by the fund, they may provide an indirect benefit to the management company. As we discussed, broker-dealers often provide research services to the investment managers who direct trading business to them. Chapter 8 discusses securities trading in detail.

Shareholder transaction fees. Shareholders may pay additional fees directly to the fund when they engage in specific types of transactions. For example, some index funds may charge a fee whenever an investor buys or sells its shares; this fee is designed to recoup the costs of trading in the underlying securities. Other funds impose redemption fees whenever fund shares are sold within a short period after their purchase—usually defined as within either 30 or 90 days; these fees discourage market timing, or frequent trading. Since shareholders pay both of these fees directly to the fund, they do not materially benefit the management company.

In addition, as we learned in Chapter 13, many transfer agents charge for maintaining certain types of accounts—individual retirement accounts or accounts with small balances, for example—or for providing special services, such as wire transfers. These fees may be paid directly by the shareholder or may be included as part of fund expenses. In either case, they are meant to cover the higher costs of these services and generate little or no profit for the transfer agent.

Fund services charges. Shareholders indirectly pay a fund's costs of providing services to its shareholders and maintaining its corporate status. These charges include:

- The transfer agent fee, which is usually the largest component in this category. A portion of this fee may be paid to subtransfer agents. See

Chapter 13 for a description of the role of the transfer agent and sub-transfer agent and the structure of this fee.

- Shareholder communication expenses related to the printing and mailing of required disclosure documents such as the prospectus and shareholder reports. If the fund is holding a proxy vote, this category might include the cost of hiring a proxy solicitation firm.
- The cost of administrative services related to keeping fund records as discussed in Chapter 14.
- Registration fees paid to the SEC and state securities commissions.
- Professional fees for the services of auditors and lawyers.
- Custodian fees for the safekeeping of securities, reviewed in Chapter 14.
- Expenses related to the board of directors.

These fees are paid by the fund to the organization that provides the service. In some cases, that provider must be a third party. The fund's auditor, for example, must be independent of the fund manager. But in other instances, the management company may be the service provider, either directly or through a subsidiary. For example, many fund management companies provide transfer agent or administrative services through affiliates, though they may outsource a portion of these functions to unaffiliated specialists.

Not all funds charge separately for these services. Some fund groups include a portion of these services in an all-inclusive management fee that shifts the risks (and rewards) of controlling total expenses from shareholders to the management company. In 2008, 19 of the 100 largest fund companies had all-inclusive fees on at least some of their funds, generally money market funds.

Management fee. While a management company may make a profit providing specific services to a fund, those profits are generally quite small relative to those from the management fee. Table 15.2 shows the annual expenses for the hypothetical Avon Hill Stock Fund, a $6 billion actively managed stock fund distributed through the intermediary channel. (This table includes only those costs that are part of the expense ratio.)

As you can see, the management fee is usually the largest component of a fund's ongoing expenses. It specifically pays for investment management services from portfolio managers who work for either the management company or an outside subadviser. And it more generally compensates the management company for the use of its brand name, for taking the risk of setting up the fund and for organizing its distribution. It is normally the main source of a mutual fund management company's earnings.

Management fees are expressed in basis points, representing a percentage of a fund's assets. Since investment management services are included

TABLE 15.2 Annual Expenses for the Avon Hill Stock Fund

Expense Type	Amount ($000)	Percent of Total
12b-1 distribution fees	12,723	22%
Transfer agent fees	9,937	17%
Shareholder communications expenses	3,504	6%
Administrative services, including fund accounting	1,696	3%
Registration fees	183	<1%
Professional fees	326	<1%
Custodian fees	135	<1%
Board of director expenses	189	<1%
Total services charges	15,970	27%
Management fee	29,722	51%
Total	58,415	100%

in the management fee, the level of these fees varies by the type of assets the fund invests in. Equity funds have the highest fees on average, while money market funds have the lowest. Table 15.3 shows the range of management fees from the bottom of the third quartile to the top of the second quartile at the end of 2008 (excluding the top 25 percent and bottom 25 percent of fees). It also shows the median fee.

For many funds, the basis point charge declines once assets reach a certain level, called a *breakpoint*. For example, an equity fund might have a management fee of 50 bp for the first $500 million of fund assets and 45 bp for fund assets above that threshold. The breakpoint may be based on just that fund's assets, on total assets in the entire fund complex or on the assets of a subset of the funds within the family, such as all equity funds. Breakpoint pricing is extremely common; Lipper reports that, at the end of 2008, more than 80 percent of the 100 largest funds used that design.

TABLE 15.3 Fund Management Fees in Basis Points (2008)

Type of Fund	Fee Range for 2nd and 3rd Quartile	Median Fee
Stock funds	65 to 100 bp	80 bp
Bond funds	45 to 62 bp	53 bp
Money market funds	20 to 45 bp	27 bp

Source: Lipper.

Given the large dollar amounts involved and the profitability of the companies that earn them, the level of management fees has attracted considerable attention.

MANAGEMENT FEE REVENUE: THE DEBATE

Why so much concern about fees? Because fees can have a significant impact on shareholder returns, especially when compounded over time. Figure 15.2 illustrates this effect. Suppose that an investor puts $100,000 in three identical equity funds—identical, that is, except for the fees they charge. One has an annual expense ratio of 0.5 percent, while the other two have annual expense ratios of 1.0 percent and 1.5 percent. If all three portfolios generated an average return of 7 percent per year before fees, the portfolios would produce net returns after fees of 6.5 percent, 6.0 percent, and 5.5 percent, respectively. At the end of a 20-year period, the $100,000 would be worth $425,000 if invested in the fund with the lowest fees and just $352,000 in the fund with the highest fees. That's a difference between the highest and lowest net return of $73,000, or over 70 percent of the original investment, solely due to fund expenses. The differential is illustrated in Figure 15.2.

The impact of fund expenses is more than just theoretical. A recent study by Morningstar found that expense ratios were good predictors of fund performance. For the five years ending 2010, the lowest-cost funds in every asset class had, on average, consistently better returns than the highest-cost funds.[2]

Because of the critical impact of fees, the SEC wants to make sure that investors are fully aware in advance of all the charges they'll incur in

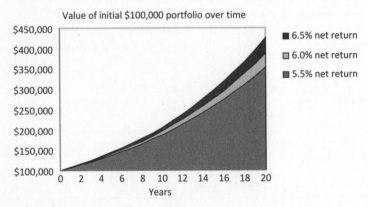

FIGURE 15.2   The Impact of Expenses

connection with a mutual fund they may buy. Expense information must be displayed prominently in virtually all material that is presented to shareholders and prospective buyers, including the summary prospectus, the statutory prospectus, shareholder reports, and advertisements.

This information is presented in many different ways so that investors can see the full expense picture from many different angles: fees are shown as a percentage of investment, as a dollar amount, and as a component of performance. Specifically, funds must provide:

- The maximum front-end sales load, if any, along with details on how investors can reduce those sales charges by taking advantage of break-points
- The maximum contingent deferred sales charge, if any, and details on its application
- The fund's annual expense ratio, broken down into management fee, 12b-1 fee (if any), and other expenses
- The actual expenses paid during the year on a $1,000 investment in a fund
- The expenses that hypothetically would be paid during the year on that $1,000 investment if it generated a 5 percent return
- The expenses that hypothetically would be paid over 1, 3, 5, and 10 years on a $10,000 investment that generated a 5 percent annual return
- Fund investment returns that reflect both the payment of a front-end load and the imposition of a back-end contingent deferred sales charge, if any

To help investors find low-cost alternatives, FINRA provides an online fund analyzer that allows consumers to screen funds based on their expense ratio, along with other criteria. This tool is available at http://apps.finra.org/fundanalyzer/1/fa.aspx.

The Critics' Case

Yet despite all these disclosures, industry detractors believe that fees are still too high. In their eyes, fund expenses may have come down in recent years (as shown in Figure 15.3), but they haven't come down enough.[3] The critics make their case with three principal arguments:

Negative 1: Insufficient benefit from economies of scale. The growth in industry assets alone should have led to even lower fees, the critics believe. They argue that the industry has enormous economies of scale, meaning that expenses rise a lot more slowly than revenues. "It doesn't cost much more to manage a $7 billion fund than it does to manage a $1 billion fund," they

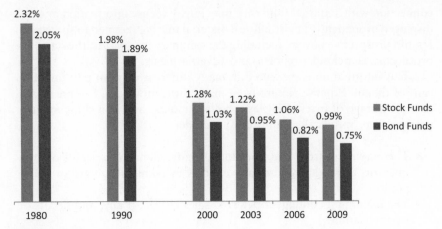

FIGURE 15.3 Total Shareholder Costs for Stock and Bond Funds
Source: Investment Company Institute.

claim, "So why does the industry charge shareholders seven times as much to manage the larger fund?" (Remember that management fees are based on assets.)

Negative 2: Other investors pay less. And, say the critics, "It's not just that management companies haven't passed on their savings to their mutual fund shareholders, they're actually charging other clients significantly less." (Fund managers often run accounts for other large institutions, such as government and corporate pension plans, as well as for mutual funds.) One much-cited 2001 study found that, on average, management companies charged their public pension plans half as much as they charged mutual funds, expressed as a percentage of assets under management.[4]

Negative 3: Noncompetitive market. Underlying both of these complaints is a more basic concern: that the market for mutual funds is not competitive. Critics claim that investors are either unaware of the fees they're paying or unable to switch to lower-cost funds because they'd incur capital gains taxes or back-end loads—and can present academic research to support this view.[5]

At the same time the critics argue, the investors' representatives, the members of the fund's board of directors, are in the pocket of the management company and not diligent in driving down fees. They take a check-the-box approach to reviewing fees, without vigorously fighting for shareholder interests. For evidence, they point to the dearth of performance fee structures, as discussed in "Paying for Performance." (Also see Chapter 2 for a review of the debate regarding fund boards.)

PAYING FOR PERFORMANCE

Another concern expressed about mutual fund fees: that they don't align the interests of the investor and the management company. And it's true that fund managers generally don't get paid specifically for producing the thing that shareholders care about most—investment performance. In fact, fewer than 250 of the 7,600-plus funds in existence at the end of 2008 paid a *performance fee* according to Lipper. Performance fees have been used mainly with equity funds.

Performance fees increase the management fee if fund performance exceeds that of a benchmark index or peer group, and they reduce the management fee if performance falls short. Note that the SEC requires that mutual fund performance fees have this symmetry, providing a reward for good performance with an identical penalty for poor performance. (Hedge funds, as we saw in Chapter 12, have a very different performance fee structure. The manager of a hedge fund usually is paid a base fee plus 20 percent of the fund's realized gains, but do not absorb 20 percent of the fund's realized losses.)

If performance fees so perfectly align the interest of the fund's manager and its shareholders, why are they so rarely used? It's partly because fund managers don't like the additional volatility in their revenues. They note that their income already depends on performance since a fund's sales—and, therefore, the management fees based on the assets determined by the level of sales—are driven by recent results. On the other hand, their costs don't vary much with performance.

At the same time, if the fee uses an index as a benchmark, it can be very difficult to actually earn positive performance fees, since fund performance—net of fees—is being compared to index performance before fees. Finally, if the manager does well and earns a performance fee, they could, ironically, be penalized by cost-conscious investors for having a higher expense ratio, since performance fees must be included in the calculation.

One other drawback: Performance fees can change portfolio manager behavior. A fund manager who is already earning a high performance fee may be too conservative to protect existing gains. On the other hand, a fund manager deep in negative territory has nothing to lose from taking a lot of risk.

According to the critics, power in the industry is highly concentrated. They note that at the end of 2009, the top 10 fund families managed over half of industry assets, and the top 25 percent managed almost three-quarters. And firms are consolidating at a rapid pace.

The Rebuttal

The mutual fund industry's defenders take issue with all of these points, contending that the industry is, in fact, extremely competitive. Their arguments include:

Positive 1: Fees decline with increasing assets. First of all, fees do decline as the level of assets increase: The prevalence of breakpoints in management fee contracts makes that a certainty. But the benefit to shareholders is not apparent when looking at an entire asset class, because the mix of funds changes over time. For example, within the equity category, many of the new fund launches in recent years have been international stock funds, which are more costly to manage and usually have higher fees than U.S. stock funds. So, for equity funds on average, a decline in fees on U.S. stock funds will be offset by the increased representation of higher-fee international funds. Because of this changing mix, comparisons over time can be tricky.

Positive 2: No fee discrimination. Industry defenders contend that evaluating fees paid by mutual funds against those paid by institutional investors is comparing apples and oranges, because the two types of investors are contracting for very different services. Institutional investors hire money managers to make investment decisions only; they take care of portfolio administration themselves. Mutual fund management companies, on the other hand, take on all of these functions for fund shareholders. A study from the Investment Company Institute found that when only investment advisory services are considered, mutual funds pay fees that are remarkably similar to those paid by institutional investors.[6] And in a recent decision on the *Jones v. Harris* case involving mutual fund fees, the U.S. Supreme Court recognized that the services provided to different types of clients may not be comparable.

Positive 3: Competitive market for funds. More importantly, the market for mutual funds is very competitive, say the industry's defenders. There's lots of evidence that investors, management companies, and boards of directors all pay close attention to fees.

- Investors focus their purchases in funds with lower fees. As we've already learned, they're unlikely to pay a front-end load. And some studies show that they appear to be sensitive to annual expense ratios as well.

In fact, Investment Company Institute analysis of the 10 years ending with 2009 found that 79 percent of investor cash flow into stock funds went into funds with expense ratios in the lowest quartile.

- Management companies frequently take steps to ensure that the annual expense ratio does not get too high and become a deterrent to new investors. To do this, they may waive a portion of the management fee; in some instances, they may even pay for, or subsidize, other operating expenses. Fund sponsors often do this for smaller equity funds that have not yet achieved economies of scale, so that service fees are still high as a percentage of assets. It is also common practice for money market funds and some higher quality fixed income funds, especially during periods of low interest rates; for these funds, the management company will adjust its fee until the fund yield is competitive.
- Fund boards of directors frequently negotiate breakpoints in management fees, and many boards today require a cap on fund expenses. Under these caps, if annual expenses exceed a certain limit, the management company must reduce its fee or even subsidize some of the fund's other expenses until the cap is reached.

And, overall, the industry just isn't concentrated enough to be anything less than competitive. One of the best-known ways of measuring the competitiveness of industry structure is with the Herfindahl-Hirschman Index. ("Trying Not to Concentrate" has a detailed explanation.) As of December 2009, the HHI for the U.S. mutual fund industry was 457, well below the standard for even moderate concentration, as calculated by the Investment Company Institute.

Why the relatively low score for the mutual fund industry? Because market share is fairly evenly distributed across many different fund complexes, as you can see in Table 15.4, which excludes ETFs. The mutual fund business is very different from the oil or auto business, where the top four or five companies control the overwhelming majority of the market. In the mutual fund world, by contrast, even the top 10 fund complexes controlled only slightly over half of industry assets at the end of 2009. In that same year, there were another 14 fund complexes with over 1 percent of assets under management each. And mutual funds compete with many other types of investment vehicles—such as separately managed accounts, collective trust funds, and hedge funds.

The table also shows at a glance how dynamic firm rankings have been. Only half the firms ranked in the top 10 in 2009 were in that elite group at the start of the decade, namely Fidelity, Vanguard, Capital Research, BlackRock

TRYING NOT TO CONCENTRATE

How do you determine whether an industry is highly competitive, with lots of smaller firms fighting it out for market share, or an oligopoly, where only a few companies set the terms for everyone? The antitrust division of the U.S. Department of Justice often uses a measure called the Herfindahl-Hirschman Index.

The HHI is calculated by squaring the market share of each firm competing within an industry and then adding up the resulting numbers. As a result, firms with larger shares get a much heavier weight in the calculation. For example, let's look at an industry that has four firms competing in it. Two of those firms have market shares of 30 percent each; the other two have 20 percent shares. The HHI for this industry is $30^2 + 30^2 + 20^2 + 20^2 = 900 + 900 + 400 + 400 = 2,600$. The two larger firms have been given more than twice as much weight as the smaller firms.

The HHI is lowest for industries that consist of a large number of companies of relatively equal size. For these industries, the HHI approaches zero. If the HHI is between 1,000 and 1,800, the industry is considered moderately concentrated; if over 1,800, it is concentrated. The theoretical maximum—for a monopoly industry with only one competitor—is $100^2 = 10,000$. The Department of Justice may look closely at mergers that increase the HHI by 100 points or more.

(which acquired the Merrill Lynch fund management group), and Franklin Templeton. And two of the firms currently in the top 10—PIMCO and Goldman Sachs—weren't even in the top 25 in 2000. It's a similar story for Dimensional, Dodge and Cox, John Hancock, Northern Trust, and Wells Fargo; all five of these firms ranked among the top 25 in 2009 but were not among the highest-ranked in the earlier period. The only consistency in the rankings has been among the top three firms. We'll talk later in this chapter about why Fidelity, Vanguard, and Capital Research have held their top-ranked positions for so long.

In short, the industry's defenders assert that it isn't a stable oligopoly—it's a highly dynamic business in which competition is rife. Shifts in relative fund performance often lead to major shifts in asset shares, so that complexes emphasizing stocks surge ahead during bull markets, while firms focusing on bond or money market funds come to the fore in more unsettled times.

New companies enter the business fairly easily: there were 209 new entrants between 2005 and 2009 alone, while only slightly below the 229 firms that left the industry over the same period, according to the Investment Company Institute. It's relatively cheap and easy to start up a mutual fund: all you need is $100,000 in seed capital and a dream (plus the resources to file the necessary paperwork with the regulators). You can obtain instant access to the distribution by signing on with a fund supermarket, and paying the operator an annual fee based on fund assets. Moreover, there are many firms that will, for another annual fee, handle all of the administrative services

TABLE 15.4 Largest Mutual Fund Complexes by Assets Under Management

	2000			2009	
Rank	Fund Complex[7]	% Share	Rank	Fund Complex	% Share
1	Fidelity Investments	11.8%	1	Fidelity Investments	11.6%
2	Vanguard Group	8.1	2	Vanguard Group	11.3
3	Capital Research & Management (American Funds)	5.2	3	Capital Research & Management (American Funds)	9.5
4	Putnam Funds	3.8	4	JP Morgan Chase & Co.	4.0
5	Morgan Stanley	3.3	5	BlackRock Funds (includes Merrill Lynch)	3.1
6	Janus	3.0	6	PIMCO Funds	3.0
7	Invesco	3.0	7	Franklin Templeton Investments	2.9
8	Merrill Lynch	2.7	8	Federated Investors	2.8
9	Franklin Templeton Investments	2.5	9	Bank of New York Mellon/ Dreyfus Co.	2.6
10	Salomon Smith Barney/Citi	2.4	10	Goldman Sachs & Co.	2.2
	Subtotal: Top 10	**45.6%**		**Subtotal: Top 10**	**52.9%**

(*Continued*)

TABLE 15.4 (*Continued*)

	2000			2009	
Rank	Fund Complex[7]	% Share	Rank	Fund Complex	% Share
11	TIAA-CREF	2.4%	11	T. Rowe Price	2.1%
12	Federated Investors	2.3	12	Wells Fargo	2.1
13	Schwab Funds	2.0	13	Columbia Management Group (formerly Bank of America)	1.9
14	Dreyfus Co.	1.9	14	Schwab Funds	1.8
15	Oppenheimer Funds/Mass Mutual	1.8	15	TIAA-CREF	1.8
16	MFS	1.7	16	Oppenheimer Funds/Mass Mutual	1.5
17	American Express Funds	1.6	17	Legg Mason (includes Salomon Smith Barney/Citi)	1.4
18	Zurich Scudder	1.6	18	Morgan Stanley	1.4
19	Bank of America	1.6	19	Invesco	1.1
20	T. Rowe Price	1.6	20	Deutsche Asset Management (includes Zurich Scudder)	1.1
21	AllianceBernstein	1.6	21	John Hancock Financial Services	1.0
22	American Century	1.4	22	Dodge & Cox	1.0
23	Prudential Mutual Funds	1.4	23	Prudential Mutual Funds	1.0
24	JP Morgan Chase & Co.	1.3	24	Dimensional Fund Advisors	1.0
25	SEI Investments	1.2	25	Northern Trust Mutual Funds	0.9
	Total: Top 25	71.0%		Total: Top 25	73.9%

Source: Investment Company Institute. Percentages may not add due to rounding.

required. With so many essential services available for hire as needed, small funds can find it quite profitable to serve a particular niche of investors.

It's only once a fund manager gathers a substantial amount of assets that it reaches a decision point. Should it stay small and continue to stay focused in a particular area, or should it broaden out and try to move in to the top tier of fund families? To do this, the manager will need access to broad distribution, capital to develop a more extensive product line, and sophisticated technology, together with specialized teams to support the required recordkeeping and shareholder services. Finally, most of the top-tier players have developed a well-known brand over a long period of time.

Faced with these challenges, many fund managers interested in growing have decided to combine with another firm. They may decide to pool resources with a similar firm in a merger, they could decide to act as an acquirer and buy another fund firm, or they might put themselves up for sale and be acquired by another company. All of this activity is collective referred to as *mergers and acquisitions,* or M&A, for short. "The Acquisition Two-Step" provides some background on the process.

THE ACQUISITION TWO-STEP

The acquisition of a fund management company is a two-step process. In the first step, a majority of the shareholders of the company being bought must agree to the transaction. They do this by either voting to approve a merger agreement in a proxy vote or by selling their shares to the acquirer. This first step is no different from mergers or acquisitions in any other industry.

It's the second step that's unique to the mutual fund industry: the acquirer must obtain the approval of both the independent directors and the shareholders of the mutual funds that the acquired firm manages. That's because, under the federal securities laws, a change in control of the investment manager of a mutual fund automatically terminates the management contract between the fund and the manager.

If the acquirer would like to continue to manage those funds, it must secure a new advisory contract through another two-step process. First, a majority of the independent directors of the funds must determine that the transfer of the advisory contract does not impose an unfair burden on shareholders. Then the shareholders themselves must approve the contracts through a proxy vote. In reality, the acquiring manager is buying the assistance of the prior manager in obtaining these approvals from fund directors and fund shareholders.[8]

MERGERS AND ACQUISITIONS INVOLVING FUND SPONSORS

Merger and acquisition activity for fund complexes during the last decade roughly followed the rise and fall of the U.S. stock market—with a modest time lag. To see the pattern, take a look at Figure 15.4, which summarizes all transactions in which a fund sponsor combined with another firm in a deal with a publicly disclosed value of $50 million or more. The peak in M&A deals during 2000 reflected the end of the Internet bubble; once it burst, deal volume declined along with the stock market for several years after that. Then, when the U.S. stock market resumed its climb in 2005, so did the number of M&A transactions involving fund sponsors—though both were to fall again in 2008 when the credit crisis broke. The jump in transactions in 2009 was a bit of a mirage. It was mainly the result of one deal: BlackRock's acquisition of Barclays's U.S. fund business for approximately $13 billion.

The prices paid in these M&A deals in asset management also tracked the movement in stock prices. Figure 15.5 portrays the median price paid for acquisitions in each year of the past decade expressed as a percentage of assets under management, or AUM. The median deal price peaked in 2000, along with the stock market, at 3.8 percent of AUM, and then declined steeply to a low 1.0 percent of AUM in 2004. When stocks recovered, so did

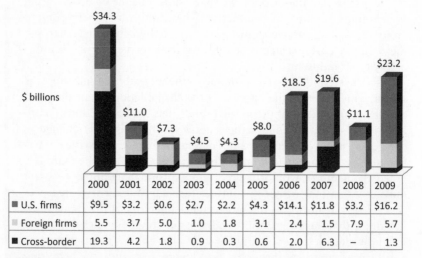

	2000	2001	2002	2003	2004	2005	2006	2007	2008	2009
■ U.S. firms	$9.5	$3.2	$0.6	$2.7	$2.2	$4.3	$14.1	$11.8	$3.2	$16.2
Foreign firms	5.5	3.7	5.0	1.0	1.8	3.1	2.4	1.5	7.9	5.7
■ Cross-border	19.3	4.2	1.8	0.9	0.3	0.6	2.0	6.3	–	1.3

FIGURE 15.4   Global Asset Management Mergers and Acquisitions (Total Deal Value)

Source: Thomson Reuters information provided by Goldman Sachs.

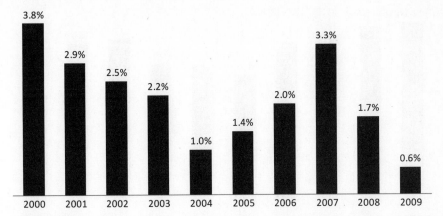

FIGURE 15.5 Median Deal Price (Percent of Assets under Management)
Source: Thomson Reuters information provided by Goldman Sachs.

the median deal price, which rose steadily until reaching 3.3 percent of AUM in 2007, before plunging again in 2008. Deal valuations were particularly low in 2009, partly as a result of the credit crisis and partly because of the special circumstances of the BlackRock-Barclays deal. The price paid in that transaction was quite small as a percentage of AUM because Barclays managed primarily low-fee index funds.

Since price as a percentage of assets under management is so sensitive to the types of funds managed, many professionals prefer to look at the *EBITDA multiple,* which is the deal price as a multiple of the manager's *earnings before interest, taxes, depreciation, and amortization*—essentially the cash produced by the business. This is shown in Figure 15.6. On this measure, the highest-priced deals were still in 2000 and the lowest-priced deals in 2009. However, the decrease in the EBITDA multiple during the first half of the decade, along with the increase in the EBITDA multiple during the second half of the decade, were much more gradual than the fall and rise of deal price as a percentage of AUM.

There are two other important perspectives on the trends in asset management deals over the last decade—the geographical locus of the acquirer relative to the target, and the industry of the institution acquiring the asset manager.

Looking back at Figure 15.4, you'll see the breakdown of mergers and acquisitions into those involving two U.S firms, those involving two non-U.S., or foreign, firms and those involving a U.S. firm on one side of the deal with a non-U.S. firm on the other side of the deal in a cross-border transaction. Cross-border deals dominated for two years at the start of the

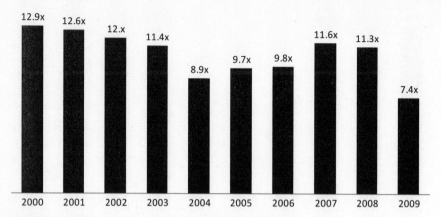

FIGURE 15.6   Median Deal Price (Multiple of EBITDA)
Source: Thomson Reuters information provided by Goldman Sachs.

decade, continuing a trend begun in the late 1990s, when European financial institutions began to buy U.S. firms in an effort to build global franchises in asset management. Foreign deals showed the highest dollar value only in 2002 and 2008, both years when total deal volume was very low. U.S. deals had the highest dollar value in the other six years.

Figure 15.7 segments the same M&A data based on the type of acquirer. The boom in activity at the start of the decade was led by other types of financial institutions—banks and insurers. Firms in the "other" category

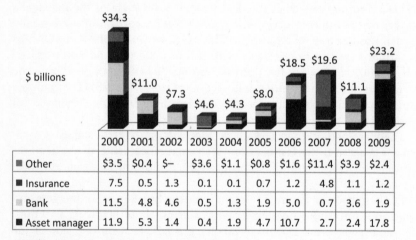

	2000	2001	2002	2003	2004	2005	2006	2007	2008	2009
■ Other	$3.5	$0.4	$–	$3.6	$1.1	$0.8	$1.6	$11.4	$3.9	$2.4
■ Insurance	7.5	0.5	1.3	0.1	0.1	0.7	1.2	4.8	1.1	1.2
■ Bank	11.5	4.8	4.6	0.5	1.3	1.9	5.0	0.7	3.6	1.9
■ Asset manager	11.9	5.3	1.4	0.4	1.9	4.7	10.7	2.7	2.4	17.8

FIGURE 15.7   Deal Value by Acquirer Industry
Source: Thomson Reuters information provided by Goldman Sachs.

predominated in 2003, when M&A activity was at a very low level and again in 2007, when deal value was high. In 2003, brokerage firms Lehman Brothers and American Express were big buyers; in 2007, leveraged buyouts by managements such as those at Nuveen and Marsico topped the charts. In other years, asset managers have been the main buyers.

In the next three sections, we discuss in more detail the asset manager deals during the start, middle, and end of the most recent decade. The web site for this book contains a selected list of asset manager deals during the last decade, organized first by geographical locus of the acquirer relative to the target and then by the type of financial institution of the acquirer.

Trends Early in the Decade

At the start of the most recent decade, many of the M&A deals were cross-border, predominantly European financial firms buying U.S. asset managers. Some of the largest deals involved European banks. For example, Deutsche Bank bought Zurich Scudder, and Société Générale bought Trust Company of the West. But European insurers and asset managers were also active acquirers. Allianz became a significant force in the U.S. fund industry through its purchase of the PIMCO Funds during the 1990s and of Nicholas Applegate in 2000, while CDC Asset Management from France bought NVest.

These firms were generally looking to increase exposure to an industry that they believed had higher growth prospects than the mature banking and insurance businesses at home. The income stream from asset management also promised to provide significant diversification. For a banking institution, asset management fee income is relatively independent of the main drivers of a commercial bank's profitability—loan volume and interest rate spreads. For insurers, asset management fees were linked to a different business cycle than revenues from selling life insurance policies—and the higher margins in the asset management business were attractive, too.

Overall, these European banks and insurers wanted to build a global franchise in asset management with a major U.S. presence as a key component of that strategy. Success was elusive for some; for example, despite the purchase of Pioneer in 2000, Unicredito Bank did not realize its goal of becoming a major player in the U.S. asset management industry.

Other European institutions were able to build a large U.S. presence through acquisitions. For example, Invesco (then known as AMVESCAP) bought U.S.-based AIM in the 1990s and soon after consolidated its U.S. position by acquiring National Asset Management in 2001 and Stein Roe in 2003. Invesco AIM is a truly global player in asset management: it has been an acquirer in Canada (Trimark), the United Kingdom (Perpetual), and Australia (Country Investment Management) in addition to the United States and has recently moved its corporate base to Bermuda.

Acquisitions of European asset managers by U.S. firms were limited during this period. The only major deal was Chase Manhattan's purchase of U.K.-based Robert Fleming.

U.S. fund sponsors, however, were active acquirers at the start of the decade within the United States—concentrating on asset managers with expertise working with wealthy individuals, known in the trade as *high net worth customers*. Managing money for these clients often requires a high level of personalized customer service as well as different approaches to investment management—capabilities that some firms decided to obtain through acquisitions rather than internal development efforts.

Two of the most prominent transactions of this type occurred in 2000. The larger of the two was the acquisition of Sanford C. Bernstein, Inc., a well-respected firm that specialized in managing money for institutions and wealthy individuals, by Alliance Capital Group, a mutual fund manager. (The combined firm is now known as AllianceBernstein.) That same year, Franklin Resources, which manages the Franklin Templeton Fund group, bought Fiduciary Trust, a private bank.

Mid-Decade Trends

During the middle of the decade, the U.S. acquisition scene was dominated by two asset managers: BlackRock and Legg Mason. Both made numerous purchases over the period to expand their asset management capabilities, whether to better serve institutional and high net worth investors (Legg Mason's acquisition of Private Capital), to grow a hedge fund business (BlackRock's purchase of Quellos and Legg Mason's acquisition of Permal), or to increase exposure to equity funds (BlackRock's purchase of State Street Research). More importantly, both took over the asset management subsidiaries of major brokerage firms: In 2005, Legg Mason acquired Smith Barney's asset management business (Smith Barney was owned by banking giant Citigroup), while the following year BlackRock bought a majority stake in Merrill Lynch's asset management arm.

The sale of their fund businesses by wirehouses Smith Barney and Merrill Lynch represented an about-face, as we mentioned in Chapter 10. Until the 1990s, both firms managed major proprietary fund groups that were sold through their own brokerage networks. This strategy was undermined, however, by stricter regulations on potential conflicts of interest and by client demand for open architecture. As a result, both brokers decided to exit fund management to focus on distribution. Smith Barney and Merrill

Lynch were not alone in this trend toward specialization. In 2006, broker-dealer Charles Schwab sold US Trust, a manager of high net worth assets that it had acquired only six years before, to Bank of America.

While brokerage firms were leaving the fund management world, many insurance companies continued to buy asset managers. Principal, a mid-size life insurer from the Midwest, and AXA—a giant French life insurer that had purchased a majority stake in Alliance Capital Management (which later become AllianceBernstein)—were both active acquirers in this period. As already discussed, they were looking for higher growth and margins, along with diversification in their revenue streams and, in AXA's case, a larger global presence. And, as we explained in Chapter 10, asset management is a particularly comfortable fit for insurance companies because of their presence in the variable annuity business.

Not all insurance companies were buyers. In 2006, Nationwide Insurance actually sold Gartmore—a U.K. manager it acquired in 2002—back to its management in a leveraged buyout with the financial support of Hellman & Friedman, a private equity firm. In a leveraged buyout, managers borrow a lot of money to buy ownership from current stockholders; they then use the cash generated by the business to pay off the loans over time.

The Gartmore deal was not the sole leveraged buyout in this period. We've already mentioned two others—the buyouts at Nuveen and Marsico—and there were at least thirteen more between 2004 and 2007. This flood of leveraged buyouts of asset managers was driven by the availability of cheap financing. Private equity firms had large amounts of funds to invest, while interest rates were relatively low and other loan terms were quite flexible. Asset management firms were attractive leveraged buyout candidates because their fees based on assets produced steady streams of cash to pay off debt. And a rising stock market meant that the prospects for asset management firms were only brightening.

Closing Years of the Decade

Merger and acquisition activity at the end of the decade was largely driven by forces external to the fund industry. Many corporate owners of mutual fund management companies were forced to sell their healthy asset management subsidiaries when trouble surfaced at the parent company. For Marsh McLennan, the problem took the form of accusations of bid rigging in its insurance brokerage operations; the solution was to sell mutual fund manager Putnam Investments to Great-West Life of Canada.

In more cases, however, the external force driving the sales was the credit crisis. After it was rescued by the U.S. government in 2008, AIG sold its asset management units (along with other businesses) to raise needed capital, while Lincoln National sold its Delaware Management unit to Australia's Macquarie Group for the same reason. Lehman Brothers, after filing for bankruptcy, sold Neuberger Berman to the latter's management group. To help raise money to pay back the federal government's capital contribution, Bank of America sold Columbia Management to Ameriprise. In a successful effort to obviate the need for a capital contribution from the U.K. government, Barclays sold its U.S. fund manager to BlackRock.

In essence, the deals at the end of the decade reversed much of the effect of the deals at the beginning of the decade. In that earlier period, non–asset managers such as banks and insurers bought mutual fund managers to diversify their revenue base. However, after the credit crisis, some banks, brokers, and insurers were forced to sell their mutual fund operations back to firms dedicated solely to asset management. If there was one big theme to the M&A activity in the past 10 years, it is that a strong focus on asset management is the best route to success in the mutual fund world.

The Impact

Many diversified financial firms have not realized the benefits they anticipated when they purchased an asset manager. They expected that they would be able to package together the asset manager's mutual funds with traditional banking and insurance services to sell to their high net worth customers. In this age of open architecture, however, high net worth customers want the best products regardless of source, and regulators monitor closely any potential conflicts of interest. As a result, diversified firms have not seen the hoped-for revenue synergies that were often used to justify a high purchase price for an asset manager.

These firms often find that they are uncomfortable with the volatility of investment performance, which is not very predictable and can vary significantly with market movements. Yet most diversified financial firms are public companies that report results to its shareholders every three months. Asset management is a more comfortable business for private firms owned by professionals that are better prepared for the ups and downs of the securities markets.

The benefits of dedication to asset management can be seen in the fund family rankings in Table 15.4. Two of the largest acquirers—BlackRock and Legg Mason—are investment-focused firms that climbed up quickly in the rankings when they bought fund complexes from brokerage firms. Other dedicated asset managers, including firms such as Franklin Templeton and T. Rowe Price, gradually expanded their market share. In contrast, the only route to the top of the fund rankings for more diversified financial firms, including J.P. Morgan, Bank of New York Mellon, and Goldman Sachs, was by concentrating on managing money market funds for institutional investors.

The benefit of focus was most evident in the three firms that have topped the charts—Fidelity, Vanguard, and Capital Research—whose combined market share rose from 25 percent to over 32 percent during the last decade. All three are dedicated asset managers, and their increase in market share was entirely the result of internal growth rather than of acquisitions. Another thing they have in common: all three of these managers are essentially run as private partnerships. Based on this small sample, the most effective organizational structure for asset managers seem to be as stand-alone entities, without public shareholders, with a long-term dedication to asset management.

In contrast, diversified financial firms often have trouble retaining the investment management professionals who are key to the success of any asset manager firm. These firms usually have an elaborate budgeting process with many formal processes for approval—a bureaucratic approach that doesn't sit well with fund executives—they want to run a semi-autonomous unit with the informal culture that tends to be correlated with investment success. Diversified firms can find it hard to pay portfolio managers at competitive rates, especially when the income of a star manager exceeds that of the firm's CEO. And they may find it politically difficult to structure special compensation programs for portfolio managers that give them an equity ownership stake in the high-margin asset management unit, rather than the whole diversified firm.

The partnership format has a significant drawback, however—it can be very difficult to plan for management succession. Somehow, the upcoming generation of managers must raise money to buy out the ownership stakes of those who are retiring. Many firms find it easiest to do this by selling shares to the public. So far, the three largest fund managers have met the challenge of providing for management succession without a public offering, by using a variety of approaches. Fidelity remains largely in the hands of its founding family, while Capital Research has a structured partnership program similar to those in certain professional service or investment firms. Vanguard avoids the issue altogether—it's owned by all the shareholders in its funds, making Vanguard a *mutual* mutual fund management company.

Smaller fund management partnerships facing a succession challenge have benefited from the availability of fund consolidators, publicly traded firms that have bought all or a majority of the interests of managers looking to cash out all or some of their ownership interests. "The Consolidator" discusses one firm's approach.

THE CONSOLIDATOR

If you look through the list of asset manager M&A deals available on the web site, you'll see one name keeps coming up: Affiliated Managers Group. AMG's strategy is to consolidate smaller management firms under a single corporate umbrella that provides centralized services supporting broader distribution and more efficient operations. At the end of 2009, AMG had 25 money management affiliates responsible for over $250 billion in assets.

The secret to AMG's success? It buys only 51 to 70 percent of an established money management firm, leaving the rest of the ownership in the hands of the key employees who continue to manage their firms independently. This substantial ownership stake gives these employees plenty of reward for building the firm's business.

In adopting this approach, AMG learned from the mistakes of United Asset Management, which pursued a similar consolidation strategy in the 1990s. UAM generally acquired 100 percent ownership of its affiliate companies—which meant that the individuals who manage money for the acquired firm, who were often the firm's founders, didn't have much incentive to stay with the firm after the buyout and continue to grow revenues. Once they departed, the acquired firms often floundered. UAM strategy was not successful, and it was eventually acquired itself in 2000.

In the final analysis, successful fund managers must foster a culture that attracts and retains top investment professionals throughout the market cycle. The value of a fund franchise depends heavily on these professionals who are extremely mobile. Partnership-type firms focused on asset management have generally found fewer obstacles in structuring compensation programs and creating work environments that enable talented investors to do their best work for shareholders.

CHAPTER SUMMARY

Shareholders pay various charges when they invest through a mutual fund. These fees fall into five categories: distribution charges, securities transaction costs, shareholder transaction fees, fund services charges, and the management fee. Fund expenses can have a significant impact on shareholder returns, especially when compounded over time. The SEC requires detailed disclosure of these charges.

The management fee is usually the largest component of a fund's ongoing expenses. It compensates the management company for providing investment management services, for the use of its brand name, for taking the risk of setting up the fund and for organizing its distribution. It varies based on the type of assets the fund invests in. The management fee is the principal source of the management company's profitability.

Historically, management companies have been quite profitable. Critics of the industry suggest that this is because management fees are too high. They believe that shareholders do not get sufficient benefit from economies of scale, that mutual fund investors pay more than other types of investors and that the market for mutual funds is noncompetitive. Industry defenders argue that fees do decline with assets, that mutual funds pay similar fees for similar services, and that the industry is highly competitive. They note that market shares within the industry are not particularly concentrated, as measured by the Herfindahl-Hirschman Index, and that there are many new entrants through start-ups and acquisitions.

There has been considerable merger and acquisition activity in the mutual fund industry over the past decade. Both the volume of these transactions and their pricing vary with market conditions. At the beginning of the past decade, many of the deals involved European firms acquiring U.S. asset managers in cross-border transactions. U.S. managers also bought asset managers with expertise working with high net worth customers. In the middle of the decade, mutual fund management firms acquired the proprietary fund businesses of brokerage firms that chose to concentrate on distribution. Insurance companies were also significant acquirers in this period, and there were several leveraged buyout transactions as well. Much of the acquisition activity toward the end of the decade was the result of the financial stress caused by the credit crisis. Many of these deals reversed the activity that took place near the beginning of the decade.

Acquisitions allow firms to rapidly increase market share. The largest fund management companies, however, increased market share entirely through internal growth. These firms are dedicated asset managers that are essentially run as private partnerships. In contrast, diversified financial firms have often not realized the benefits they anticipated when they purchased an asset manager, partly because star managers do not like to work for large conglomerates and partly because clients prefer nonproprietary funds in an age of open architecture.

Five

The Internationalization of Mutual Funds

In this section, we look outside the borders of the United States and examine the growing internationalization of mutual funds over the past three decades—a phenomenon with two distinct, but related, aspects. Mutual funds registered in the United States are increasingly likely to invest at least some of their assets overseas. At the same time, fund management companies—both U.S. and non-U.S.—are looking to gather assets from investors in other countries. That's particularly true for fund sponsors based in more mature markets like the United States and Western Europe.

While the two trends have the same root causes, they have each developed at a very different pace. Overseas investment by U.S. funds has grown significantly over the past 30 years, and is now widely accepted by the U.S. investing public. By contrast, fund management companies have had mixed success in their efforts to gather assets from overseas investors. That's because fund markets around the world are usually walled off from one another by local tax and regulatory policy.

As a result, fund distribution remains a largely local business, giving fund managers based within a country a home court advantage. Firms aspiring to global reach can't easily capture market share by distributing existing products around the world—even if those products have more desirable features, are combined with superior service, and are provided at lower cost. Fund sponsors instead must often first develop a presence in each foreign country, launching funds customized for that market and working with local distributors.

Yet the world is slowly changing when it comes to the market for investment funds. The acceptance of cross-border products—most notably the UCITS funds based in Europe—has steadily increased. The asset management industry is responding by building truly global expertise in fund management, distribution, and administration—through organic growth, alliances, or acquisitions. It's easy today for an investor in Germany to buy shares in a Luxembourg-registered fund sponsored by a subsidiary of a U.S. fund management company that invests in Thai stocks selected by a portfolio manager based in Hong Kong.

This section has three chapters:

Chapter 16 explores overseas investing by U.S. mutual funds, looking at the cross-border investment environment in general, then at the advantages, risks, and operational challenges of investing overseas. It concludes with a discussion of the special issues facing portfolio managers of international and global funds, as distinct from funds investing only in the United States.

Chapter 17 reviews the worldwide market for investment funds and the models for building a global fund business. It then focuses on Europe, discussing the success of the UCITS structure for cross-border funds and the potential for cross-border pension plan management. To illustrate these European trends, we examine the market for investment funds in Germany.

Chapter 18 takes a detailed look at selected markets for investment funds around the world. It analyzes trends in the Asian Tiger markets, with a special focus on China, and then turns to Japan. It next moves to Latin America, taking a close look at Chile. It concludes with a review of the funds market in Canada.

CHAPTER 16

Cross-Border Investing

Millions of Americans are traveling to the far corners of the globe—at least with their money. Over the past three decades, U.S. investors have been steadily increasing their exposure to foreign securities. They've taken to the road in the hopes of finding better returns than are available at home, in economies that have a higher potential for growth. And American investors believe that investing in foreign markets will increase the diversification of their portfolios because investment returns outside the United States are often different from those inside the United States.

Mutual funds have acted as travel agents for many U.S. investors who want to venture abroad but are concerned about the possible hazards and hassles involved. Fund managers monitor the investment risks and deal with the operational complexities on behalf of their shareholders, to make going overseas no more work than staying at home. In this chapter, we talk about why international investing has become easier—and why it can still be quite difficult.

This chapter reviews:

- The reasons for the growth in cross-border investing
- The advantages and risks of investing overseas
- The operational challenges of international investing
- Managing a global or international fund

THE GROWTH IN CROSS-BORDER INVESTING

Since the early 1990s, U.S. investors have been building up their portfolios of international securities, as shown in Table 16.1. By the end of 2009, U.S. investors held close to US$6 trillion of international securities. That's almost seven times the amount held only 15 years earlier despite a sharp drop during the credit crisis of 2008.

TABLE 16.1 U.S. Portfolio Holdings of Foreign Securities (US$ billions)

	Foreign Stocks	Foreign Bonds	Total
1994	US$ 567	US$ 304	US$ 870
1997	$1,208	$ 547	$1,755
2001	$1,613	$ 704	$2,317
2004	$2,560	$1,226	$3,787
2005	$3,318	$1,291	$4,609
2006	$4,329	$1,662	$5,991
2007	$5,253	$1,967	$7,220
2008	$2,748	$1,543	$4,291
2009*	$3,995	$1,981	$5,977

*Preliminary
Source: U.S. Treasury. Figures may not add due to rounding.

Figure 16.1 shows how overseas investment activity by U.S. mutual funds has mirrored this growth trend. Over roughly the same time, assets in mutual funds focused on investing outside the United States quintupled, while the number of such funds almost doubled. Assets in global and international funds went from 9 percent of total industry assets in 1994 to 13 percent in 2009.

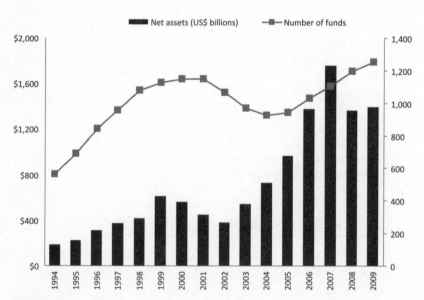

FIGURE 16.1 Global and International Mutual Funds (U.S.-Registered)
Source: Investment Company Institute, *2010 Investment Company Fact Book.*

The expansion in international investing by U.S. funds became possible because other nations have opened up their markets to greater amounts of foreign capital. Countries with fewer restrictions on money flows are more attractive to foreign investors—who want to know that they can take their money out at any time. Therefore, eliminating or reducing capital controls tends to increase the supply of foreign capital available to local companies—and more capital for local businesses creates the potential for stronger economic growth.[1]

On the other hand, opening the doors of a financial system to all who wish to enter can lead to greater volatility in the amount of capital available at any one time. Foreign investors can pour large amounts of money into a country and then decide to pull it out on short notice—causing real economic damage in the process. For example, between 2000 and 2008, foreign investment equaled 20 percent of both England and Ireland's gross domestic product and a massive 50 percent of Spain's GDP. Foreign capital allowed tiny Iceland to grow its banking system to nine times the size of its GDP during that same time. Much of this foreign money seemed to find its way into housing—either directly or through bank lending—creating a bubble that burst after the inflows of capital stopped, resulting in great economic stress.

It's important to note that not all foreign capital is *hot money* that's likely to flow in and out of a country quickly. For example, Investment Company Institute research suggests that U.S. mutual funds were a stable source of capital for the emerging markets during the 1990s, which were a period of high volatility for many of these markets.[2] Overall, however, foreign capital is—by its nature—less stable than domestic sources of funding.

The emerging markets—with their less-developed financial infrastructure—are particularly vulnerable to sudden capital outflows. (See "Developing Terminology" for a definition of *emerging market*.) As a result, these countries often try to insulate themselves from global economic pressures and maintain better control of their internal affairs by regulating the amounts or types of foreign investment that they allow in their financial markets.

For example, China has restricted foreign ownership of its corporations' stock. Foreign investors who want to buy shares of Chinese companies can invest through one of two classes of shares. Anyone can buy the H class of shares, which trade on the Hong Kong stock exchange. On the other hand, a foreigner who wants to buy the A shares that trade in mainland China must obtain recognition as a QFII, or *qualified foreign institutional investor*. But since the Chinese government has placed a strict quota on QFII licenses, the designation is difficult to obtain. China has been only gradually relaxing the restrictions on foreign investment by increasing the quota.

DEVELOPING TERMINOLOGY

What exactly is an *emerging market*? While the term is not precise, it's generally used to refer to a less-well-off country that's quickly becoming wealthier because its economy is growing at a rapid clip. The emerging markets are a subset of what used to be called *Third World nations*, *less developed countries*, or LDCs, but are now more often referred to as *developing economies*.

There's no universally accepted list of emerging markets. For example, some observers would classify Hong Kong and Singapore as emerging, while others feel that the two now belong in the ranks of *developed markets*. Among the largest emerging market economies are Brazil, Russia, India, and China, often lumped together as the BRIC countries. The smallest emerging markets are sometimes called *frontier markets*.

Because there are a limited number of QFII licenses, there are few foreign buyers to help support the price of A shares. But the number of non-QFII foreign buyers wanting to invest in China exceeds the supply of H shares. As a result, the H shares usually trade at a higher price than A shares, which means there's a significant investment advantage to obtaining a QFII license.

China is not alone in opening some doors to foreign investment. Over the past 25 years, many nations have entirely eliminated capital controls. Brazil, Mexico, and South Korea are among the countries that have opened up their capital markets to foreign investment relatively recently. Even many of the nations that continue to regulate capital flows have reduced and simplified their regulatory requirements as a means of encouraging greater levels of foreign investment.

An important caveat: while the overall trend has been toward the easing of capital restrictions, countries on occasion have imposed new regulations when they perceive that their economy is under threat. Chile, for example, responded to a massive inrush of overseas money in the early 1990s by imposing capital controls. Foreigners wishing to buy Chilean securities had to deposit 20 percent of their investment in a non-interest-bearing account, or *encaje*, with the central bank, and there was a 3 percent penalty for early withdrawal. This policy aimed to leave the door open for long-term investors, while keeping out hot money. These policies were short-lived; by 2001, the Chilean central bank had removed all controls on capital inflows.[3]

In another instance of retightening, Malaysia reestablished controls on foreign exchange during the Asian financial crisis of 1998 and 1999 when many currencies in the region plunged in value. While domestic economic factors appear to have been the primary cause of the crisis, the Malaysian government was reacting to public perception that the damage was the result of foreign speculation.

As the world's capital markets have gradually opened up—despite the occasional setbacks—businesses have increasingly come to rely on publicly issued debt and equity securities—as opposed to bank loans and family investments—as their primary source of raising capital. The development of the European capital markets is a case in point. In a market sense, Europe is a microcosm of the world as a whole, since it includes some of the world's oldest and most mature markets (London and Amsterdam), emerging markets (the former Communist bloc countries in Eastern Europe), and developed countries that were generally considered emerging just a few decades ago (Portugal and Ireland).[4] In 1994—five years after the fall of the Berlin Wall—there were fewer than 6,000 stocks trading on European exchanges; by 2008, just 14 years later, the number had more than doubled. Similarly, net issuance of corporate debt—which in 1994 amounted to just €3 trillion (euros)—had soared to €337 trillion by 2008.[5]

All these trends have greatly expanded the number of overseas investments available to U.S. investors. As Table 16.2 illustrates, although the U.S. stock markets are by far the largest in the world, they accounted for less than half of the world's stock market capitalization at the end of 2009—a drop of more than eight percentage points compared to just five years earlier. But the United States wasn't alone in losing share. Most of the other developed markets also saw declines—with Canada and Australia as notable exceptions. Both of these countries were major exporters of natural resources, which were in high demand during this period. The emerging markets, on the other hand, saw their share of world market capitalization surge ahead—from 6.4 percent in 2004 to 14.7 percent just five years later.

Even though assets flow across borders much more easily, investors still tilt their portfolios toward their local market—a preference that academics call the *home bias puzzle*. While home bias has decreased over the decades, it has not entirely gone away. For example, if U.S. investors had no geographic preferences at all, they'd have 41.9 percent of their stock holdings in U.S. companies and the balance in foreign stocks—matching the weighting of the U.S. in the world index. Yet, at the end of 2009, only about 25 percent of U.S. stock mutual fund assets were in global or international funds.

TABLE 16.2 Percent of MSCI All Country World Index
Market Capitalization

Country	2004	2009
United States	50.1%	41.9%
Japan	9.2%	8.5%
United Kingdom	10.5%	8.8%
Developed Europe ex U.K.	18.9%	18.4%
Canada	2.8%	4.2%
Australia	2.1%	3.4%
Total Developed Markets	93.6%	85.3%
Brazil	0.5%	2.2%
China	0.4%	2.3%
South Korea	0.9%	1.7%
Taiwan	0.7%	1.5%
India	0.3%	1.0%
Russia	0.2%	0.8%
Other emerging markets	3.4%	5.2%
Total Emerging Markets	6.4%	14.7%

Source: MSCI. Percentages may not add due to rounding.

Investors often buy local because they feel that they have an information advantage in their own market. They're more likely to receive regular reports on an investment in a language they understand both from management and in the media—and they may even have first-hand knowledge of the company's products and services. They may also be more comfortable with the home country's system for enforcing shareholder rights. At the same time, investors may feel discouraged from buying in other markets—which may be dominated by insiders and large local shareholders.[6]

ADVANTAGES AND RISKS OF INVESTING OVERSEAS

Despite their lingering concerns, U.S. investors have been increasingly willing to venture outside their home market—mainly because the potential rewards have been very attractive, especially in the developing world. The emerging markets have grown as a percentage of total world market capitalization because stocks in those countries have done extremely well in recent years, reflecting the higher growth in their economies. Table 16.3 provides a comparison of returns in the emerging markets to those in the developed world.

TABLE 16.3 Annual Returns (periods ending December 31, 2009)

	1 Year	3 Year	5 Year	10 Year
U.S. (S&P 500 Index)	26.5%	−5.6%	0.4%	−1.0%
Developed Markets ex U.S. (MSCI EAFE Index)	32.5%	−5.6%	4.0%	1.6%
Emerging Markets (MSCI Emerging Market Index)	79.0%	5.4%	15.9%	10.1%

Source: S&P and MSCI.

Many U.S. investors also believe that adding exposure to emerging markets allows them to reduce portfolio risk as well as increase return. That may seem counterintuitive, since—on a stand-alone basis—risks in the emerging markets are significantly greater. But making higher-risk investments can reduce total portfolio risk—as long as the returns of those higher-risk holdings are not highly correlated with those of the balance of the portfolio.

To see how this works, assume that an investor holds just low-risk Asset A, with an expected return of 6 percent. He's thinking about adding Asset B—with an expected return of 10 percent and a higher level of risk—to his portfolio. The two assets have a weak positive correlation—which means that they tend to move in the same direction, but to different degrees and not exactly at the same time. Figure 16.2 shows all the possible combinations of Asset A and Asset B in a graph that's called an *efficient frontier*. (See this

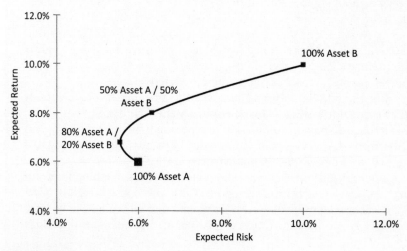

FIGURE 16.2 The Efficient Frontier

book's web site for more on the math behind the graph.) Because the stocks don't go up and down in lock step, adding some Asset B to the portfolio both increases expected return and reduces expected risk. A portfolio with 80 percent in Asset A and 20 percent in Asset B is estimated to have the lowest risk. In this case, shifting 20 percent of the portfolio into Asset B was the investment equivalent of a free lunch: more return with less risk.

Many investors believe that it's reasonable to substitute *developed markets* for Asset A and *emerging markets* for Asset B. Developed stock markets are relatively low risk–low return, while emerging markets are comparatively high risk–high return, and—at least in the past—the returns of these two categories of stock markets had not been highly correlated. In fact, it wasn't that long ago that advocates of international investing would substitute "the U.S." for Asset A and "all non-U.S. markets" for Asset B. Unfortunately, recent market movements have raised doubt about both the correlation data and the conclusion, especially for the United States and other developed markets. See "Does International Investing Really Reduce Risk?" for more on the debate.

DOES INTERNATIONAL INVESTING REALLY REDUCE RISK?

Over the past decade, market observers began to question whether international diversification does, in fact, reduce risk. At first, the evidence was largely anecdotal. Investors began to notice that markets were moving together more—especially when things went wrong. In times of crisis, all the markets around the world—U.S. and non-U.S., developed and emerging—all went down together. Perhaps that shouldn't have been a surprise. World economies are much more tightly intertwined than they were in the past, so it would make sense that financial markets would be more interconnected as well.

But the parallel movements created a dilemma for advocates of international investing. If markets were highly correlated, that would mean that adding a riskier market to a portfolio might still add potential return—but it wouldn't reduce risk. In fact, it might increase risk instead. In other words, "Goodbye, free lunch!"

To the dismay of everyone who prefers getting something for nothing, the academic research supported the anecdotal evidence. Correlations among markets—both developed and emerging—have been increasing over time, and those correlations are indeed higher in periods of market turmoil.[7] Making for a double misfortune, those periods of crises are occurring with increasing frequency. One study counted 139 financial crises (including defaults of sovereign debt) somewhere in the world between 1973 and 1997, compared to just 38 in the preceding 26 years.[8]

That doesn't mean that international diversification is irrelevant to reducing overall portfolio risk. The emerging markets are still less correlated than the developed markets and more influenced by country-specific factors, especially at the extremes. Within the developed markets, international investors must be more selective and attuned to changes in trends if they want to realize the benefits of diversification. For example, one recent study focused on the correlations of the United States, German, and Japanese markets. It found that the U.S. and Japanese markets were significantly correlated before the 9/11 attack in 2001—but that the U.S. and German markets were most correlated afterward.[9]

Many portfolio managers now believe sector exposure has become more important than country exposure, particularly in developed markets. (Remember that a sector is a group of related industries.) As businesses have become globally integrated, an adverse development affecting an industry in one part of the world is likely to hurt the share prices of all companies in that industry, regardless of where their shares are traded or where they have their headquarters. This ripple effect is most noticeable in global industries dominated by multinational companies, such as energy or autos, and less of a factor for industries that are necessarily more local, such as real estate or retailing.

While international exposure might reduce portfolio risk, investors who wander overseas still face a number of risks that they don't face at home. These risks are often most pronounced in the emerging markets.

Currency risk. Cross-border investing typically involves currency risk. That's because a U.S. investor will normally have funds in U.S. dollars, while foreign securities are usually priced in the local currency. As a result, exchange rate fluctuations can have a significant impact on total return measured in U.S. dollars. During a period when the foreign currency is strong compared to the U.S. dollar, returns to U.S. investors will be boosted—but they'll be hurt if the value of the foreign currency falls. For example, if a U.K. stock gains 12 percent over the course of a year, but the value of the British pound declines 5 percent against the U.S. dollar over that same period, the stock's return to a U.S. investor will be closer to 7 percent than 12 percent.

Political and regulatory risk. Government policies in other countries are often less investor-friendly than they are in the United States. Disclosure can be significantly less extensive. For example, many foreign companies are not required to provide detailed information on pension liabilities, mergers and acquisitions, or business segment results. Laws to prevent abusive practices such as insider trading or market manipulation may not be enforced effectively. And, as we saw in Chapter 9, shareholder rights may be less well protected. There's even the chance that a government will confiscate investor assets by nationalizing companies or entire industries. That happened recently in Venezuela, when the government announced in the summer of 2008 that it would take over private companies in strategic sectors such as cement and steel. Many countries have nationalized banks when they encounter difficulties.

Special standards may apply to nonlocal investors. Foreigners may be prohibited from buying large positions in companies that are connected with national security or prestige, such as airlines or telecommunication companies. (Note that this can be an issue for foreign companies trying to buy U.S. assets as well. China National Offshore Oil Corporation, for example, was forced to abandon its attempt to acquire Unocal Corporation in 2005 after Congress expressed reservations about the transaction.)

Trading. Buying and selling securities can be difficult and costly overseas. While the markets in major financial centers such as London and Tokyo are quite efficient, securities in many foreign markets—especially the emerging markets—may trade almost by appointment, making it hard to accumulate the substantial positions that institutional investors such as mutual funds often seek. Commission rates can be much higher than they are in the United States's electronic markets. In some markets, brokerage rates may still be fixed by law. And some countries impose a stamp duty, or transaction tax, whenever a security is bought or sold, which can add significantly to trading costs. The United Kingdom, for example, imposes a stamp duty on trading the stocks of companies listed there, equal to 0.5 percent of the value of the trade.

Financial infrastructure. Markets overseas may lack the basic infrastructure to handle transactions efficiently. Perhaps the classic example of the problems this can cause was in India where, until the 1990s, the settlement of securities transactions still involved the exchange of paper certificates of ownership. While the system functioned well when volumes were low, once India became a popular place to invest and trading soared, the antiquated system couldn't handle the volume. That led to long delays in settling trades—in some cases exceeding six months—and to the circulation of a large number of fraudulent shares. India has since moved to electronic recordkeeping of share certificates.

Russia and some of the former Eastern bloc countries today have no independent, centralized securities registration system—similar to DTCC in the United States. (We say more about the role of central securities depositories in a moment.) Instead, companies maintain the only official records of share ownership. In consequence, if a Russian company should eliminate an ownership record, a shareholder can't correct the error by referring to the separate entries in the central database. Another concern: Paper certificates are held by the company's registrar—not by the central depository or the investor's custodian as is the norm elsewhere in the world. If securities should go missing, investors have little recourse other than to press the issuer and its registrar to fix the mistake or pay damages.

OPERATIONAL CHALLENGES OF INVESTING OVERSEAS

Investing overseas also raises a host of operational issues. Funds generally can't use the accounts that they have established in the United States to buy securities in other markets.

- *Custody*. Instead, most mutual funds buy securities locally and entrust them to local custodian banks—called *subcustodians*—for safekeeping. (Turn back to Chapter 14 for a refresher on the role of the custodian.) Most funds have a number of subcustodians around the world forming a *global custody network*, which is discussed further in "Network Management." The subcustodians are often a key source of information about developments in the local market, particularly from a regulatory perspective.

  Opening a subcustody account is easy in some countries—taking only one or two days. In others, it's a time-consuming process that can extend for several months, often requiring the approval of a local regulator or exchange board. Portfolio managers who want to invest in these markets must allow plenty of lead time before making their first trades. For some funds, opening an account in a particular country may prove impossible. For example, funds that are created as a Massachusetts business trust may find that certain foreign regulators don't recognize that legal form of organization.

  If opening foreign securities accounts is a challenge for mutual funds, it has been nearly impossible for individuals—at least until recently. Several brokerage firms have now established international

NETWORK MANAGEMENT

A fund's board of directors begins the process of establishing a global custody network by selecting a *foreign custody manager,* or FCM—which is usually the fund's U.S. custodian bank. The board delegates responsibility for day-to-day management of the network to the FCM—but only after the directors have carefully reviewed the FCM's qualifications and the FCM agrees to exercise "reasonable care, prudence and diligence" in performing its duties.

The FCM chooses local subcustodian banks for the network that it believes will exercise that same "reasonable care, based on the standards applicable to custodians in the relevant market." In making its selections, the FCM will consider a bank's reputation, financial strength, and system of internal controls. The bank must agree to indemnify, or insure, the fund against the loss of securities held by that bank, clearly identify assets as belonging to the fund, provide access to independent auditors, and allow assets to be transferred freely. The FCM must monitor how the local bank performs it duties and take assets away from any bank that fails to meet these requirements.[10]

FCMs must also confirm that central securities depositories in other markets meet minimum standards. Like DTCC in the United States, these depositories are clearing and settlement agencies established by the government or the national stock exchange to maintain the official records of security ownership—either in paper or dematerialized electronic form. Investors in a country are often required to use these depositories—though an FCM can stop a fund from dealing in a country if it believes that a mandatory central depository doesn't do enough to protect fund assets. For example, an FCM might not allow a fund to trade in a country in which the central depository commingles its own assets with fund assets.

One final responsibility for FCMs: They must report periodically to the fund's board of directors. These reports review the performance of the subcustodians and assess the risks associated with using central securities depositories.

accounts that enable do-it-yourself investors—and usually only those with substantial assets—to trade directly in a limited number of markets around the world. It's still more common for individuals investing overseas to use *American Depositary Receipts,* or ADRs, as "Security Deposits" explains.

SECURITY DEPOSITS

Investors who don't want to—or can't—open a securities account overseas can still invest outside the United States using a tool that's been around for more than 90 years: the *depositary receipt,* which is a share of a foreign company that trades outside its local market. Depositary receipts are a popular way of investing internationally. BNY Mellon reports that there are 3,000-plus depositary receipt programs for companies based in more than 70 countries outside the United States; most involve stocks, though depositary receipts can be used for other securities. An American Depositary Receipt, or ADR, trades on a U.S. stock exchange, while a Global Depositary Receipt, or GDR, is listed on a European exchange.

To create ADRs or GDRs, a depository bank buys shares of a stock in its local market and then issues receipts to U.S. investors as evidence of share ownership. The bank handles all of the currency exchange, so that the receipts are priced in dollars. Larger companies usually sponsor the ADR, agreeing to register the offering with the SEC and provide shareholder disclosure that meets SEC requirements—allowing the ADR to be listed on an exchange. For multinational companies, trading volume in its ADRs in the United States can be as high—or even higher—than volume in its home market. At a customer's request, however, banks can create receipts that trade over the counter for any foreign stock—even without the company's sponsorship.

Why ever invest locally? Why not just buy depositary receipts? For one thing, there may be more liquidity in the stock in the local market, especially for smaller companies. Investors in local shares may be able to react more quickly to news announcements because they don't have to wait for the U.S. market to open before they can trade. Finally, local owners may have access to more information, because companies may be required to report to direct holders of its stocks but not to owners of depositary receipts.

As a result, mutual funds that invest the bulk of their assets outside the United States generally establish a global custody network and buy shares locally. Funds and individuals that make only the occasional foreign purchase often opt for the convenience of a depositary receipt.

- *Foreign institutional investor registration.* In some countries, a fund or its manager may need to register as a *foreign institutional investor,* or FII. This can be a paperwork-intensive process involving the local subcustodian, the foreign custody manager, the fund manager, and the fund itself, not to mention the foreign regulators. If the country places a quota on FII investment, as China does, the fund may need to stand in a queue until capacity is available. And the FII may be subject to greater compliance requirements and investment restrictions than local investors.

Another country that requires FII registration is India. Just deciding which entity should register is a complex process. The FII could be:

1. The fund itself, known as a *single entity FII*
2. The investment manager with each fund listed as a subaccount under the manager's license (the most popular choice for mutual funds)
3. The sponsor of the fund family, in which each fund is managed by a separate investment manager. This is called a *multimanaged account*

All Indian FIIs are required to have a designated compliance officer, who helps ensure that investments comply with all relevant regulations—including those related to the payment of tax.

- *Foreign taxation.* Investments made overseas may be subject to tax overseas—as well as tax in the United States. If funds do end up paying foreign taxes, they normally provide information on each fund investor's share of those taxes on the annual Form 1099-DIV tax report. Shareholders can claim a credit or deduction for those amounts on their U.S. income taxes—assuming both that they pay sufficient U.S. income taxes and that they hold shares of the fund in a taxable account and not in a retirement fund.

  Because not every fund investor can offset foreign taxes in this way, funds work with local tax consultants to minimize their tax bills by taking full advantage of any exemptions or credits available. Since many of the taxes that funds ultimately end up paying are withholding taxes on dividends, funds may limit positions in stocks with large dividends. Alternatively, they may engage in *cross-border dividend arbitrage,* lending those high-yielding stocks to local investors just before they make dividend payments in exchange for a lending fee—equivalent to the dividend—that's not subject to tax.

- *Foreign share ownership compliance.* Most countries have regulations regarding ownership concentration. Many require that investors file a notification with the regulator whenever their percentage ownership of a company exceeds a certain threshold. In the United States, for example, investors must notify the SEC whenever their holdings of a company exceed 5 percent of its shares outstanding. In the United Kingdom, the equivalent limit is 3 percent, while French companies may establish reporting thresholds as low as 0.5 percent in their by-laws. Countries may also establish absolute limits on ownership for certain types of companies for certain foreign investors.

The rules are myriad—but mutual funds must be prepared to abide by all of them. The penalties for failing to do so can be quite steep, ranging from loss of shareholder voting rights to substantial fines to loss of foreign institutional investor qualifications. A mutual fund's compliance team will work closely with local experts to make sure that their systems monitor all the requirements.

Given all the complexities of overseas investing, it's no wonder that few individual investors attempt it. Instead, they have generally turned to mutual funds—which have greater resources to tackle the research, trading, operations, and compliance issues in multiple markets.

PUTTING IT ALL TOGETHER: MANAGING A GLOBAL OR INTERNATIONAL FUND

You've just been appointed the portfolio manager of a U.S.-registered stock mutual fund that invests overseas. In many respects, you'll be doing the same work as the manager of a fund that stays at home, but there are some key differences, as we'll see.

Prospectus. As with any mutual fund management assignment, you'll start by reading the prospectus, which will define the objectives, investment approach, and restrictions that apply to the fund. One of the most important things you'll learn is where specifically the fund can invest. Your fund may be:

- *Single country.* Confined to a specific country such as India or Japan.
- *Regional.* Focused on a particular geographic region, such as Europe, Latin America, or Southeast Asia.
- *Emerging market.* Investing in developing economies only.
- *International.* Investing exclusively outside the United States, perhaps in developed markets only or in a combination of developed and emerging markets.
- *World or global.* Investing in both the United States and other countries.

To comply with SEC regulations, your fund will generally need to invest at least 80 percent of its assets in investments that are economically tied to the area of focus. The prospectus will list the criteria that you'll use to determine whether a specific investment will help you meet the test. Within these categories, you might even focus on a specific industry or sector.

We'll assume that your fund is actively managed—though index funds are used for overseas investing, too—and your prospectus specifies that you will use a value approach to stock selection.

Benchmark. You're acutely aware that both your positioning and your performance will be judged in relation to a benchmark index. MSCI is the best-known provider of indexes for international and global, so there's a good chance you'll be judged against one of these indexes. The most commonly used ones are:

- *MSCI All-Country World Index.* A common benchmark for global funds. The MSCI ACWI (pronounced *ack*-wee) covers both the

---

BUILDING AN INDEX

Constructing an international market index is not for those who are comfortable with the status quo. There's so much happening in the world markets—particularly in the developing economies—that the indexes must change regularly to keep pace.

To begin with, you'll want the index to represent the investable universe—the stocks that are available for the average portfolio manager to buy—so you'll eliminate all the corporate cross-holdings and the blocks held by insiders from index weightings. To do that, you'll have to keep on top of all the changes in ownership at a company.

And what do you do if a country surprises everyone by imposing currency controls, as Malaysia did in 1998? You have a legitimate reason to remove the country from the index, since it's effectively closed to foreign investments. But that will put portfolio managers with existing positions in a real bind: they can't sell their positions, but are still being evaluated against a benchmark that suddenly has no exposure to the country. (In this case, MSCI compromised by dropping Malaysia from its indexes, while at the same time offering to create parallel indexes that continued to include it.)

At times, you might even have to consider completely revamping your approach. MSCI did just that in May 2008, when it segmented its indexes according to market capitalization: large-, mid-, and small-cap. They previously had two sets of indexes: standard indexes that included a wide range of market caps for both developed and emerging markets and a separate small cap family of indexes for the developed markets only. The change acknowledged the increasing specialization of markets and investors around the world.

developed and emerging markets. As of July 2010, it included more than 1,725 stocks in 45 countries, roughly half of which are developed and half emerging.

- *MSCI EAFE Index.* EAFE—referred to as *Ee*-fuh, or *Ee*-fee—stands for Europe, Australasia, and the Far East. It's representative of the developed markets excluding Canada and the United States.
- *MSCI EM Index.* As its name suggest, the MSCI Emerging Markets Index is a common benchmark for funds that focus on emerging economies.

Constructing indexes in the the emerging markets can be particularly challenging—as "Building an Index" explains.

You'll have to think about the breakdown of the index along four different axes: country, currency, sector/industry, and issuer. A manager of a U.S. stock fund only has to think about the last two dimensions! Specifically:

1. *Country.* As we've seen, country exposure is much less important than it once was, but it can still be critical at times. At the very least, you'll want to avoid exposure to countries where the government is particularly hostile to investors. At the same time, you may want to favor countries where the economy is growing rapidly.

2. *Currency.* It wasn't that long ago that country and currency were synonymous, but that's just not the case today. Many countries in Europe—though not all—are part of the European Monetary Union and use the euro as the currency. On the other hand, some emerging markets tie their currencies to the either the euro or the U.S. dollar in order to demonstrate the stability of their economic policies. You'll need to keep track of all the linkages.

3. *Sector.* Like the manager of a U.S. stock fund, you'll monitor your sector and industry exposure. If you're managing a fund that focuses on large cap stocks in the developed world, you may be more concerned with your sector weights than your country weights. Many of the companies you'll be investing in are truly multinational, with businesses that reach around the world.

4. *Issuer.* You'll want to make sure you're familiar with the largest positions in the index. They'll have a significant impact on index performance, so you'll consider your investment decisions in these stocks particularly carefully.

Peer group. You'll take a look at the other funds that you will be compared against, to get a sense for their biases. For example, many fund managers continually overweight the emerging markets—believing that return prospects are better for stocks in those markets. In consequence, if you decide to underweight these markets compared to the index, you'll be even more heavily underweighted versus your competitors.

Quantitative screening. Because there are so many stocks and so little time, you'll try to use quantitative analysis to narrow down the universe of stocks that you'll consider for investment. As a value manager, you'll look for stocks with low P/E, price/book, and price/cash flow ratios. (Chapter 5 covers quantitative analysis, value investing, and other approaches to stock investing in more detail.)

But data constraints make this type of screening much more difficult for a fund that invests internationally than for a fund investing only in U.S. stocks. There are problems with both data availability and comparability:

- *Data availability.* Generally, more data are available for U.S. companies than for companies in other developed markets, and much more data are available for the developed markets than for the emerging markets. Particular types of data may not be available at all in certain markets and, if available, may have been collected for only a short period, limiting the usefulness of any back test.
- *Data comparability.* Making matters even more difficult, the same data point may not be comparable across markets. For example, a P/E ratio in the United States can't necessarily be compared to a P/E ratio in Germany, which, in turn, may not be comparable to a P/E ratio in Japan. That's because each of these countries use different accounting standards to arrive at the earnings per share figure that makes up the denominator of the P/E ratio. U.S. companies keep their accounts using Generally Accepted Accounting Principles specifically adapted to U.S. requirements, usually referred to as *U.S. GAAP.* Europe relies on International Financial Reporting Standards, or IFRS, while Japan has its own standards. These standards differ in how they measure something as basic as revenue and as philosophical as the value of intangible assets, such as acquired patents.

There's a general agreement among investors that they'd be better off with a single global standard, and most regulators around the world have endorsed convergence—at least in principle. In the United States, for example, the SEC has announced that the United States is trying to adopt the international standard by 2014 if all the issues can be resolved. But many observers expect that this timetable will be pushed back, given the much more pressing regulatory issues raised by the credit crisis. Other countries have not yet established any definite time frames for the changeover, and many companies have little enthusiasm for changing accounting systems.

In any event, it will be a long time before the accounting convergence makes quantitative analysis easier. In countries that have already made the transition—for example, Chile adopted IFRS in 2009—only a limited amount of historical data will be restated. In short, even if all countries were to adopt IFRS tomorrow, back tests would still need to use historical data based on different accounting standards.

Because of the issues with cross-border comparisons, you'll rely on relative valuation within countries more than you might like. This is another reason why you still need to monitor country weightings, even though sector now plays a bigger role in returns. You'll evaluate a market's overall valuation, and if it appears to get out of line—as it did in Japan in the late 1980s—you'll want to adjust your exposure to that country.

Fundamental analysis. Now that you've used quantitative screens—however imperfect—to narrow down the universe, you're ready to work with your analysts to delve into company fundamentals. Obviously, the challenges here are much greater than they are for domestic fund managers—and not just because non-U.S. companies often disclose less information, as we've discussed. You'll probably want foreign language capabilities on your team. While many companies conduct their daily operations in English—and many more translate at least key documents into what has become the business world's lingua franca—you may not catch many of the nuances if you're not fluent in the local language. You may even miss an opportunity in a smaller company that hasn't yet started to cater to the preferences of international investors.

To ensure that you're getting the full picture, you might decide that you'd like your analysts to be based in the regions they're researching. To that end, many fund management companies have set up offices with analytical staff in hubs like London, Singapore, and Tokyo. You'll hope to get better information from company managements and have a clearer picture of local trends. But foreign investment offices are very expensive. Furthermore, it may be tougher to coordinate the efforts of analysts around the world and ensure that they all use a similar approach. As a result, you may decide to keep both your international and U.S. teams based at your U.S. headquarters.

In either case, you'll be traveling extensively. You'll want to meet with managements yourself, especially for your largest holdings. And if you have analysts based overseas, you'll try to meet with them often, to pull them together as a team.

Currency. But having a style for picking stocks is not enough. You'll also need to have an approach to managing currency exposure. To hedge or not to hedge? If you hedge, you'll use derivatives—usually foreign currency forwards but often futures or swaps—to convert the value of the shares from the local currency back into U.S. dollars. There are three possible approaches:

1. *Never hedge.* You may decide that you'll never hedge, that you'll simply accept the foreign currency risk and factor it into your decision about whether to buy a particular stock. For example, if you think that the Japanese yen will be especially weak versus the U.S. dollar, you'll expect lower returns from stocks in Japan and probably reduce your weighting. Many fund managers use this approach, which involves the lowest transaction costs.
2. *Always hedge.* Maybe you don't want to accept any foreign currency risk, so you'll convert back into U.S. dollars at all times. One problem with this approach: Your returns might differ significantly from those of the benchmark index or of your peer group. That will be a particular problem when foreign currencies are strong and your performance lags behind. As a result, few managers use this approach, which involves the highest transaction costs.
3. *Hedge sometimes.* Many managers try to improve returns by hedging when they believe that foreign currencies will be weak and the U.S. dollar will be strong. Since currency values often move in sustained trends, technical analysis can be helpful in predicting their direction.

Trading. Once you've made your security selections, you'll send your buy and sell orders to the trading desk—or trading desks, as may well be the case. As with your analytical team, you may decide to spread your traders around the world. Local knowledge can be extremely important, especially in smaller markets where trading volumes are low and automation is less prevalent. But wherever your traders are based, be prepared for phone calls in the middle of the night. Your fund's trading team will track the sun around the world, and you can be asked to clarify instructions at any time.

While we've emphasized the differences between managing a fund that invests overseas and one that stays at home, the process is the same at the core. You and your team need to see beyond the consensus to find winning investment ideas. Figure 16.3 presents an actual research note presenting what turned out to be a successful sell recommendation on a Swiss stock.

MFS RESEARCH NOTES

NOBEL BIOCARE AG CHF2.00(BR) (CH;NOBE)

Rating: 3-Sell (Downgraded)   Quant Rank: 57
Previous Close: CHF425.25   Mkt Cap: CHF10,923M   Avg. Daily Vol: 0.1M

Health Care, Medical Equipment

Div Yield	0.8% 18.6	Price to Book	
% of Index (EAFE)	0.060%	ROE	43.3%
MFS Price Target	--	EV | EV/Sales	10,070M | 13.4
MFS Downside Risk	--	LT EPS Growth Est.	23.0%

Estimates - FYE Dec 31	2006	2007	2008	2009
P/E	40.9	32.0	26.4	28.1*
EV/EBITDA	-- 28.2	*	23.2*	19.5*
* Consensus Estimates Used				
Earnings (MFS)	10.40	13.30	16.10	--
Revenue (MFS)	--	--	--	--
EBITDA (MFS)	--	--	--	--
Earnings (Consensus)	10.01	12.48	15.15	--
Revenue (Consensus)	971.63	1,162.09	1,359.97	--
EBITDA (Consensus)	356.92	433.62	515.42	--
Earnings Growth (MFS / Consensus)		-- / 24.76%		
Revenue Growth (MFS / Consensus)		-- / 19.60%		
EBITDA Growth (MFS / Consensus)		-- / 21.49%		

CH:NOBE (738572)   2/1/2005 to 2/1/2007   High: 416.25   Low: 212.5   Last: 416.25

Business Description

Nobel Biocare Holding AG. The Group's principal activity is the development, production and marketing of dental implants and IT-based industrialized dental prosthetics. The Group operates two business units: Dental Implants, which makes permanent replacements for lost teeth and Procera, which produces dental copings and dental bridges using a computer-aided manufacture based process.

Investment Thesis

In a nutshell this is a stock that will probably continue to outperform in the short 2, 3 or 5 years from now - growth is going to hit a brick wall. When it does earnings will be downgraded and the hefty rating implode (40x 06, 33x 07, and 27x 08) would leave you with well over 50% downside risk.

Note Conclusion

Nobel Biocare is a stock that I have looking at and thinking about for quite a while now. The multiple was unappealing but I forced myself to look at the company and about a week ago after I met the CEO. In a nutshell this is a stock that will probably continue to outperform in the short maybe even medium-term - and I don't know whether that is 2, 3 or 5 yrs from now - growth is going to hit a brick wall. When it does earnings will be downgraded and the hefty rating implode (40x 06, 33x 07, and 27x 08) would leave you with well over 50% downside risk. I am prepared to miss the excitement in the short and even medium-term as I am not clever enough to be able to time an exit and don't want to be the greater fool left holding the shares when the story implodes.

The dated MFS Equity Research example above should not be considered a recommendation to buy or sell any security.

FIGURE 16.3   An Actual Research Note

CHAPTER SUMMARY

U.S. investors have increased their holdings of overseas securities. Opportunities for investing abroad have expanded because other countries have reduced controls on capital flows and non-U.S. markets have grown. Because returns in foreign markets are not perfectly correlated with returns in the United States, adding overseas holdings to a portfolio can reduce overall risk. The correlation among markets, however—particularly in the developed world—has been increasing, especially during times of crisis. Investors continue to show a preference for their local market, though this home bias has been decreasing over time.

Compared to investing in the United States, investing overseas involves special risks. The value of the local currency may fluctuate against the dollar. Government policies in other countries may not be particularly investor-friendly. Trading costs may be high, and some countries may lack the financial infrastructure to ensure that records are kept accurately and transactions processed promptly.

Funds that invest overseas by trading locally must establish a global custody network, hiring a foreign custody manager to select local subcustodian banks. These funds may be required to register with local regulators as a foreign institutional investor. They must also comply with local tax rules and limitations on share ownership. Investors can avoid the difficulties involved with trading locally by buying depositary receipts, which represent shares of foreign companies that trade outside their local market.

Mutual funds that invest overseas may focus on a single country or region, may invest only outside the United States, or may invest globally, holding both U.S. and non-U.S. securities. Portfolio managers of these funds must monitor country and currency exposure in addition to sector and issuer exposure—all relative to a benchmark index that will change fairly often to reflect the rapid pace of change in many non-U.S. markets.

Quantitative screening is more difficult to use in overseas investing than for U.S. investing because fewer data points are available for non-U.S. companies and data may not be comparable across markets. That's because different countries use different accounting standards. Regulators have endorsed a convergence toward International Financial Reporting Standards, but movement toward the single standard has been slow. Some fund management companies may have analysts and traders based around the world to increase the level of local knowledge, while others prefer to keep the investment staff in a single location to ensure consistency of approach. Portfolio managers must decide whether to hedge currency exposure and, if so, to what extent.

CHAPTER 17

Cross-Border Asset Gathering

T he relaxation of controls on cross-border financial flows has made more than investing overseas easier—it has made doing business globally easier as well. As the world economy has become increasingly integrated, more and more companies are reaching beyond their home base in search of growth in other countries. They're looking to increase revenues and profits by selling into a larger market.

Mutual fund management companies are part of this globalization trend, creating new funds and setting up operations around the world. The math is compelling. The United States is the largest mutual fund market—yet it accounts for less than half of worldwide assets—meaning that firms establishing themselves overseas can at a minimum double the size of their target market. And there's a good chance that those overseas markets are growing at a faster pace than the fund business is at home.

In our concluding two chapters, we look at mutual fund management companies as businesses trying to expand internationally. In this chapter, we explain the models that fund sponsors have used to build a presence in other countries. We then take a look at how those models have been used in Europe to develop a successful structure for cross-border asset gathering. In the next chapter, we look at the market for asset management services in countries outside the United States and Europe. In both chapters, we provide snapshots of the markets for investment funds in key countries, with overviews of their historical growth, regulation, and methods of distribution.

This chapter reviews:

- The past growth and future potential of the worldwide market for investment funds
- The possible models for building a global fund business
- The success of the European UCITS funds
- The potential for cross-border pension plan management in Europe

We conclude this chapter with a snapshot of the German investment funds market as an illustration of the growth of UCITS within a major European country.

THE GLOBAL MARKET FOR INVESTMENT FUNDS

Mutual fund management companies can significantly increase their growth potential by expanding overseas. At the end of 2009, assets of mutual funds worldwide were US$23.0 trillion—having grown 6.9 percent per year over the preceding 10 years. Let's take a look at the markets for funds and growth trends in each region, which are shown in Figure 17.1:

- *United States.* The United States, with US$11.1 trillion in assets, accounted for almost half of worldwide fund assets at the end of 2009. But it's been the slowest-growing region, experiencing only 5.0 percent annual gains in the past decade. Even so, the United States is where the money is, so non-U.S. fund sponsors who want to expand their global reach generally try to establish a presence here, usually through acquisitions. Since most of this book has examined the U.S. market for funds in detail, we will not review it further in this chapter, except to highlight differences versus the rest of the world.
- *Americas ex U.S.* While the Americas outside the United States is a small portion of the worldwide market, growth within that portion has been spectacular. Assets tripled over the 10-year period, adding up to annual growth of 13.4 percent, led by gains in Latin America. Brazil is the largest market in this region, having taken over the number one spot from Canada (now ranked second) over the course of the decade.

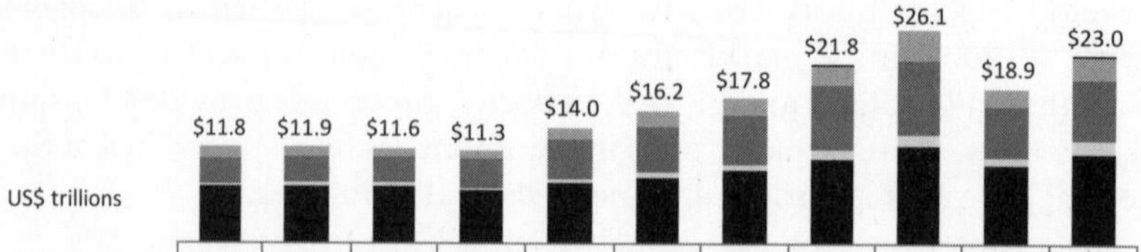

US$ trillions	1999	2000	2001	2002	2003	2004	2005	2006	2007	2008	2009
	$11.8	$11.9	$11.6	$11.3	$14.0	$16.2	$17.8	$21.8	$26.1	$18.9	$23.0
■ Africa	$0.0	$0.0	$0.0	$0.0	$0.0	$0.1	$0.1	$0.1	$0.1	$0.1	$0.1
■ Asia and Pacific	1.3	1.1	1.0	1.1	1.4	1.7	1.9	2.5	3.7	2.0	2.7
■ Europe	3.2	3.3	3.2	3.5	4.7	5.6	6.0	7.8	8.9	6.2	7.5
■ Americas ex U.S.	0.4	0.5	0.5	0.4	0.6	0.7	0.9	1.1	1.4	1.0	1.5
■ U.S.	6.8	7.0	7.0	6.4	7.4	8.1	8.9	10.4	12.0	9.6	11.1

FIGURE 17.1   Worldwide Mutual Fund Assets
Source: Investment Company Institute, *2007 to 2010 Investment Company Fact Books.*

- *Europe.* Europe was the second-largest region, at almost one-third of world assets. Growth there has been above average, averaging 8.9 percent per year over the 10-year period. Luxembourg is the largest market within Europe, with over 30 percent of European fund assets. That may be surprising, since Lux—as it's familiarly known by many in the fund industry—is a small country. Yet it has become a hub for the management of fund assets not only from the rest of Europe, but also from around the globe. France is the second-largest market, while Ireland—another fund management hub—ranks third. The United Kingdom is fourth. We talk more about Europe's role as an asset management center later in this chapter.
- *Asia and Pacific.* Asia-Pacific accounted for a little over 10 percent of world fund assets and grew at an above-average 7.8 percent yearly rate over the past decade. Strong growth in Australia—the largest market in the region—and in some of the emerging markets, notably India, was offset by sluggish gains in the second-largest market, Japan.
- *Africa.* Fund assets in Africa were very small. South Africa is the only significant mutual fund market on that continent.

Not surprisingly, wealthier countries tend to have larger mutual fund markets—not just in absolute terms but also relative to the size of their economies.[1] Figure 17.2 shows fund assets in 2009 for the world's largest economies as a percentage of gross domestic product. In the United States, mutual fund assets equaled 78 percent of GDP that year, but most other countries had a significantly lower ratio. For example, fund assets in Japan amounted to only 16 percent of GDP, meaning that assets would need to increase by US$2,566 billion dollars for funds in Japan to have the same presence as they have in the United States. The chart shows how much fund assets would need to grow in each country to equal 78 percent of GDP. Only in Australia—which, as we'll see, has a mandatory private retirement system—do assets exceed that level.

On the other hand, the smaller mutual fund markets are often faster-growing. In total, fund assets in countries outside the United States rose from US$4.9 trillion at the end of 1999 to US$11.8 trillion 10 years later. That's an annual gain of 9.2 percent, almost double the growth rate in the United States. A number of factors have contributed to these high levels of fund growth outside the United States—factors that are likely to continue in force over the next decade.

- *Growing middle class.* In the emerging markets in particular, economic development has supported an expansion of the middle class—a group with a rapidly growing pool of savings and an increasing appetite for investing them for a higher return. The middle class, as opposed to the

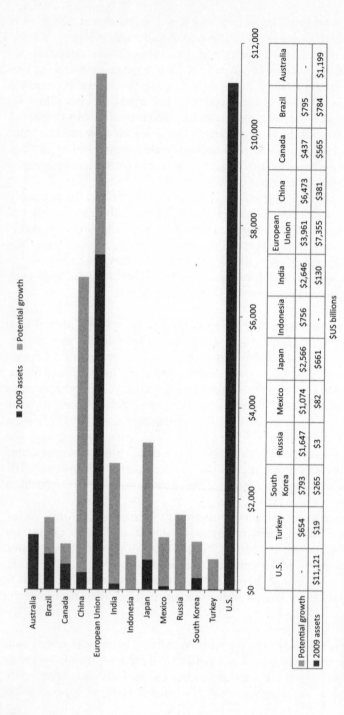

	U.S.	Turkey	South Korea	Russia	Mexico	Japan	Indonesia	India	European Union	China	Canada	Brazil	Australia
Potential growth	-	$654	$793	$1,647	$1,074	$2,566	$756	$2,646	$3,961	$6,473	$437	$795	-
2009 assets	$11,121	$19	$265	$3	$82	$661		$130	$7,355	$381	$565	$784	$1,199

$US billions

FIGURE 17.2 Potential Global Fund Industry Growth

Potential growth assumes fund assets equal 78 percent of GDP.

Source: Investment Company Institute, *2010 Investment Company Fact Books*, and Central Intelligence Agency, *The World Factbook.*

poor and the very rich, are the primary market for mutual funds in most countries.

■ *Increasing awareness of advantages of mutual funds.* At the same time, middle class investors are becoming more aware of the advantages of mutual funds, turning to them for professional management, a higher level of diversification and access to a wider range of investments. The transparency of mutual funds—combined with a significant degree of regulatory oversight—provide shareholder protections that may not be available with other investment options. Researchers have found that funds are generally most accepted—and least costly—in countries in which investor protections are the strongest.[2] On the other hand, in some markets, investors believe that investing through mutual funds allows them to compete effectively in countries where there are many favored insiders and large shareholders.

■ *New product introductions.* As in the United States, fund sponsors in foreign countries have introduced new types of funds to appeal to different market niches. For example, they have created funds with hedge fund–like features that are designed for more aggressive investors, and funds with guaranteed minimum returns, or floors, for risk-averse investors.

■ *Increased competition.* Countries have allowed new types of competitors to enter the mutual fund market. Banks, for example, may now be permitted to sell funds where only securities firms were allowed to deal in them before, or offshore funds registered in other countries may be authorized for sale in a market in which only locally registered offerings had been available. Lower barriers to entry contribute to growth in fund assets.

■ *Aging populations and increased retirement savings.* Many countries have rapidly aging populations that are increasingly turning to mutual funds to help them save for retirement. Figure 17.3 shows the trend in the percentage of the population age 65 and over for China, Europe, India, Japan, and the United States. The United States may be aging quickly, but China is aging even faster, the result of its one-child policy. Similarly, in Europe and Japan, retirees will soon constitute a larger percentage of their total populations than in the United States.

Retirees in developed countries other than the United States generally expect that the state-sponsored pension system will provide them with most of their income. However, as with Social Security in the United States, current workers generally support payments to current retirees in these largely pay-as-you-go systems. Yet many of these systems are watching the number of workers per retiree dwindle. As a result, many public pension plans may soon have difficulty making the

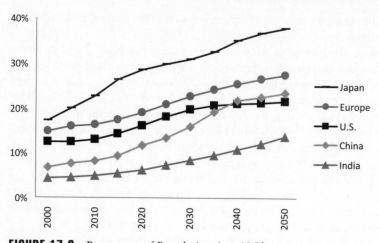

FIGURE 17.3   Percentage of Population Age 65-Plus
Source: Population Division of the Department of Economic and Social Affairs of
the United Nations Secretariat, *World Population Prospects: The 2008 Revision.*

books balance—and may be forced to reduce the growth of benefits to
remain solvent.

   To reduce the burden on the public systems, many countries are encouraging private retirement savings—by individuals or
employers—usually through tax incentives. As in the United States,
mutual funds are often used as an investment option in these private
retirement programs. For just two examples, the United Kingdom has
established "Self-Invested Personal Pensions" that are similar to U.S.
individual retirement accounts, while Australia has a "Superannuation
Guarantee" based on a mandatory savings program that looks like
somewhat like a 401(k) plan with a required employer contribution.
The Australian program has been particularly successful, accumulating approximately US$1 trillion in assets by mid-2010. "Contrasting
Schemes" explains in more detail how retirement programs in other
countries compare to U.S. 401(k) plans.

CONTRASTING SCHEMES

Defined contribution retirement savings schemes in other countries
are often compared to 401(k) plans—mainly because they all provide a retirement income benefit that's determined by the value of the
assets in an individual's account without a continuing benefit guarantee from the employer sponsoring the plan. But they differ in an

equally important respect: U.S. 401(k) plans are entirely voluntary, while the programs in most foreign countries are often compulsory in at least some respects. Table 17.1 summarizes some of the key differences. (Turn back to Chapter 11 for details on 401(k) plans.)

TABLE 17.1 Non-U.S. Defined Contribution Plans versus U.S. 401(k) Plans

Feature	Non-U.S. Defined Contribution Plan	U.S. 401(k) Plan
Individual account	Worker has individual account; value of account based on contributions and investment earnings.	Worker has individual account; value of account based on contributions and investment earnings.
Employee participation	Worker participation compulsory in some countries.	Workers may be automatically enrolled but have ability to opt out.
Employee contribution	Mandatory at fixed percentage of salary in some countries.	At worker's discretion, subject to caps and nondiscrimination rules.
Employer contribution	Normally mandatory at fixed percentage of salary.	At employer's discretion, subject to caps and nondiscrimination rules.
Plan provider	In most countries, either workers choose among limited number of providers or government administers plan.	Chosen by employer.
Investment allocation	Investment allocation determined by plan administrator, or participants given limited number of alternatives.	Employer chooses array of options; worker has complete freedom to allocate assets among those options.
Benefits	Determined by the value of assets in the account, although some countries guarantee a minimum benefit.	Determined by the value of assets in the account.
Payout of benefits	Participant may be required to receive all or part of their benefits in the form of a life annuity.	Participant decides when to withdraw money from the account, subject to a required minimum distribution.

One other key distinction: Defined contribution plans overseas are often referred to as *schemes*—a term that doesn't have the negative connotation abroad that it has in American English. We take a closer look at some defined contribution plans in other countries in the next chapter.

MODELS FOR A GLOBAL FUND BUSINESS

While the long-term growth potential in overseas markets is tantalizing, fund management companies face formidable obstacles in establishing viable operations abroad. Investment management is very much a local business. No single mutual fund can be sold in every country throughout the world. That's because regulation, accounting standards, and tax regimes vary from country to country—and are often incompatible. Fund sponsors need to tailor their offerings to local predilections—and not just by publishing documents in the local language and denominating the NAV in the local currency. They must adjust their product mix to match preferences for different investment types. For example, within Scandinavia, Danes are most likely to buy bond funds, while Swedes lean toward stock funds.

Moreover, competition from local players is fierce. They're familiar with the ins and outs of the local market and have had a long time to build a dominant position. The top five companies often control a majority of the market, as Figure 17.4 shows, making most foreign mutual fund markets significantly more concentrated than the U.S. market for mutual funds.

A fund management company looking to enter a new market and take share from entrenched competitors must establish its own local presence in that market—developing a line of funds that conforms to the regulatory requirements and investor tastes in that market while creating a distinct brand name and reputation. That local presence must be built market by market—which makes it difficult for a fund sponsor to reduce start-up expenses by taking advantage of economies of scale. Therefore, the challenge for fund management companies with global aspirations is to define a business model that allows the firm to distribute products that are competitive in each local market, while keeping costs manageable.

Although there is no perfect way to structure a global growth strategy for mutual funds, firms have generally relied on one of six different models: mutual recognition, master-feeder structures, clone funds, joint ventures, subadvisory relationships, and acquisitions. Let's take a look at each.

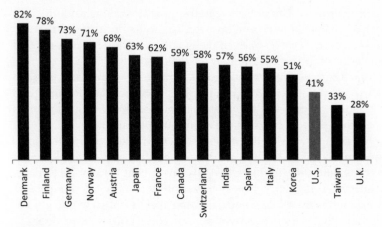

FIGURE 17.4 Market Share of Top Five Providers (June 2009)[3]
Source: Strategic Insight.

Mutual recognition. The first model is mutual recognition. It's a regulatory arrangement that allows a fund organized and regulated in one jurisdiction—the home country—to be sold in other host countries—without having to reregister the fund in each of those host countries. (A brief note on terminology: when a fund is registered with regulators in a particular country, it's said to be *domiciled* in that *jurisdiction.* We use *domicile* and *jurisdiction* interchangeably to refer to registration and regulation in a country.)

Mutual recognition agreements in other spheres are very common. For example, drivers' licenses are mutually recognized throughout the 50 states and often internationally as well. A driver licensed in Massachusetts can take a car trip anywhere in the United States and can even rent a car in London—without having to take the rigorous U.K. road test. Mutual recognition makes life much easier for businesses and consumers, and it rarely raises eyebrows as long as there's a basic agreement on principles—on what makes for a qualified driver, for example.

When it comes to mutual funds, unfortunately, there's rarely much international agreement on which investor protections are needed and what taxation is appropriate. And there's little incentive for local firms or local regulators—who are both protecting their turf—to compromise. They prefer *national treatment,* which requires that all funds comply with the same local rules. As a result, mutual recognition in the fund world is rare.

But it does exist in Europe. Perhaps that's not surprising given that the European Union was initially formed to increase economic cooperation and given that the European Union has created supranational institutions, such as the European Council and the European Commission to foster that co-operation. However, as we'll see, even the European Union has encountered local obstacles to implementing mutual recognition.

Master-feeder structures. If selling the same fund in different jurisdictions won't work, perhaps it would be possible to repackage the same fund to meet the requirements of different regulators. Electronics manufacturers do this when they provide users' manuals in multiple languages.

In the investment world, the *master-feeder,* or *hub and spoke,* funds are designed to fill this need. In a master-feeder structure, multiple feeder funds invest in a single master fund; the only investment held by the feeder is shares of the master. In theory, master-feeder funds should be less expensive than establishing separate local funds, because there's only one portfolio in the master fund that supports a number of feeder funds sold in different distribution channels. The feeder funds are registered locally, while the master fund may be formed and regulated in another jurisdiction. Figure 17.5 diagrams how an ideal master-feeder structure would look.

In practice, however, the accounting and administration in a multi-layered master-feeder structure is quite expensive. That's because each of the feeder funds is a separate legal entity. As result, master-feeder funds are not commonly used within the United States to provide customized fund offerings for different customers. Instead, to achieve the same end, most fund sponsors have chosen to set up multiple share classes within the same legal entity. (We review share classes in Chapter 10.) Share classes

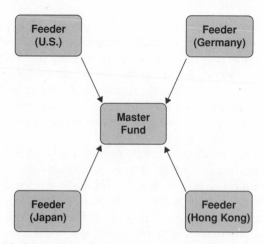

FIGURE 17.5   Ideal Master-Feeder Structure

are a lot cheaper to administer, although they are also less flexible than a master-feeder structure. Share classes enable funds to charge different distribution and servicing fees to different types of shareholders, but otherwise generally require that shareholders receive identical treatment.

One problem with master-feeder structures is that regulators in many countries are concerned that they can be used to circumvent local rules and tax regimes and, therefore, place severe restrictions on their use in publicly

ISLAND HAVEN

While master-feeder structures are difficult to establish for mutual funds, they're very popular with hedge funds. A sponsor establishes a master fund in a low-tax—or even no-tax—jurisdiction such as the Bahamas, Bermuda, or the Cayman Islands. The master fund then typically has at least two feeder funds: a domestic feeder for taxable U.S. investors and an offshore feeder for tax-exempt U.S. investors, such as pension plans, and for non-U.S. investors. The domestic feeder is usually a limited partnership, while the offshore feeder is normally structured as a corporation.

This structure allows the master fund to benefit from economies of scale while meeting the needs of a diverse set of investors. Taxable U.S. investors must invest in the domestic feeder, since U.S. tax rules prevent them from putting money in offshore funds. Only the domestic feeder provides reports to the IRS—which means that investors in the offshore feeder don't have to worry about being caught in the U.S. tax net. And only the domestic feeder needs to worry about the accredited investor tests that allow a hedge fund to avoid regulation. (Chapter 12 has more on these rules.) At the same time, the corporate form of the offshore feeder is attractive to U.S. tax-exempt investors who might be subject to tax on unrelated business taxable income if they invest through the limited partnership.

The hedge fund manager is usually registered or licensed offshore, though not in the United States, placing it clearly outside the scope of U.S. regulation. The manager must still comply with country-specific rules, however, when raising money from non-U.S. investors for the offshore feeder—rules that are about to become much stricter in the European Union once the new Alternative Investment Fund Manager directive becomes effective.

offered funds. In the United States, for example, the SEC prohibits the sale of U.S.-registered feeder funds if the master fund is organized in another country. Again, the exception is Europe. The recently approved UCITS IV directive—which we discuss in greater detail shortly—will make master-feeder structures possible within the European Union. Another exception: Some investment managers have created master-feeder funds to capture assets from wealthy individuals—often from Latin America—who have moved a substantial amount of their assets offshore.

By contrast, master-feeder structures are very common in the hedge fund world, as "Island Haven" explains.

Clone funds. In light of the obstacles, many managers have given up trying to sell the same fund in several countries at the same time. They establish different funds in each country, instead, and then manage them as clones of one another. As we discussed in Chapter 8, clone funds have essentially identical investment objectives and policies—and essentially identical portfolios. They are managed by the same portfolio manager, who replicates the holdings in one fund in all the other funds, often with the help of the trading desk. The portfolio manager may handle the largest fund personally or may create an investment template; in either case, the trading desk then copies the holdings in the base fund in the clone funds.

Again, while the process is straightforward in theory, in practice it can be quite difficult to keep the portfolios perfectly aligned. Local regulatory requirements frequently oblige funds to follow slightly different investment policies. For example, each country might set a different limit on maximum position size or on the use of derivatives. The cloned funds will experience different cash flows from shareholder purchases and redemptions—which means that they won't always be trading at the same times, and securities available to all funds last month may not be available to the fund that needs to invest excess cash today. This is a particular problem for bond funds.

Despite its drawbacks, cloning is the simplest model from a regulatory and operations standpoint. As a result, it is the one that is used most often, at least for smaller-scale efforts.

Joint venture. For larger investments—particular in the markets that are hardest to enter—many mutual fund management companies may enter into joint ventures with a local partner. JVs were once quite popular in India, though they are now used less since rules on foreign investment have been relaxed. At times, a JV may be the only way to enter a market: that's currently the case in mainland China, where foreign fund sponsors must partner with a local bank or securities company.

JVs can be formed in one of two ways: The fund sponsor can create a new entity together with the local partner, or the fund sponsor can buy a large stake in an existing company. The advantage of JVs is that fund sponsors can hit the ground running in the new market since they gain instant access to local knowledge and connections, and the local partner can usually help speed up the necessary regulatory approvals.

Even with a head start, the JV will still need to establish its own brand identity before it can reach critical mass, especially if it's an entirely new entity. The JV might still need to create locally registered funds, limiting the ability to capitalize on economies of scale. In addition, working with a partner can be difficult, especially for a minority owner. In China, foreign fund sponsors are limited to a 49 percent stake in a JV, ceding ultimate control to the local partner. To reduce the tensions inherent in JVs, fund management companies must pick their JV partners very carefully.

Subadvisory relationships. In a watered-down variant of the joint venture, fund management companies can agree to provide investment management services for a fund that is organized by a local firm. This type of arrangement is called a *subadvisory relationship*. It's a low-cost way for local fund sponsors to add new types of funds to their product lineup, even when they don't have the investment expertise in-house. The local firm simply pays the subadviser a fee based on assets under management, without having to invest in setting up a portfolio management team. Hiring well-known fund managers as subadvisers can also enhance the fund family's brand reputation and boost sales. For the subadviser, the arrangement is an easy way to boost fee income with little expense. The subadviser simply starts managing another clone fund, leaving all the distribution and operational headaches to the local fund sponsor.

On the negative side, the foreign fund manager isn't entitled to any of the profits should the venture prove successful—although there's no exposure to potential losses, either. Perhaps more importantly, it's difficult for a fund manager to establish a local presence through a subadvisory relationship, since it's the local fund firm that has direct client contact. A subadviser may find that an agreement is terminated once the local manager has had time to build up its own expertise.

Note that while the fund needs to be registered with the local securities regulator, the subadviser usually does not—as long as the foreign fund manager does not have a local investment office and is subject in its home country to regulations that are as stringent as those imposed in the host country. (In essence, this is a form of mutual recognition.) Since U.S. regulation is quite strict, U.S. fund managers generally encounter no obstacles in subadvising a non-U.S. fund. At least that's the case right now, although there is increased attention being paid to this issue in the wake of the credit crisis.

Acquisitions. Finally, a management company can simply buy its way into a market—assuming that there are no restrictions on foreign ownership, of course. As mentioned, many foreign fund sponsors decide to enter the U.S. market by this route—it's almost a necessity because of the size of the market, the tough competition from the big players in the U.S. industry, and the tight regulation based on national treatment. (Chapter 15 reviews acquisitions of fund managers in the United States.)

However, if the acquirer wants to generate cross-selling opportunities or to realize cost savings, it must incorporate some of the other models into its post-purchase operational plans. For example, it may establish clone funds or subadvisory relationships that enable its newly acquired portfolio team to manage funds sold around the world. Without this kind of integration, the merger is likely to fail to produce the expected benefits.

In practice, fund management companies building a global presence generally use a variety of models, considering what will work best under particular circumstances. Thus, firms will take advantage of mutual recognition regimes in regions where they are well established, such as Europe. They'll use master-feeder funds in markets in which regulation allows them, such as in Latin America. They'll establish locally registered clone funds if they believe they can gather enough in assets to justify the cost, either because the market is sufficiently large or the competition is sufficiently weak. They'll partner in joint ventures with domestic firms when that model will provide the most efficient access to the local market. And firms may layer these approaches. For example, a fund management company may clone a U.S-based portfolio in a fund registered in Dublin and then rely on mutual recognition to distribute the Irish fund throughout Europe.

At the same time, they'll centralize as many functions as possible in an effort to achieve lower operating costs. For example, portfolio management and trading teams will be housed in just a few offices in major financial centers, such as London, Tokyo, or Singapore. Similarly, shareholder servicing, fund accounting, and investment operations will be consolidated into multilingual service centers, using a single technology platform to process transactions involving multiple currencies.

THE UCITS MODEL

Cross-border distribution has been most successful within Europe. A mutual fund registered in any country that is a member of the European Union may be sold throughout the EU merely by filing a notice with regulatory authorities in a host country, using what is referred to as a passport. The framework for this mutual recognition was established in 1985 with the passage of the first *Undertakings for Collective Investment in Transferable Securities* directive—better known as the UCITS (*Yoo*-sits) directive. (A *directive* is legislation passed by the European Parliament.) "Hail, CESR!" provides a brief introduction to the structure of securities regulation in Europe.

HAIL, CESR!

The key components of European Union securities regulatory structure are:

European Council. The European Council—often referred to as the Council of Ministers—is composed of appointed representatives of the member states. The Council elects a president for a term of two and a half years.

European Parliament. Members of the European Parliament are elected by EU citizens. The number of seats held by a country is determined by population.

Directives. The European Council and the European Parliament must both approve new legislation, called *directives*.

MiFID. The Markets in Financial Services Directive—more commonly known as MiFID (pronounced with a short *i*)—aims to harmonize the regulation of investment services across the European Union. It was passed in 2007, replacing the Investment Services Directive. Under MiFid, member states may not impose additional regulations to protect companies in their home markets against competition from firms in other member states.

UCITS. The Undertakings for Collective Investments in Transferable Securities is a series of directives that allow pooled investment vehicles to operate throughout the European Union after registering in one country.

European Commission. The European Commission is the executive branch of the EU. It is headed by a group of 27 commissioners from the member states, supported by an extensive civil service.

CESR. The Committee of European Securities Regulations—referred to as *Caesar*—is the agency within the European Commission responsible for securities-related matters. It coordinates the activities of local securities regulators and advises the Commission on potential new directives. It also provides guidance on the implementation of directives. CESR is roughly akin to the SEC in the United States, although it does not have enforcement powers. Member states perform that task, though they often rely on CESR's guidance. European courts may also pass judgments on the appropriateness of a member state's implementation of a directive.

ESMA. CESR will be reorganizing in 2011 and taking on a new name: the European Securities Markets Authority or ESMA.

Consultations. CESR does much of its work through consultations. If CESR makes a proposal with regard to a securities-related directive, it sends that proposal to the European Council, which in turn sends it to the Parliament for consultations. Effectively, CESR proposals are subject to a comment period before their implementation.

To qualify for mutual recognition and become a UCITS fund, pooled investment vehicles must meet certain minimum standards.[4] They must protect assets by entrusting them to an independent custodian, they must diversify their investments, and they must obtain board or shareholder approval of significant changes in the management contract. Overall, these restrictions are quite similar to the ones that apply to U.S. mutual funds, though they are more restrictive and more precise in some instances and less restrictive and broader in others. One key difference between U.S. and European funds is that UCITS are not required to distribute all income annually, though most offer that option to investors. A second notable difference is that UCITS need not accept redemptions more than twice a month, although most allow investors to redeem daily.

The UCITS system has been very successful despite obstacles raised by some local regulators. Today, the most common type of investment fund in Europe is the UCITS fund, which accounts for approximately 75 percent of assets under management in the fund industry in Europe, according to EFAMA, the European Fund and Asset Management Association. Roughly 25 years after the scheme was first established, there are now more than 50,000 cross-border registrations of UCITS funds. The average fund is registered in eight countries, while more than a third are registered in 10 countries or more.[5] In many European countries, the number of cross-border UCITS funds exceeds the number of domestic funds.

In short, UCITS have established themselves as the preeminent investment funds for retail investors throughout Europe—and UCITS are becoming increasingly accepted outside the European Union. In 2009, they were distributed in more than a dozen non-EU countries, notably Bahrain, Chile, Singapore, and South Africa. Many non-European fund management companies—including most major U.S. firms—have subsidiaries in Europe that have established fund families in Luxembourg or Ireland. Most UCITS sold cross-border are based in one of these two countries, as we discuss in "Fund Focus."

FUND FOCUS

Two small countries—Luxembourg and Ireland—have become giants in the mutual fund world. That's because each has become a preeminent jurisdiction for the registration of UCITS funds.

Luxembourg—located in the heart of Europe, tucked between Belgium, France, and Germany—was the first country to adopt the UCITS directive in the mid-1980s and to make cross-border funds a core element of its economic growth strategy. Lux built an easy-to-understand regulatory system that responded quickly to applications from mutual funds and established a favorable tax regime. At the end of 2009, it was home to more than $1.8 trillion in fund assets—UCITS and non-UCITS—representing about one-quarter of the European fund total—making Lux the largest fund domicile in the European Union.[6]

Ireland followed Luxembourg's lead and now ranks number 4 in Europe, with more than $1 trillion in fund assets, equal to roughly four times its GDP! It has recently taken steps to increase its market share by making it easier for fund management companies to move funds from other jurisdictions into Irish registration.

France and Germany technically fill the number 2 and number 3 spots, though funds domiciled in these countries are normally dedicated to the local market and are less likely to be sold cross-border. In fact, over 75 percent of UCITS registered in at least three countries are set up in Lux, while Ireland has a 13 percent share of these cross-border UCITS. In this ranking, it's the United Kingdom that places third with less than a 3 percent share.

Luxembourg and Ireland are working hard to keep their top rankings, because other countries are finding the business of hosting investment companies attractive. Malta—a tiny island nation in the Mediterranean—has made a name for itself in the hedge fund world. (In some European countries, hedge fund managers have long been required to register with regulators.) And there's talk that some of the Baltic countries will soon be entering the fray.

You can learn more about mutual fund industries in Luxembourg and Ireland from their respective trade associations: ALFI, the Association for the Luxembourg Fund Industry, and IFIA, the Irish Fund Industry Association. Their web sites are www.alfi.lu and www.irishfunds.ie, respectively.

The success of UCITS has not come easily. Many local regulators have tried to undermine the mutual recognition regime by imposing burdensome notice and reporting obligations on UCITS that seek to register in their country. Some have established their own regulatory requirements—which can be incompatible with those imposed by other countries. They might demand that a fund maintain a local paying agent, translate fund documentation into the country's national language, and publish certain information regarding the fund in local media, or they might create rules regarding the content of performance advertisements, prospectuses, and marketing disclosures. Moreover, each nation has its unique set of tax laws and established marketing practices that must be taken into account in designing products that will sell in that market. Thus, even in a relatively integrated region such as Europe, some local customization of funds is still necessary before a UCITS can be distributed successfully in any particular country.

While local difficulties remain, the European Union continues to work to make cross-border distribution of funds simple in practice. In 2009, the most recent UCITS directive—known as UCITS IV—was passed, amending the prior directives.[7] UCITS IV:

- Permits a UCITS registered in one country to hire a management company based in another EU country. (This was previously not permitted.) This flexibility has become known as the *management company passport*.
- Enables UCITS funds based in different countries to merge.
- Authorizes master-feeder structures.
- Simplifies host country notification procedures.
- Requires funds to supply investors with a *key information document*, or KID, rather than a prospectus.

Though the ease of cross-border distribution has been key to the UCITS success story, another important component has been its investment flexibility. While the investment guidelines in the original directive were quite restrictive, the UCITS III directive, which was adopted in 2002—combined with the Eligible Assets Directive, approved in 2007—have broadened the range of investments and strategies available within the UCITS format.

Most significantly, UCITS are now permitted to use sophisticated investment strategies that employ derivatives extensively. In consequence, UCITS can now replicate hedge fund investment strategies such as long-short or other absolute return approaches, even though UCITS still don't have the ability to sell short directly. (Chapter 12 reviews hedge fund strategies.)

Funds that take advantage of these enhanced capabilities are known officially as *sophisticated UCITS*—or more informally as *NewCITS*. Their fund management companies are required to have a strong risk management

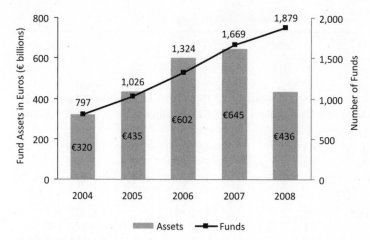

FIGURE 17.6 Trends in Alternative Mutual Funds in Europe[8]
Source: Cerulli Associates.

process—independent of the portfolio manager—that evaluates and controls the fund's exposure to market, credit, counterparty, and liquidity risk. In addition, intermediaries who sell these funds must confirm that these funds are suitable for a particular investor, given that investor's profile. France's financial regulator recently suggested that fund promoters set higher investment minimums for these products to help ensure that they are sold only to investors who have the resources to assume a high level of risk.

As Figure 17.6 illustrates, the number of these alternative mutual funds—and their assets—have been growing slowly but steadily. But there's speculation that numbers will increase dramatically as more hedge funds register as UCITS. Hedge funds could well find the UCITS format more attractive than they did in the past—and that's not just because UCITS now have more investment flexibility. It's also because hedge fund managers in the European Union are facing the prospect of more extensive regulation under a directive approved in 2010, called the Alternative Investment Fund Managers Directive. That directive would require every EU country to regulate local managers of hedge funds and would prohibit managers based outside the EU from raising money for hedge funds from local investors unless they were subject to significant regulation in their home country. Hedge fund managers might conclude that the UCITS format allows them to engage in most of the strategies they would use in a hedge fund—while UCITS offer access to a larger market.

Despite its success, the European model faces a number of challenges—almost literally. There were over 33,000 funds in Europe at the end of 2009—contrast that to only 7,600 funds in the United States with a

TABLE 17.2 Number of Funds and Assets by Region (US$)

	2000	2009	Change
United States			
Number of funds	8,155	7,691	–464
Total assets	US$7.0 trillion	US$11.1 trillion	+ US$4.2 trillion
Assets per fund	$854 million	$1,446 million	+ $592 million
Europe			
Number of funds	25,503	33,054	+ 7,551
Total assets	$3.3 trillion	$7.5 trillion	+ $4.2 trillion
Assets per fund	$129 million	$226 million	+ $97 million
Asia			
Number of funds	13,158	14,795	+ 637
Total assets	$1.1 trillion	$2.7 trillion	+ $1.6 trillion
Assets per fund	$86 million	$137 million	+ $51 million

Source: Investment Company Institute, *2008* and *2010 Investment Company Fact Books.*

significantly larger asset base. As a result, the average European fund has less than a fifth of the assets of the average U.S. mutual fund. (Table 17.2 has figures on numbers of funds and assets for the United States, Europe, and Asia. Note that these numbers include non-UCITS funds that are generally distributed only locally rather than cross-border.) With smaller fund sizes, European funds tend to be more expensive than U.S. funds—quite a bit more expensive, in fact. The average expense ratio for a fund in Europe is almost double that of a U.S. fund.

The less favorable asset-to-fund ratio in Europe is the result of an unfavorable sales pattern: a large portion of European fund sales are made into new funds. In other words, in order to gather assets, fund families must continually create innovative funds. In contrast, most fund flows in the United States go into existing funds. That has allowed the number of U.S. funds to decline over in the past decade, while assets still grew.

Why the difference? Distributors of funds in Europe tend to emphasize new features, while distributors in the United States emphasize long track records. Those long records are particularly important to the employers sponsoring defined contribution retirement plans, which don't change investment options often. In general, the substantial presence of retirement plans in the U.S. mutual funds has helped to stabilize the industry's asset base and product line. As we've discussed, private retirement plans play a large role in the United States. However, as we'll see in the next section, the development of pan-European pensions is in its early stages.

EUROPEAN PENSION POOLING

While encouraging higher levels of private retirement savings, the European Union is also working to reduce the cost of investing those savings. Pension plan management in Europe is a highly local business—much like the mutual fund industry before UCITS gained wide acceptance. This fragmented system discourages employers from establishing plans, since they need to create a separate plan in each country in which they have employees. And each country has its own set of rules—often inconsistent with one another. Some countries require that assets be managed by a local company or that a minimum percentage be invested in government securities. An employer with operations in several countries generally can't hire one manager to handle everything related to the retirement plan.

To make life easier for employers, the European Union adopted a directive in 2003 that authorizes cross-border *occupational pensions,* which in U.S. terminology would be employer-sponsored plans. In Europe, most of these plans are defined benefit plans, which were reviewed in Chapter 11. Under the terms of the directive, an employer can set up a pension fund in one EU country that will cover all of its workers in the European Union, and the investment manager for this cross-border plan can be based in any EU country. The directive also established common standards for plan governance and for the management of pension fund assets, based on a broad prudent-person rule. Put another way, the directive did not contain a list of specific investment guidelines or restrictions; instead, it stated that the plan's manager must invest its assets in a way that a prudent person would deem appropriate.

At the same time, tax obstacles to cross-border pension plans are being chipped away. In most EU member countries, contributions to pension plans are tax-deductible while investment income accrues tax-free. Earnings are taxed only when withdrawn from the account. (This tax treatment is similar to that of a U.S. qualified retirement plan, also described in Chapter 11.) In the past, however, many countries provided these tax benefits only to plans within its borders, imposing taxes on contributions made across borders. These discriminatory taxes have become less common after a series of court decisions found that they were inconsistent with the basic principles of the European Union, specifically the right to move and reside freely, which includes the right to move to find a job.

Despite the favorable rulings, pensions are not portable throughout the European Union. For example, workers may be taxed when they transfer balances between certain countries. The European Commission has proposed that tax deferral for occupational pension schemes be a universal principle throughout the European Union. But any sort of tax harmonization proposal is always extremely controversial—touching as it does on fundamental questions of national sovereignty—so a true alignment of pension plan taxation is unlikely in the near future.

While problems remain, cross-border occupational pensions might still present a significant asset-gathering opportunity for fund management companies. Private retirement savings are growing, and employers—who are more likely to operate across borders themselves—are increasingly interested in simplifying their retirement offerings. To date, the countries that have established themselves as the frontrunners for the creation and promotion of cross-border pension plans are Luxembourg and Belgium—which have created vehicles specifically for pan-European pension funds—as well as the United Kingdom and the Netherlands—which themselves have the largest private occupational pension systems, with combined assets of more than $2 trillion.

Luxembourg and Ireland hope to take cross-border pensions a step further with pension pooling or asset pooling, which allow companies in many countries to pool their pension scheme assets together into a single investment vehicle. Plan sponsors can choose from various subfunds, each focused on a different asset type (stocks, bonds, and so forth). They can adjust this mix as needed to comply with local regulation.

In the "Country Snapshot," we take a look at one of the larger markets within Europe: Germany.

COUNTRY SNAPSHOT: GERMANY

To get a better sense for the European fund market we take a closer look at one of its largest markets. Germany has a substantial local fund market, but has also been very involved in the move to cross-border funds, as we'll see.

Historical Growth

Assets in German mutual funds have remained fairly flat for the past six years. Figure 17.7 shows how, after climbing steadily until 2007, assets dropped sharply during the credit crisis. The recovery the following year was subdued, partly because a new capital gains tax was imposed on investments purchased after December 31, 2008. At the end of 2009, retail fund assets were US$318 billion.

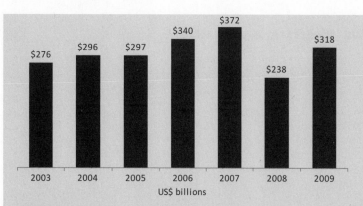

FIGURE 17.7 German Mutual Fund Assets
Source: Investment Company Institute, *2010 Investment Company Fact Book.*

Cross-border funds make up a significant—and growing—part of these assets, as Figure 17.8 illustrates. In 2009, more than half of German fund assets were in funds registered outside the country—most of them UCITS funds. At first, the growth in UCITS was driven by tax considerations. When the German government introduced withholding taxes in the late 1980s, banks responded by sponsoring funds in Luxembourg, selling them to German investors from offshore and thereby avoiding the tax.[9] While this tax avoidance mechanism is no longer available, UCITS remain popular because of the wide variety of options available.

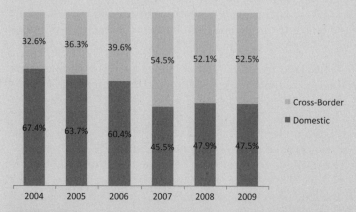

FIGURE 17.8 German Fund Market: Domestic versus Cross-Border
Source: Cerulli Associates, *Quantitative Update: Global Markets 2009.*

Regulation, Structure, and Taxation

From a regulatory standpoint, Germany and other European Union members reside in two worlds simultaneously. While each has its own securities regulator, EU members coordinate their activities with pan-European regulator CESR (soon to be ESMA), as we have discussed.

Germany's financial markets regulator is the Federal Financial Supervisory Authority, or *Bundesanstalt für Finanzdienstleistungsaufsicht*, usually referred to as BaFin. It was created in 2002 by uniting the Federal Banking Supervisory Office (BAKred) and the Federal Securities Supervisory Office (BAV).[10] Its role varies with the type of fund:

- *Institutional funds*, or *Spezialfonds*. Funds sold to institutional investors do not require BaFin approval and are very lightly regulated. They are a significant factor in the German funds market, accounting for about 60 percent of total assets in mid-2010, according to the local fund industry association BVI, or *Bundersverband Investment und Asset Management*.
- *Local retail funds*. Mutual funds sold to the public—called *Publikumsfonds*—that are registered in Germany must receive BaFin approval. These funds are called Open Ended Investment Companies, or OEICs (pronounced *oyks*).
- *Cross-border retail funds*. For cross-border funds—including UCITS funds—that are registered in another country, BaFin reserves the right to review marketing materials before those funds may be sold. It may also monitor their ongoing compliance with securities statutes.

BaFin's role is particularly important given the growing consumer interest in innovative funds, especially those in the "mixed and other" category. (Figure 17.9 shows the gains in this category.) While BaFin has so far allowed these alternative structures to be distributed broadly, it may in the future need to restrict access to them to conform with the rules of conduct and suitability principles in MiFID and with the proposed Alternative Investment Fund Management, should it become final.

As mentioned before, tax rules changed significantly on January 1, 2009. The new law imposes a flat 25 percent capital gains tax, a higher tax than under the previous regime. This same tax applies to

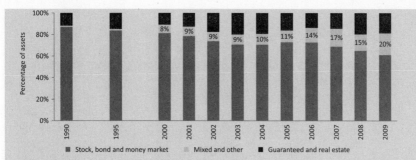

FIGURE 17.9 Investment Objectives of Funds in Germany
Source: BVI.

cross-border UCITS funds, which are required to provide German tax authorities with information on interest and dividend income and on fund distributions—all in the format required by German regulators. If the fund fails to supply this information, the investor will be subject to onerous taxation.

Distribution

Domestic banks have traditionally dominated the distribution of mutual funds in Germany, as Figure 17.10 illustrates. Banks sell funds

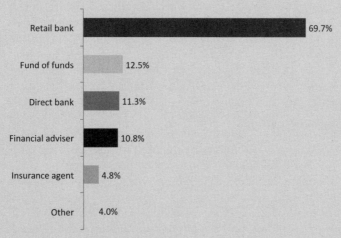

FIGURE 17.10 German Fund Purchases by Distribution Channel (2009)
Source: Survey by BVI. Adds to over 100 percent due to multiple responses.

through their retail branches, directly to the public either online or by telephone (direct bank), and indirectly through bank-sponsored fund of fund platforms similar to U.S. brokerage wrap programs, which have been gaining in popularity.

The financial adviser channel is particularly extensive in Germany. There were about 300,000 financial advisers in the country at the end of 2008, accounting for more than one-half of the advisers in all of Europe.[11] That equals roughly one financial adviser for every 300 German citizens! Another important distribution channel for investment funds is insurance companies. Insurance agents may sell funds directly to consumers, though more often they are sold as part of *unit-linked* insurance policies. (The equivalent U.S. term is *variable*.)

For the new entrant to the German market, even negotiating selling agreements with key distributors can be a daunting task, since the requirements imposed by German law are quite detailed and vary with each channel. The good news is that German distributors are more willing to distribute nonproprietary funds than they have in the past, because open architecture has become more widely accepted. (Chapter 10 discusses open architecture in a U.S. context.) According to McKinsey & Company, more than one-third of retail sales in 2004 were in third-party funds.[12]

Moreover, regulations adopted in the mid-2000s have made it easier for local asset managers to hire non-German subadvisers for German-registered investment funds. Subadvised funds, called Master KAGs—for *Master-Kapitalanlagegesellschaft*—experienced solid growth as a result, largely because of purchases by institutional investors. The market continues to evolve and new structures have been developed that allow investors to hire asset management and fund administration services separately. (Master-KAGs combine the two.)

Retirement Savings

In 2001, Germany—anticipating the need for more private retirement savings—made significant changes in its pension system. Until then, most Germans relied exclusively on a state-sponsored system that promised a retirement income equal to 70 percent of an individual's earnings while working. This system is deemed so secure that it's called retirement insurance, and the payroll deductions made to fund it are referred to as premiums.[13] But it isn't really insurance at all: Like Social Security in the United States, Germany's public retirement plan is a pay-as-you-go system that relies on current workers to support current retirees.

The 2001 reform—called the *Riester reform* after the labor minister in office at the time it was enacted—created a new pension regime based on three pillars:

1. *Pillar 1: Statutory insurance.* The first pillar is the existing state pension system, which accounted for about 85 percent of retiree household income in 2006.[14] Plan benefits were actually reduced for future retirees in 2003, by raising the retirement age from 65 to 67 and by providing for a benefit adjustment to reflect the number of workers supporting the plan.
2. *Pillar 2: Occupational pension schemes.* The second pillar consists of employer-sponsored pensions, which accounted for about 5 percent of retirement income in 2006. About two-thirds of workers were covered by these plans in 2006—almost double the number covered before the Riester reforms were passed.[15]
3. *Pillar 3: Individual pension provisions.* The third pillar is composed of voluntary individual retirement savings programs, or *Riester-Rente*. They accounted for 10 percent of retiree income in 2006.

Tax incentives were created to encourage contributions by both employers and individuals. To qualify for these incentives, occupational pension schemes must be defined benefit plans, while individual pension plans must provide a lifetime annuity upon retirement. That's a key departure from the U.S. model, where individuals generally bear investment risk throughout retirement. (Turn back to Chapter 11 for key retirement plan terms.)

CHAPTER SUMMARY

Fund management companies can significantly increase their growth potential by expanding overseas. The United States is the world's largest market for mutual funds, but still accounts for only half of global fund assets. With a few exceptions, penetration of mutual funds—as measured by assets as a percentage of gross domestic product—is much lower in other countries than in the United States. However, the growth rate in assets has generally been higher outside the United States, especially in the emerging markets. Establishment of private retirement savings schemes often leads to increased demand for mutual funds as investment options within those programs.

Fund sponsors use one of six different models to establish operations in other countries. They may:

1. Rely on mutual recognition to allow them to take a fund set up in one country and sell it in another country without have to reregister it there
2. Establish master-feeder structures by creating a master fund in one country and feeder funds in other markets
3. Clone a fund managed in another country and register it locally
4. Enter into a joint venture with a local partner
5. Subadvise funds for a local fund sponsor
6. Acquire a local fund manager

Fund management companies may use more than one of these models, adapting their approach to each market they are trying to enter.

Cross-border distribution has been most successful within the European Union. A mutual fund registered in any EU member state that complies with the provisions of the UCITS directives may be sold in any other member state with minimal notice filings in the host country. UCITS funds now account for three-quarters of mutual fund assets in the European Union and are accepted in many non-EU countries as well. Most cross-border UCITS funds are registered in either Luxembourg or Ireland. UCITS funds are now permitted to use derivatives and sophisticated investment strategies extensively, allowing managers to use the UCITS structure for hedge fund strategies. Sales of UCITS are concentrated in new funds, and there are still many local funds. As a result the average UCITS fund is quite small and has a higher expense ratio than the average U.S. mutual fund.

The market for pension fund management in Europe remains very fragmented. However, the European Union has recently adopted a directive that should make it easier for employers to establish cross-border pension plans. Since tax harmonization is politically controversial in the European Union, the pooling of pension assets from multiple countries for investment purposes is the most likely result.

A large portion of the mutual funds sold in Germany are UCITS funds. Banks dominate the distribution of funds in that country. Open architecture is becoming more widely accepted, and opportunities for independent fund managers have been increasing. Germany has recently reformed its retirement system to place a greater emphasis on private savings and individual accounts.

CHAPTER 18

The Market for Investment Funds: Beyond the United States and Europe

Because investment management is primarily a local business, mutual fund sponsors expanding around the world must be prepared to adapt to the specific requirements of each market they enter. In Chapter 17, we surveyed the models for growing internationally and examined how one of those models has been implemented in Europe, where there is a substantial cross-border fund business.

In this chapter, we look at how the models have been used in a few markets for asset management outside the United States and Europe. Our survey is not comprehensive; rather, we try to illustrate how major trends are playing out around the world. Specifically, we explore the varied challenges that global fund management companies face when establishing a presence overseas—in the form of regulatory restrictions, investor preferences, tax considerations or entrenched competition. Our survey includes both developing and developed markets. While the emerging markets may provide highest future growth potential, the established markets already have a large base of assets that presents an opportunity for investment managers today.

> **Note:** Before you read on, please note that we refer to the concepts discussed in Chapter 17, which reviewed models for cross-border asset gathering (especially UCITS funds), and in Chapter 11, which provided an overview of retirement plans.

This chapter provides an overview of major trends in the investment funds markets in:

- Asia, including the fast-growing *Asian Tiger* countries of South Korea, Taiwan, Hong Kong, Singapore, and China as well as the mature market in Japan
- The Americas outside the United States, with an emphasis on Chile and Canada

The chapter summary reviews the international trends affecting fund managers seeking to gather assets in local markets.

ASIA

The growth opportunities in Asia have captured the attention of many expansion-minded global corporations—mutual fund management companies among them. The region has experienced exceptionally strong economic gains, especially after the recent credit crisis. Consumer demand for investments has soared, even overriding cyclical downturns. According to Strategic Insight, investors in Asia put more than US$80 billion into funds in 2008—the year of the credit crisis—while investors in Europe withdrew US$500 billion at the same time.

On the other hand, the region is quite fragmented with no equivalent of the European Union institutions to coordinate policy. Each country is a separate market, with its own set of regulations and distribution system. We look at the fund management industry in the fast-growing Asian Tiger countries, with a special focus on China, and then at the more mature financial market in Japan.

The Asian Tigers

Much of the growth in the region has been in the Asian Tiger markets—South Korean, Taiwan, Hong Kong, and Singapore, as well as China. Economic gains in these countries have been extremely strong, driving renewed growth in the middle class, which had been hit hard by the late 1990s Asian financial crisis—a middle class with savings to invest.

Two other factors have made these countries particularly attractive to offshore investment managers. First, government-sponsored savings plans have expanded the pool of assets in need of investment management services—and these plans are increasingly likely to be able to invest overseas. Second, cross-border funds—particularly UCITS funds registered in Ireland

and Luxembourg—have gained acceptance from both regulators and retail investors in all the Tiger countries except China—significantly reducing barriers to entry into those markets.

South Korea. South Korea illustrates both the opportunities and challenges in the region. Growth potential in the country is substantial. In 2009, fund assets of US$265 billion amounted to just 19 percent of gross domestic product—well below the 78 percent figure for the United States discussed in Chapter 17.[1]

Retirement savings are growing rapidly as well. In 1988, Korea established its National Pension Plan, which is a compulsory savings system now covering 40 percent of the population. In 2010, National Pension Fund assets stood at US$230 billion, ranking it among the largest pension plans in the world. While these assets are invested primarily in domestic bonds, exposure to local stocks, overseas investments, and alternative investments has been increasing. Non-Korean managers have been hired for the last two categories.

In addition, South Korea has opened up its market to foreign asset management companies. Until recently, the market for investment advisory services was dominated by a small number of locally owned investment trust companies, or ITCs, which focused on selling closed-end bond funds. These contractual-type funds were structured as investment trusts that issued beneficiary certificates to investors.

In the late 1990s, however, the government began to permit the sale of *offshore funds*—meaning those registered in another country. These offshore funds must comply with certain investment restrictions—for example, they must invest at least 60 percent of their assets outside Korea—and be sold through exclusive distribution arrangements with local broker-dealers. Foreign companies are now allowed to own up to 100 percent of a new form of investment manager, called investment trust management companies, or ITMCs—which can manage a new type of fund, called a security investment company, or SIC. Like U.S. mutual funds, SICs use a corporate form of organization and issue shares to investors.

With this new freedom, foreign asset managers have established a presence in Korea, though most still find it a challenging place to do business. To begin with, the demand for funds investing abroad has been quite limited. Savers continue to favor local investments, partly because tax advantages enjoyed by local funds have only just been eliminated. There is also considerable uncertainty about the long-term strategic impact of recent financial services industry reform—and even about how it will be implemented practically. The new legislation is designed to increase the level of competition by allowing firms greater latitude to diversify. For example, banks are now permitted to charge an advisory fee when distributing investment funds.

To reduce risk in this uncertain environment, many foreign funds have decided to enter the Korean market through a joint venture.

Taiwan. Like Korea, Taiwan has opened up its market to foreign investment managers, though through different avenues. Most notably, sales of offshore funds have become a common means of entry into Taiwan. Offshore funds took off after the principal regulator established rules governing their sale in 2005. These regulations require that a single master agent—a local investment trust, investment consulting firm, or securities broker—be appointed to oversee the sale and marketing of funds by local agents. Foreign firms may apply for a Securities Investment Consulting Enterprise or SICE license to distribute offshore funds, and many firms have done so, usually choosing this route over a joint venture with a local partner. The government controls the pace of new fund introductions by allowing master agents to request the registration of just one fund at a time.

Offshore funds have proved very popular. In fact, within a few years of their introduction, the assets of offshore funds exceeded those of local funds. While interest in local funds rebounded during the credit crisis, by 2009, assets in offshore funds were again equal to those of domestic funds. Figure 18.1 shows the asset figures in Taiwan dollars for both types of funds.

More than 90 percent of the offshore funds distributed in Taiwan are UCITS funds.[2] In response to their growing popularity, the government formed a task force to address the differences between the regulation of UCITS and domestic funds. As a result of this group's recommendations, regulations for Taiwan-based funds in the areas of investment operations, corporate governance, and disclosure were harmonized with those of UCITS.

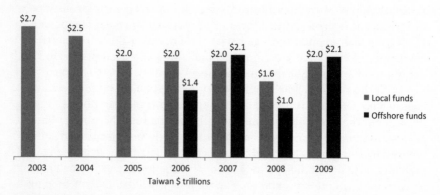

FIGURE 18.1 Mutual Funds Assets in Taiwan
Source: Securities Investment Trust & Consulting Association of the R.O.C., *Annual Report 2009.*

Despite the recent growth, Taiwanese mutual fund assets of US$58 billion at the end of 2009 represented just 8 percent of GDP. Retirement plan assets are growing as well, and local plans generally outsource investment management, often awarding mandates to overseas firms.

Hong Kong. Hong Kong maintains a uniquely open market for foreign financial institutions, a result of its historic status as an international free trade zone. Global fund managers have long been permitted to sell offshore funds to retail investors rather than developing a local product line, and these offshore funds—which are usually UCITS—have gained a high degree of acceptance in the marketplace. In fact, UCITS funds account for approximately 70 percent of the authorized funds in Hong Kong according to ALFI, the Association of the Luxembourg Fund Industry.

Mutual funds play an important role in the retirement savings system in Hong Kong—most notably the government-sponsored Mandatory Provident Fund, which was established in 1995. Hong Kong residents contribute 5 percent of their wages to the scheme, while their employers contribute an additional 5 percent. (There are exceptions: workers making less than a specified minimum are not required to contribute. And there is a relatively low annual cap on contributions for both employees and employers.) Employers select a *master trust scheme* from a provider registered with the Hong Kong regulator. Employees allocate their assets among the mutual funds available for that particular scheme. To be eligible for inclusion in a master trust, funds must comply with certain investment restrictions and agree to limit their fees.[3] Some of the leading fund managers are overseas firms.

The Capital Investment Entrant Scheme—adopted in 2003—provides another opportunity for asset managers. This program allows individuals to establish residence in Hong Kong after agreeing to invest a substantial amount in local real estate or in certain types of financial assets; that's unlike similar schemes in other countries, which usually require that potential residents invest in local businesses directly. Mutual funds are on the list of eligible investments, but only if they are managed by a firm licensed in Hong Kong, invest the bulk of their assets locally, and price their shares in Hong Kong dollars. While it may be difficult for funds sponsored by overseas managers or offshore funds to meet all these requirements, the scheme serves to illustrate how open Hong Kong is to foreign capital.

Singapore. Hong Kong is vying with Singapore for leadership in asset management within the region. Singapore has positioned itself as a gateway to the Asia Pacific region, becoming a major financial center in the process. A combination of business-friendly regulation, a highly skilled and multilingual labor force, cost-competitive infrastructure, stable political environment, and central location between Malaysia and Indonesia has made this small nation one of the world's most competitive countries—and it's also one of the easiest to do business in, according to the World Economic Forum. As a result, some of the largest financial institutions in the world have established hubs in Singapore to provide a spectrum of banking, insurance, and fund management services throughout the region.

Because its capital markets are very well developed—trading stocks, bonds, and derivatives for companies from many countries in Asia—Singapore has become a center for investment management of assets from around the region. Over 2,500 investment professionals—many working for U.S. and European firms—were based there in 2009.

In that same year, assets in investment funds exceeded Singapore$850 billion, more than double the amount just five years earlier—despite a 20 percent decline in 2008 as a result of the credit crisis. (These asset figures exclude Central Provident Fund and GIC assets. We discuss both of these programs in a moment.) Almost two-thirds of assets in these funds are invested within the region. [4]

While many of these funds are distributed cross-border to other Asian countries, investors within Singapore have a growing appetite for asset management services. Offshore funds—especially UCITS funds—have developed a strong presence in the country. The Code on Collective Investment Schemes, adopted in 2002, established consistent regulations governing the distribution of all types of funds, both locally registered and offshore, making it easy to register a UCITS in Singapore. Private banking and independent financial advisory services have also developed to meet the needs of sophisticated local investors—who are growing in both number and net worth. At the end of 2007, approximately 14 percent of fund assets held in Singapore had been sold by independent financial advisers, according to Cerulli Associates.

At the same time, the Singaporean government sponsors two pension programs of considerable size:

1. The Central Provident Fund—established in 1955—is a compulsory retirement scheme, which also provides a more general social safety net, by allowing savings to be used for education and health care expenses as well as for home purchases. Although most fund assets earn a fixed rate of return paid by the Singaporean government, participants may invest a portion of their account in other investments, including locally-registered or offshore mutual funds.
2. As its full name suggests, GIC—or the Government of Singapore Investment Corporation—invests the government's assets in what is called a *sovereign wealth fund*. Assets in GIC were over US$100 billion in 2010. Investment management of this fund is largely handled by an internal staff, though a portion is allocated to external managers, which may be foreign firms.

In sum, the markets for asset management in Korea, Taiwan, Hong Kong, and Singapore are quite similar in many ways. All four countries are relatively open to foreign investment managers—though to varying degrees. UCITS funds are a significant factor in all but Korea—though each country has steered its own course when it comes to regulating these funds, and government-sponsored savings programs are large investors in Korea, Hong Kong, and Singapore. The current situation in China is quite different, as the "Country Snapshot" explains.

COUNTRY SNAPSHOT: CHINA

The size of the Chinese economy—together with its rapid growth—has attracted the attention of investment management firms looking to expand globally. Entering the market has proved very challenging, because China is behind the other Asian Tigers in opening up its capital markets.

Historical Growth

The growth in mutual fund assets in China has been dramatic—as Figure 18.2 illustrates—mirroring the tremendous growth in the economy as a whole. The Chinese fund market hardly existed at all until 2001, when regulators approved the first mutual fund, yet by mid-2009 assets totaled US$327 billion. Cerulli Associates reports that an increasing proportion of assets are invested in stocks, which accounted for 55 percent of assets in June 2009.

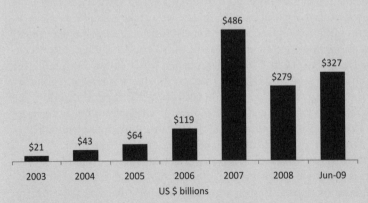

FIGURE 18.2 Mutual Fund Assets in China
Source: Cerulli Associates, *The Cerulli Edge: Global Edition.*

Even after the recent gains, growth potential in China for fund management companies is still enormous. Mutual fund assets equal less than 5 percent of GDP—compared to 78 percent in the U.S. And there is considerable wealth within the country: One recent study found that, in 2006, over 400,000 individuals in China had at least US$1 million to invest.[5]

Opportunities for Cross-Border Investing and Asset Gathering

Even though the market for mutual funds is still in its infancy, the China Securities Regulatory Commission, or CSRC—the primary regulator of the securities industry—has allowed both institutions and individuals to invest outside the country to some extent. That's unusual because most countries with closed systems have given their domestic industries more time to develop before opening markets to foreigners. But China's savings were growing much faster than opportunities to invest in them locally, forcing regulators to act quickly to make other options available to savers.

Cross-border investments must go through a *qualified domestic institutional investor,* or QDII, a financial institution—a bank, fund manager, insurer, or securities company—that has registered with the regulators.[6] QDIIs were first authorized in April 2006. China's State Administration of Foreign Exchange, or SAFE, determines the permitted level of overseas investments.

In practice, Chinese authorities impose strict controls on the investments that can be purchased through a QDII. Initially, investments were structured to replicate an index or track a single asset class, though regulations have since become more flexible, allowing greater exposure to stocks or foreign-based funds. The China Banking Regulatory Commission, or CBRC, determines which countries qualify for investment through a QDII and then establishes a bilateral regulatory cooperation agreement with those countries. By the end of 2009, the CBRC had negotiated a Memorandum of Understanding with more than 35 countries, including the United States, Japan, the United Kingdom, Singapore, Ireland, and Luxembourg.

While cross-border investing is growing, the real opportunity in China is in the domestic market: Cerulli Associates reports that some 97 percent of mutual fund investments in 2007 were made onshore. That means that fund management companies looking to build a meaningful presence there must open up shop inside China. Joint ventures have emerged as the most popular option for doing so, though prices for buying into a Chinese fund manager have been quite steep. Another key drawback: current regulations prohibit outsiders from owning more than 49 percent of joint ventures, so that the local partner has the ability to exercise full management control. According to the China Securities Regulatory Commission, by October 2009, there were 33 Sino-foreign joint ventures.

In general, while China has opened the door to its capital markets slightly, it has been quick to slam it shut whenever there is turmoil in the outside world. During the credit crisis, the State Administration of Foreign Exchange temporarily stopped issuing new QDII quotas.

Distribution

The Chinese fund industry is extremely dynamic. Banks were early market leaders, but they have faced increasing competition from new entrants, many of them joint ventures. According to Cerulli Associates, of the top 20 Chinese mutual fund managers at the end of 2007, eight were recently formed joint ventures, but these initial winners are already battling even newer entrants.

Distribution of funds in China is complicated by the very short-term perspective of many Chinese investors. As Figure 18.3 illustrates, flows in and out of funds are highly variable, suggesting that many investors view funds more as a quick trading play than as vehicles for long-term investment.

Retirement Savings

China faces a looming retirement crisis that could dwarf similar problems in other large nations. Its ratio of workers to retirees is dropping rapidly—from six-to-one in 2000 to two-to-one just 40 years later, a direct consequence of China's one-child policy.[7] In contrast, it will take the United States twice as long—80 years (from 1960 to 2040)—to experience the same decline, giving the United States much longer to prepare for the strains that will result. As of 2006, the implicit pension debt in China stood at approximately US\$1.5 trillion, a liability that primarily rests on the country's 31 provinces.

Hoping to forestall a problem, the Chinese have been working since the 1990s to diversify retirement funding and increase retirement

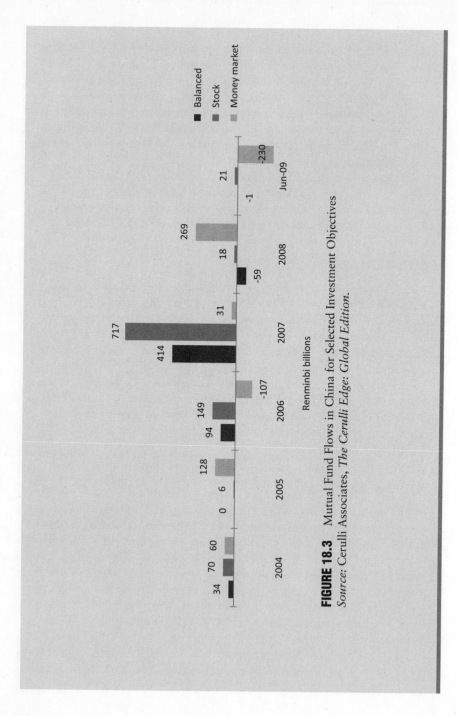

FIGURE 18.3 Mutual Fund Flows in China for Selected Investment Objectives
Source: Cerulli Associates, *The Cerulli Edge: Global Edition.*

savings. Retirement incomes are now funded from four different pillars:

Pillar I. A public pay-as-you-go pension scheme, providing basic benefits and financed by payments by employers

Pillar II. A mandatory defined contribution system, administered through employers, with contributions from both workers and employers

Pillar III. A voluntary defined contribution system, called the *enterprise annuity system*

Pillar IV. Voluntary private savings through employers

Informal family support also makes up a large part of the retirement system, though that support is declining.

Unfortunately, only 50 percent of urban workers and 11 percent of rural workers actually pay into formal plans. And the system is very fragmented, so that both coverage and funding vary widely. For example, each province is responsible for pension payments for its own residents, and expenditures vary dramatically from region to region. From time to time, particularly hard-pressed provinces have decided to use contributions from Pillar II to pay off obligations under Pillar I; these provinces have received some financial assistance from the central government and the National Social Security Fund.

In 2000, China established the National Social Security Fund, or NSSF, as a national long-term strategic reserve to supplement Pillar I. The NSSF is funded by government contributions and by 10 percent of the proceeds from the sale of shares in publicly owned companies, known as state-owned enterprises. At the end of 2008, the NSSF had US$82 billion in assets, making it the largest institutional investor in China. Up to 40 percent of the NSSF assets may be invested offshore, which has created opportunities for foreign asset managers, who have been awarded mandates for overseas investments.

Overall, the opportunities in China are large—but so are the hurdles to establishing an investment management business there. Nevertheless, many fund management firms are keen to move into the country—believing that the size of the opportunity will eventually outweigh the regulatory barriers.

Japan

In contrast to the Asian Tigers, Japan is a very mature market—literally. One of the most powerful factors driving the outlook for mutual funds in Japan is demographics. The Japanese have the longest life expectancy in the world: 82 years for men and women combined. (The comparable figure for the United States—which ranks twenty-eighth in the world—is 78 years.[8]) At the same time, the birth rate is very low and immigration is severely limited, so Japan has the fastest-aging population in the world. The percentage of people over 65 has increased from 5 percent in 1955 to 20 percent in 2008 and is set to rise to 35 percent by 2040.

Since retirees usually draw income out of savings accounts—rather than put money into them—growth in private savings in Japan is expected to be modest at best. In fact, as Figure 18.4 illustrates, assets in mutual funds (denominated in Japanese yen) have been relatively stable for much of the past two decades. The low growth early in the period was partly due to a stagnant economy—and gains in assets have been stronger recently as the economic growth has begun to rebound. Nevertheless, with US$660 trillion in assets, Japan is the seventh-largest fund market in the world—making it one that can't be ignored.

Before the 1990s, Japan's mutual fund industry essentially was closed to foreign competition. Regulatory practices effectively prohibited foreign firms from obtaining the licenses needed to manage yen-denominated investment

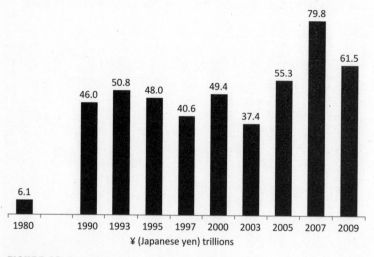

FIGURE 18.4 Mutual Fund Assets in Japan[9]
Source: The Investment Trusts Association, Japan.

trusts, the Japanese equivalent of a mutual fund. (The relevant regulator is the Financial Services Agency, which is charged with oversight of banking, insurance, and securities companies.) Foreign firms were permitted to sell offshore funds through local broker-dealers, but since those funds could not be denominated in Japanese yen, they enjoyed little success with local investors.

The regulatory landscape has become much more accommodating to foreign managers since 1990, when a trust manager's license was granted to a foreign firm for the first time. The investment trust industry was significantly deregulated later that decade as part of a series of changes known as the Big Bang initiative. These reforms:

- Expanded the types of financial institutions that were permitted to distribute investment trusts. Specifically, banks were allowed to offer mutual funds alongside brokers, which had been the traditional channel for fund sales previously.
- Significantly streamlined regulatory procedures and requirements for establishing an investment trust business in Japan.
- Encouraged greater financial innovation, permitting both the use of a corporate structure for funds (similar to that used for U.S. mutual funds) and the sale of privately placed investment trusts.
- Eliminated restrictions that had made it difficult for trust management companies to use overseas affiliates as investment managers.
- Allowed offshore funds to be denominated in Japanese yen to be sold publicly with regulatory approval.

Even though the regulatory environment has become more welcoming, foreign fund management companies still find Japan challenging. Investment trust management continues to be dominated by domestic asset managers selling through an affiliated distribution channel—for example, Nomura's broker-dealer selling funds managed by Nomura's asset management arm. In 2007 and 2008, nine of the top 10 management companies were local, according to Cerulli Associates. Table 18.1 provides market share by type of sponsoring firm.

Foreign asset managers are generally sought out mainly for their expertise in specific asset classes or styles that are in vogue, such as the currency selection funds that have been popular recently. These funds allow investors to choose the currency exposure separately from the underlying investment. For example, a fund might buy U.S. junk bonds but be denominated in the Brazilian real. These funds have opened up opportunities for non-Japanese managers.

TABLE 18.1   Market Share of Mutual Funds in Japan by
Type of Sponsoring Company (2007)

Type of Company	Number of Firms	Market Share
Security firm	4	50%
Bank	11	30
Insurance company	7	3
Independent	17	2
Foreign company	32	16
Total	71	100%

Source: Nomura Institute of Capital Markets Research, *The Future of Japan's Mutual Fund Industry.* Percentages may not add due to rounding.

The regulatory landscape continues to change. In 2006, following a series of high profile corporate scandals, Japan enacted a new Financial Instruments and Exchange Law to enhance investor protections.[10] This law broadened the application of regulations across the financial system, increased the level of disclosure and required firms to maintain a system of internal controls—and imposed much tougher sanctions for failure to do any of these things. This law was amended in 2008 to allow for development of a market in securities for institutional investors only. It will take some time for the full impact of the changes to be seen.

Perhaps more importantly, the distribution channels for funds are in a state of flux. Securities firms once controlled the market for distribution of mutual funds, though their share has eroded significantly since 1998, as Figure 18.5 illustrates. The big gainers have been the banks, which could surpass securities firms as the leading distribution channel within the foreseeable future. However, the shift in sales patterns has done little to make life easier for foreign fund management companies. That's because banks—like securities firms—prefer to sell their own line of proprietary funds rather than provide access to outsiders. Financial advisers are still largely compensated by commissions on transactions, which means that they often prefer to promote a new foreign fund every few years, encouraging clients to switch from one to the other. Unfortunately for new entrants to the fund market, Japanese investors prefer that their financial advisers be affiliated with larger institutions. An independent adviser channel—that might be more open to nonproprietary products—has yet to take root in Japan.

The big wild card is Japan Post. The government-owned company is more than the country's postal service—with 25,000 branches throughout the country—and one of its largest employers; it's also the world's largest

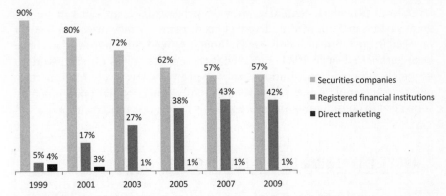

FIGURE 18.5 Mutual Fund Assets in Japan by Distribution Channel
Source: The Investment Trusts Association, Japan. May not add to 100 percent due to rounding.

savings bank and a major insurer that controls upward of US$3 trillion in consumer savings accounts.

Consumer dissatisfaction with Japan Post as a savings vehicle has been growing. That's because most deposits have to be invested in government bonds and generate very low returns as a result.[11] Steps to increase options available to consumers—by offering mutual funds in a limited number of Japan Post branches—haven't provided the comprehensive solution that seemed needed.

In the mid-2000s, the government proposed a radical solution—to sell a majority stake in the postal system to the public, allowing a privatized Japan Post the freedom to offer a wide range of investment alternatives to consumers. To prepare for the sale, the company was broken up into four more focused entities—Japan Post Service Company, Japan Post Network Company, Japan Post Bank, and Japan Post Insurance—under the umbrella of Japan Post Holdings.

The privatization process has stalled—perhaps permanently—during recent political turmoil in the country. In 2009, Japanese voters tossed out the long-reigning Liberal Democratic Party after a lengthy recession, and the new government headed up by the Democratic Party of Japan struggles to find a stable footing. But whether privatization moves forward or not, Japan Post is likely to prove tougher competition for existing distribution channels than it has in the past.

In sum, despite regulatory changes that should have served to increase competition—from both within the country and from overseas firms—Japan's investment management industry remains dominated by large local providers. Similarly, over 95 percent of Japan's private retirement savings are still held in defined benefit plans—which are often heavily invested in government bonds—even though defined contribution plans have been authorized since 2001. But even if these newer types of plans were to be widely adopted, contributions are capped at very low levels, limiting their ability to accumulate assets.[12] Given its rapidly aging population, Japan may soon need to consider moving more actively to increase retirement savings.[13]

ASSET GATHERING IN THE PERSIAN GULF STATES

The accumulation of income from oil and gas production has led to a growing demand for investment management services from the resource-rich countries bordering the Persian Gulf, especially Dubai and Bahrain. Traditionally, asset managers tapped this market by obtaining mandates from large institutional funds, which were often government-owned *sovereign wealth funds*.

More recently, overseas asset managers have begun offering funds for individual investors, often using the UCITS format, generally sold through partnerships with local intermediaries and private banks. Funds focused on this market often invest in accordance with Shari'ah, or Islamic law. Shari'ah-compliant funds don't invest in companies involved in alcohol, tobacco, gambling, pork, or pornography. And since Shari'ah prohibits earning of interest, or *riba*, these funds don't own bonds or other fixed income securities or invest in companies—such as banks—that earn significant interest income.

Many funds establish a Shari'ah supervisory board of Muslim scholars to advise them on the application of Islamic law and ensure that the fund complies with its principles. They may invest in financial instruments called *sukuk* that, like bonds, provide a steady income, although they generate this return by investing in assets rather than through payment of interest. In general, managing Shari'ah-compliant funds requires dedicated resources and specialized expertise—which has limited the number of managers in the arena.

While distributors of these funds have focused on the Persian Gulf states, these funds have gained traction in other regions with larger Islamic populations, including Asia and Europe. According to Cerulli Associates, assets in Shari'ah-compliant funds stood at US$800 billion in 2008, and the demand for them is expected to experience strong growth.

The experience of foreign fund management companies in Japan illustrates that culture is as important as regulation in determining the openness of a particular market. "Asset Gathering in the Persian Gulf States" discusses how nonregulatory issues play an important role in that market.

THE AMERICAS EX U.S.

In many ways, the market for investment management services in the Americas outside of the United States is quite similar to the market in Asia. It can be divided into two segments: the smaller, high-growth markets—in this case in Latin America—and the asset-rich developed market of Canada. As in Asia, the region has no coordinating body comparable to the European Union working on financial services harmonization, so the market is quite fragmented. Some of these markets have been more open to foreign fund managers and cross-border mutual fund flows than others.

What distinguishes the Americas is the emphasis on private management of government retirement programs. We take a quick look at trends in Argentina and Colombia and then examine Chile and Canada in greater depth.

Latin America

The trends in Latin America are conflicting—sometimes even within the same country. Wealthy investors—with long memories of the hyperinflation and expropriation that once plagued the region—have historically been quite open to placing assets overseas. A number of fund management companies have organized offshore master-feeder funds targeted at high net worth Latin American investors. However, there are still many instances of regulations that place strict restrictions on the outward investment of capital and that seriously discourage foreign entrants.

Countries in the region have been in the forefront of implementing private retirement savings programs—though results have been mixed. Colombia is one of the success stories. In 1993, the country established a defined contribution pension scheme alongside its pay-as-you-go system. Workers decide which better suits their needs—and have opportunities to switch between the two—though they are required to participate in one of the two systems. Beginning in 2010, workers in the defined contribution program have a choice of three funds with different risk profiles—conservative, moderate, and aggressive—that can invest up to 40 percent of their assets abroad. By April 2010, the system had accumulated over US$80 billion in savings.

Argentina, on the other hand, illustrates how private systems are vulnerable to political or economic instability. The government never seemed quite comfortable with private plans, which it authorized in 1993. Asset managers were required to produce minimum returns that could only be reasonably guaranteed through investments in local fixed income securities. Although regulations were eventually relaxed somewhat, ability to invest overseas remained severely limited.

In 2008, the government moved to nationalize the US$30 billion in these funds. It claimed that it needed to protect investors who had suffered severe losses during the credit crisis—the second major financial crisis to strike Argentina in a decade. The move was controversial, especially since some observers believed that the takeover was designed as much to reduce the growing national debt in Argentina as to protect retirees. Under the government's plan, private pension assets in individual accounts would be transferred to the state's mandatory pay-as-you-go retirement system. A court ruling blocked a complete nationalization, however. As a result, individuals with private pension accounts were allowed to transfer assets to either a locally authorized management company or to the government pension system. If they chose the latter option, the value of their accounts would be factored into the benefit calculation upon retirement. In the wake of the nationalization attempt, investment managers have become much more cautious about the outlook for raising assets in the country.

In establishing defined contribution retirement programs, Colombia and Argentina—like many countries around the world—were following the lead of Chile. Let's take a closer look at asset management in Chile in the "Country Snapshot."

COUNTRY SNAPSHOT: CHILE

Chile was one of the first developing countries to privatize its pension system, creating a pool of savings that has helped support economic growth.

Historical Growth

Mutual fund growth in Chile has been robust. As Figure 18.6 shows, assets have more than doubled in the short period from 2003 through early 2009—despite the credit crisis, as Figure 18.6 illustrates. These assets equaled 20 percent of 2009 GDP, a substantial figure for an emerging economy.

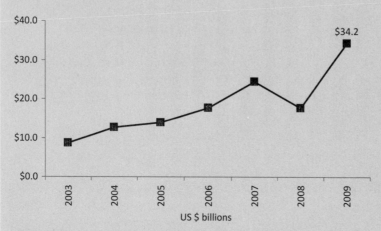

FIGURE 18.6   Mutual Fund Assets in Chile
Source: Investment Company Institute, *2010 Investment Company Fact Book.*

Assets in locally registered funds are heavily tilted toward money market and bond funds, and the emphasis on safety only increased during the credit crisis, as Figure 18.7 shows.

Opportunities for Cross-Border Investing and Asset Gathering

Any discussion of regulation of the investment industry in Chile is necessarily intertwined with the Chilean pension system—which is the largest single source of asset gathering, not just in Chile, but in all of Latin America, according to Cerulli Associates. Chile was one of the first developing countries to introduce a defined contribution system for its retirees—perhaps not surprising since it has long been a leader in providing social benefits. It established its own public retirement income program in 1924, more than a decade before the United States created its Social Security system.

Chile established its mandatory defined contribution system in 1980, and by 2007 two-thirds of Chilean workers were covered by the program, which had assets of US$111 billion at the end of that

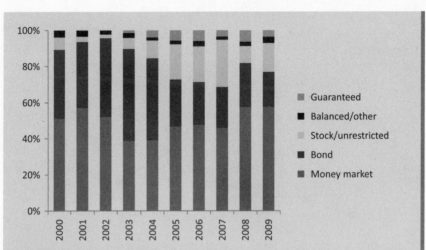

FIGURE 18.7   Locally Registered Mutual Fund Assets in Chile by Type of Investment
Source: Superintendencia de Valores y Seguros.

year.[14] Workers contribute at least 10 percent of their income to individual retirement accounts overseen by single-purpose private-sector firms known as *Administradoras de Fondos de Pensiones,* or AFPs. An AFP cannot be a local bank.[15] Workers choose an AFP, and the AFP handles investment management, often by hiring subadvisers.

AFPs may invest up to 60 percent of assets overseas—a limit that has been steadily raised over the life of the program. They normally buy shares of offshore mutual funds registered with the Comisión Clasificadora de Riesgo, meaning "risk classification commission," or CCR. Funds seeking registration must prepare detailed applications describing their investment policies, risk management practices, operational features, and management. They must also have at least US$100 million in assets at all times and agree to provide certain information to the CCR. Funds from various jurisdictions—including the United States and European Union—have been approved. An AFP may place up to 5 percent of its assets in a single fund. Chileans are also now permitted to place non-AFP personal savings—often held in other types of tax-advantaged retirement accounts—in overseas investments.

Both the AFPs and individual investors are taking advantage of the increased investment flexibility. UCITS funds have been a particularly popular format for cross-border investing. In sharp contrast to the investment pattern in locally registered funds, cross-border funds are likely to be invested aggressively. According to Cerulli Associates, 16 percent of the AFP assets under management of the top 10 cross-border fund sponsors were invested in the emerging markets.

Some of the world's largest fund companies have vied for AFP cross-border assets. Ten non-Chilean managers control almost two-thirds of AFP assets invested overseas, as Table 18.2 shows.

TABLE 18.2 Top Cross-Border AFP Fund Managers (May 2009)

Rank	Manager	Market Share (Percent of Cross-Border Assets)
1	Barclays	14.1%
2	Schroder	8.6%
3	Fidelity	7.7%
4	Vanguard	5.5%
5	Gartmore	5.2%
6	Dimensional	4.5%
7	J.P. Morgan	4.3%
8	Franklin Templeton	4.3%
9	BlackRock	3.7%
10	Baring	3.4%
	Top ten total	61.3%
	Others	38.7%

Source: Cerulli Associates.

The Chilean pension system continues to evolve. Chile still must support the substantial cost of maintaining a pay-as-you-go system for older workers and for retirees who were not in the new system for long enough to accrue benefits, and it must continue to provide a minimum pension for its poorest citizens who simply cannot afford to save. The system has also been criticized for its high costs—and the resulting high profits earned by the AFPs—though, in their defense, AFPs promise minimum returns and need to be financially sound to back those guarantees.

Canada

While a high percentage of Canadians have long-term investments in stocks, mutual fund assets equal only 44 percent of GDP compared to 78 percent of GDP in the United States. This relatively low level of penetration—combined with a more open attitude toward foreign entrants into its marketplace—makes Canada an attractive growth opportunity for global fund management firms.

Mutual funds have a long history in Canada. The first Canadian fund—the Canadian Investment Fund Ltd.—was established in 1932, and it still operates today as the CI Canadian Investment Fund. But investing through mutual funds didn't take off until the 1990s, when a sharp decline in interest rates made stock investing more attractive.

Growth in private retirement savings has also played a role. Individuals can save for retirement through Registered Retirement Savings Plans, or RRSP, which are tax-deferred savings accounts similar in many ways to individual retirement accounts in the United States. Mutual funds are very popular investment options in these accounts, although these funds must be dedicated to tax-deferred vehicles. That's significantly different from the United States, where the same mutual fund can accept investments from both taxable and nontaxable accounts.

RRSP contribution limits are quite generous—at a maximum of roughly US$21,000 per year. When owners of an RRSP reach age 71, they can use accumulated assets to purchase an annuity that provides a guaranteed income, or they can transfer assets to Registered Retirement Investment Funds, or RRIFs, and continue to invest them on a tax-deferred basis. Some employers offer Group RRSP plans to their workers.

Defined contribution plans—called *capital accumulation plans,* or CAPs—have also been introduced in Canada. Unlike 401(k) plans in the United States, participation in CAPs through salary deduction is normally mandatory. These plans generally offer a wide range of investment options, and—unlike similar plans in many other markets—workers are almost always permitted to determine the asset allocation in their account.[16]

However, CAP plan growth has not proved a boon to mutual fund sponsors. Growth in defined contribution plans has been less robust than expected, as Figure 18.8 illustrates. Few employers have switched from their existing defined benefit plans to capital accumulation plans when compared to the experience in the United States. And all Canadian employers must also contribute to a public defined benefit plan—the Quebec Pension Plan for residents of that province or the Canadian Pension Plan for all other Canadian citizens. These public plans invest contributions in a diversified portfolio of securities, using both internal and external managers.[17]

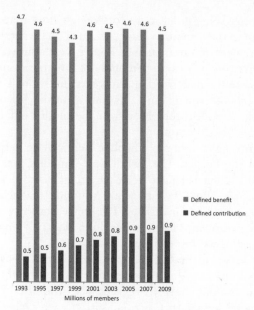

FIGURE 18.8   Membership in Canadian Pension Plans by Type
Source: Statistics Canada.

Regulations make it difficult to use mutual funds as investment options within a CAP defined contribution plan. That's because Canada has strict suitability requirements when it comes to the sale of securities, including mutual funds. A registered dealer must confirm that each purchase is consistent with the investor's stated profile and risk tolerance—a rule that applies even to all the individual orders within a defined contribution retirement account. Complying with the rule in a CAP—with its high volume of transactions—requires elaborate workarounds that make the program less than ideal for employers.

Institutional funds offered by insurance companies aren't subject to such a strict suitability requirement—and they often have lower fees than mutual funds as well. As a result, the CAP market is dominated by four Canadian insurance companies—Sun Life Financial, Great-West Life, Standard Life, and Manulife Financial—which have achieved significant economies of scale in plan recordkeeping.[18] Insurance companies can also offer their CAP clients health care and group life insurance, providing convenient one-stop shopping for employee benefit programs. As a result, barriers to entry into the CAP market have become quite high.

There has been some good news for foreign fund management firms wanting to tap in to the Canadian market. Limits on ownership of offshore securities in retirement accounts such as RRSPs were removed in 2005. (Before then, foreign content laws capped offshore fund positions at 30 percent of assets.[19]) Despite the new freedom, however, individuals have generally continued to prefer investments in Canadian securities. Also, foreign fund sponsors face considerable competition from the handful of large local banks that dominate fund distribution.

Canadian firms have been more likely to set up shop in the much larger market south of the border. The insurance companies that dominate the defined contribution market have been particularly active as acquirers of U.S. asset managers. Sun Life Financial, Manulife Financial, and Power Corporation (the parent of Great-West Life) have bought well-known U.S. fund firms: MFS Investment Management, John Hancock Financial Services, and Putnam Investments, respectively.

The border between the United States and Canada—at least when it comes to financial services—has become more porous in other ways. Canadian broker-dealers don't have to register with the SEC if they want to continue to provide service to Canadian citizens who have moved to the United States but still have retirement plan assets in Canada. And Canadian brokers can continue to recommend foreign securities and Canadian funds for those accounts without having to register those investments in the United States. Similarly, Canadian mutual funds don't need to register with the SEC under the 1940 Act if owners of a large number of their shares move to the United States. Canada provides similar exceptions for the investment accounts of U.S. citizens who move to Canada.

Yet despite this modest degree of mutual recognition, the markets remain quite separate. Strict Canadian regulations on fund distribution that vary by province—combined with different tax laws—have prevented U.S. funds from easily entering the market. At the same time, the relatively small size of the opportunity—combined with entrenched local competition—can make establishing a local presence in Canada very challenging. It also appears to have led to high fees for Canadian mutual funds relative to those in the United States.[20]

CHAPTER SUMMARY

Despite increased openness to cross-border investing and asset gathering over the past few decades, investment management remains largely a local business. Fund management firms wishing to build their business overseas must generally establish a local presence in each market they wish to enter, complying with local regulations and adapting to local preferences. Some countries impose more restrictions on offshore funds and on foreign fund sponsors than others.

- The United States—which has a national treatment regime—is one of the most closed markets. It does not permit the retail sale of offshore funds within its borders, and the managers of U.S.-based funds that can be sold within the country must register with the SEC as investment advisers.
- The European Union has developed a mutual recognition scheme for retail mutual funds within its borders. A similar scheme for pension fund management is still under development.
- Japan has removed many of the restrictions on cross-border investing and asset gathering, but entrenched competition and cultural preferences keep asset management a largely local business.
- Select emerging markets, including Chile, Hong Kong, Singapore, and Taiwan, are quite open to cross-border flows. European-registered UCITS funds account for a large proportion of fund assets in these countries.
- Other emerging markets, such as China, remain closed to foreign fund sponsors unless they are prepared to own a minority interest in a joint venture.

Fund management companies rely on a wide variety of models in their overseas expansion efforts:

- *Mutual recognition.* As mentioned, UCITS funds may be sold throughout the European Union and in other markets around the world through a system of mutual recognition. However, mutual recognition of foreign funds is very limited in most countries. Mutual recognition is more commonly applied to registrations of investment managers than to registrations of mutual funds.
- *Master-feeder structures.* While master-feeder structures are often used for hedge funds that make private offerings, regulations often prohibit their use for publicly sold mutual funds. Master-feeder structures for mutual funds are sometimes available in Latin America and have recently been authorized within the European Union.
- *Clone funds.* Clone funds are the most common model for global expansion. U.S. firms distribute UCITS funds by establishing a management company subsidiary in the European Union and registering funds there. These funds are often clones of funds managed in the United States, though it's often impossible to eliminate all differences among clone funds.

- *Joint ventures.* Fund management firms must use joint ventures to establish a local presence in China and often use them in Korea. These joint ventures can involve managerial tensions, especially when the foreign fund manager has only a minority interest.
- *Subadvisory relationships.* Dominant local companies often look to foreign subadvisers for specialized expertise. For example, pension fund managers in Chile, proprietary fund companies in Japan and the National Pension Fund in Korea often hire foreign firms to manage specialized mandates in overseas assets for their funds.
- *Acquisitions.* Foreign fund management firms wishing to establish a presence in the United States usually do so through acquisition.

The markets that present the greatest opportunity for fund management companies are often those in which governments encourage prefunding of retirement income—through defined benefit or defined contribution plans—and no longer rely exclusively on pay-as-you-go systems. Two of the most developed fund markets in the world—the United States and Australia—have popular tax-deferred retirement savings programs. Emerging countries that have adopted prefunded programs—such as Chile, Colombia, Hong Kong, South Korea, and Singapore—have rapidly accumulated a substantial pool of savings, some of which may be invested abroad.

Notes

Preface

1. All data in Preface from Investment Company Institute, *2010 Investment Company Fact Book* (2010).

CHAPTER 1:   Investing through Mutual Funds

1. Except as noted, all statistics in Chapter 1 in text, figures, and tables are from the Investment Company Institute. See *2010 Investment Company Fact Book* (2010), "The U.S. Retirement Market, 2009," "Ownership of Mutual Funds, Shareholder Sentiment, and Use of the Internet, 2009," and "Profile of Mutual Fund Shareholders, 2009."
2. Brian K. Bucks et al., "Changes in U.S. Family Finances from 2004 to 2007: Evidence from the Survey of Consumer Finances," *Federal Reserve Bulletin* 95 (February 2009): A1.
3. John Campbell et al., "Have Individual Stocks Become More Volatile? An Empirical Exploration of Idiosyncratic Risk," *Journal of Finance* 56 (1) (February 2001); Dale L. Domian, David A. Louton, and Marie D. Racine, "Diversification in Portfolios of Individual Stocks: 100 Stocks Are Not Enough," *The Financial Review* 42 (4) (November 2007); and Zakri Bello, "How Diversified are Equity Mutual Funds?" *North American Journal of Finance and Banking Research* 1 (1) (2007).
4. For more on the history of mutual funds, see Matthew P. Fink, *The Rise of Mutual Funds,* (New York: Oxford University Press, 2008).
5. Pioneer Fund, Inc., "Policies Objectives Management Record" (1952), quoted in Philip L. Carret, *Classic Carret* (Boston: The Pioneer Group, Inc., 1998), 86.
6. Inflation adjustment based on the Consumer Price Index from the U.S. Bureau of Labor Statistics; real gross domestic product from the U.S. Bureau of Economic Analysis.
7. Before the legislation was passed, the interest income from municipal bonds held in a mutual fund was subject to tax.
8. Net investments in funds include new cash and reinvested dividends. Funds are defined as mutual funds (including those held in variable annuities), exchange-traded funds, and closed-end funds.
9. These are median figures. The average household invested $180,000 in six different funds.

10. Securities and Exchange Commission, "The Investor's Advocate: How the SEC Protects Investors, Maintains Market Integrity, and Facilitates Capital Formation," www.sec.gov/about/whatwedo.shtml (accessed December 30, 2009).

11. The action against Goldman Sachs involved its marketing of investments related to the subprime mortgage market. In 2004, there were actually two split decisions. The first instance involved a proposal requiring hedge fund managers to register with the SEC; the second involved a proposal requiring that the chair of a mutual fund board of directors be independent of the management company. Though adopted by the Commission, both proposals were nullified by subsequent lawsuits.

12. FINRA, "Get to Know Us," www.finra.org/web/groups/corporate/@corp/@ about/documents/corporate/p118667.pdf (accessed June 1, 2010).

13. See www.opensecrets.org.

CHAPTER 2: How Mutual Funds Work

1. Mutual funds may be either a corporation or a business trust. While there are technical differences between the two formats, they are—for all practical purposes—identical in all but name. We'll refer only to the corporate form throughout the book.

2. Funds reserve the right to make payment for redemptions in kind—by distributing some of the investments that the fund holds—rather than in cash. They very rarely invoke this authority, and then only for very large investors who agree to receive the securities proffered.

3. Matthew P. Fink, *The Rise of Mutual Funds* (New York: Oxford University Press, 2008), 26.

4. Investment Company Institute, *2010 Investment Company Fact Book* (2010), 195.

5. If the fund is formed as a business trust, it's called a board of trustees, though its function is identical to that of a board of directors. Again, to keep things simple, we use the term *directors* throughout this book.

6. Median size was seven members. Source: Investment Company Institute and Independent Directors Council, "Overview of Fund Governance Practices: 1994–2008": 7.

7. *Gartenberg v. Merrill Lynch Asset Management, Inc.* 694 F.2d 923 (2d Cir. 1982).

8. The 1940 Act requires that only 40 percent of directors be independent, but the SEC does not permit funds to engage in certain activities unless they comply with its more stringent rules on board composition and procedures. As a result, virtually every fund conforms to the SEC's rules.

9. Management Practice Inc. reports that in 2008 directors for a fund family with $9 billion to $25 billion in assets earned median compensation of $117,500. The comparable figure for fund families with more than $100 billion in assets was $191,820. See Meyrick Payne & Jay Keeshan, "2008 Director Compensation Survey," www.mpiweb.com/content/view/70/ (accessed June 3, 2010).

10. Investment Company Institute and Independent Directors Council, "Overview of Fund Governance Practices: 1994–2008": 1.
11. In the past, the term *Chinese wall* was often used instead of firewall.
12. FINRA prohibits individuals registered with FINRA from giving gifts valued at more than $100. (See Chapter 1 for an introduction to FINRA registration requirements.) Investment adviser codes of ethics generally extend this policy to all employees and to both the giving and the receiving of gifts.
13. Securities and Exchange Commission, *Compliance Programs of Investment Companies and Investment Advisers*, (IA-2204, December 2003), I.C.2.
14. FormulaInvesting, AlphaClone, FolioInvesting, Wealthfront (formerly kaChing) and Covestor, respectively.
15. There are other types of commingled investment vehicles, but these are not available for direct purchase by individuals. Bank common trust funds are available for investment only when the bank serves as "trustee, executor, administrator or guardian," per the Code of Federal Regulations § 9.18(a)(1). A particular subset of bank common trust funds, collective trust funds, may be used only within ERISA-regulated plans, such as 401(k) plans. We talk more about these accounts in Chapter 11. Insurance company separate accounts provide investment options for life and annuity products only. (As an aside, mutual funds are often used as the investment option within these accounts.) Other commingled funds support defined benefit pension plans. Consumers generally do not have direct ownership of the assets in these accounts. On the contrary, to receive distributions from a defined benefit plan, individuals must meet a series of tests with regard to age and tenure at the sponsoring company.
16. Statistics on closed-end funds, exchange-traded funds, and unit investment trusts in this section are from Investment Company Institute, *2010 Investment Company Fact Book* (2010).

CHAPTER 3:   Researching Funds: The User Guides

1. More precisely, funds that use *tax-exempt* in their name must invest in securities that generate income that is exempt from both ordinary income taxes and the alternative minimum tax. Securities in funds using *municipal* in their name may be subject to AMT. If a fund uses a state name along with *tax-exempt* or *municipal,* income must be exempt from that state's tax as well.
2. Investment Company Institute, "Shareholder Assessment of Risk Disclosure Method" (Spring 1996).
3. After-tax returns are not required if a fund is sold only as a part of an investment vehicle that is not subject to tax, such as a 401(k) plan or variable annuity.
4. Investment Company Institute, "Understanding Investor Preferences for Mutual Fund Information" (2006), 6.
5. Cited in Securities and Exchange Commission, *Enhanced Disclosure and New Prospectus Delivery Option for Registered Open-End Management Investment Companies* (33-8861, November 21, 2007), 6.

6. NewRiver, Inc., "New River Summary Prospectus Index as of April 30, 2010," http://www1.newriver.com/documents/NewRiverSummaryProspectusIndex_043.pdf (accessed June 3, 2010).
7. Advertisers who have never previously filed with FINRA must submit materials 10 days *before* first use for one year.
8. FINRA, "Communications with the Public," Rule 2210(d)(1).
9. A few funds report to shareholders quarterly, but these are exceptions.
10. Specifically, all funds except money market funds are required to list their top 50 holdings, plus any other holdings that exceed 1 percent of net assets. A full list of holdings must also be filed with the SEC quarterly, although some funds release information about holdings more frequently. The shareholder report explains how you can access holdings data.

CHAPTER 4:   Comparing Mutual Funds

1. This calculation is referred to as the Sharpe measure of risk.
2. Diane Del Guercio and Paula A. Tkac, "Star Power: The Effect of Morningstar Ratings on Mutual Fund Flows," *Federal Reserve Bank of Atlanta, Working Paper 2001-15*, August 2001 (updated January 2007).
3. Russel Kinnel, "The Star Rating at Its Best and Worst," *Morningstar Fund Spy* (November 30, 2009), http://news.morningstar.com/articlenet/article.aspx?id=317169 (accessed March 21, 2010) and "How Expense Ratios and Star Ratings Predict Success", *Morningstar Fund Spy* (August, 9. 2010), http://news.morning star.com/articlenet/article.aspx?id=347327&part=2 (accessed September 13, 2010).
4. For more information, go to www.imoneynet.com.
5. Lipper, "U.S. Open-End, Closed-End, Variable Annuity, and Overseas Fund Classification Descriptions" (April 2010).
6. Source: Morningstar. Excludes sector funds and funds with expense ratios of 0.0 percent. Total of 184 index funds and 1,931 actively managed funds on June 20, 2010.
7. For a review of the literature on performance persistence, see Eero J. Pätäri, "Do Hot Hands Warm the Mutual Fund Investor? The Myth of Performance Persistence Phenomenon," *International Research Journal of Finance and Economics* 34 (2009).
8. Researchers attribute the persistence of negative performance to investor inertia. Some investors will just not sell fund shares at a loss, no matter how consistently bad long-term results have been.
9. W. V. Harlow and Keith C. Brown, "The Right Answer to the Wrong Question: Identifying Superior Active Portfolio Management," *Journal of Investment Management* 4 (4) (2006).
10. Investment Company Institute, *2010 Investment Company Fact Book* (2010).
11. Convertible securities funds invest in bonds or preferred stocks that can be exchanged, or *converted,* into stocks. These securities may behave like either bonds or stocks, depending on market conditions and the specific

terms of the security. We discuss conversion features in the Appendix to Chapter 6.

CHAPTER 5: Portfolio Management of Stock Funds

1. Stock is also often referred to as *common stock* to distinguish it from *preferred stock,* an investment much closer to a bond than a stock. Like bonds, preferred stocks appeal to income-oriented investors because they pay out a fixed amount annually, though in the form of dividends rather interest. They do not carry any ownership or voting rights. There are, however, two critical differences between preferred stocks and bonds. First, the income payments on preferreds are made at the discretion of management and are not contractual commitments, as are interest payments; companies in financial difficulty will suspend preferred stock dividends before stopping payment of bond interest. Also, preferreds are *perpetual,* meaning that they have no maturity date; they remain outstanding until the company takes steps to redeem them.

2. In a notable exception, Google initially sold its stock to the public directly, without the intermediation of an investment bank.

3. Any subsequent sales of shares by the company are often dubbed *secondary offerings,* though the term can also refer to the sale of a large amount of stock by a single shareholder.

4. The model for this example was provided by Phil Roth of Miller Tabak + Co.

5. Technical analysis is often used in commodity and currency investing, where price trends are particularly important.

6. The *accrual anomaly,* as it's called, was first documented by Richard G. Sloan in 1996. "Do Stock Prices Fully Reflect Information in Accruals and Cash Flows about Future Earnings?" *The Accounting Review* 71 (3): (1996).

7. AIM Basic Value Fund, *Annual Report to Shareholders* (December 31, 2009), 5.

8. Columbia Acorn Fund, *Columbia Acorn Family of Funds Annual Report* (December 31, 2009), 8.

9. T. Rowe Price Growth Stock Fund, *Annual Report* (December 31, 2009), 2.

10. This effect has become less pronounced in recent years. See Standard & Poor's, "The Shrinking Index Effect" (November 2008), http://www2.standardand poors.com/spf/pdf/index/The_Shrinking_Index_Effect.pdf (accessed March 21, 2010).

11. This is the popular definition of alpha. A quant will note that, technically, alpha is the difference between portfolio return and *beta-adjusted market return,* which equals the market return times the portfolio's beta.

12. Portfolio managers often casually refer to weighting decisions as *bets.*

13. Distinct portfolios only. Excludes index and sector funds.

14. If all the funds in a fund family buy a large proportion of a company's shares, it becomes more difficult to sell those shares simply because of a lack of other buyers. Also, if the holdings of a fund complex in a company exceed 15 percent

of its voting shares, the funds involved run increased risk of becoming subject to filing or other requirements under various federal and state laws.

CHAPTER 6: Portfolio Management of Bond Funds

1. Effective maturity, which reflects mortgage prepayments, puts, and coupon adjustments.
2. Those guarantees turned out to be very costly to the agencies when home values were falling during the credit crisis of 2008.
3. For a full discussion, see Michael Lewis, *The Big Short* (New York: Norton, 2010).
4. The issuer was Sperry Lease Finance Corporation.
5. Most ABS are *overcollateralized,* meaning that there are more loans in the underlying pool than are needed to pay all investors. As a result, Tranche D would experience losses only after the cushion was exhausted.
6. The creator, or originator, of the ABS also retains the rights to any excess income above and beyond what is needed to pay obligations to the tranches. This is referred to as the *seller's interest;* it technically absorbs the first set of losses, before the junior tranche is affected.
7. *Inside Mortgage Finance* data, cited in Robert Pozen, *Too Big to Save?* (Hoboken, NJ: John Wiley & Sons, 2010), 11.
8. Drexel Burnham Lambert went bankrupt as a result. Michael Milken served time in prison after pleading guilty to charges that he violated securities laws.
9. Eurodollar bonds are issued and traded outside the United States, Yankee bonds within.
10. Yield to worst.

APPENDIX TO CHAPTER 6: Bond Basics

11. SIFMA, *Fact Book 2009* (2009). Excludes money market securities.
12. The illustration assumes annual coupon payments.
13. For more information on the credit ratings, visit: www.fitchratings.com, www.moodys.com, and www.standardandpoors.com.

CHAPTER 7: Portfolio Management of Money Market Funds

1. This was due to Regulation Q, which prohibited banks from paying interest on checking accounts and limited the interest payable on savings accounts. See Chapter 1.
2. Rule 2a-7 was adopted in 1982, when the SEC decided to codify the guidance it had previously given to money market funds through "no action" letters. The rule has been expanded to reflect the creation of new security types and strengthened to prevent a recurrence of credit quality issues that have arisen at times.

3. The cost basis is adjusted for amortization of premium or discount, which is essentially the accretion in zero coupon securities. (See the appendix to Chapter 6 for a definition of *accretion.*)
4. There is significant concern within the fund industry that removing the references to credit agency ratings could increase the risks for at least some money market funds. Many insiders believe that the ratings helped ensure consistency across funds and that, without them, it will be easier for fund managers to boost yields by buying securities of less than the highest quality.
5. This is a *demand,* or *put* feature. A put gives the holder of the security the right to sell the security back to the issuer at any time at a set price.
6. Congress increased the limit on deposit insurance from $100,000 to $250,000 in October 2008 as one of the measures designed to stem the credit crisis. The Dodd-Frank financial reform legislation made the temporary increase permanent.
7. With non-U.S. government securities, more than 102 percent collateral would ordinarily be required.
8. The bonds may be held directly with the issuer, or they may held in an asset-backed structure sponsored by a third party. The latter is a *synthetic VRDN.*
9. Check writing is usually provided by a bank on behalf of a money market fund.

CHAPTER 8: Implementing Portfolio Decisions: Buying and Selling Investments

1. John Chalmers, Roger M. Edelen, and Gregory B. Kadlec, "An Analysis of Mutual Fund Trading Costs" (November 1999), in SSRN, http://ssrn.com/abstract=195849 (accessed June 11, 2010).
2. Cited in Securities and Exchange Commission, *Concept Release on Equity Market Structure* (34-61358, January 2010), 6.
3. The name initially stood for "National Association of Securities Dealers Automated Quotations." It was an electronic version of a pre-existing dealers' market that did business over the telephone and through the publication of paper *pink sheets.*
4. The *order handling rule,* adopted by the SEC in 1996, requires that market makers include customer orders in bids and offers, if those customer orders are at a price equal to or better than the market maker's own bid or offer.
5. The regional exchanges, such as the Boston and the Philadelphia Stock Exchanges, serve almost as adjuncts to the NYSE. The American Stock Exchange was acquired by NYSE Arca in 2008.
6. This rule technically applies only to market makers whose trading exceeds 1 percent of nationwide trading volume in a stock.
7. James J. Angel, Lawrence E. Harris, and Chester S. Spatt, *Equity Trading in the 21st Century* (February 2010), 8, www.knight.com/newsRoom/pdfs/EquityTradinginthe21stCentury.pdf (accessed June 11, 2010).
8. BATS originally stood for *Better Alternative Trading System,* although the exchange now uses the acronym exclusively.

9. Technically, a *broker* arranges trades for its clients, charging a commission for its services. It does not take ownership of the securities as part of the transaction. A *dealer,* in contrast, buys and sells securities for its own account; it expects to earn a spread when it trades. Many firms are broker-dealers that can engage in both activities.

10. Angel, Harris, and Spatt, 14.

11. The market circuit breakers were implemented after a similar computer program–driven crash in 1987.

12. Mao Ye, "A Glimpse into the Dark: Price Formation, Transaction Cost and Market Share of the Crossing Network" (January 2010), in SSRN, http://ssrn.com/abstract=1521494 (accessed June 11, 2010).

13. Confusingly, sometimes the term *soft dollar research* is used to refer only to research sourced from third parties.

CHAPTER 9: Mutual Funds as Institutional Investors

1. While mutual funds are also substantial owners of corporate bonds, bondholders generally do not have voting rights at the companies that issue the bonds. Therefore, this chapter does not address the role of mutual funds as institutional investors in corporate bonds.

2. *Mutual funds* include exchange-traded and closed-end funds. *Pension plans* include private pension funds, state and local government retirement funds, and federal government retirement funds. *Other* includes broker-dealers, state and local governments, savings institutions, and commercial banks.

3. As discussed in Chapter 3, open-end mutual funds are an exception to this rule. Closed-end funds must hold a proxy vote annually.

4. Shareholders have the right to amend bylaws that bind the company, but there is controversy regarding the use of bylaw amendments to take away the board's discretion to manage the company.

5. Investment Company Institute, "Proxy Voting by Registered Investment Companies: Promoting the Interests of Fund Stockholders," *Research Perspective* (July 2008), 3.

6. See Tom Lauricella, "Mutual Funds Get Mad," *Wall Street Journal,* October 2, 2007.

7. Diane Del Guercio, Laura Cole, and Tracie Woidtke, "Do Boards Pay Attention When Institutional Investor Activists 'Just Vote No'?" (January 2008), in SSRN: http://ssrn.com/abstract=575242.

8. Social Investment Forum, "Socially Responsible Investing Facts," www.socialinvest.org/resources/sriguide/srifacts.cfm (accessed June 12, 2010) and Investment Company Institute, *2010 Investment Company Fact Book* (2010).

CHAPTER 10: Retail Sales

1. This 75 percent includes the more than 17 percent of industry assets in individual retirement accounts, which we discuss in detail in the next chapter.

2. One study documenting this effect is Ronald T. Wilcox, "Bargain Hunting or Star Gazing? Investors' Preferences for Stock Mutual Funds," *Journal of Business* 76 (4) (2003): 645–663.

3. Diane Del Guercio and Paula A. Tkac, "Star Power: The Effect of Morningstar Ratings on Mutual Fund Flows," *Federal Reserve Bank of Atlanta, Working Paper 2001-15,* (August 2001, updated January 2007).

4. Investors appear to be less sensitive to differences in the annual expense ratio than to sales loads. See Brad M. Barber, Terrance Odean, and Lu Zheng, "Out of Sight, Out of Mind: The Effects of Expenses on Mutual Fund Flows," *Journal of Business* 78 (6) (2005).

5. Prem Jain and Joanna Wu, "Truth in Mutual Fund Advertising: Evidence on Future Performance and Fund Flows," *Journal of Finance* 55 (April 2000): 937–958. This study does not consider whether the profits from the incremental sales exceed the cost of advertising.

6. Investment Company Institute, "Understanding Investor Preferences for Mutual Fund Information" (2006).

7. Mutual fund supermarkets include distribution through discount brokers.

8. Virtually all larger money managers are registered with the SEC as investment advisers, but they are not normally referred to as RIAs. The term is reserved for firms serving individual clients directly.

9. All the licensing programs are administered by FINRA.

10. There's one other difference between financial advisers and registered investment advisers. Only FAs can engage in principal trades with clients. (See Chapter 8 for an explanation of principal trading.)

11. According to an Investment Company Institute survey (see note 5), 40 percent of investors prefer to receive fund information from advisers in person.

12. Insurance companies previously used proprietary accounts as investment options in variable annuities.

13. Statistics on variable annuities are from Insured Retirement Institute, *2010 Annuity Fact Book* (2010).

14. Variable annuities can be sold in an unbundled format with a menu of choices. This means that the insurance contract that comes with the VA may be fairly basic in regard to coverage. Then the client has the option of adding—and paying for—additional features, such as guaranteed levels of retirement payments.

15. Data on sales loads are from Investment Company Institute, "Trends in the Fees and Expenses of Mutual Funds, 2009," *Research Fundamentals* 19 (2) (April 2010).

16. When Rule 12b-1 was adopted in 1980, funds were experiencing significant redemptions as a result of a severe economic recession. Increasing fund assets was seen as a way to reduce fund expenses through greater economies of scale—helping both shareholders and fund management companies.

17. Class B shares have fallen out of favor partly because they create significant financial risk for fund management companies. As explained, a fund distributor pays the load to the intermediary up front, earning it back only over time through 12b-1 fees and contingent deferred sales charges. The risk: The payback period can be extended significantly. That may happen if fund assets fall because

of a decline in the market or if the fund's board of directors suspends the 12b-1 program, maybe because the fund has become very large and is no longer accepting new investments. To reduce the risk, many fund sponsors chose to sell the rights to future 12b-1 payments at a discount to a third party. However, as noted, many firms no longer offer B shares and therefore avoid the risk altogether.

18. One fund complex has introduced another class of shares—Class N—specifically for retirement plans. This class is limited to retirement plans with assets exceeding $500,000 and typically charge a 0.50 percent 12b-1 fee and a 1 percent contingent deferred sales charge on redemptions made within 18 months of purchase. This Class N is used by fund complexes which sell through intermediaries and should not be confused with the Class N used by no-load fund complexes.

19. For load funds, these are usually Class A shares with the load waived. For no-load funds, this is usually Class N.

20. Both UTMA and UGMA are model state laws. Most states have adopted the newer UTMA statute, replacing preexisting UGMA laws.

21. Mutual fund companies establish nonprofits that hold the contributions from donors and establish guidelines for donations. Generally, these guidelines permit donations to 501(c)(3) public charities and to other donor-advised funds, such as community foundations. Donations to private foundations are severely restricted.

CHAPTER 11: Retirement Plans and Mutual Funds

1. Defined contribution plans and individual retirement accounts each accounted for roughly the same percentage of mutual fund assets. Retirement plans account for 50 percent of household investments in non–money market funds. Investment Company Institute, *2010 Investment Company Fact Book* (2010).

2. These are the tax benefits for traditional 401(k) plans. Roth 401(k)s are also available, although few of these plans have been established; they provide tax benefits that are similar to those of the Roth IRAs that we review in a moment.

3. Sometimes, but rarely, employees also make contributions to defined benefit plans.

4. Technically, to be fully funded, a defined benefit plan must have sufficient assets—considering both current value and expected investment earnings—to pay out all benefits accrued to that date, excluding promised benefits for future service.

5. ERISA also applies to many other employee benefit programs, including health care plans.

6. Median job tenure in 2008 according to the Bureau of Labor Statistics, September 26, 2008.

7. Employers who have been unable to terminate a defined benefit plan for tax or contractual reasons often convert them to cash balance plans, which are hybrids of defined benefit and defined contribution plans. These plans don't guarantee

a specified level of income throughout retirement. Instead, they agree to pay workers a specific lump sum upon retirement—or possibly upon termination of employment before retirement—based on contributions to the plan and an assumed rate of return. Employers prefer cash balance plans to traditional DB plans because they reduce their exposure to investment risk. Plan conversions have been controversial because benefits for older workers may be reduced in the process, an effect called *wear away*. In 2007, less than 10 percent of DB plans were cash balance plans, but these plans covered 25 percent of the workers participating in those plans. Statistics are from the U.S. Department of Labor, Employee Benefits Security Administration, *Private Pension Plan Bulletin: Abstract of 2007 Form 5500 Annual Reports* (2010) and *Private Pension Plan Bulletin: Sixth Edition, 1993.*

8. The Pew Center on the States, *The Trillion Dollar Gap* (2010).
9. Ronald Snell, National Conference of State Legislatures, "State Retirement System Defined Contribution Plans" (September 2009), www.ncsl.org/Portals/1/Documents/employ/StateGovtDCPlansSept2009.pdf (accessed May 20, 2010).
10. J. Mark Iwry, Peter R. Orszag, and William G. Gale, "The Automatic 401(k): A Simple Way to Strengthen Retirement Savings," *The Retirement Security Project* 2500-1, www.brookings.edu/papers/2005/03saving_gale.aspx (accessed June 28, 2010).
11. Under the antidiscrimination rules, the average contribution rates for highly compensated employees, or HCEs, and for non–highly compensated employees, or NHCEs, must be calculated and compared by the 401(k) plan administrator each year. The plan passes the antidiscrimination test if HCEs contribute at an average rate no more than 125 percent higher than that for NHCEs, or if the average contribution rate for HCEs is less than two percentage points greater than the average rate for NHCEs. Catch-up contributions are excluded from the calculation. The antidiscrimination rules do not apply to 403(b) or 457 plans.
12. Collective trust funds were originally designed to allow banks to commingle assets of smaller defined benefit plans in a single group trust. The bank offering the CTF acts as the group trustee of the assets held in the pool on behalf of the investors in the pool.
13. The manager of a mutual fund may be exempt from those requirements.
14. Investment Company Institute, "401(k) Plan Asset Allocation, Account Balances, and Loan Activity in 2008," *Research Perspective* 15 (2) (2009): 26.
15. Plan sponsors generally prefer stable value pools over guaranteed investment contracts because they provide greater protection against the bankruptcy of the issuer. GICs are issued by insurance companies and are secured only by its corporate assets; if the insurer should fail, the investors in the GIC could lose everything. Stable value pools can be issued by many different financial institutions, including insurers. While backed by that institution, investors have recourse to a segregated set of assets that has provided the pool's annual income should the issuer go bankrupt.
16. SEP, or Simplified Employee Pension, Plan individual retirement accounts are also designed for small employers. SIMPLE IRAs more closely resemble 401(k) plans since they allow for both employer and employee contributions; SEP IRAs

involve employer contributions only. Congress had previously authorized SAR-SEP (Salary Reduction Simplified Employee Pension Plan) IRAs; employers may no longer establish new SAR-SEP plans, although existing ones may continue to be used. SIMPLE plans can be structured as 401(k) plans or IRAs; virtually all employers have chosen IRAs because of their greater simplicity.

17. Patrick Purcell, "Retirement Savings and Household Wealth in 2007," *Congressional Research Service* 7-5700, April 2009.

18. Seasonal or part-time work is defined as fewer than 1,000 hours per year.

19. SIMPLE plan participants are eligible for the Saver's Credit.

20. Jason Furman, *Policy Basics: Top Ten Facts on Social Security's 70th Anniversary* (August 2005), www.cbpp.org/cms/index.cfm?fa=view&id=531 (accessed June 28, 2010).

CHAPTER 12: The Competition from Exchange-Traded Funds and Hedge Funds

1. Data derived from Cerulli Associates, Inc., *The Cerulli Report: Exchange-Traded Funds: Threat or Threatened?* (2009) and Investment Company Institute, *2010 Investment Company Fact Book* (2010).

2. See "Leland O'Brien Rubinstein Associates Inc.: SuperTrust," *Harvard Business School Case Study 9-294-050* (1995) for an account of the challenges faced in the development of the first exchange-traded fund.

3. In 2010, some discount brokers eliminated commissions on ETF trades. At the time this chapter was written, it's unclear whether this is a temporary promotion or a permanent change.

4. This investment return is often structured to be taxed at more favorable capital gains rates. The IRS is currently reviewing the tax treatment of this income.

5. National Stock Exchange, *ETF Data: Monthly ETF Reports, Month End April 2010;* www.nsx.com/content/etf-assets-list (accessed May 11, 2010).

6. The redemption basket is based on the portfolio at the time of the next calculation of NAV.

7. U.S. Commodity Futures Trading Commission and U.S. Securities & Exchange Commission, *Preliminary Findings Regarding the Market Events of May 6, 2010* (May 2010), 5–6.

8. *Tracking error* is defined here as the difference between the performance of the NAV and the performance of the index. Some analysts define it as the difference between share performance and index performance, which would reflect changes in the premium or discount of the share price versus the NAV.

9. Mutual funds are limited in the amount of exchange-traded fund shares they may purchase. Under the 1940 Act, a fund may not invest more than 5 percent of its assets in any other single mutual fund or more than 10 percent of its assets in other mutual funds in total. Also, it may not acquire more than 3 percent of the shares of another fund. These rules prevent *fee pyramiding*. Target date

funds and other funds of funds must request an exemption from this rule from the SEC.

10. Richard A. Ferri, *The ETF Book: All You Need to Know About Exchange-Traded Funds* (John Wiley & Sons, 2009).

11. Selling short before borrowing shares is called *naked shorting* and is prohibited in the United States.

12. See Burton G. Malkiel and Atanu Saha, "Hedge Funds: Risk and Return," *Financial Analysts Journal* 61 (6): 80–88 (November-December 2005), and Roger G. Ibbotson and Peng Chen, "The A, B, Cs of Hedge Funds: Alphas, Betas, and Costs," *Yale ICF Working Paper No. 06-10* (September 2006).

13. Stephen J. Brown and William N. Goetzmann, "Fees on Fees in Funds of Funds," *Yale ICF Working Paper No. 02-33* (June 2004).

14. The Global Investment Performance Standards—or GIPS standards—are designed to minimize backfill and survivorship bias in an investment firm's performance reporting. Firms that adhere to the standards must keep historical records of the performance of all portfolios managed by the firm. The CFA Institute created and administers the standards.

15. A growing number of investment managers are offering hedge fund strategies in mutual fund structures. This is most common in Europe, as we see in Chapter 17. Some of these funds seek to replicate the returns of a hedge fund not available to the average investor. On the plus side, these replication products offer lower initial investment thresholds, lower fees, greater transparency, and more frequent liquidity. On the negative side, these funds generally do not offer genuine access to star managers and may have high fees.

16. For more, see Roger Lowenstein, *When Genius Failed: The Rise and Fall of Long-Term Capital Management* (New York: Random House, 2000).

17. Smaller hedge fund managers—those with less than $150 million in assets—still need not register with the SEC if they have fewer than 15 clients and do not publicly market their services. However, smaller hedge fund managers may be subject to state-level investment adviser regulation.

CHAPTER 13: Customer Service

1. Under the Securities Exchange Act of 1934, the transfer agent must register with the SEC.

2. Investment Company Institute, *2010 Investment Company Fact Book* (2010).

3. A few fund management companies have established a network of branch offices, and prospective investors may hand in completed applications at these branches.

4. Transfer agents generally do not send confirmations for purchases made through systematic investment plans; these transactions will be included only in quarterly statements.

5. The effective date of the new law varies by type of investment, and it applies only to shares acquired after that date. For stocks, the new requirements kick in

for shares acquired after January 1, 2011. For mutual funds, the relevant date is January 1, 2012. For other securities, there's no impact until January 1, 2013.

6. BNY Mellon Asset Servicing was PNC Global Investment Servicing before it was acquired by BNY Mellon in mid-2010. Before joining the PNC financial group, it was PFPC.

CHAPTER 14: Portfolio Recordkeeping and Valuation

1. There is an exception to the T+1 rule: institutional money market funds post transactions—both securities trades and capital stock activity—on the trade date, or T+0.

2. Under "Fair Value Measurements and Disclosures (Topic 820)," under the new Financial Accounting Standards Board codification system. When it was initially adopted, this guidance was referred to as Financial Accounting Standard 157, or FAS 157.

3. Intermediaries using omnibus accounts, including many 401(k) plans, may need time to total the day's orders after the market close and therefore must submit them to the fund after 4 P.M. This practice is acceptable if the intermediary has a written contract with the fund that requires it to affirm that no trades have been placed by investors after 4 P.M.

4. Includes PNC Global Investment Servicing, which was acquired by BNY Mellon in 2010.

5. Fund managers are not legally required to reimburse funds for losses incurred as the result of errors, but most do so as a matter of practice.

CHAPTER 15: The Financial Dynamics of the Fund Management Industry

1. This group includes BlackRock, Eaton Vance, Federated Investors, Franklin Resources, Invesco, Janus Capital, Legg Mason, T. Rowe Price, and Waddell & Reed. Source: Morningstar, Inc.

2. Russel Kinnel, "How Expense Ratios and Star Ratings Predict Success", *Morningstar Fund Spy*, (August, 9. 2010), http://news.morningstar.com/articlenet/article.aspx?id=347327&part=2 (accessed September 13, 2010).

3. For a detailed review of the debate over mutual fund fees, see R. Glenn Hubbard et al., *The Mutual Fund Industry: Competition and Investor Welfare* (New York: Columbia University Press, 2010).

4. John P. Freeman and Stuart B. Brown, "Mutual Fund Advisory Fees: The Cost of Conflicts of Interest," *The Journal of Corporate Law* 26:609–674 (2001).

5. Brad M. Barber, Terrance Odean, and Lu Zheng, "Out of Sight, Out of Mind: The Effects of Expenses on Mutual Fund Flows," *Journal of Business* 78 (6) (2005).

6. Sean Collins, "The Expenses of Defined Benefit Pension Plans and Mutual Funds," *Investment Company Institute Perspective,* December 2003.
7. Current name used for substantially similar firms.
8. Also, at least 75 percent of the directors of the funds must remain independent for at least three years after the transfer of the advisory contract.

CHAPTER 16: Cross-Border Investing

1. For a comprehensive study of the benefits of trade and investment liberalization, see Organisation for Economic Co-Operation and Development, "Open Markets Matter: The Benefits of Trade and Investment Liberalization," *OECD Policy Brief* (October 1999) and *Trade, Investment and Development: Reaping the Full Benefits of Open Markets* (Paris, France: Organisation for Economic Co-Operation and Development, 1999).
2. John Rea, "U.S. Emerging Market Funds: Hot Money or Stable Source of Investment Capital?" *ICI Perspective* 2 (6) (December 1996) and Mitchell A. Post and Kimberlee Miller, "U.S. Emerging Market Equity Funds and the 1997 Crisis in Asian Financial Markets," *ICI Perspective* 4 (2) (June 1998).
3. The *encaje* was increased to 30 percent in 1992. In mid-1998, it was reduced to 10 percent, and the early withdrawal penalty was lowered to 1 percent. It was eliminated entirely in September 1998. Direct investment was subject to different restrictions. From 1982 through 1991, direct investment needed to stay in the country for 10 years. The required holding period was reduced to three years in 1991 and one year in 1993. See Christopher J. Neely, "An Introduction to Capital Controls," *Federal Reserve Bank of St. Louis Review* (November-December 1999).
4. These last countries are sometimes informally referred to as the PIIGS, for Portugal, Ireland, Italy, Greece, and Spain. They are the least well-off of the countries using the euro as a currency and experienced significant financial stress as a result of the credit crisis.
5. Piero Cinquegrana and Willem Pieter de Groen, *ECMI Statistical Package 2009,* www.eurocapitalmarkets.org/?q=node/408 (accessed June 23, 2010).
6. See Amir Andrew Amadi, "Equity Home Bias: A Disappearing Phenomenon?" (May 5, 2004), in SSRN: http://ssrn.com/abstract=540662, and Bong-Chan Kho, Francis E. Warnock, and Rene M. Stulz, "Financial Globalization, Governance, and the Evolution of the Home Bias," *BIS Working Paper No. 220* (June 2007), in SSRN: http://ssrn.com/abstract=911595.
7. See Peter F. Christoffersen, Vihang R. Errunza, Kris Jacobs, and Xisong Jin, "Is the Potential for International Diversification Disappearing?" (March 16, 2010). In SSRN: http://ssrn.com/abstract=1573345, and Roberto Ribogon, "International Financial Contagion: Theory and Evidence in Evolution" *Research Foundation Publications* (August 2002).
8. Barry Eichengreen and Michael Bordo, "Crisis Now and Then: What Lesson from the Last Era of Financial Globalization," *NBER Working Paper* No. 8716 (January 2002).

9. Burhan F. Yavas, PhD, "Benefits of International Portfolio Diversification," *Graziadio Business Report* 10 (2) (2007), http://gbr.pepperdine.edu/072/ diversification.html (accessed June 23, 2010).

10. "Custody of Investment Company Assets Outside the United States," Rule 17f-5 promulgated under the Investment Company Act of 1940.

CHAPTER 17: Cross-Border Asset Gathering

1. Ajay Khorana, Henri Servaes, and Peter Tufano, "Explaining the Size of the Mutual Fund Industry Around the World," *Darden School of Business Working Paper No. 03-04; Harvard NOM Working Paper No. 03-23; EFA 2003 Annual Conference Paper No. 804* (January 2004), in SSRN: http://ssrn .com/abstract=573503.

2. Ajay Khorana, Henri Servaes, and Peter Tufano, "Mutual Funds Fees Around the World," *HBS Finance Working Paper No. 901023* (July 2007), in SSRN: http://ssrn.com/abstract=901023.

3. Data for Switzerland are as of December 2008.

4. A UCITS fund may be either a SICAV, which stands for *société d'investissement à capital variable*, meaning "investment society with variable capital," or an FCP, for *fond commun de placement*. A SICAV is a separate legal entity, roughly equivalent to a U.S. open-end mutual fund, while an FCP is established by contract between the management company and the custodian.

5. Information on cross-border registrations in this section is from Pricewater-houseCoopers, *Global Fund Distribution 2010* (2010). Cross-border funds are defined as those registered in at least three countries.

6. European fund market share data from EFAMA, "Trends in the European Investment Fund Industry in the Fourth Quarter of 2009 and Results for the Full Year 2009," *Quarterly Statistical Release* 40 (March 2010), www .efama.org/index.php?option=com_docman&task=cat_view&gid=72&Itemid =-99 (accessed September 16, 2010).

7. The original UCITS directive was adopted in 1985. A proposed amendment to the original directive—which was to have been known as UCITS II—was abandoned before it was implemented. This failed amendment was modified and adopted as UCITS III in 2002.

8. Alternative mutual funds include absolute/total return, commodity, property, infrastructure, specialty funds (includes 130/30, private equity, and funds investing primarily in derivatives), fund of hedge funds, and hedge funds deemed UCITS-compliant.

9. John C. Coates IV, "Reforming the Taxation and Regulation of Mutual Funds: A Comparative Legal and Economic Analysis" (December 30, 2008): 50, in SSRN, http://ssrn.com/abstract=1311945 (accessed June 27, 2010).

10. BAKred is short for *Bundesaufsichtsamt für das Kreditwesen*, while BAV is the acronym for *Bundesaufsichtsamt für das Versicherungswesen*.

11. Fédération Européenne des Conseils et Intermédiaires Financiers, *Annual White Book – December 2008*, www.fecif.org/library/FECIF%20white% 20book%202008%20FINAL.pdf.

12. McKinsey & Company, *The Asset Management Industry in 2010*, www .mckinsey.com/clientservice/bankingsecurities/latestthinking/The_Asset_ Management_Industry_in_2010.pdf (accessed June 17, 2010).
13. Axel H. Börsch-Supan and Christina Wilke, "The German Pension System: How It Will Become an NDC Look-Alike," *Pension Reform* (World Bank, 2006).
14. Statistics on contributions from each of the three pillars are from Axel Oster, *Risk-Based Pension Supervision—German Approach* (March 2006), www.oecd.org/dataoecd/43/52/36344245.pdf (accessed June 25, 2010).
15. The Social Protection Committee of the European Commission, *Privately Managed Funded Pension Provision and their Contribution to Adequate and Sustainable Pensions* (2008) and *Synthesis Report on Adequate and Sustainable Pensions* (2006), http://ec.europa.eu/employment_social/spsi/adequacy_ sustainability_en.htm (accessed July 6, 2010).

CHAPTER 18: The Market for Investment Funds: Beyond the United States and Europe

1. U.S. dollar fund asset figures in this chapter are from the Investment Company Institute, *2010 Investment Company Fact Book* (2010). GDP figures are from the Central Intelligence Agency, *The World Factbook*.
2. U.S.-registered mutual funds are included in the 10 percent represented by non-UCITS funds. Taiwan is one of the few countries that permit their distribution.
3. Before Hong Kong's Consumer Council took steps to limit fees in 2007, expenses on some funds were as high as 4 percent a year.
4. Statistics on Singapore from Monetary Authority of Singapore, *2009 Singapore Asset Management Industry Survey,* www.mas.gov.sg/resource/eco_research/ surveys/AssetMgmt09.pdf (accessed August 4, 2010).
5. Capgemini and Merrill Lynch, *Asia-Pacific Wealth Report 2008* (2008).
6. Foreign investors wishing to purchase investments in China must register as qualified foreign institutional investors, or QFIIs. See Chapter 16 for more on the QFII regime.
7. Chinese retirement system information from Robert C. Pozen, *An American Perspective on the Chinese Pension System, EBRI Notes* 27 (8) (August 2006) and Stuart P. Leckie, *A Review of the National Social Security Fund in China,* www.actuaries.org/PBSS/Colloquia/Tokyo/LECKIE_StuartP.pdf (accessed July 3, 2010).
8. Of countries with a population of at least one million. Central Intelligence Agency, *The World Factbook*.
9. Publicly offered investment trusts of the contractual type.
10. The law has been likened to Sarbanes-Oxley in the United States and is often referred to as J-SOX.
11. Carol Wood, "Special Delivery: Japan Post to be Privatized," in *Bloomberg Businessweek,* www.businessweek.com/investor/content/apr2006/pi20060405 _205672.htm (accessed July 4, 2010).

12. Individuals who are not covered by a defined benefit plan may contribute ¥552,000 (or roughly $5,200) to a defined contribution plan annually. Contributions for others are capped at ¥276,000 (or $2,600).

13. For the history of Japan's retirement system, see David Rajnes, "The Evolution of Japanese Employer-Sponsored Retirement Plans," *Social Security Bulletin* 67 (3) (2007), www.ssa.gov/policy/docs/ssb/v67n3/v67n3p89.html (accessed July 4, 2010).

14. Assets fell to US$74 billion in 2008 during the credit crisis, but have since rebounded. Not all workers are included in the program. For example, military personnel and the self-employed are exempt. For more information on the Chilean system, see Superintendency of Pension Fund Administrators, *The Chilean Pension System, Fourth Edition,* www.safp.cl/573/article-3523.html (accessed July 4, 2010).

15. Citi recently announced plans to sell its indirect stake in an AFP to focus on its core banking business in Chile.

16. Canadian Institutional Investment Network, *2009 Cap Benchmark Report* (2009).

17. Canadians are also covered by a pay-as-you-go system, which provides a modest level of benefits.

18. Brooke Smith, "Closing the Gap," *Benefits Canada* (December 2009).

19. Before the restrictions were removed, clone funds used derivatives to replicate the performance of foreign markets while complying with the local content laws.

20. Ajay Khorana, Henri Servaes, and Peter Tufano, "Mutual Funds Fees Around the World," HBS Finance Working Paper No. 901023 (July 2007), in SSRN: http://ssrn.com/abstract=901023.

About the Authors

ROBERT POZEN

Robert C. Pozen is chairman emeritus of MFS Investment Management. He works with MFS and its management team in an advisory capacity, and also serves on the board of directors of the MFS Funds.

Bob joined MFS in 2004 as chairman and served in that role until 2010. He is currently a senior lecturer at Harvard Business School and is a senior fellow at the Brookings Institution. He recently served as chairman of an SEC advisory committee focused on improving the U.S. financial reporting system, and was a member of two private sector commissions studying global market competitiveness.

Before joining MFS in 2004, Bob was the John Olin Visiting Professor at Harvard Law School during 2002 and 2003. During 2003, he also served as Secretary of Economic Affairs for Massachusetts governor Mitt Romney.

In late 2001 and 2002, Bob had the distinction of serving on President Bush's Commission to Strengthen Social Security, and he developed a Social Security solvency proposal that was later embraced by the president.

From 1987 to 2001, Bob held numerous senior positions at Fidelity Investments, ending as vice chairman and president of Fidelity Management and Research Company. Before joining Fidelity, Bob served as associate general counsel for the SEC and taught at New York University.

Bob graduated summa cum laude from Harvard College with a Bachelor of Arts degree and earned a law degree from Yale Law School. He has authored many articles and books, including *Too Big to Save? How to Fix the U.S. Financial System.*

THERESA HAMACHER, CFA

Theresa has been the president of NICSA since March 2008. NICSA (the National Investment Company Service Association) is the leading provider of independent education and networking forums to professionals in the global investment management community.

She has served as chief investment officer for Pioneer Investment Management USA in Boston, Massachusetts, where she oversaw a team of more than 50 investment professionals managing more than $15 billion in global equity and fixed income assets for mutual fund and institutional clients. She was previously the chief investment officer for Prudential Mutual Funds in Newark, New Jersey, where she supervised over $60 billion in assets. In 1984, she was the portfolio manager of the top-performing mutual fund in the United States, the Prudential-Bache (Tax-Managed) Utility Fund. She began her career in the investment industry in 1983 as a securities analyst.

Theresa is the co-author of *The Pocket Idiot's Guide to Investing in Stocks (Alpha, 2006)*. She is a summa cum laude graduate of Yale College and a Chartered Financial Analyst.

Index